RECOVERING
THE RESURGENCE OF I  ᴜ LAW

Canada is ruled by a system of law and governance that largely obscures
and ignores the presence of pre-existing Indigenous regimes. Indigenous law, however, has continuing relevance for both Aboriginal
peoples and the Canadian state. In this in-depth examination of the
continued existence and application of Indigenous legal values, John
Borrows suggests how First Nations laws could be applied by Canadian
courts, while addressing the difficulties that would likely occur if the
courts attempted to follow such an approach. By contrasting and comparing Aboriginal stories and Canadian case law, and interweaving political commentary, Borrows argues that there is a better way to constitute
Aboriginal–Crown relations in Canada. He suggests that the application
of Indigenous legal perspectives to a broad spectrum of issues will help
Canada recover from its colonial past, and help Indigenous people
recover their country. Borrows concludes by demonstrating how Indigenous peoples' law could be more fully and consciously integrated with
Canadian law to produce a society where two world-views can co-exist
and a different vision of the Canadian constitution and citizenship can
be created.

JOHN BORROWS is Professor and Law Foundation Chair in Aboriginal
Justice at the University of Victoria.

Fort Nelson Public Library
Box 330
Fort Nelson, BC
V0C-1R0

SEP - - 2014

JOHN BORROWS

Recovering Canada:
The Resurgence of
Indigenous Law

UNIVERSITY OF TORONTO PRESS
Toronto Buffalo London

Fort Nelson Public Library
Box 330
Fort Nelson, BC
V0C-1R0

© University of Toronto Incorporated 2002
Toronto Buffalo London
Printed in Canada

Reprinted 2006, 2007

ISBN 0-8020-3679-1 (cloth)
ISBN 0-8020-8501-6 (paper)

∞

Printed on acid-free paper

National Library of Canada Cataloguing in Publication

Borrows, John, 1963–
Recovering Canada : the resurgence of Indigenous law / John Borrows.

Includes bibliographical references and index.
ISBN 0-8020-3679-1 (bound).   ISBN 0-8020-8501-6 (pbk.)

1. Native peoples – Legal status, laws, etc. – Canada.
2. Customary law – Canada.   I. Title.

KE7709.B68 2002   340.5′271   C2002-902472-2

The University of Toronto Press acknowledges the financial assistance to
its publishing program of the Canada Council for the Arts and the
Ontario Arts Council.

University of Toronto Press acknowledges the financial support for its
publishing activities of the Government of Canada through the Book
Publishing Industry Development Program (BPIDP).

Contents

Preface

This book follows contours of thought developed over the past ten years in my research into Aboriginal legal issues. During this period I have attempted to transmit and test these ideas in many forums, and this work has, I hope, benefited from the reflective and (sometimes) more fervent interactions that law professors enjoy in the course of their year. The frequent testing of ideas through the immediacy of the spoken word, in the classroom and elsewhere, has reminded me of the need to strive for relevance and coherence. Ultimately, my work flows from an orientation to and preference for the oral tradition as a method of communication. It is in that mode that I feel most comfortable. However, I have also published my ideas, as another test of their worth, in law reviews and journals. These publications create an environment of exchange in which authors of similar training can share their views and receive comments and criticism on their interpretation of the issues under study. I have enjoyed and been challenged by the feedback I received as a result of this process. The scope of a law review's readership is, however, somewhat limited and I wanted to expand the circle of conversation about my ideas. This book thus stems from a desire to further build on the thoughts developed through both personal exchange and professional legal writing. In revising and building connections between the ideas found in my presentations and articles, this book represents the next stage in testing their value. The ensuing chapters largely build on articles published in Canadian law journals.[1] In republishing this work in a book format, however, I have tried to introduce a theme and unity not always present or apparent in earlier manifestations of my ideas. I do not know if I have been successful, but I hope that the ideas expressed will continue to generate exchange and undergo further refinement.

I wish to acknowledge the support I have received from numerous institutions and individuals in the production of this work. In the past seven years I have taught at the law schools of the universities of British Columbia, Toronto, and Victoria, as well as at Osgoode Hall, York University and Arizona State University (proof that I cannot hold a job). Each institution has its own distinctive character that I hope has worked its way into these pages. I am appreciative of Deans Lynn Smith, Marilyn Pilkington, Joost Blom, Ron Daniels, Patricia White, and Andrew Petter, and colleagues at the faculties of each law school who put up with my wandering as this work developed. I am continuously surprised, yet grateful, for the willingness of people to understand and encourage a broad spirit of intellectual exploration and tolerate my somewhat peripatetic life. That this can occur in an atmosphere of friendship and good-natured criticism seems almost too much to expect. Nevertheless, I have enjoyed such company along the way and feel a kinship with those who have welcomed me in their own particular ways. Among those who have encouraged or read parts or all of this manuscript, include: Alex Clapp, Loreena Fontaine, Sakej Henderson, Shin Imai, Michael Jackson, Patrick Macklem, June McCue, Kent McNeil, Kent Roach, Doug Sanders, Brian Slattery, David Schneiderman, Rebecca Tsosie. I have also treasured the work and wisdom of various research assistants who have contributed to this book. Lisa Dufraimont, in particular, helped me further refine the structure and detail through her diligent and painstaking review of the manuscript. It would be hard to overestimate Lisa's contribution to the final form of this work. Others who assisted, and whose help is appreciated, include: Kristen Clark, Colin Desjarlais, Janelle Dwyer, Kerry Jimmerson, Matt Kirchener, Sunny Larson, and Sandra Leland. Thanks also go to Virgil Duff, Allyson May, and the staff at the University of Toronto Press for their valuable assistance in helping to prepare the manuscript for publication.

Finally, I am grateful for my mother, Jean Borrows, for stories told and lessons well lived. She is an incredibly inspirational woman, and her influence lies at the root of much of what follows. I have also benefited from the encouragement of my father, Joseph, and from his loving, thoughtful, and measured responses to my inquiries and needs through the years. Most of all, I am thankful to my partner, Kim, for her willingness to move (again, again, and again) and experience new dimensions to life as the work in this book unfolded. In our companionship is reflected the hope I feel for future.

Introduction

The University of Toronto's Faculty of Law is situated on Philosopher's Walk, a quiet footpath that winds its way among some of the city's grandest buildings. Philosopher's Walk is a place of both visible and hidden power. At its mid-point, between Bloor Street and Hoskin Avenue, stands the law school. Climbing the short hill east from this part of the Walk, you approach the school's three-storey, pillared side entrance. Going through its doors and down the hall you encounter oak panelling, fifteen-foot ceilings, and opulently adorned rooms. The walls of these rooms, adorned with portraits of deans who later became university presidents, Supreme and appellate Court judges, and members of the Order of Canada, testify that this place is an important source of economic and political strength. Further into its heart the corridors are lined with pictures of graduates who are well represented in the upper realms of Ontario's social caste. Stepping into its classrooms and meeting its students you seem to be meeting the future face of power in the province.

The law school is made up of two grand former residences, Flavelle House and Falconer Hall. These structures, built in a classical Greco-Roman style, were originally occupied by wealthy-businessmen. Flavelle House was first owned by the industrialist Sir Joseph Wesley Flavelle, while Falconer Hall was once the residence of Edward Rogers Wood, an influential financier and investment banker. Flavelle House, the larger building on the south of the site, was originally known as Holwood. It was built between 1901 and 1903 and, as one author observed, 'succeeded in recreating the permanence and grandeur of the classical tradition. The building was heavy and solid, built to last, and built to impress the viewer with its grand scale and dignity, its exceptional lawns and gardens, and impressively-furnished interior spaces.'[1]

Falconer Hall, the smaller residence to the north, was originally named Wymilwood to memorialize the name of its owner, Mr Wood. When built, it was situated on a small rise beside a beautiful stream. The house boasted one of the finest private gardens in the city, and the property included stables and a coach house. 'The home itself,' it has been said, 'stood as a fine example of modernized Elizabethan architecture, with its rosy brick exterior, high gables and tall chimneys.'[2] Eventually, Wymilwood was renamed Falconer Hall in honour of a one-time president of the University of Toronto. When acquired by the university, Falconer Hall became part of the Faculty of Law in 1972. In 1992, the attached law library was renovated and named after Bora Laskin, one of the school's founding members and former chief justice of the Supreme Court of Canada. It is a grey post-modern product, looking like the walls of a Bay Street lawyer's library turned inside out.[3]

The two houses of the University of Toronto law school are built on a ravine that was once a headwater and home to spawning salmon and trout. The school has displaced this earlier presence with the green space now known as Philosopher's Walk. Buried far beneath it is a stream, known to the Anishinabek as Ziibiing[4] and later to the settlers as Taddle Creek. If followed to its mouth this stream led to Wonscodonahk,[5] where Queen's Quay now stands, on the Lake Ontario shoreline. By covering living reminders of a previous landscape, the systems of planning and architecture that created the law school have nearly erased the Ojibway people's relationship with this place.

When I look at Philosopher's Walk I see that 'Western' forms have blanketed patterns once indigenous to the area. Yet enough of the land's contour and shape survive to evoke memories of its former use.[6] As the Walk passes between the law school and the Royal Ontario Museum on one side, and Trinity College and the Royal Conservatory of Music on the other, it winds its way between the green banks of the ancient stream. A mere two hundred years ago, a short time in the history of the area, streams in places like Philosopher's Walk witnessed the reproduction of a pattern of life which was replicated throughout the area.[7] These streams were the springtime gathering places for my people.[8] In early March my ancestors would have been north and west of the Creek in the woodlands that surrounded Lake Ontario. The Anishinabek would assemble in small, winter kin-based camps and engage in small-scale hunting and gathering activities. In late March or early April they would begin gathering with members of their extended family in slightly larger camps. They would take sap from the trees for the approaching spring. In mid-April to May the Anishinabek would then move to the heads of the rivers and streams and engage in fishing, as the streams became full of spawning aquatic life. Congregations of people would be found at places like 'Philosopher's Walk' using gill nets, spears, hooks, and fish weirs.

Philosopher's Walk was then the source of another kind of power. The place did not reproduce the power of people, politics, or capital; it reproduced itself, and its own power. The Anishinabek believed that any particular physical feature on the landscape contained its own powerful spirits.[9] For example, unusually productive or fast rivers possessed a spirit power. These places were approached timidly, with sacred tobacco left on a rock nearby as an offering. Philosopher's Walk would have been one such place. The spirits at the Walk would have manifested themselves in audible ways. It has been written of similar places, where waters flowed into Lake Ontario: 'At the head of the Lake Indians frequently heard sounds like explosions or the shooting of a gun. The elders told Sacred Feathers (a young Anishinabek in 1820) that the spirits living in the escarpment's caverns immediately west of Burlington Bay caused the volleys by blowing and breathing. The deep, awful sound of the spirit of the falls of Niagara could be heard at sixty kilometers, shaking the air and the earth itself. At the Credit River the Indians often heard the river God (who lived at the foot of a high hill in a deep hole, three kilometers from the river's mouth) singing and beating his drum.'[10] Philosopher's Walk once enjoyed this type of audible power. When the landscape was changed, the ancient power of the place fell silent. The spirits of the land and water on which the law school was built were buried and submerged. The stream is concealed, the fish are gone, and Anishinabek people no longer gather at this site to witness the spectacular reproduction of life.

During my time as a student, I discovered that law school has the power to hide many things. As an Anishinabek person involved in legal studies, I found that Aboriginal laws were concealed and submerged by a system that privileges Western legal narratives. Although Indigenous law predates the arrival of Europeans, principles of Aboriginal order are rarely recognized or affirmed by the settlers' legal establishment. In effect, the common law in Canada built over Anishinabek law and obscured these prior customs from public view, just as Philosopher's Walk covers and conceals an ancient past. Architecture and Planning have joined Law in privileging Western forms,[11] building over Anishinabek relationships and obscuring ancient customs from public view. Yet

Philosopher's Walk retains a muted sense of its former power. From a place just off Hoskin Avenue, looking north up the ravine, the outlines of a design that pre-existed its Classical, Elizabethan, and postmodern additions can be made out. Somewhere beneath them one can discern an older power at work.

A similar insight motivates this book: the power of Aboriginal law can still be discerned despite the pervasiveness of imported law. While Canada and its laws have largely built over Indigenous legal structures, other legal cultures have not been entirely obscured. Their contours are evident at a level just below Canada's legal imagination. Indigenous legal values form the hidden but underlying bedrock upon which the Crown and its assignees have built their claims. This study attempts to reveal the Aboriginal legal structures that have been built over, but not destroyed, by the common law by bringing together viewpoints from the two worlds in which I have been schooled: Aboriginal and Canadian legal narratives. Engaging a vocabulary of comparison, I will examine the common law's stories as understood through and evaluated by Anishinabek stories. I have pursued this methodology in an attempt to reverse the flow of judgment between Aboriginal and Canadian legal structures. In the rare instances in which they have entered into Canadian legal discourse, Aboriginal legal perspectives have been evaluated by stories that are alien to this land.[12] It is now time for the common law's treatment of Aboriginal peoples to be judged by stories indigenous to this continent.

RECOVERING CANADA:
THE RESURGENCE OF INDIGENOUS LAW

Chapter One

With or Without You:
First Nations Law in Canada

Neesh-wa-swi'ish-ko-day-kawn arose and said:

> *in the time of the Seventh Fire an Osh-ki-bi-ma-di-zeeg' (new people) will emerge. They will retrace their steps to find what was left by the trail ...*
>
> *The task of the new people will not be easy. If the new people remain strong ... [t]here will be a ... rekindling of the Sacred Fire ...*
>
> *It is at this time that the Light-skinned Race will be given a choice between two roads. If they will choose the right road, then the Seventh Fire will light the Eighth and Final Fire – an eternal Fire of peace ... If the Light-skinned Race makes the wrong choice of roads ...*[1]

There are over one million people of Indigenous ancestry in what is now called Canada.[2] These peoples, variously known as the 'Aboriginal,'[3] 'Native,' or 'First' peoples of North America, include, among others, the ancient and contemporary nations of the Innu, Mi'kmaq, Cree, Anishinabek, Haudenosaunee, Dakota, Métis, Blackfoot, Shuswap, Salish, Haida, Dene, and Inuit.[4] First Nations are as historically different from one another as are other nations and cultures in the world. For example, Canadian Indigenous peoples speak over fifty different Aboriginal languages from twelve distinct language families, which have as wide a variation as do the language families of Europe and Asia.[5] These nations' linguistic, genealogical, and political descent can be traced back through millennia to different regions or territories in northern North America.[6] In these geographic spaces Indigenous peoples developed spiritual, political, and social customs and conventions to guide their relationships.[7] Each group created its own distinctive ceremonies and formalities to renew, celebrate, transfer, or abandon their legal relationships. The ceremonies of the Potlatch on the West Coast produced entirely different legal relationships from those of the Sundance on the Prairies or of the Midewiwin and False Face societies of central Canada. The stories told in the Big Houses of the Salish differ fundamentally from those told in the teepees of the Assinaboine, which might likewise be very different from those spoken in the Longhouses of the Haudenosaunee or the lodges of the Mi'kmaq. The ceremonies and stories of the different groups varied according to their history, material circumstances, spiritual alignment, and social structure. The diverse customs and conventions which evolved became the foundation for many complex systems of law,[8] and contemporary Canadian law concerning Aboriginal peoples partially originates in, and is extracted from, these legal systems.[9]

Of course, Canadian law concerning Aboriginal people also draws on British and American common law, and to a lesser extent on international law.[10] Like Aboriginal systems, these legal sources are similarly grounded in the complex spiritual, political, and social customs and conventions of particular cultures, in this case those of European nations.[11] Canadian law concerning Aboriginal peoples thus originates in a culturally mixed medium drawn together from diverse jurisprudential sources. This is consistent with R. Cover's observation that 'The creation of legal meaning – jurisgenesis – always takes place through an essentially cultural medium.'[12] However, most accounts of Canada's jurisgenesis do not recognize the importance of its Indigenous sources. Distinctive European legal customs have sometimes been applied to First Nations as if there were no differences between cultures.[13] More disturbingly, Canadian law has often been applied as if First Nations cultures were inferior to European law, legal institutions, and culture.[14] In these instances, the legal systems of First Nations were ignored, repressed, or concealed. Yet Indigenous customs and conventions have, in fact, at times been incorporated into Canadian law.

Much of the history of Canadian law concerning Aboriginal peoples is often seen as conflictual, a contest between ideas rooted in First Nations, English, American, and international legal regimes[15] in which one source of law must become ascendant. Courts taking this view have frequently refused to apply First Nations law, preferring to recognize the common law as the sole or pre-eminent source of law in Canada. I will argue that it is unnecessary for courts to approach the interpretation of Aboriginal rights as though each source of law was in competition with the others.[16] The Supreme Court of Canada has defined Aboriginal rights in such a way that these sources can often be harmonized, and need not obstruct each other.[17] As Brian Slattery has pointed out, Canadian law applying to First Nations is an autonomous body of law, not fully bound to any one of the legal systems identified above.[18] It 'bridges the gulf' between First Nations and European legal systems by embracing each without forming a part of them.[19] While it is true that legal doctrines from Britain, the United States, and the international community (or, for that matter, First Nations) have had a persuasive influence on the development of Canadian law, the body of case law dealing with Aboriginal issues is, in the end, 'indigenous' to Canada.[20] Thus, while Canadian law dealing with First Nations may borrow legal notions from various Aboriginal and non-Aboriginal cultures,[21] it is also a uniquely Canadian amalgam of many different legal orders.[22] It is therefore incumbent upon Canadian judges to draw upon Indigenous legal sources more often and more explicitly in deciding Aboriginal issues.[23]

This chapter describes how Canadian jurisprudence on Aboriginal issues compels the courts to analogize and apply principles from First Nations laws. Canadian courts have recognized Indigenous law as a legitimate source in formulating legal principles dealing with Aboriginal rights. What is more, Indigenous legal principles have survived despite the constraints often imposed by Canadian judges. First Nations rights, after all, have not been extinguished,[24] even under the most oppressive weight of Western legal control.[25] After identifying the persistence of Indigenous law, I will provide an example of contemporary Aboriginal law and explain how its principles can be more fully received into the Canadian legal framework.[26] There are sources of First Nations laws that can be rendered 'cognizable' to European-based law. As described below, for instance, Anishinabek environmental law can be articulated so as to apply to disputes before Canadian courts. This chapter identifies mechanisms that are currently in place to allow for the communication, interpretation, reception, and application of First Nations law in Canada.

I Taking the Court ... Seriously: Sources of Law in Canadian Aboriginal Rights Jurisprudence

Some courts have recognized from the outset that Canadian law as applied to First Nations draws on Aboriginal and non-Aboriginal sources. In the first year of Canada's Confederation the Quebec Superior Court affirmed the existence of Cree law on the Prairies and recognized it as part of the common law. In arriving at this position Justice Monk wrote: 'Will it be contended that the territorial rights, political organization such as it was, or the laws and usages of Indian tribes were abrogated – that they ceased to exist when these two European nations began to trade with [A]boriginal occupants? In my opinion it is beyond controversy that they did not – that so far from being abolished, they were left in full force, and were not even modified in the slightest degree ...'[27] In keeping with this early recognition of Indigenous law, Aboriginal rights have been called, among other things, pre-existing,[28] un-extinguished,[29] customary,[30] sui generis,[31] and beneficial.[32] While these designations are by no means synonomous, each implies that the rights of Aboriginal peoples in Canada cannot be understood without looking beyond the common law. The various descriptors counsel the courts to look outside the common law: 'pre-existing' and 'un-extinguished' seem to refer to a time prior to its arrival; 'customary' involves a set of practices parallel to the common law; 'sui generis' communicates the incompleteness of conventional common law categories, and 'beneficial' implicates the rules of equity. These designations illustrate that courts have conceived the sources of the Canadian law of Aboriginal rights in a way that references their separate origins. Canadian courts are thus alive to the possibility that Canadian law dealing with Aboriginal peoples draws upon non-European law in giving meaning to the content of Aboriginal rights.[33]

It should come as no surprise, therefore, that Canadian law may draw upon First Nations legal sources. Courts have long recognized the unextinguished continuity of those pre-existing legal relationships. Since the common law did not alter First Nations law, Indigenous customs and conventions give meaning and content to First Nations' legal rights. For example, Stellaquo adoption laws were recently recognized by the common law and by the constitution of Canada in *Casimel v. Insurance Corporation of British Columbia* (B.C.C.A.).[34] In that case, Louise and Francis Casimel, two biological grandparents, applied for 'no fault' death benefits as 'dependent parents' under provincial insurance regulations when their grandson Ernest Casimel was killed in a car crash. The issue to be resolved was whether Louise and Francis could be legally classified as parents, for the purposes of the statute, when this status depended solely on Ernest's customary adoption. The court held that they could, and that Louise and Francis could therefore collect benefits. It accepted adoption under Stellaquo law by relying on 'a well-established body of authority in Canada' which established 'that the status conferred by

Aboriginal customary adoption will be recognized by the courts for the purposes of application of the principles of the common law and the provisions of statute law to the persons whose status is established by customary adoption.'[35] In arriving at this conclusion the court rejected the insurance company's argument that the customary relationship between the Casimels gave rise to moral rights and obligations only in the absence of any federal or provincial action. The *Casimel* case can be regarded as representative of a string of cases that incorporates Aboriginal law into Canadian law. Similar results can be found in cases involving Aboriginal peoples and land, governance, trade, marriage, adoption, and death.[36] In each such case courts have had to sift through Aboriginal and non-Aboriginal legal sources to determine answers to the question in dispute.

Nevertheless, a parallel line of cases has discounted the idea that First Nations legal sources can be part of Canadian law concerning Aboriginal peoples.[37] A particularly strong statement in this regard is that 'the common law is not part savage and part civilized,' written as obiter in *Sheldon v. Ramsay* in 1852.[38] Cases such as *Sheldon* portray the intersection of Indigenous North American and European legal genealogies as necessitating conflict.[39] In such instances, the Aboriginal source of law is generally not applied because of its perceived incompatibility with, or supposed inferiority within, the legal hierarchy.[40] Under these formulations, Aboriginal rights are labelled personal, usufructuary, and dependent on the goodwill of the sovereign.[41]

For example, two of the most important cases in Canadian jurisprudence concerning First Nations have stated that Crown law and interests were paramount to those of Aboriginal peoples. The 1888 case of *St. Catherines Milling and Lumber Co. v. The Queen* held that Crown title was superior to Aboriginal title because 'there has been all along a substantial and paramount estate, vested in the Crown, underlying the Indian title.'[42] Similarly, the Supreme Court of Canada announced more recently in *R. v. Sparrow,* that 'there was from the outset never any doubt that sovereignty and legislative power, and indeed the underlying title, to such lands [meaning Aboriginal lands] vested in the Crown.'[43] These cases, and others like them,[44] illustrate the view that Aboriginal law is an inferior legal source in Canadian law and must give way to non-Aboriginal sources. Under such interpretations, Canadian law seems to be more attentive to non-Aboriginal legal sources, which consider Indigenous legal rights as emanating only from the sovereign.[45]

On the whole, Canadian courts have emphasized the latter line of cases, which favours non-Aboriginal over Aboriginal legal sources. This overreliance on non-Aboriginal legal sources has resulted in very little protection for Indigenous peoples.[46] Aboriginal land rights were obstructed,[47] treaty rights repressed,[48] and governmental rights constricted.[49] This judicial discourse narrowed First Nations' social, economic, and political power.[50] However, First Nations legal sources and their derivative rights need not be obscured; many Indigenous and non-Indigenous legal principles can be consistent[51] and coexist without conflict.[52] While the case law does not often reveal instances of compatibility, this is largely due to the adversarial process. The oppositional paradigm conceals the broader context in which Aboriginal and non-Aboriginal laws generally co-exist. Perhaps unwittingly, the Supreme Court of Canada reconciled this 'appearance of conflict'[53] by simultaneously referring to the origins of Aboriginal rights as being both pre-existing and personal and usufructuary. As Chief Justice Dickson noted in *R. v. Guerin*: 'It appears to me that there is no real conflict between the cases which characterize Indian title as a beneficial interest of some sort, and those which characterize it as a personal usufructuary right. Any apparent inconsistency derives from the fact that in describing what constitutes a unique interest in land the courts have found themselves applying a somewhat inappropriate terminology drawn from general property law.'[54] The court found that different descriptions of Aboriginal rights were apparently inconsistent because judges had used inappropriate terminology and incorrect legal categories to describe those rights, and it held that, in general, Aboriginal and non-Aboriginal legal sources were consistent with each other and could operate together.

Of course, finding consistency between Aboriginal and non-Aboriginal interests in general does not address the more difficult issue of which of the two laws should prevail if these interests are found incompatible. While the Supreme Court has not expressly invoked the doctrine of incompatability in defining Aboriginal rights protected by the Canadian constitution, such a doctrine may ultimately find its way into the law.[55] Though it would be preferable (and consistent with past judicial practice) to harmonize First Nations and Canadian interests through a process of reconciliation that respects both Crown and Aboriginal legal orders,[56] the potential issue of incompatability cannot be ignored. While this chapter focuses on the often-neglected instances of compatibility between Crown and Aboriginal legal sources, later chapters will examine the paths courts and other bodies have followed in the event of conflict. The courts have not always given preference to Indigenous legal sources when finding such inconsistency, but there are tests aimed at reconciliation which suggest First Nations laws should receive substantial protection from conflicting non-Aboriginal laws in these circumstances.[57] In fact, the court in *Guerin*, despite delineating consistency between First Nations and Crown interests, did not close its eyes to possible conflict in some instances. In the event of such a conflict the court ruled that the Crown's interest should yield to that of the Indians.'[58] Tests that narrow the scope of conflict in federalism jurisprudence generally could also be applied by way of analogy to Indigenous issues. These tests would require actual operational conflict between two laws in order for one to be held invalid.[59] The *Guerin* court was principally concerned, however, with the general compatibility between First Nations and non-Aboriginal legal sources.

Since the pre-existing rights of First Nations can often function alongside western legal principles, the task for the courts is to find more appropriate terminology to describe Aboriginal rights. Ultimately this requires recognizing a category of Canadian law to receive First Nations law. The judiciary has already taken steps in this regard by noting that First Nations law protects sui generis interests.[60] Sui generis is a Latin term meaning 'forming a kind by itself; unique, literally of its own particular kind,'[61] or class. In defining Aboriginal rights as unique, the judiciary has acknowledged that it cannot use conventional common law doctrines alone to give them meaning.[62] Aboriginal rights have always been regarded as different from other common law rights.[63] They do not wholly take their source or meaning from the philosophies that underlie the Western canon of law.[64] Although equal in importance and significance to other rights,[65] Aboriginal rights are different because they are held only by Aboriginal people in Canadian society.[66] A sui generis approach to interpreting Aboriginal rights is appropriate because, in some respects, Aboriginal peoples are unique within the wider Canadian population.[67] The existence of this doctrine suggests the possibility that Aboriginal rights stem from alternative sources of law[68] that reflect the unique historical presence of Aboriginal peoples in North America.[69]

While the sui generis doctrine of Aboriginal rights places significant emphasis upon Aboriginal difference, it does not ignore the similarities between Aboriginal and non-Aboriginal peoples. A legal doctrine focused exclusively upon the differences between Aboriginal and non-Aboriginal people would distort the reality both of Crown-Aboriginal relations and Aboriginal peoples' lives. Aboriginal and non-Aboriginal people have developed ways of relating to one another which, over the centuries, have produced numerous similarities between the various groups.[70] Moreover, Aboriginal and non-Aboriginal people often share interests in the same territories, ecosystems, economies, ideologies, and institutions. While imperfect, and often skewed to the disadvantage of Aboriginal people, these points of connection cannot be ignored. The sui generis doctrine expresses the confidence that there are sufficient similarities between the groups to enable them to live with their differences. Under this doctrine, points of agreement can be highlighted and issues of difference can be preserved to facilitate more productive and peaceful relations. The sui generis doctrine reformulates similarity and difference and thereby captures the complex, overlapping, and exclusive identities and relationships of the parties.[71]

In describing Aboriginal rights as sui generis, the court observed that an Aboriginal right 'derives from the Indian's historic occupation and possession of their tribal lands.'[72] This interpretation takes account of the fact that 'when the settlers came, the Indians were there, *organized* in societies and occupying the land as their forefathers had done for centuries.'[73] As stated in *Van der Peet*, '[A]boriginal rights [exist] ... because of one simple fact: when Europeans arrived in North America, [A]boriginal peoples were already here, living in communities on the land, and participating in distinctive cultures, as they had for centuries.'[74] In that case, the Supreme Court was perhaps at its clearest in holding that that Aboriginal rights arise from the traditional laws and customs of Aboriginal peoples.[75] Lamer C.J.C. held that, just as Aboriginal rights cannot be categorized using conventional common law doctrines alone, neither can they be defined using only Indigenous legal principles. Their essence lies in their bridging of Aboriginal and non-Aboriginal legal cultures.[76] The court thus found that Aboriginal rights are a 'form of intersocietal law that evolved from long-standing practices linking the various communities.' This view was supported by drawing from Professor Walters's writings. The court stated: 'The challenge of defining [A]boriginal rights stems from the fact that they are rights peculiar to the meeting of two vastly different legal cultures; consequently there will always be a question about which legal culture is to provide the vantage point from which rights are to be defined ... a morally and politically defensible conception of rights will incorporate both legal perspectives.'[77] Therefore, the sui generis conception of Aboriginal rights exists to respect and incorporate the presence of Canada's two vastly different legal cultures. A sui generis approach will place 'equal weight' on each perspective and thus achieve a 'true reconciliation' between the cultures.[78]

This same point was recognized in *R. v. Delgamuukw*, where the court wrote, 'what makes [A]boriginal title sui generis is that it arises before the assertion of sovereignty.'[79] Chief Justice Lamer furthered this point by writing that Aboriginal title 'is also sui generis in the sense that its characteristics cannot be completely explained by reference to either the common law rules of real property or to the rules of property found in [A]boriginal legal systems. As with other [A]boriginal rights, it must be understood by reference to both common law and [A]boriginal perspectives.'[80] This formulation of Aboriginal title gives legal recognition and force to the systems by which First Nations organized themselves, 'with a legal as well as a just claim to retain possession' of their territory 'and to use it according to their discretion.'[81] Since Aboriginal organization and occupation of land is dependent on the existence of Indigenous laws, these laws become a source of Aboriginal rights. The fact that the sui generis interest in land has its roots in Aboriginal law means that these laws must form a part of the contemporary meaning of Aboriginal rights. Because Aboriginal legal systems of occupancy were not irretrievibly interrupted or altered by the reception of the common law,[82] there is a continuity of First Nations legal relationships 'in the lands they traditionally occupied prior to European colonization, [which] both pre-dated and survived the claims to sovereignty' by non-Native peoples.[83] In this way, the sui generis formulation of Aboriginal rights attests to the continued existence of First Nations law.

Finally, the pre-existing and contemporary status of Indigenous law was made very plain by the Supreme Court of Canada in *Mitchell v. M.N.R.*[84] In declaring the source of Aboriginal rights Chief Justice McLachlin wrote that 'English law ... accepted that the Aboriginal peoples possessed pre-existing laws and interests, and recognized their continuation ...'[85] As such, she held, '[A]boriginal interests and customary laws were presumed to survive the assertion of sovereignty, and were absorbed into the common law as rights.'[86] McLachlin C.J.C.'s declaration that Aboriginal laws secured the protection of the common law following the assertion of sovereignty by the Crown demonstrates why Aboriginal laws may be held to exist despite the intervention of foreign (non-Aboriginal) legal systems.[87] The common law (and since 1982 constitutional law) status of Indigenous law is what makes possible the submission that Aboriginal laws have relevance in contemporary legal disputes.

Since one source of Aboriginal rights is 'the relationship between common law and pre-existing systems of [A]boriginal law,'[88] Canadian courts and lawmakers charged with developing Aboriginal rights law must grapple with First Nations laws and legal perspectives. Creating law that accounts for both parties' legal perspectives makes sense in the context of Aboriginal and treaty rights litigation because these disputes involve the interaction of legal interests from Aboriginal and non-Aboriginal societies. The use of First Nations law in these instances creates an effective check on inappropriate analogies drawn from other legal sources. The application of Indigenous law by Canadian courts helps to ensure that interactions between the Crown and First Nations are perceived as being fair. It can counteract the powerful influence of non-Aboriginal laws in the development of sui generis principles and help to ensure that this law is as impartial and free of bias as possible. Thus, the explicit reception of Aboriginal perspectives and principles more firmly establishes an autonomous body of law that bridges Aboriginal and non-Aboriginal legal cultures.[89] The sui generis doctrine allows for this *intermingling* of common law and Aboriginal conceptions.[90] Such symmetry allows for the recognition of Aboriginal difference while building strong ties of cooperation and unity between Aboriginal and non-Aboriginal people.

Given that First Nations laws continue to give meaning and content to Aboriginal rights[91] and form a part of the 'laws of Canada,'[92] reference to these laws in Canadian law recognizes a foundational and unifying principle in Aboriginal rights jurisprudence. Indigenous laws have 'always constituted an integral part of their distinctive culture ... for reasons connected to their cultural and physical survival,'[93] and they constitute a principled reference point in the interpretive framework of Aboriginal rights.[94] Since Indigenous laws are integral to the exercise of Aboriginal rights they must be implied into the very fabric of this unique jurisprudence.[95] In considering the existence of any Aboriginal right, it is necessary to recognize that such rights are manifestations of an integral and overarching phenomena. A pervasive and unifying principle that underpins the existence of Aboriginal rights is the existence of Indigenous law and legal perspectives. By inquiring into the First Nations legal viewpoint which gives meaning to particular Aboriginal rights, courts can approach these cases on a more principled and global basis, while retaining their fact- and site-specific context. When courts incorporate Indigenous laws into Canadian Aboriginal rights law they give fuller meaning to them as sui generis interests.

II   First Nations Law: Traditions, the Trickster, and Transformations

'I want you to remember only this one thing,' said the Badger. 'The stories people tell have a way of taking care of them. If stories come to you, care for them. And learn to give them anywhere they are needed. Sometimes a person needs a story more than food to stay alive. That is why we put these stories in each other's memories. This is how people care for themselves.' [96]

How can a court discover Indigenous law in order to receive it into Canadian law concerning Aboriginal peoples? Indigenous law originates in the political, economic, spiritual, and social values expressed through the teachings and behaviour of knowledgeable and respected individuals and elders.[97] These principles are enunciated in the rich stories, ceremonies, and traditions within First Nations.[98] Stories express the law in Aboriginal communities, since they represent the accumulated wisdom and experience of First Nations conflict resolution.[99] Some of these narratives predate the common law, have enjoyed their effectiveness for millennia, and have yet to be overruled or abrogated.[100] They can be communicated in a way that reveals deeper principles of order and disorder, and thereby serve as sources of normative authority in dispute resolution.

For example, Navajo courts use stories to answer legal questions in cases they are called upon to adjudicate. One particularly strong example of this practice comes from their decision *In Re Certified Question II: Navajo Nation v. MacDonald.*[101] In *MacDonald*, the Navajo court was asked to consider, among other things, whether their tribal chairman had breached any fiduciary duties by receiving 'bribes and kickbacks from contractors doing business with the Navajo Nation.'[102] This case was significant for the Navajo courts because it asked them to solve their nation's most pressing problem without resorting to external legal institutions. In finding that the chairman did possess fiduciary duties to the nation, the court referred to a story concerning two 'Hero Twins' who slew monsters and overcame other troubles faced by the Navajo at the time of their creation. The court held that this story embodied the 'Navajo traditional concept of fiduciary trust of a leader (*naat'aanii*).' In applying the principles embedded in this story the court wrote:

> After the epic battles were fought by the Hero Twins, the Navajo people set on the path of becoming a strong nation. It became necessary to elect *naat'aaniis* by consensus of the people. A *naat'aanii* was not a powerful

politician nor was he a mighty chief. A *naat'aanii* was chosen based on his ability to help the people survive and whatever authority he had was based upon that ability and the trust placed in him by the people. If *naat'aanii* lost the trust of his people, the people simply ceased to follow him or even listen to his words ... The Navajo Tribal Council can place a Chairman or Vice Chairman on administrative leave if they have reasonable grounds to believe that the official seriously breached his fiduciary trust to the Navajo people ...[103]

The court's use of the Hero Twins story illustrates the relevance of stories to contemporary Indigenous jurisprudence. It enabled the Navajo to solve a pressing constitutional crisis in their nation by fitting general principles to the specific realities of their community. Stories are clearly central to the normative legal structure of Navajo adjudication.

When used in this manner, Indigenous traditions and stories are both similar to and different from case law precedent.[104] They are analogous to precedent because they attempt to provide reasons for, and reinforce consensus about, broad principles and to justify or criticize certain deviations from generally accepted standards.[105] Common law cases and Aboriginal stories are also similar because both record the fact patterns of past disputes and their related solutions.[106] Furthermore, both Aboriginal stories and common law precedent are interpreted by knowledgeable keepers of wisdom and presented in a manner suitable to a particular dilemma.[107] Finally, both Indigenous stories and common law cases are regarded as authoritative by their listeners, and there are natural, moral, and cultural sanctions for the violation of their instructions.[108] The interpretation of these stories encourages a basic personal and institutional adherence to underlying values and principles.[109] Each of these factors permits First Nations to look upon their stories as a body of knowledge that fulfils many of the same functions as common law precedent.[110]

First Nations stories, however, can also be distinguished from common law precedent in both form and content because of the way they are recorded and applied.[111] First Nations use an oral tradition to chronicle important information,[112] which is stored and shared through a literacy that treasures memory and the spoken word. The oral transmission allows for a constant recreation of First Nations systems of laws.[113] This system of law does not depend on finding the 'authentic' first telling of such an event, uncorrupted by subsequent developments. In fact, the reinterpretation of tradition to meet contemporary needs is a strength of this methodology, although it purportedly distinguishes Indigenous law from the common law.[114] While the common law is itself continually reinterpreted to meet contemporary demands, the degree of fluidity is arguably greater within Aboriginal oral cultures than it is within the common law. At present, there is no tangible library to refer to in the study of First Nations law, and there are sharp cautions from people within the communities against collection and codification.[115] It is understood 'that the teller of the story is so much a part of the event being described that it would be arrogant to presume to classify or categorize the event exactly for all time.'[116]

The application of Indigenous memories and words can thus be quite different from the application of common law precedent. But while non-ceremonial stories can change from one telling to another,[117] such changes do not mean that the story's truths are lost. Rather, modification recognizes that context is always changing, requiring a constant reinterpretation of many of the account's elements.[118] The fluidity of First Nations stories reflects an attempt to convey contextual meaning relevant to the times and needs of the listeners.[119] While the timeless components of the story survive as the important background to the event being heard, its ancient principles are mingled with the contemporary setting and with the specific needs of the hearers.[120]

The Supreme Court of Canada has reflected on the similarities and differences between Aboriginal and non-Aboriginal traditions in its recent jurisprudence. In *Delgamuukw*, Chief Justice Lamer observed: 'In the Aboriginal tradition the purposes of repeating oral accounts from the past is broader than the written history of western societies. It may be to educate the listener, to communicate aspects of culture, to socialize people into a cultural tradition, or to validate the claims of a particular family to authority or prestige.'[121] This description of the social role of Aboriginal oral histories is striking not because it is inaccurate – indeed, the court is sensitive to the various roles these traditions can play – but because it betrays the court's lack of awareness of the social function of the common law. The claim validation aspect of Aboriginal stories obviously parallels the common law's function; it may be also argued that the 'broad social role' of Aboriginal tradition, in the 'expression of the values and mores' of culture, is not very different from the role played by the common law.[122] Yet by contrasting Aboriginal and non-Aboriginal traditions in a dichotomous manner, the Supreme Court does not appear to have acknowledged the common law's broad social function.

The differences between Aboriginal and non-Aboriginal legal systems can give rise to many misconceptions about Aboriginal traditions and stories. It is sometimes tempting to make broad, almost irreconcilable distinctions between Aboriginal legal traditions and Western legal sources, given the different histories, social organization, and values of the two groups. The court may have fallen into this trap in *Delgamuukw*. Such overgeneralization can be problematic, however, when it neglects the common law's own role as a cultural medium that educates, communicates to, and socializes people. It makes Aboriginal principles and tradition appear overly subjective and 'non-legal.' It is only too easy to detach the common law from its cultural context, especially when common law culture seems almost invisible as it corresponds with the values shared by a wide portion of society. A fair account of the similarities and differences between Aboriginal and common law legal systems would pay equal attention to the cultural aspects of each form of law.

Perhaps the best way to illustrate the parallels between Indigenous and non-Indigenous law is by providing an example,[123] using the case method.[124] I will do this by recounting an Anishinabek story in a manner intended to demonstrate the ancient and contemporary stability and flexibility of Anishinabek law. Just as the common law is only understood through a grid of intersecting judgments, the content of First Nations law cannot be understood without an appreciation of how each story correlates with others. A full understanding of First Nations law requires familiarity with the myriad stories of a particular culture and the surrounding interpretations given to them by their people. Nevertheless, within these limitations, I will try to provide a glimpse into how the combination of First Nations stories creates law. The stories recounted below were told to me by my relative John Nadjiwon of Neyaashiinigming, and reinforced by reference to the writings of Basil Johnston, also of Neyaashiinigming.[125] These stories are retold below in a way that combines ancient principles with the contemporary requirements of our people.[126]

A   *Nanabush v. Deer, Wolf et al.*: A Case Comment on First Nations Law

In the distant mists of time, the Anishinabek Nation rendered its judgment in the case of *Nanabush v. Deer, Wolf et al.*[127] The decision signifies an important principle in the development of Anishinabek environmental law. After weighing strong competing factors, the Elders of the Nation proclaimed an important societal/legal position with respect to the governance of natural resources. In their discussion of natural resource use, the Elders stressed the significance of the intersection of relationships in the natural and human world. The case provides an opportunity to illustrate this principle. My commentary examines the *Deer and Wolf* decision to demonstrate its implications with respect to the use of resources situated in Anishinabek territories surrounding the Great Lakes. While the following is not meant as a codification of law, as problems could arise in freezing oral tradition in this manner, the structuring and communication of law in this way may help those unfamiliar with Aboriginal law to gain a sense of its application and principles.

i   The Facts

Nanabush, the woodland Trickster, was journeying through the forest when he saw a deer coming towards him to get a drink. Nanabush stopped the deer and asked, 'What's the matter with your eyes? They look so very red. They certainly must be quite sore. I have some medicine here for sore eyes.' The deer answered that his eyes were not sore, and that redness was their natural condition. Nanabush interjected: 'I never saw them like they are today. My eyes were like that for some time, but I cured them with this.' Nanabush showed the deer some berries he had in his hand and eventually persuaded the deer to take some of the medicine. He took a handful of the berries and rubbed them in the deer's eyes. It was so painful that the deer dropped to the ground. As the deer went down, Nanabush beat it with a club and killed it. He then dressed the deer and roasted the deer, leaving only the head for his grandmother.

When Nanabush sat down to eat, he saw a tree nearby. Every time the wind blew, one of its branches would screech. Nanabush did not like this, and he said to the branch, 'Don't you bother me just when I want to eat, for I am very hungry.' Yet every time he was about to take a bite, the branch began to screech. So Nanabush got up and climbed into the tree to break off the branch that was screeching. But just as Nanabush broke off the branch, his wrist got caught between two branches and he was forced to hang in the tree for some time.

As he was hanging there, unable to free himself, he saw a pack of wolves running along the river. They were about to run by, when Nanabush shouted out: 'Run right on, don't look in this direction.' When they heard this, the wolves said to each other, 'Nanabush must have something there, for he would not tell us to run ahead if he didn't.' So they all went to Nanabush, where they found and ate all the deer that had been roasted. When they were finished, Nanabush said, 'Now go right ahead, don't look up in that tree there.' So the wolves looked up and saw the deer's head hanging in the branches. They pulled it down and ate all the meat that was on it. Just as the wolves were leaving, Nanabush managed to release his wrist and come down from the tree. He could not find the slightest piece of deer meat. He turned the head around but could find nothing.

Then Nanabush thought of the deer brains. So he transformed himself into a very small snake and burrowed his way into the head. He ate all the deer brains, but when he tried to get out, he found that he was unable to do so. So he transformed himself into Nanabush again. But now he had a deer skull on his head. With this he went to the river, but there he came upon some people who mistook him for a deer and chased him. As he ran away, he tripped and fell down. The deer head struck a stone and broke open, and Nanabush was freed once again.

ii   *The Issue: Do Nanabush's Actions Violate the Balance*
Required by Law in the Relationship between Humans and Animals?

The Anishinabek attributed some of their society's problems to the imbalance of the hunting relationship between humans and animals. In this case, Nanabush failed to respect the dignity and body of the deer. But how do we know that Nanabush broke the law in doing so? Just as in the common law, the legal significance of these facts can only be appreciated by reference to previous Anishinabek cases. One cannot understand First Nations law without an appreciation of how each story correlates with others. A full understanding of First Nations law, and their principles for governance, requires familiarity with other stories of the particular culture and the surrounding interpretations given to them by their people. The court in this case answered the issue identified in the Nanabush case by accepting the earlier case of *Crow, Owl, Deer et al. v. Anishinabek.*[128]

In the *Crow* case, the deer, moose, and caribou left the land of the Anishinabek and were captured by the crows. The crows kept them in confinement, and when the Anishinabek discovered this they went to battle against the birds. There was a long and bitter battle in which neither side prevailed. During the battle, the deer looked on with seeming indifference to the outcome. Eventually a truce was called and the Anishinabek met with the crow and deer in council. The Anishinabek asked: 'Why are you unconcerned with our efforts to rescue you from your forced confinement? We have endured hardship, and risked death on your behalf. Still you appear indifferent.' The Chief Deer replied: 'You have assumed wrongly that we are here against our wishes. On the contrary, we choose to remain here and are quite content. The crows have treated us better than you ever treated us when we shared the same country with you.'

The Anishinabek were astonished and asked the deer how they had offended. The deer spoke sadly 'You have wasted our flesh; you have despoiled our haunts; you have desecrated our bones; you have dishonoured us and yourselves. Without you we can live – but without us, you cannot live.' The Anishinabek then asked how they could make amends, and said their negligence was not motivated by ill will. They asked: 'How shall we atone for your grief?' The Chief Deer answered, 'Honour and respect our lives and our beings, in life and in death. Cease doing what offends our spirits. Do not waste our flesh. Preserve fields and forests for our homes. To show your commitment to these things and as a remembrance of the anguish you have brought upon us, always leave the tobacco leaf from where you take us. Gifts are important to build our relationships once again.' The Anishinabek promised to follow the words of the Chief Deer, and the crows released their captives from bondage.

iii   Resolution of the Issue

The *Crow* case applies to the *Nanabush* case because it is clear that Nanabush broke the law by disregarding the promise of respect embodied in the treaty between the Anishinabek and the deer. These covenants are central to Anishinabek resource law, as well as general governance. Through disrespectful trickery and foolish ruse, Nanabush violated the Nation's oath of honour and respect. In particular, Nanabush's method of killing the deer, the way in which his actions caused the deer to be despoiled by the wolves, the breaking of the skull of the deer, and his failure to leave tobacco all point to the creation of an imbalance in the relationship of human to animal and constitute a violation of Anishinabek resource law. This was the finding of the majority in *Deer, Wolf*, who convincingly responded to the cases Justice Wendigo relied on in dissent:

> Justice Wendigo would have us find that the deer was a thin skulled plaintiff, and caused his own death by his pride and susceptibility to Nanabush's flattery. Wendigo, J. arrived at this conclusion by relying on the reasons in *Rest of the Forest v. Birch Tree*,[129] where the birch tree was whipped by the pine needles for its vanity in boasting about its pre-eminent strength and

beauty. In that case, the pine tree was held not to be liable for the dark lateral marks placed on the white bark of the birch because the birch created an imbalance by asserting its greater worth relative to others. However, this reasoning does not apply to excuse Nanabush in this case because it fails to respect the generous and liberal interpretation that should be accorded to the treaty the Anishinabek made with the deer. This conclusion is thus not sensitive to the broader historical context in which the Anishinabek Nation's promise of respect was made. The deer was justified in exercising trust in Nanabush because this is the balance the relationship was intended to have at the time the Anishinabek agreed to respect the deer. Therefore, I must respectfully disagree with the suggestion that the vanity of the deer made him contributorily responsible for his fate.

The minority's narrow focus on the deer's actions to the exclusion of the treaty fails to preserve the spirit and intent of the covenants made between the Anishinabek and the deer. If the minority was followed, it could create a serious problem for the deer and the Anishinabek: the deer would once again disappear from Anishinabek territory. The majority decision in the *Deer, Wolf* case is, therefore, a powerful precedent for Anishinabek people in governing their resources. It represents principles their governments aspire to follow. If the Anishinabek do not honour and respect their promises, relations, and environments, the eventual consequence is that these resources will disappear. When these resources are gone, no matter what they are, the people will no longer be able to sustain themselves because, as the *ratio* of the case states, while the resources have an existence without us, we have no existence without them.[130]

B   Giving and Receiving Gifts: The Application and Scope of First Nations Law

The *Deer, Wolf* case demonstrates many of the similarities and differences between First Nations law and the common law described above. It is true that the stories as told here have been translated and stylized to make them more readily accessible to common law readers. However, all law requires a translation process.[131] Law is 'a culture of argument' that 'provides a place and a set of institutions and methods where this conversational process can go on, as well as a second conversation by which the first is criticized and judged.'[132] The stories in this chapter are translated into the language of legal culture to be recognizable within Canadian law, and to remind Canadian law-makers of their reluctance to engage in legal conversations with First Nations cultures. The changes made are also quite consistent with a genre of First Nations storytelling, which allows the narrator to become the Trickster, transforming the content of the stories into a new, previously unaccepted form.

Regardless of the form of First Nations stories, however, they function together to guide people in the resolution of disputes. Indigenous peoples frequently access their historic experiences and cultural epics in order to formulate and apply their own law. The stories are flexible enough to be applied as answers to different questions. They often contain multiple meanings and their deceptive simplicity hides a sophisticated structure and substance. Indeed, while I have related the stories in question to resolve issues concerning resource use, they contain an important principle with respect to Canada's relationship with First Nations people generally, which could be used to judge the justice of the parties' interactions. However, in keeping with the conventional methods of Anishinabek legal process, and to illustrate its operation, I will leave it up to the readers to go back in the text, study the stories for themselves, and draw their own conclusions about their messages in this regard. My retelling of these stories demonstrates that the most important messages in First Nations stories may be the least obvious on first hearing. The speaker may even intentionally bury the primary motivation in relating a story to deflect its directness and thereby avoid outright confrontation. Clearly, this path to judgment leaves much to an individual's analytical reflections and contains a very different understanding of legal reasoning from that most familiar to Canadian courts. In these circumstances, it is no wonder that common law judges have had so much trouble recognizing First Nations law.

It is evident that the distinctive elements of Indigenous legal reasoning present challenges in communicating and applying First Nations law. Yet, such intellectually challenging work is found in all legal reasoning processes. Answers to tough legal questions are not formulaic or self-evident; they require hard choices concerning the appropriate inferences to be drawn from the facts and cases in any dispute. Despite the difficulties that may be encountered in working with First Nations law, it is important that Canadian judges have a suitable understanding of these legal institutions and narratives. When this law is more widely proclaimed, Indigenous laws and legal perspectives can influence *sui generis* categories of Canadian law concerning Aboriginal peoples. Courts frequently draw useful analogies from international law and various areas of the common law, including contract and property, in developing Canadian Aboriginal law; principles from Indigenous law can be extracted in a similar manner. That is, Aboriginal legal principles can be accepted by analogy into the common law to bridge the gap between Aboriginal and non-Aboriginal laws. They can be used in a culturally appropriate way to answer many of the contemporary challenges encountered by Canadian courts. The incorporation of such a broad base of legal principles would make the law more truly Canadian and, as a result, more equitable and fair.[133]

If courts begin to use First Nations law regularly, questions may still arise about the nature and scope of such an exercise. For example, it may be suggested that while First Nations law may work to resolve issues within First Nations, it should be strictly limited to that sphere of activity. It may be argued that First Nations laws are of little assistance in resolving intercultural disputes between First Nations and non-Aboriginal people, and that they have no relevance in cases involving non-Aboriginal peoples. I myself would not be so quick to dismiss the potential of First Nations law to resolve disputes between non-Aboriginal people. This line of argument would misapprehend the way the common law works. If a principle from tort law is relevant to a dispute in contract or property law, the courts apply it regardless of category of law to which it owes its origin.[134] While there are always limits to this kind of exercise, developments in the common law frequently arise from cross-fertilization among its categories.

Furthermore, First Nations legal principles have the respect of many non-Aboriginal people, and they have a long history in mediating intercultural disputes. For example, early treaties were often negotiated and ratified according to First Nations form and content and have been remarkably successful in maintaining peace and friendship over long periods of time.[135] Contemporary notions of First Nations dispute resolution are finding increasing acceptance in many Western institutions.[136] The future may see the continued development and use of First Nations law to answer questions plaguing Western society today.[137] For example, in many Canadian jurisdictions, traditional Aboriginal practices regarding justice are modified to interact with courtroom procedures.[138] Often, Aboriginal practices will be employed at the pretrial stage,[139] and sometimes they function at the end of the conventional criminal justice process.[140] The operation of First Nations law in conjunction with the criminal law demonstrates the role First Nations institutions can play in intercultural disputes.[141]

Sentencing circles provide an interesting illustration of the inter-cultural interaction of First Nations institutions and principles with Canadian law,[142] drawing upon both the customary conflict resolution processes used by some Aboriginal peoples and Canadian criminal law. Traditionally, the circle consists of people interested in participating in the resolution of a dispute. These people are usually the offender; his or her family; and friends, the victim, and other individuals with informa-tion, interest, or skills that may be used to restore harmony between the people involved and within the community more broadly. Those present gather in a circle, both to symbolize a connection to the order of the non-human world and to confirm the equality of all the participants. Once in a circle, conversation flows in one direction with one person speaking at a time. People speak in this manner to imitate the trajectory of the sun, earth, and moon and to ensure that everyone has the oppor-tunity to contribute without being interrupted. People speak about what can be done to help the offender, the victim, and the wider community.

The principles used in the sentencing circle are heavily influenced by some prairie peoples' traditional law and world-view. At the same time, the topics of conversation within the circle are those of contemporary Western society. This mingling of forms indicates that there is indeed room for Aboriginal law in the resolution of intercultural disputes.[143] In fact, one judge has decided that the circle may be useful to guide the resolution of disputes when Aboriginal peoples are not involved: according to Justice Milliken of the Saskatchewan Court of Queen's Bench in *R. v. Morin*, a judge may approve the use of a sentencing circle even if the offender is non-Aboriginal.[144] First Nations legal institutions may thus have a role to play in resolving disputes wholly outside of Aboriginal involvement.[145] This reasoning creates an even stronger justi-fication for the application of First Nations law where there is conflict between Aboriginal and non-Aboriginal peoples.[146]

III   Epilogue: At the Beginning

Tradition ... cannot be inherited, and if you want it you must obtain it by great labour.[147]

The question of how to implement the reception of First Nations law more fully in Canadian law is just beginning to unfold. Full respect for and acceptance of First Nations law will not be easy to accomplish,[148] even though there is legal precedent that would allow it as well as strong and clear evidence of existing Indigenous law. The contemporary dynamics of political, economic, and social power place the common law in a superordinate position relative to Indigenous law.[149] Lawyers and judges trained in conventional legal reasoning are bound to encounter difficulties in interpreting Indigenous law[150] because they are accustomed to looking to reported cases to assist them in defining and applying the law. It will be a great challenge to present First Nations laws to decision makers unfamiliar with non-European cultures.[151] Changing the cultural power of conventional Western law will also be difficult.[152] Legal principles derived from communities outside the cultural mainstream often encounter daunting obstacles before they are accepted.[153]

Bias and prejudice will also be hard to overcome;[154] despite recent case law, some people will continue to believe that First Nations laws are inferior.[155] This problem has arisen in the United States, where tribal law is more prominent.[156] It is exemplified in the following account of the Chief Justice of the Navajo Court speaking to a six-state conference of judges on the meaning of 'Indian traditional law' or 'Indian common law.' After Chief Justice Yazzie spoke, 'Jim Zion, our court solicitor, dashed outside for a cigarette. He overheard two Wyoming judges talking about what I had to say. The first judge said, "What did you think of Chief Yazzie's presentation on Navajo common law?" The second laughed and said, "He didn't mention staking people to anthills."'[157] Inappropriate caricatures of First Nations will inevitably persist for many years, and prejudices rooted in racial and cultural bias will continue to suppress the legitimacy and acceptance of First Nations law.[158] The unique characteristics of Indigenous law, moreover, will make its reception into Canadian common law more complex.[159] As a result, it may take longer for these laws to enjoy the same respect accorded to other categories of the common law.

Yet there are mechanisms currently in place that would allow for the communication, proof, interpretation, reception, and application of First Nations law.[160] Ethnography,[161] recorded precedent,[162] learned treatises,[163] judicial notice,[164] expert testimony,[165] and skilled advocates can all assist judges in this venture. Properly trained lawyers of all cultures would conceivably be able to learn and articulate First Nations law, given appropriate access to, and support from, the community they represent. Among this cadre of lawyers are legally trained members of First Nations.[166] Many of these people are bicultural and/or bilingual and have learned law from their Elders as well as from Canadian legal and academic institutions.[167] They can interpret Western common law precedent, but they also know where to find resolutions to the same questions within First Nations customary or common law. They have access to an alternative source of knowledge and their contributions can help courts resolve troublesome issues.[168] They can bridge the gulf between First Nations and European legal systems and help to make the law truly intersocietal.

Of course, not every First Nations person trained in Canadian law schools will be capable of providing courts with the necessary guidance.[169] Many First Nations lawyers are relatively young and have, understandably, been so busy learning Canadian law that they have not had time to invest in the study of their own traditional laws. As Jürgen Habermas noted, 'The reproduction of traditions and cultural forms is an achievement which can be legally enabled, but by no means granted.' Thus it is critical that Aboriginal people be afforded the opportunity to learn and create their own laws, and then take the personal initiative to master them. In this effort, as Habermas again suggests, 'Reproduction ... requires the conscious appropriation and application of traditions by those native members who have become convinced of these traditions' intrinsic value. These members must first come to see that the inherited traditions are worth the existential effort of continuation.'[170] The acquisition of Aboriginal law does require effort, as great, if not greater, an investment of time as is necessary to learn and apply Canadian law.[171] Individuals wanting to learn First Nations law must currently embark on a personal quest for understanding and knowledge, and it is not always easy to acquire this information by oneself.

The acquisition of First Nations law does not flow from magical rituals or mystical processes. While some may understand it through non-linear processes, this law can be discerned on other bases as well.[172] Some sources of First Nations law, such as the sacred and the ceremonial, would be inappropriate to bring before the court, but much of the information is acquired in the same way other legal education is acquired: through years of study and hard work. The fact that First Nations law can be learned in a manner familiar to most people means that the interpretation of this law for the benefit of Canadian courts is not the exclusive domain of Aboriginal people, though caution should always be exercised in this regard. Cultural knowledge should remain under community control, and to educate non-Aboriginal people in the details of Indigenous law poses a risk of unjust appropriation of this knowledge. However, it is conceivable that a non-Native person who received the training, confidence, and certification of a First Nations community may be able to provide the bridge by which First Nations law is communicated to Canadian courts. Discussions have only recently begun with respect to establishing an institutional way for First Nations law to be communicated to First Nations and non-Aboriginal lawyers, law students, and other interested people.[173] An important step in this regard was taken when the University of Victoria Faculty of Law recently partnered with the Akitsiraq Law Society of Nunavut to deliver Inuit legally oriented education in that territory. The creation of an Indigenous Traditional Law School or Program would go a long way to articulating and diffusing knowledge of Indigenous law. The courts' continued recognition of the importance of First Nations laws within the Canadian legal framework would also encourage this learning. Until such initiatives receive support from universities, law societies, courts, and First Nations, we will have to rely upon individuals who make the effort to become educated in both legal systems. These people are waiting to be called upon, but much more could be done to facilitate their efforts.

The institutional apparatus of Canadian law, and the community whose legal interests are represented, must recognize those who can traverse the divide between First Nations and non-Aboriginal legal sources in any specific dispute and allow them the opportunity to speak to the law. They could speak as would any other lawyer in addressing the relevant law. If we are to take the court seriously in its pledge to treat Canadian law concerning Aboriginal peoples as intersocietal and sui generis, people of all cultures must be permitted and encouraged to express First Nations law for application. If Aboriginal people are going to take seriously the challenge to change Canadian jurisprudence and transform legal principles to accommodate their understanding of law and justice, they must devote thoughtful consideration and effort to an articulation of their own laws.[174] Efforts to define and apply these laws will assist First Nations to fulfil important philosophical and social responsibilities in the communities of Nations and peoples.[175]

None of the statements made in this chapter regarding First Nations laws providing analogies for Canadian law or First Nations being able to articulate their laws in a Western format should be taken to mean that First Nations will only work to implement their laws through the formal institutions of Canadian law.[176] In fact, as discussed in the next chapter, Aboriginal laws should be regarded as even more relevant in less formal settings, both within Indigenous communities and in the interactions of Indigenous peoples with their neighbours.[177] Courts should only be the smallest corner in which Aboriginal laws are applied. In fact, the chances of Canadian law accepting Indigenous legal principles would be substantially weakened if First Nations did not continue to practise their own laws within their own systems.[178] Aboriginal systems of law can and do operate, with or without the reception of their principles in Canadian courtrooms. They should continue to provide the greatest guidance through their application in family, community, and intracommunity disputes. In less formal settings these stories will retain more of their flexibility and subtlety, and thus be of even more assistance in answering people's questions.

First Nations legal traditions are strong and dynamic and can be interpreted flexibly to deal with the real issues in contemporary Canadian law concerning Aboriginal communities. Tradition dies without such transmission and reception. Laying claim to a tradition requires work and imagination, as particular individuals interpret it, integrate it into their own experiences, and make it their own. In fact, tradition is altered by the very fact of trying to understand it.[179] It is time that this effort to learn and communicate tradition be facilitated, both within First Nations and between First Nations and Canadian courts. There is persuasive precedent in Canadian law recognizing the pre-existence of Aboriginal rights and their associated laws. Furthermore, the courts have created an opportunity to receive these laws into Canadian law by analogy and through sui generis principles. These principles must be allowed to influence the development of law in Canada. When First Nations laws are received more fully into Canadian law, both systems will be strengthened.[180] As both an Anishinabek and Canadian citizen, it is my hope that Canada will not disregard the promise of respect that Canadian law holds for First Nations.[181] Canadian legal institutions will soon determine if First Nations law will continue with or without them.

Neesh-wa-swi'ish-ko-day-kawn arose and said:

in the time of the Seventh Fire an Osh-ki-bi-ma-di-zeeg' (New People) will emerge. They will retrace their steps to find what was left by the trail.

The task of the new people will not be easy. If the new people remain strong in their quest, the Waterdrum of the Midewiwin Lodge will again sound its voice. There will be a ... rekindling of old flames. The Sacred Fire will again be lit.

It is at this time that the Light-skinned Race will be given a choice between two roads. If they will choose the right road, then the Seventh Fire will light the Eighth and Final Fire – an eternal Fire of peace ... If the Light-skinned Race makes the wrong choice of roads, then the destruction which they brought with them in coming to this country will come back to them and cause much suffering ...

We might be able to deliver our society from the road to destruction. Could we make the two roads that today represent two clashing world views come together to form [a] mighty nation?

Are we the New People of the Seventh Fire?[182]

Chapter Two

Living Between Water and Rocks: The Environment, First Nations, and Democracy

The western shores of Georgian Bay are a place of ancient life. Prehistoric limestone escarpments rise hundreds of feet into the air, and then advance into cool turquoise waters. Piled at the feet of these giants are the chronicles of a storied past. There, flat grey shale stones narrate the traditions of tens of thousands of years. Entombed within these rocks are the remains of the territory's earlier spirits. The genealogy of this coast records the fossilized memories of cone-shaped squid, brain-sized coral, and silver-black crustaceans. Intermingled are the impressions of Palaeozoic sponges, long tendrils of flowing kelp, and stiff, hollow reeds. If you follow the escarpment underwater, you discover eight-thousand-year-old forests,[1] and the hushed campfires[2] of my ancestors, the Anishinabek.[3]

Our presence continues to endure in these margins. Between the shadows of the escarpments and the waters of the lake lies home, Neyaashiinigming.[4] This place is also known as the Cape Croker Indian Reservation, the heart of the Chippewas of the Nawash First Nation. The reserve is on a peninsula surrounded by the waters of Lake Huron's Georgian Bay, in an area now known as southern Ontario. A mile across the water to the east is Kookoominiising,[5] or Hay Island, used and occupied by our people since time immemorial.[6] In its forests we hunt deer, on its shores we collect medicines, and off its coast we fish in the waters.[7] On the north end of the Island below the bluff, where there is a flat plain and lagoon, we buried our dead.[8] The island has the same characteristics as the reserve. Rare plants flourish on the long, fossil-strewn shores sandwiched between high limestone escarpments and deep, rich waters. A variety and abundance of fish frequent its underwater cliffs. Hay Island is mostly forested, with a small clearing on its upper plateau that provides a range of important wildlife habitats. Several intermittent streams carry surface water from the plateau down the bluff, where ravines have been created, and across the shoreline.[9] The 1,600-acre island is about one-tenth the size of the reserve.

The Chippewas of the Nawash First Nation live at the margins of more than just lakes, islands, and land. They exist just beyond the borders of the North American legal imagination.[10] In land-use planning processes, my people are caught between the peripheries of competing political jurisdictions.[11] The relationships of federalism have been almost exclusively attentive to national and provincial interests and have thus constricted the political space within which Neyaashiinigming operates.[12] The community has little or no opportunity to influence environmental ideas, design, and decision making. Towering behind it are the escarpment-like barriers and constraints of a racist and outdated Indian Act.[13] This archaic federal document casts long, dark shadows across First Nations governmental powers.[14] The Indian Act hinders participation in environmental planning by limiting the steps Indigenous peoples can take to directly address environmental challenges.[15] Compressing First Nations from the other side are the deep waters of provincial authority. Indigenous peoples are often submerged and invisible in their own land because the province does not make provision for a representation of their interests.[16] These federalist structures organize, separate, and allocate water and rocks in a manner that promotes unequal distributions of political influence.[17] Federalism constucts a 'legal geography of space' that marginalizes Indigenous peoples in significant environmental decision making. Neyaashiinigming's residence in the legal spaces between competing political boundaries exemplifies the ailing condition of our democracies in North America.

The process of Indigenous exclusion within North American democracies has been greatly assisted by the operation of law. Despite its potential to do otherwise, the law has both inadvertently ignored and purposely undermined Indigenous institutions and ideas, and thus weakened ancient connections to the environment. The culture of the common law has imposed a conceptual grid over both space and time which divides, parcels, registers, and in peoples and places in a way that is often inconsistent with Indigenous participation[18] and environmental integrity.[19] As I discovered in my time at the law school on Philosopher's Walk,[20] this mapping of knowledge has repressed and concealed both Indigenous participation and ecological systems in the configuration of North American settlements. The law rarely recognizes forests, fields, roads, or settlements that owe their founding and pre-European existence to prior Indigenous environmental use.[21] Indeed, we scarcely appreciate that the early possibility and pattern of settlement in North America often depended upon an appropriation or a systematic erasure of Indigenous environmental use.[22] Furthermore, North American law rarely recognizes the integrity of watersheds, air-sheds, or biotic zones.[23] Again, the very possibility for and pattern of many settlements in North America was based on the appropriation and separation of certain resources from their ecosystems, and the denial of their interconnections.[24] The law has employed a culturally exclusive vision of geography that severs the relationship between local, Indigenous use of the natural environment and democratic institutions.[25] Consequently, the knowledge and experience that Indigenous peoples might contribute to the formulation of institutions and ideas to better live with our environment have been suppressed.

There is a real need to reformulate how we plan and participate in the design and governance of human settlements. Increasing alienation from our natural and social environments has nearly overwhelmed our ability to effectively function in the places we choose to live.[26] Cities and towns are being eviscerated through pollution, poverty, congestion, crime, and a loss of control over the political means to change this situation.[27] Our farms and villages are similarly being decimated.[28] There are significant problems of desertification, deforestation, and soil erosion.[29] Furthermore, we are witnessing the collapse of fisheries, the draw-down and pollution of ground water, the extinction of species,[30] the depletion of stratospheric ozone, and an increase in atmospheric carbon dioxide.[31] As in the cities, people living in rural environments perceive that the decisions precipitating their problems are taken without their influence or participation.

The degradation of our biophysical and sociological ecosystems is deeply disturbing. North American environmental and democratic systems are straining to sustain their current level of economic activity and material consumption.[32] Pressure is intensified by a hegemonic alignment of interests, institutions, and ideas that enable some to gain enormous political and economic power by over-exploiting the environment.[33] This intersection of certain individuals' preferences, their organization into powerful coalitions, and the subsequent entrenchment and reproduction of their ideas has frustrated the integration of environmental considerations into our democracies.[34] Yet at a primary level human society is a subset of the ecosphere.[35] The viability of our settlements requires that our ideologies and decision-making structures take account of the fact that we are embedded in nature.[36] Therefore, our democracies must strengthen the relationship between the natural environment and democratic institutions, and harness those forces that weaken this tie. The objective of this simultaneous release and restraint of different environmental orientations is the strengthening of our local, regional, and national environments.

The publication of *Our Common Future* popularized a vital clue about how we might start to reframe our relationship with the environment.[37] This report by the World Commission on Environment and Development (the Brundtland Commission) suggested that our activities should 'meet the needs of the present without compromising the ability of future generations to meet their own needs.'[38] The notion of 'sustainable development'[39] advocated a renewed approach to planning human settlements that attempts to integrate human economic and natural ecological activities.[40] The Brundtland Commission recognized that some communities have at times realized this objective. These communities, the so-called Indigenous or tribal peoples of the world,[41] '... are the repositories of vast accumulations of traditional knowledge and experience that links humanity with its ancient origins ... These groups' own institutions to regulate rights and obligations are crucial for maintaining the harmony with nature and the environmental awareness characteristic of the traditional way of life. Hence the recognition of traditional rights must go hand in hand with measures to protect local institutions that enforce responsibility in resource use. And this recognition must also give local communities a decisive voice in the decisions about resource use in their area.'[42] As the commission notes, significant Indigenous institutions and ideas can be built upon to halt the deterioration of places we call home.[43] Allowing local Indigenous communities a democratic voice in regulating environmental rights and obligations may contribute to the improvement of human settlements.[44] Over the centuries, these peoples have enjoyed great success in meeting the needs of the present without compromising the ability of future generations to meet their needs.[45]

The fact that Indigenous peoples may contribute to the creation of better communities should not be taken to mean that all of our environmental problems will vanish if we heed their knowledge.[46] Given the scale of our current troubles, there are many intricacies these peoples have not faced. Indigenous settlements, villages or towns are different organisms from the great cities of North America.[47] To try to understand all of our environmental afflictions through Indigenous knowledge would only compound our confusion about how to overcome environmental degeneration. A successful response to particular historical, environmental, and social circumstances may not always be translated appropriately to other settings. Ecological systems are often unique and require the application of specialized knowledge to ensure their continuation as well as to more universal principles of wise use. While instructive, Indigenous knowledge is also imperfect, and only one of many sources to be consulted in working through our environmental challenges.[48] Many stereotypes concerning 'the ecological Indian,' moreover, do not accord with current or even past Aboriginal practices, and if followed, could lead to serious environmental degradation.[49] Furthermore, many Indigenous peoples have themselves become colonized[50] and are implicated in serious environmental destruction.[51] Aboriginal peoples are as capable of environmental degradation as anyone else, despite their rhetoric or the popular view of their environmental sensitivity. Self-interest and cultural blindness to the potential dangers of one's own group's practices can be found everywhere, and any group's claim to a better path of environmental preservation should be met with a healthy degree of scepticism.[52]

Despite these cautions, we cannot entirely diregard Indigenous environmental knowledge because, as the Brundtland Commission noted, some of these peoples have enjoyed substantial and long-term environmental successes. These lessons have not yet been integrated with broader North American institutions and ideologies.[53] Indigenous knowledge has often been delegitimated and thus concealed from wider public view. So-called democratic institutions repress Indigenous participation, degrade their environments, and thereby hinder the extension of knowledge about how to successfully live with the environment.[54] The result is detrimental to all because many Indigenous communities may function as 'canaries in the coal-mine' to provide an early warning of environmental dangers other people may later encounter.[55] Since many First Nations still live close to the land and directly depend on its health for their livelihood, they will often be the first to face any problems that may subsequently affect society as a whole.[56] Thus, the suppression of Indigenous institutions has potentially detrimental consequences for all human settlements.[57]

This chapter addresses the barriers within North American democracies that currently prevent First Nations from participating in the governance of their environments, preclude the articulation and acceptance of Indigenous knowledge, and in doing so, obscure an important perspective about how humans are ultimately embedded in nature. The loss incurred is illustrated through a case study that examines a proposed development on Hay Island, lands in which Indigenous peoples have a continuing interest. I have chosen an event focus to emphasize how law is interpreted in settings other than courts. While courts are obviously an important site for marking legal boundaries, the drawing of legal margins also occurs 'on the ground.'[58] Communities, politicians, bureaucrats, and developers interact with each other to draw, erase, and redraw legal borders to include and/or exclude certain peoples, institutions, and ideas. These dialogical engagements create and interpret a kind of customary law and produce a legal geography that remains largely uncharted. A decentred map of law refocuses attention on how these informal, customary practices of law continue to operate simultaneously with the often more visible and formal institutions of law.[59] This study illustrates how contemporary processes of customary law have inhibited the reception of Indigenous knowledge and thereby frustrated the design of sustainable settlements.

A case study of contemporary customary law also has the advantage of highlighting more general lessons that can be applied within a wider North American context, where the formalities of law might vary between jurisdictions. While the events described occur within Canada, Indigenous peoples experience strikingly similar forms of exclusion on both sides of the (comparatively) newly created U.S./Canadian border,[60] and planning institutions throughout the hemisphere could greatly benefit by considering Indigenous legal knowledge. Effective consultation with First Nation communities could dismantle many of the barriers separating them from their traditional environments. Indigenous inclusion and involvement in existing institutions potentially facilitates sustainability by suggesting important reconnections of biological relationships within ecosystems.

After examining the barriers Indigenous peoples and ecosystems encounter in North American democracies, this chapter takes a constructive turn and identifies First Nations legal principles concerning sustainable communities. If North Americans are going to improve their settlements, it is not enough merely to consult Indigenous peoples within existing structures. North Americans require different principles to judge Indigenous contributions because contemporary legal rules were developed within a cultural logic that erased prior Indigenous presence and ecological relationships.[61] Reinscribing Indigenous laws on the North American landscape brings into sharper relief the socially constructed notions of space currently passing as neutral facts in land-use planning processes. It also reveals the cultural contingency of the ideas that currently dominate North American legal thought. Indigenous legal principles form a system of 'empirical observations and pragmatic knowledge' that has value both in itself and as a tool to demonstrate how people structure information.[62] First Nations laws embrace ecological protection, and they could be woven into the very fabric of North American legal ideas.

As illustrated in the previous chapter, Indigenous laws often find expression in traditional stories, which are a primary source of precedents guiding environmental and land-use planning. These narratives have been persuasive for centuries. Placing Indigenous traditions in an intersocietal context, through a culturally appropriate methodology that allows access to oral tradition and community knowledge,[63] reveals ways in which traditional legal knowledge could enhance democracy and facilitate sustainability. Locating Indigenous accounts of law within and beside Western interpretations of contemporary customary law encourages more inclusive democratic conversations. This chapter sketches a tentative pathway to reintegrate democracy and law with environmental concerns, and thus contains general lessons North American democracies might consider in the design and governance of their settlements.

I   Lost in (Legal) Space: Neyaashiinigming and Hay Island

The law's spatial severance of North America's pre-existing ecosystems and societies continues despite the government's numerous legal guarantees to protect Indigenous interests. For example, in 1764 we entered into a treaty of peace and friendship with representatives of the British Crown, who recognized our responsibilities and jurisdiction relative to Hay Island, Neyaashiinigming, and other lands.[64] In 1836, at Treaty 45½, our title to the island was confirmed by the then lieutenant governor, Sir Francis Bond Head.[65] In 1847 Queen Victoria issued a declaration specifically stating that these lands would be held for us in trust for future generations.[66] In 1854, Treaty 72 again confirmed our rights.[67] However, in 1899 the government-appointed Indian agent, in an apparent conflict of interest, took a legal surrender of Hay Island and sold it to his daughter.[68] In this transaction Anishinabek spatial consciousness encountered a different orientation to both land and place. The possessive accumulation of resources by individuals disrupted the shared relationship the Anishinabek cultivated with the surrounding ecosystem. This transaction meant that Hay Island was no longer an Indian reserve, despite our continued use and interests.[69] The validity of this transaction is the subject of an outstanding land claim.[70]

Uncertainty surrounding underlying title did not stop others from pressing their interests on this land, despite the fundamental challenge Anishinabek property rights pose to the ownership of subsequent claimants. In January 1989 the owners of Hay Island applied for an amendment to the Bruce Peninsula Official Plan to redesignate the north end of Hay Island from rural to 'resort.'[71] This amendment would have dramatically changed the character of the island through the creation of 135 linear waterfront lots. It was intended that these lots would be purchased by summer cottagers, who would make the four-hour drive from Toronto or Detroit. The application was supported by the township and county but turned down by the Province of Ontario. The province expressed concerns about the impact of the proposed lots on the surrounding waters due to poor septic system suitability and site servicing.[72]

Undaunted, the owners of Hay Island brought forward an application for an amendment to the official plan in 1992. This time they proposed a cluster development, in an attempt to meet the earlier-identified concerns. They wanted to site ninety-eight seasonal residences in a smaller, hundred-acre envelope on the northern tip of the island. Support was again forthcoming from the township and the county, and this time the provincial ministries were also supportive.[73] This result was not satisfactory to the Chippewas of the Nawash. In their view the process leading to the proposal and tentative approval of the project did not involve them sufficiently, nor did it adequately evaluate the impact of this development on the local environment.[74]

A   Feeling Out of Place: Neyaashiinigming's Procedural Exclusion in Land-Use Planning

Environmental issues have not been satisfactorily addressed in the design of the Hay Island project because of significant inequities in the interactions of the parties concerned. Many people at Neyaashiinigming believe that the non-Native participants responsible for deciding project involvement have provided interpretations of law that direct political influence away from the reserve. It could be argued that these interpretations, arrived at through informal legal reasoning, produced customary law judgments that excluded Neyaashiinigming from the planning process. This apparent exclusion seems to have raised serious issues of notice, misrepresentation, and conflicts of interest.

Ontario's Planning Act does not require official and direct notice to, or participation from, the First Nation. The legislative and policy framework thus produces institutions that seem to minimize the existence of Indigenous communities. In this case, the local planning agencies appear never to have disclosed the proposed development to the officials of the reserve. The people of Neyaashiinigming did not know about it until almost immediately before Bruce County Council's final approval meeting, despite the fact that plans for the development of Hay Island had been circulated for three and a half years at the highest levels of both the local and provincial governments.[75] The perceived lack of notice and involvement of the reserve is inappropriate from a planning and environmental perspective because Neyaashiinigming would be the community most affected by the development.[76] Hay Island is in much closer proximity to the reserve than to the Abelmarle township office that was working on the plan's approval. In fact, Neyaashiinigming lies between the township and the island, and separates them. The island completely dominates the eastern skyline of the reserve and any development would have a very strong impact.[77]

However, the depth of Indigenous exclusion appears to extend beyond issues of notice. Many at Neyaashiinigming feel that their interests have been seriously distorted in Hay Island's plan. The Band Council of Neyaashiinigming was not involved in the development's proposed design and claims that the plan falsely represents their interests. In both the developer's planning report and the county's planning development report the council is said to have agreed to allow the developer mainland access from the reserve. The planning development report submitted to County Council stated: '[t]he applicants propose to gain access to the Island development from the Cape Croker reserve. The applicants are currently in the negotiation stage of obtaining some type of long term arrangement with the reserve authorities in order to permit the establishment of docking facilities.'[78] The Band Council objects to this statement of its actions and intention. According to the chief and council: 'there have been no formal negotiations with the Chippewas of Nawash council concerning mainland access.'[79] In the view of the Band Council, the planning department report that went to County Council contained a 'very serious misrepresentation.'[80] The other planning report, submitted by the developer to the planning department, was also of concern to the Band. The developer's planning report indicates that both an individual on the reserve and the council were prepared to agree to mainland access for the development. This reports states: 'Mr Jones is prepared to ... enter into a formal agreement to insure the security of use of this site. The council of the Nawash First Nation is also prepared to enter into any required agreements to insure access to the King's Point facility. Discussions have taken place with both Mr. Jones and the Nawash council and general agreement has been reached on the contents of such agreements.'[81] The chief replied:

> [o]n behalf of the Chippewas of Nawash First Nation I wish to officially register an objection to the [developer's planning report]. I wish to specifically dispute the statement 'the council of the Nawash First Nation is also prepared to enter into any required agreements to ensure access to the King's Point facility.' Never has the Chippewas of the Nawash First Nation council negotiated any agreements on access as referred to in that statement.
>
> Back in 1990, the Chippewas of Nawash First Nation was made aware of the establishment of a landing area at lot 19, concession 5 east on the property of Howard Jones. I should like to inform you that Howard Jones has permission to service the existing facility but would require the permission of the Chippewas of the Nawash First Nation council for further expansion which at this time has not been granted.[82]

This correspondence reveals the Band's disavowal of statements in both the county's and the developer's plans. The developer's approach to Mr Jones raises important issues concerning the legal capacity of Aboriginal individuals to enter into agreements alienating a long-term interest over collectively held reserve land to a non-Native party. The legal uncertainty surrounding such conveyances,[83] coupled with the council's repudiation of its involvement in such an agreement, illustrates the problems created when the community is not involved more fully. Since the reserve community was unable to participate in the design of the proposal, the potential for its sense of being misrepresented increased. Lack of notice not only prevented the disclosure of vital information about the environment, it also assisted in the propagation of what, according to the council, is false information.

Finally, the lack of Indigenous participation also seems to have contributed to an apparent conflict of interest. The planner who wrote the Hay Island proposal eventually became one of the parties responsible for its approval.[84] He changed jobs between writing the plan and the time at which it was accepted by the province, and acted as an advising official for the Ministry of Housing when the proposal came before that department for approval. This possible conflict of interest was not noted until the plan came to the Band's attention. Their participation in a more fully democratic process could have resulted in the more timely elimination of what seemed to be serious procedural flaws, which in this instance would also have strengthened environmental protection.

In the interaction between the developers, the planner, the local municipalities, and the provincial government the parties drew legal boundaries 'on the ground' to exclude the community of Neyaashiinig-ming. The Planning Act neither mandated nor prohibited consultation with the Band regarding the proposal, and the parties developing and considering the proposal were free to interpret legal procedures concerning the notice, and participation of the First Nation. Similar types of interpretations regarding standing, notice, and participation are made by more formal institutions of law all the time.[85] In this instance, the groups' informal institutional alignment interpreted both the Act and customary rules regarding notice and participation in a restrictive way to exclude the Band. By construing the rules in this seemingly narrow way, the developer, the municipality, and the province located the First Nation outside the relevant jurisdictional line that required participation. Similarly, the federal government's jurisdiction over Indians and Indian lands was not triggered to direct First Nations participation.[86] The band was assigned a site of legal residence outside of the parties' procedural rules for participation, beyond the boundaries of the parties' legal imagination.

B   (Re)placing Knowledge: Bringing Anishinabek Ideas to Community Design

Procedure and process are not the only areas that could have benefited from Indigenous participation. The community of Neyaashiinigming could have contributed concrete and valuable information respecting issues most pertinent to the settlement's sustainability, such as water quality, fish habitat, deer migration, mainland connections, burial grounds, and the social and cultural effects of siting new villages. A brief outline of these various potential contributions reveals an alternative orientation to spatial relationships, one more fully representative of broader ecologies. It also underscores the value and significance of the empirical contributions Aboriginal people could make during environmental planning.

The substantive inclusion of Indigenous knowledge in the area of water quality, for example, could have led to a fuller examination of the proposal's impact on this resource. No investigation was made into the effects of boat traffic and associated pump-out facilities on delicate fish habitats and spawning sites. The Anishinabek people still depend upon the fish of the area as a primary dietary staple. Many members of the reserve worried that increased boat traffic from the development might directly affect the reproduction of fish in the area, and consequently have a negative impact on their food and on the commercial fishery.[87] The people know the fish biology of the area and are aware of the intricacies of the water system that supports the aquatic populations. The fishers of Neyaashiinigming have specialized techniques specifically adapted to secure sustainable harvests in the freshwater limestone cliff formations characterized by numerous caves and pockets of deep water.[88] White fish, trout, sturgeon, and deep-water herring frequent these waters. The white fish, trout, and sturgeon live closer to the top of the underwater escarpments and are taken by five-inch meshed nets onto twelve-foot-long open boats to conserve stocks and allow smaller fish to escape.[89] The Anishinabek rarely take the herring, which live in the deeper waters and caves, for food or commercial sales. The herring are lower on the food chain, and the people of Neyaashiinigming carefully preserve this species to ensure an adequate diet for larger species. In this respect the Anishinabek are very different from the larger, non-Native commercial fishers, who take these herring in their catches. There are also certain times of the year in which fish are not harvested to allow for undisturbed spawning,[90] and the Neyaashiinigming fishers frequently consult with their community to place moratoria on fishing at other times of the year if certain species become scarce.[91] Anishinabek participation in the Hay Island proposal could have helped to identify the development's impact on these aquatic populations, just as the community's knowledge of the waters could have shown where increased boat traffic could increase water turbidity and disturb underwater pools and spawning grounds. Acceptance of this knowledge could improve both the quality of the settlement for the people who eventually reside there, and the quality of the natural environment if the resort is built.[92]

Plant and animal habitats were similarly not investigated in the Hay Island proposal. The loss of delicate plants and animals would have a serious effect on the Indigenous community's health, culture, and relationships, and it would profoundly alter the diversity and sustainability of the environment. The Anishinabek have very specific knowledge about plants and animals because of their long dependence on these resources.[93] Many plants located on Hay Island have medicinal properties. The Midewewin Lodge or Medicine Society remains an important institution in collecting information relative to the uses of plants in the area.[94] A pre-settler, traditional, complex, social and cultural institution that exists in most Anishinabek communities throughout the Great Lakes,[95] the Lodge recognizes many formal degrees of tested and accredited learning and performs ceremonies and services to the community. The focal point of this organization is knowledge of plants, and at Neyaashiinigming its influence is still heavily dependent on knowledge of plants on the island.

Plants in the area are used for medicine, food, and ceremonies that feed both the physical and cultural body of the community.[96] Plants are considered primary elements among the Anishinabek and are thought of as foundational to their lives.[97] In my research I discovered a valuable collection of traditional formulas to produce healing medicines from the many plants found around Neyaashiinigming. These formulas were written in Anishinabek by a Christian missionary who lived among our people in the late 1800s and learned of the ingredients from the women in the community.[98] They have yet to be translated into English and compared with current knowledge of plant medicines on the reserve, nor has any inventory of plants on Hay Island been taken in the creation of the developer's proposal. Given the incomplete information about the Island's plant resources, the fragile soils they grow in, and their isolated location, the commencement of the development could have very deleterious impacts on the Island's vegetation. Islands are notoriously sensitive to the introduction of new species and land-disturbing activities. Anishinabek participation in the design of the resort could have identified significant plants and thereby assisted in the retention of important fauna and flora. [99]

Knowledge of local burial grounds could have also been called upon in designing the settlement. The people of Neyaashiinigming have experience with burial site profiles and characteristics on the opposite side of our reserve;[100] members of the community could have assisted planners by pointing out where burials were likely to be found.[101] However, the legal order frustrates First Nations participation in decision making with respect to Indigenous burial sites. Not marked in conventional Western ways, these sites are considered by the Cemeteries Act to be 'unapproved Aboriginal cemeteries.'[102] This offensive designation of the places in which our ancestors rest grants to the Provincial Director of Cemeteries sole discretion to determine how to treat the remains of those so interred. Since burial sites are sacred to the Anishinabek, as they are to most people, the director's broad discretion creates a powerful disincentive for Aboriginal people to reveal their knowledge about them. Why would any Anishinabek person want to reveal where a sacred site is, only to have someone else decide how to treat the area? Most people would prefer to take their chances with developers and hope that they have the decency to respect burial sites. At least developers can be appealed to on a personal basis, whereas appeals to the Director of Cemeteries can be bureaucratic, formalistic, and humiliating. Aboriginal participation in creating better settlements is severely hindered by a system that devalues First Nations knowledge of spiritual and historic sites. Such environmental racialization also hinders environmental protection because so many storied sites can be lost.[103]

Had the developer, planner, and municipalities, the provincial and federal governments, not drawn the Anishinabek's legal jurisdiction to exclude the reserve, substantive ecological considerations would have received greater attention and standing; the Indigenous community's interpretation of customary law concerning environmental planning would have encompassed water, fish, plants, animals, past generations, and broader public policy issues. The inclusion of Anishinabek knowledge in these informal interpretations of statutory and customary law would also challenge the current separation, allocation, and distribution of space. Water, fish, plants, animals, and ancestors would have a more prominent place if Indigenous learning was admitted. Reintroducing a shared spatial orientation to Hay Island destabilizes the boundaries between humans and their surroundings and deconstructs the seemingly neutral and natural façade of contemporary geo-legal ideas. Indigenous knowledge has the potential to problematize prevailing assumptions and to envelop the surrounding environment because, as a system of perceiving, transmitting, and transforming ideas, this knowledge developed within a different grid of relationships. The restraining of Anishinabek jurisdiction obscured these influences and extended the potential for adverse impacts in the creation of the settlement on Hay Island.

C   Locating Institutions: First Nations, Land-Use Planning, and Implications for Democracy

The people of Neyaashiinigming were not included in the environmental planning process because they reside between jurisdictional boundaries.[104] The reserve's interests are being pinched from both sides and function within very narrow margins. In the province's view, First Nations are not conventional municipalities,[105] nor do they resemble concerned citizens' groups that have standing in the environmental planning process. Indigenous peoples are considered a federal responsibility and thus are not accounted for in provincial planning. Provinces are reluctant to assume duties relative to Indigenous peoples because of the high financial cost associated with such action.[106] Thus, the province has not implemented legislation to mandate Indigenous notice and participation.

While the federal government recognizes limited powers for Indigenous peoples, they have failed to establish any mechanisms to allow them to successfully interact with their non-Native neighbours. The federal government is reluctant to create positive duties that might oblige it to spend more money on Aboriginal peoples. Some assert that successive governments have been 'moving deliberately and systematically to end [their] Indian policy making role.'[107] Thus, the federal government is reluctant to expand the jurisdiction of Indigenous peoples to protect rights with respect to off-reserve environmental issues. With no federal legislation or policy to compel others to consider their interests, Indigenous peoples have little power to oblige parties that may affect their environments to consider them. In the absence of formal tools to allow for communication, Indigenous peoples must use very blunt instruments to make their point, such as highly charged political demonstrations, blockades, and litigation.[108] These adversarial approaches often serve to increase hostility and intransigence on the other side and to escalate the conflict. The perceived necessity of direct confrontation and violence to protect a way of life thwarts the potential of law within democracy to mediate such conflict. In this exchange, federalism does not distribute sovereignty in a peaceful way. The approach First Nations are often forced to take to protect their environment pulls the parties further from constructive solutions and further restricts democracy.

North American democratic institutions, including bureaucracies,[109] should more effectively link democracy and the environment and provide for the participation of Indigenous peoples. This participation would allow a better approach to the design of more sustainable communities. At present, as exemplified by the Hay Island proposal, First Nations interests are excluded from the representative process. This lack of representation has repercussions for both First Nations and environmental concerns. As this case demonstrates, the way representative democracy is currently administered, those charged with designing, enacting, and implementing laws often have little or no concern for environmental consequences that do not directly and immediately affect their constituencies. Linking natural and social environments and internalizing the costs of negative environmental decisions has thus been difficult.[110] Such an approach is destructive of sustainability, which strives to 'meet the needs of the present without compromising the ability of future generations to meet their own needs.' Since even members of the present generation are not squarely represented in the current construction of representative democracy, the needs of future generations are unlikely to be adequately addressed.[111] Future generations, much like Indigenous peoples, are given insignificant influence in the design of human settlements.[112] Neither Indigenous peoples, past and future generations, nor the environment itself are treated as proper subjects of democracy. Indigenous peoples are cast instead in the role of its passive objects, those which are acted upon rather than active agents able to participate on their own terms in the formulation of decisions regarding our settlements. They are drawn out of the geography of law and their ideas and institutions are erased from the philosophical maps that guide our legal imagination. This racist, ageist, and anthropocentric approach does not bode well for environmental revitalization.

The filtered participation of representative democracy has thus isolated important agents from the sphere of political power.[113] Federalist structures, which favour national and provincial/state governments, have eclipsed Indigenous spheres of power. The use of 'virtual' participation and 'bi-focal' federalism has removed important constituencies from the routine operations of government[114] and replaced them with artificial persons or structures.[115] These disengagements have separated our democratic institutions from the environment. In the process, many segments of our community have been alienated. Anxiety has been expressed about the apparent debasement of public discourse concerning our constitutions,[116] the ever-increasing domination of politics by special interests,[117] low voter participation rates,[118] and cynicism about the integrity of elected individuals.[119] The net result of these trends is that many individuals and communities, of which Indigenous peoples are only one example, have lost a sense of participation in the institutions that design and control our settlements.[120]

One proposed solution to this perceived disengagement is that democracy be reinvigorated through direct participation.[121] This movement has acquired strong support over the past decade. 'Direct democracy' attempts to allow a country's citizens to vote or otherwise express themselves directly on major questions of government and policy.[122] Proponents hope that direct participation in public affairs will bestow greater legitimacy on their institutions.[123] Yet, like representative government, direct democracy itself may also prevent the improvement of our environment and frustrate the facilitation of Indigenous peoples' participation. James Madison argued that under direct forms of government, 'there is nothing to check the inducements to sacrifice the weaker party or an obnoxious individual.'[124] Direct democracy may allow an unrestricted majority to trample the interests of minorities. Contemporary writers have also noted these dangers.[125] Those with the least political power may be further disadvantaged by direct democracy if a majority can maintain its privileges by outvoting the underclass at the ballot box.[126] Since the natural environment has no voice or vote,[127] Indigenous peoples are numerically small, and future generations cannot physically cast votes, it is likely that under these conditions their interests will be disregarded. The Hay Island situation anticipates the ways in which direct democracy may frustrate and obstruct the interests of minorities. Yet, without the participation of minority constituencies in the design of human settlements, we may experience great difficulties in improving our communities.

Therefore, in partial answer to questions about how we can strengthen our environments, democracies could invite full participation from Indigenous peoples and take some guidance from their laws and their knowledge of their territories.[128] Federalist structures could be revitalized to place these communities at the centre of debates concerning their environments. This would enable the integration of political and ecological activities occurring in the same place.[129] As the Hay Island example reveals, Indigenous participation would bring important environmental knowledge to light. Indigenous participation would also strengthen the institutions of democracy by adding elements of generational and non-human representation. Incorporating First Nations people into the formal notice and participation processes in environmental planning and design would be an important step in this regard.[130] If Indigenous peoples were involved in environmental planning from the outset, they would have a greater chance of persuading proponents of the wisdom of their knowledge.

However, changes to the environmental planning process must extend beyond merely including Indigenous peoples in existing institutions. Democracy has substantive as well as procedural elements.[131]

More is required than a mere correction of procedural flaws by incorporating Indigenous peoples into the current regime.[132] Procedural realignment, through institutional reform and interest group reconfiguration, must be accompanied by an infusion of substantive ideas consistent with such reform. While the enhancement of federalist structures may assist democracies in making better environmental decisions, if the only result of Indigenous participation is the reception of their knowledge as evidence of best practices, this knowledge is unlikely to change the way our institutions relate to the environment.

Indigenous legal knowledge must be an integral part of decision-making standards within democracy. It must be considered and received as precedent in law to guide our answers to questions concerning the environment. The articulation, debate over, and acceptance of specific First Nations legal principles would facilitate an intellectual integration of language – a community of discourse – which could create a new approach to environmental and planning law.[133] It could help to reframe the culture of law. Integration of the different North American cultures would make possible new forms of legal discourse and result in more creative answers to the environmental challenges we face. In the process, local knowledge from particular areas could critique or build upon existing law in this field. The interaction of Indigenous legal knowledge with Canadian and American laws in the shadows of the courtrooms where customary law continues to unfold could help to bridge the cultural divide.[134] The representation of First Nations legal discourse could help to redraw the maps of environmental and planning law from which we draw our current orientation. Furthermore, our democracies would be strengthened by the representation in public life of the principles and values of people from different constituencies. This will be accomplished as the intellectual traditions of First Nations are received in institutions partly of their making, using Indigenous legal principles as the criteria upon which decisions can be judged and executed.

II   Describing Aboriginal Space:[135] Integrating First Nations Laws into Democracy

As discussed in the last chapter, Aboriginal peoples developed spiritual, political, and social conventions to guide their relationships with each other and with the natural environment. These customs and conventions became the foundation for many complex systems of government and law. Like other laws in North America, these principles can function as guidelines to make judgments about whether a particular course of action having implications for the environment should be undertaken. As noted previously, to accomplish this objective, Indigenous laws should not merely be received as *evidence* of a particular culture's environmental values; along with other laws they should be accepted as *legal standards* against which North American practices can be measured. Indigenous environmental protection laws are robust and contain legal principles that could be integrated into U.S. and Canadian institutions. Listening to, considering, and accepting these laws would do much to enhance the participation of First Nations in our democracies, and to promote democracy for all peoples.

The best way to illustrate the existence and democratic potential of First Nations environmental law is to provide a further example, using the case method introduced in the last chapter. I will therefore recount another Anishinabek story, and then employ its principles to evaluate the Hay Island proposal. This story, like that of Nanabush and the deer, was told to me by John Nadjiwon, and it similarly draws inspiration from Basil Johnston's writings.[136]

A   *Nanabush v. Duck, Mudhen et al.:* Environmental Planning Law

In the distant mists of time, the Anishinabek Nation rendered its judgment in the case of *Nanabush v. Duck, Mudhen and Geese*.[137] Like the earlier case of *Nanabush the Trickster v. Deer, Wolf et al.*, this decision reveals an important principle in the development of Anishinabek environmental law. Environmental responsibilities are defined by the Elders in reference to the way natural resources are used,[138] the manner in which they are monitored, and the relationships among different users in their allocation. In the Anishinabek nation environmental law has always stressed a literal connection and interaction between those things in the environment that act to use their surroundings, and those that are acted upon. A compact between humans and their surroundings must be considered when humans make governmental decisions about themselves and their neighbours.

i   *The Facts*

Nanabush was walking through the forest and, as usual, he was very hungry. He came to a lake and, looking around, he saw a nice, sandy beach.

Nanabush then looked out across the lake and saw geese, ducks, and mudhens. 'What can I do to get them?' he wondered. So he went to the woods and gathered some trees and boughs and made a lodge. Then he walked back to the bay with his packsack. One of the ducks asked:

'Nanabush, what you got in that packsack?'
'I got some songs from out west.'
'Sing us some songs,' said the ducks.
'At nightfall, come up to the lodge and I'll sing.'

Later on they all went up to the lodge, where Nanabush had lit a nice, large fire. Before entering, Nanabush told them, 'I got too much smoke. Shut your eyes or they'll turn red. You won't look good with red eyes.' The geese, ducks, and mudhens all went inside with their eyes closed. Nanabush took up his drum and began to sing. The birds danced around the lodge. As they came close he grabbed them, twisted their necks, and put them in his sack. After a while, one of the dancing mudhens opened one eye a little. She saw what was going on and shouted out, 'Nanabush is killing us!' Forty of the birds were dead already. Nanabush, who had been blocking the door, got up and chased the mudhen around the lodge. All the others escaped and flew away.[139]

Nanabush then built a good, hot fire on the beach. He buried the dead birds in the scorching sand so he could roast them, leaving their feet sticking up so he could find them later. While the birds were baking he thought he would take a little nap. To make sure nobody would steal the ducks he instructed his feet to be watchmen.[140] He asked his feet to wake him if anyone came near.

During his nap the Winnebago people passed by and saw the smoke. 'Hmmm, Nanabush is roasting something,' they said to each other. They went over and dug the birds out and took them away, leaving just the legs sticking out of the sand. The watchmen tried to warn Nanabush, but he slapped them saying, 'Don't bother me, I'm trying to sleep.' When he eventually woke up he was very hungry. He looked at what he still thought was a feast of birds spread before him. Finally he pulled at one leg. 'Oh!, it's so well done that the feet come right out.' Nanabush ate the leg; it was done to his satisfaction. But when he dug around in the sand for the rest of the duck, it wasn't there. He dug around the other feet and found it was the same.

Nanabush was furious and started to beat his watchmen. 'I'll fix you for this,' he said. He lit a great big fire, and set his feet on it. His feet hurt badly, but Nanabush was firm: 'you can cry all you want to, but I'll punish you!' He burnt his feet until they were sizzling. When he started walking his feet hurt so much that he tried to run away from them. He ran along the shore with blood trailing along behind.[141] In running, he got turned around and saw his own tracks. 'Somebody's passed here,' he said to himself when he saw them. 'They must be violent, I can see blood all around.' Nanabush became frightened that he would be chased. But he couldn't go anywhere. His feet were all blisters. So Nanabush lay down on the sand, hungry, sore, and afraid.

   ii   *The Issue: Do Nanabush's actions in killing the ducks,*
        placing his faith in his feet as watchmen, losing the ducks,
     and punishing the watchmen violate Anishinabek resource law?

As the case of *Nanabush and the Deer* illustrated, the Anishinabek attribute some of their society's afflictions to a misbalance in relationships between humans and animals.[142] Nanabush violated these principles when he killed more birds than he could possibly eat. The Anishinabek also teach care and respect in the stewardship they have over their bodies and the gifts they receive from the earth.[143] Nanabush breached these laws by trusting the birds' care to questionable watchmen, carelessly losing the birds, and not recognizing his connection to the watchmen. The court arrived at this conclusion by following the earlier case of *Bears, Bees et al. v. Rabbits.*[144]

In the *Bear* case, the bears, bees, and hummingbirds all felt that something was wrong. Roses were once the most plentiful flower to be found. Their presence lighted the forests and fields, and their rich colours blanketed the earth. Yet, despite all their brilliance no one really paid much attention to them. Eventually, they became much less visible, their numbers decreased and their bright shades paled. As the flowers became fewer and fewer, the rabbits became fatter and fatter.

Still, no one noticed. There were always cycles, periods of abundance and scarcity. The time came, though, when the Anishinabek too felt that something was not right. It was hard to say what. They knew that the bear's flesh did not taste as sweet. The bears could not find much honey anymore, and what they did find was very bland. The Anishinabek blamed the bears for not being as industrious in their search for honey. The bears in turn blamed the bees and hummingbirds. No one could figure out what was happening.

Then, one summer, there were no roses at all. The animals grew weary. At last everyone became alarmed. In great desperation a meeting was called; everyone was invited and a great council ensued. It was decided that all the winged creatures would search the earth for a single rose. Months went by and, finally, a hummingbird discovered a solitary rose perched on the sides of an escarpment. It gently removed the rose from its perch and carried it back to the council-place. When everyone was assembled they asked the rose to explain what happened.

In a voice weak from hanging on for life, the rose said: 'the rabbits ate all the roses.' The council exploded with anger. The bears, wolves, and lynxes seized the rabbits, grabbing them by their ears and batting them around. The attack stretched the rabbits' ears and split their lips in two. The enraged mob might have killed them, but the rose was heard once more. 'Had you cared for and watched over us, we would have survived. But you were unconcerned about us. Our destruction was partly your fault. Let the rabbits go.'

The animals who had rashly judged the rabbits were all ashamed, so they freed them. No one spoke or moved. Nanabush stood and addressed the silent crowd. 'We need the roses, and roses need us. They performed their duty to us; we did not do the same for them. Within our place, everything is dependent upon everything else. The loss of even one inevitably affects the well-being of the rest. The delicate balance between us must be preserved. You can take the life of plants, but you cannot give them life.'

The rabbits never completely healed and they retained some emblems of their immoderation. The roses were never the same either. They were less colorful and fewer in number. Nanabush also gave them thorns to protect them from the acquisitiveness and greed of the intemperate.

iii   Resolution of the Issues

In the *Duck* case it is clear that Nanabush broke the law by taking more than he could possibly use; as did the rabbits with the roses in the *Bear* case, Nanabush took more birds than he was entitled to. This action violated Anishinabek law because it did not respect the balance required between the species. Moreover, Nanabush's method of killing the birds (disrespectful trickery and foolish ruse), his failure to leave gifts to respect their giving their lives,[145] and the way in which his actions contributed to the birds being stolen by the others all point to the creation of an imbalance in the relationship of human to animal and thus constitute a violation of Anishinabek environmental law.

Nanabush's failure to recognize his connection to both the ducks and the watchmen he punished also demonstrates a breach of Anishinabek law. Just as the council in the *Bear* case did not realize their connection to the roses, Nanabush did not realize his connection to his feet. He punished part of himself, just as the animals punished themselves by not preventing the abuse of the roses.

If resources are not honoured and respected, and our interrelationships not recognized, these resources will no longer usefully exist in our lands. When resources become scarce, no matter what they are, our people will no longer be able to sustain themselves. As Nanabush said in council: 'Within our place, everything is dependent upon everything else. The loss of even one inevitably affects the well-being of the rest. The delicate balance between us must be preserved.' The legal principles identified in the *Duck* and *Rose* cases, like those of the *Deer, Crow* case presented in the previous chapter, assist Anishinabek people in the resolution of their disputes regarding the environment, land, habitat protection, and hunting rights.[146]

B   Creating a New Langscape:[147] Applying Anishinabek Law to Human Settlement Design and Democracy

Anishinabek law and the Nanabush cases have important implications for settlement design in both democracy and law. In democratic terms, the application of Anishinabek law could enable architects, planners, lawyers, and politicians to consider broader constituencies in building communities and ensure a more representative system of government. This is the point made in Part I of this chapter. In legal terms, the extension of precedent could enable these same actors to judge their decisions on different criteria. The presentation and reception of Indigenous knowledge would introduce new interpretive considerations to the communities entrusted with applying the law. Architects, planners, lawyers, politicians, quasi-public bodies, and tribunals could use Anishinabek law, along with the other legal sources they customarily consider, to make decisions on environmental planning. In the process, both common law and contemporary customary law would more satisfactorily integrate diverse bodies of knowledge and better connect our decisions to their environmental impact. The translation and interpretation fired in the interaction between Western and Indigenous law would recast law in a manner consistent with, while at the same time significantly extending, received legal principles. A truly North American law would emerge, forged through mingling Indigenous and Western jurisprudence.

Some might doubt the usefulness of referring to Anishinabek stories in the planing process. Their allegories may seem to give a simple answer to environmental questions that could be better resolved, in a more sophisticated way, through a number of other disciplinary approaches. As I have already indicated, however, I am not aware of any widespread common law principles in either Canada or the United States that directly raise or protect the environment in the way these cases suggest. The legal rules derived from the *Duck* and *Rose* cases, for instance, have specific implications for site plan development. The parties could have used these precedents in deciding the appropriateness of the Hay Island proposal. Judging the proposal by the standards of Anishinabek law could reduce the development's environmental impact.

First, the legal principle of designing to scale arises from both cases. Nanabush took more ducks than he could eat; the rabbits ate more roses than required to sustain themselves. The consequences in both these instances were similar: a necessary resource was lost. The application of this principle to Hay Island makes it clear that the development is too big for the island. The scale of the proposal endangers the very elements that make Hay Island attractive and viable as a settlement.[148] People would presumably be interested in living on the island because of its isolated location and relative environmental health. Increasing the population of this fragile island escarpment by one-third would threaten both isolation and environmental quality. That is, the scale of the proposal could undermine the very purpose of settlement at this site. It would render the Hay Island settlement unsustainable and negatively affect continued sustainability on the nearby reserve.

Second, the *Duck* and *Bear* cases stand for the proposition that a replenishment or restoration of the environment should follow after any use.[149] Neither Nanabush nor the rabbits followed the appropriate protocols when using resources. Nanabush failed to leave anything to restore nature's balance after taking the birds, just as the rabbits failed to leave enough roses behind to allow them to naturally regerminate.[150] Similarly, the Hay Island proposal does not attempt to replenish or restore what will be taken from the site. The developer could have included in the plan initiatives such as fish enhancement programs, the setting aside of alternative deer habitat under protected status, the cultivation of disturbed plants in another area, or the substitution of other lands to restore those removed from Indigenous use. Other ideas for restoration could be added in conversation with developers, politicians,

lawyers, and planners. The interpretation of Anishinabek legal principles concerning restoration expands the stock of precedent that can be
applied in North America. These principles more strongly connect
humans with the environment and direct our attention to our embed-
dedness in nature.

Finally, the *Duck* and *Rose* cases indicate that Anishinabek law places a
positive duty on users of natural resources to create reliable systems to
monitor the state of the environment. Both Nanabush and the animals
failed to recognize their connection to their surroundings. When Nanabush appointed his feet as watchmen, he placed himself in charge of
monitoring the ducks without realizing that he did so. He similarly
failed to recognize his connection to the monitoring process when he
punished his own feet. In the *Rose* case, failure of the rabbits and other
animals to monitor their environment resulted in a loss of resources.
The application of this principle in the Hay Island proposal would dictate a regularized review of and report on the settlement's impact on the
environment over time to ensure that such losses do not occur. It also
directs the parties to react appropriately to the results of this inquiry.

While Anishinabek law does not prescribe the form of environmental
monitoring systems, it is possible to imagine a system that would adequately monitor the environmental impact of the settlement. If the Hay
Island proposal is approved, each stage of its construction could be con-
tigent on demonstrating that the previous stage did not negatively affect
the environment. Appropriate stages for monitoring could be agreed
upon through negotiation between the parties. Once the buildings are
completed and people have moved in, a further monitoring process
could be undertaken by the new community, the Band, and the township. This review could take place according to the principles and customs of both Anishinabek and Western law. Each party could conduct its
own evaluation of any environmental impact according to its own rules
and customs, and the groups could then compare their findings to see
where improvements need to be made. Local involvement of each party
would avoid the problem illustrated in the *Duck* case of placing an in-
attentive watchperson over the resource. The comparative approach
would also address the problem identified in the *Rose* case of the moni-
tors being in conflict of interest because they enjoy greater benefits than
others from the use of the resource. If each party's evaluation provided
a check on that of the other, the likelihood of any one party degrading
the environment to the detriment of others would decrease.

The application of these principles in the Hay Island case confirms that Indigenous peoples have specific legal knowledge that can shed light on the appropriateness and proper design of human settlements. If these tenets of our mutual dependence were highlighted and applied, more communities would be sustainable and prosperous. The receipt of Indigenous law would accord to the environment a more central site in planning settlements. It would also implant Indigenous peoples more firmly in our federal structures and seed their laws into the very undergrowth of North American law. Since customary law continues to inform the development of the common law, it is conceivable that Indigenous laws could receive even greater protection over time: the development of such laws 'on the ground' could eventually provide an important source of law for more formalized decision makers. The application of Indigenous customary law in interactions between Indigenous and non-Indigenous peoples might ultimately compel courts to apply the legal principles relied upon in these exchanges. If this were to occur, both the environment and Indigenous people would evolve from passive objects within democracy to active agents in the creation of our settlements.

There is a real need to reformulate how we plan and participate in the design and governance of human settlements. The increasing disjunction between our natural and social environments could be reduced if broader constituencies of previously excluded people were more fully involved in the creation of institutions and ideological justifications for better practices. However, as the Hay Island case demonstrates, significant obstacles must be overcome before others can effectively participate in the integration of our economic and ecological systems. This chapter has suggested that the current practice of democracy has frustrated the development and growth of Indigenous legal knowledge through its failure to significantly involve Indigenous peoples in its institutions. However, it has also provided a ray of hope and suggested how Indigenous participation could be encouraged to enrich our democracies and assist in the more sustainable development of our communities. As Indigenous laws become embedded in the informal planning processes they may pull the environment more fully into view.

III   Conclusion

One July a few years ago, I was walking along the shores of the reserve outside my home with my mother, my partner, and our two daughters. The rocky starkness of the ten-foot-wide beach stretched for miles before us. Nothing seemed to grow on the heaped stones by the water. Yet our eyes were deeply filled with the immensity of blue from the sky and the bay. We didn't notice when the laughter of delight first started. When it finally caught our attention, we saw that the girls had discovered the only plant that dared grow on the barren embankment.

The plant was slender, tall, and green, with beautiful, orange flowers. Behind the flowers was a large pouch, and Meagan and Lindsay had realized that if you squeezed the pouch between your thumb and finger it would burst, explosively spreading seeds in all directions. Unfortunately, they had found the jewel weed. This very rare plant is beneficial in healing, and helps to cure poison ivy and rashes.[151] If you pop the seeds before they are ripe they will not germinate, and the reproductive capacity of the plant is extinguished. When we told the girls the consequences of what they were doing they understood, and left the plant to grow to its future purpose.[152]

From where we were standing, Hay Island lay a mile across the water to the east. We could not help but feel that something else was being pressured into existence. If the resort is built it may be of temporary beauty to watch the site explode with activity. The cottages will no doubt be very attractive, and the boats of the new marina will sparkle like the seeds floating in the summer sun. However, when everything is settled, will the environment be able to reproduce itself? Or will we lose not only healing plants such as the jewel weed, but also the ability to restore the world of the fish, the deer, and the Anishinabek? Will the pressure of living between competing legal boundaries erase the living space of the current generation of Neyaashingmiing? And what of those beings sleeping in the rocks on the beach, and the people buried by the lagoon on the shore? What of their participation? Will the stories their presence could tell to the seventh generation of my children be forever silenced? Will our participation, like theirs, be left to lie sleeping between the water and the rocks?

Chapter Three

Frozen Rights in Canada: Constitutional Interpretation and the Trickster

As I have tried to illustrate thus far, the Anishinabek have an independent legal tradition. The Elders teach these laws through stories of a character known as Nanabush, the Trickster. The Trickster offers insights through encounters that are simultaneously altruistic and self-interested.[1] Lenore Keeshig-Tobias, an Anishinabe storyteller from my reserve, has observed that 'The Trickster, The Teacher is a paradox: Christ-like in a way. Except that from our Teacher, we learn through the Teacher's mistakes as well as the Teacher's virtues.'[2] In his adventures, Nanabush roams from place to place and fulfils his goals by using ostensibly contradictory behaviours such as charm and cunning, honesty and deception, kindness and mean tricks.[3] The Trickster also displays transformative power as he takes on new personae in the manipulation of these behaviours and in the achievement of his objectives.[4] Lessons are learned as the Trickster engages in actions which in some particulars are representative of the listener's behaviour while in others they are not.[5] The Trickster encourages an awakening of understanding because listeners are compelled to confront and reconcile the notion that their ideas may be partial and their viewpoints limited. Nanabush can kindle these understandings because his actions take place in a perplexing realm that partially escapes the structures of society and the cultural order of things.[6]

This chapter further draws upon this Indigenous intellectual tradition and sites Nanabush at both the centre and edge of recent Aboriginal rights cases from the Supreme Court of Canada, thereby highlighting yet another aspect of Anishinabek jurisprudential thought: critique. Whereas earlier chapters concentrated on the constructive use of Anishinabek laws in dispute resolution, this chapter and the next employ these traditions to criticize the common law's application to Aboriginal peoples. This deconstruction will proceed by alternating between Anishinabek and Canadian jurisprudential perspectives and providing commentary on the distinctions highlighted within this encounter, accentuating where confusion, misinformation, and self-contradiction appear in the Supreme Court's story about Aboriginal rights.[7] The Trickster's unique position generates a language bridging Western and Aboriginal accounts of law[8] and incorporating intersecting and oppositional cultural perspectives.[9] The Trickster's critique reflects an Aboriginal perspective on the appropriateness of the analysis and effects of these common law cases;[10] the Trickster stands inside and outside of the court, both a member and a critic. His appearance allows alternative constitutional interpretations[11] and reveals the cultural construction and contingency of law. The Trickster's incongruous entry into legal discourse permits us to view law from a perspective that falls outside the conventional structure of legal argument and exposes its hidden cultural (dis)order.[12]

The Trickster is alive and well and living in Canada. The Supreme Court of Canada revealed this in the cases of *R. v. Van der Peet*,[13] *R. v. Gladstone*,[14] *R. v. N.T.C. Smokehouse Ltd.*,[15] and *R. v. Pamajewon*,[16] where the count considered how it would define Aboriginal rights 'recognized and affirmed' under section 35(1) of the Canadian constitution. Until these judgments were released, the country's highest court had supplied very little guidance concerning the test it would use to identify the rights protected by section 35(1). In 1982, at the insistence of many Aboriginal governments,[17] Aboriginal rights were entrenched in Canada's newly patriated Constitution Act, and outside of its Charter of Rights and Freedoms.[18] Section 35(1) protected these rights by stating that 'the existing [A]boriginal and treaty rights of the [A]boriginal people of Canada are hereby recognized and affirmed.' The problem was that no one was quite sure what Aboriginal rights were, and therefore what, if anything, was being protected.[19] After the failure to define these rights through four high-profile First Ministers' conferences and a nationally negotiated Charlottetown Accord,[20] the task of defining Aboriginal rights passed to the country's highest court. Unfortunately, the Supreme Court of Canada's definitions of Aboriginal rights fell far short of the large, liberal, and generous interpretations of Aboriginal rights considered throughout the political process[21] and mandated by previous judgments.[22]

The Supreme Court was asked to consider the meaning of Aboriginal rights in the context of charges brought against Aboriginal people under sections of the Fisheries Act and the Criminal Code. In *Pamajewon* charges were laid under the Criminal Code for keeping a common gaming house and conducting a scheme for the purposes of determining the winners of property.[23] The Supreme Court of Canada held that Aboriginal rights did not include 'high stakes gambling' and were not a defence to the convictions entered under the Criminal Code. In the *Van der Peet*, *Smokehouse* and *Gladstone* cases, charges were laid under the Fisheries Act for exchanging fish for money without possessing a commercial fishing licence. These cases were more varied in their results. In *Van der Peet* and *Smokehouse*, the court held that these particular groups did not have an Aboriginal right to sell and exchange fish, while in *Gladstone* it ruled that the group in question did possess such a right. This latter ruling is significant in Canadian jurisprudence because for the first time the court held that it is possible for Aboriginal peoples to possess contemporary, commercial-like rights to harvest and sell resources within their territories. However, in arriving at these conclusions the court seriously undermined the future commercial competitiveness and survival of Aboriginal nations in contemporary Canadian society. The court's partiality concerning the contemporary nature of Aboriginal rights is the subject of this chapter.

I   Seegwun

Ahaaw, paankii nika-tipaacim. Weshkac peshikwa seegwun – spring. Nanabush is walking up a stream. Around his ankles the water breaks free and flees to the Nottawasaga River. Imprisoned as ice for too long, it hurries its escape towards Georgian Bay and Lake Huron. Nanabush notices that the water's rush is met by travellers going in the opposite direction. Fish run into and through the water's swollen charge. In the midst of this collision there are periods of rest. In a shallow pool Nanabush spots a solitary rainbow trout. He breaks the walls of a downstream beaver dam. He waits ... Within a few minutes the water in the pool goes down. Trapped, the fish has nowhere to go. Another prisoner caught on life's precarious journey. He walks towards it, slowly puts his fingers under its belly, and feels the weight of life within. Nanabush lifts the fish, pauses, and considers its fate. He then gently places it into the next pool and watches it swim away.

II   Neebin

Neebin – summer. Nine people are dressed in red, with white ermine framing their costumes. They are wearing their traditional regalia.[24] It is the members of the Supreme Court of Canada, asked to consider the meaning of Aboriginal rights in the context of charges laid against Aboriginal people exchanging fish for money. Their chief justice, Antonio Lamer, is delegated to speak for the group. He steps into court. He notices that Aboriginal rights are held by Aboriginal people because they are Aboriginal.[25] Given his starting point, he is going to have to tell us what 'Aboriginal' means. How will he do this? Maybe Chief Justice Lamer knows what it means to be Aboriginal. He writes: 'The Court must define the scope of s. 35(1) in a way which captures both the [A]boriginal and the rights in [A]boriginal rights.'[26] He will define Aboriginal by 'capturing' the Aboriginal and the right? How is he going to do this? What will he do once he captures it? He searches for a purpose that might help him. In the jurisprudential stream behind him, he sees a purposive rationale and a foundation to explain 'the special status that [A]boriginal peoples have within Canadian society.'[27] He pulls the sticks from this structure; a deluge ensues. Aboriginal rights in section 35(1) exist 'because of one simple fact: when Europeans arrived in North America, [A]boriginal peoples were already here, living in communities on the land, and participating in distinctive cultures, as they had done for centuries.'[28]

The chief justice is nearly washed away by this flood. When he pulled the sticks he was standing on the wrong side of the weir and could have been knocked over. If Aboriginal peoples have prior rights to land and participatory governance, how did the Crown and court gain their right to adjudicate here? He has to stem the flow. He has to regain his footing. He plants a flag. '[A]boriginal rights recognized and affirmed by s. 35(1) must be directed towards the reconciliation of the pre-existence of [A]boriginal societies with the sovereignty of the Crown.'[29] Chief Justice Lamer now has a purpose with which to capture both the Aboriginal and the right – 'the reconciliation of pre-existing claims to the territory that now constitutes Canada, with the assertion of British sovereignty over that territory.'[30] The assertion of British sovereignty provides familiar ground from which to define Aboriginal.[31]

Now comes the clairvoyant moment when he will tell us what Aboriginal means. He reaches his fingers into the cold stream of past decisions, but relies on only one judgment to define Aboriginal. At his feet, in a shallow pool of reasoning, the chief justice finds the *Sparrow* court's acknowledgment that the Aboriginal right to fish for food was considered to 'ha[ve] always constituted an integral part of their distinctive culture.'[32] From this solitary line, where the Aboriginal right to fish for food was never in doubt, the chief justice tells us what Aboriginal means, and by extension what Aboriginal rights are. Aboriginal rights are those activities that are 'integral to the distinctive culture of the [A]boriginal group claiming the right.'[33] But what is integral to being Aboriginal, and claiming rights? He takes another step, and sets out to explain what is integral to Aboriginal people. '[T]he test for identifying the [A]boriginal rights recognized and affirmed by s. 35(1) must be directed at identifying the crucial elements of those pre-existing distinctive societies. It must, in other words, aim at identifying the practices, traditions and customs central to the [A]boriginal societies that existed in North America prior to contact with Europeans.'[34] Integral thus means central, significant, distinctive, defining. The chief justice notes: 'a practical way of thinking about this problem is to ask whether, without this practice, tradition or custom, the culture in question would be fundamentally altered or other than what it *was*' (emphasis mine).[35]

With this test, as promised, Chief Justice Antonio Lamer has now told us what Aboriginal means. Aboriginal is retrospective. It is about what was, 'once upon a time,' central to the survival of a community, not necessarily about what is central, significant, and distinctive to the survival of these communities today. His test has the potential to reinforce troubling stereotypes about Indians. In order to claim an Aboriginal right, the court's determinations of Aboriginal will become more important than what it means to be Aboriginal today. The notion of what was integral to Aboriginal societies is steeped in questionable North American cultural images.[36] These stereotypes will entrench the notion that a protected Aboriginal right has its 'origins pre-contact,'[37] 'prior to the arrival of Europeans:'[38] '[b]ecause it is the fact that distinctive Aboriginal societies lived on the land prior to the arrival of Europeans that underlies the Aboriginal rights protected by s. 35(1), it is to that pre-contact period that the courts must look in identifying Aboriginal rights.'[39]

Aboriginal means a long time ago, pre-contact. Aboriginal rights protect only those customs that have continuity with practices existing before the arrival of Europeans. Aboriginal rights do not sustain central and significant Aboriginal practices that developed solely as a result of their contact with European cultures.[40] The jurisprudential dam is now back in place. What will become a stagnant pool is once again filling in behind it. With this judgment the chief justice lifts the Aboriginal right and gently places it back in this pool, behind some of its centuries-long, common law encumbrances. As he set out to do, he has captured both the Aboriginal and the right. Nanabush waits.

III   A New Test for Defining Aboriginal Rights

As the above account reveals, the Supreme Court of Canada developed its definition of Aboriginal rights by using a questionable definition of aboriginality. However, the court's initial inquiry was appropriate, as it sought discover 'the purposes behind s. 35(1) as they relate to the scope of the rights the provision is intended to protect.'[41] In answer to this question the court found that the 'special legal and constitutional status of [A]boriginal peoples' existed to reconcile 'pre-existing [A]boriginal rights with the assertion of Crown sovereignty.'[42]

The chief justice advanced two reasons in support of this proposition. First, Aboriginal people enjoy constitutional protection because the First Nations occupied this land before the arrival of Europeans.[43] Second, Aboriginal rights were placed within the constitution to reconcile the assertion of British sovereignty with the pre-existing rights of Aboriginal peoples.[44] The decision might not have been as troubling had the court stopped there, since its reasons seem to recognize legal equality for Aboriginal people. However, in further searching for the intention behind the entrenchment of Aboriginal rights, the court applied disturbing images of Aboriginal culture to frame the reconciliation it suggested. It defined the time 'prior contact with Europeans' as the legally relevant date for reconciliation.[45] As a result, to establish an Aboriginal right, Aboriginal peoples have to demonstrate that the practices for which they are seeking protection were a 'central and significant part of the society's distinctive culture'[46] prior to first contact.[47] The court thus placed those activities that developed solely as a result of European culture outside of the protection of the Canadian constitution.[48] This decision relegates Aboriginal peoples to the backwaters of social development, deprives them of protection for practices that grew through intercultural exchange, and minimizes the impact of Aboriginal rights on non-Aboriginal people. The rights of Aboriginal peoples should not be completely dependent on their prior occupation of or sovereignty in North America; they should be based on the continued existence of Aboriginal communities throughout the continent today.

In its reasons for judgment, the court elaborated upon ten factors it would consider in the application of the 'integral to a distinctive culture' test. These factors were articulated to provide guidance for future courts in defining Aboriginal rights. They provide an important insight into how the court developed the integral test, and demonstrate the court's limited cultural understanding of contemporary Indigenous communities.[49]

First, in applying this new test the court noted that it must consider the perspective of Aboriginal peoples themselves on the meaning of the rights at stake. This factor was first identified in the path-breaking case of *R. v. Sparrow*[50] and elaborated upon in *Van der Peet*. While in *Sparrow* the court observed that Aboriginal peoples' perspectives on their rights were crucial, in *Van der Peet* it modified this approach and stated that the Aboriginal perspective must be 'framed in terms cognizable to the Canadian legal and constitutional structure.'[51] While this is a positive development, the court did not address the very real danger that Aboriginal law may be mischaracterized in order to make it 'fit' the common law system. Moreover, there is little mention of ways in which the common law may have to be reframed to preserve the underlying context and reason for the existence of a particular legal principle within an Aboriginal community.[52] The court nonetheless reasoned that its approach best reconciles the prior occupation of Canada with Crown sovereignty, because it bridges two legal perspectives.[53] One would have liked to see more discussion of how each system would have to change to accommodate the other, and a real engagement of the types of considerations raised in the last two chapters. Regrettably, the court did not take up these questions in its subsequent decisions of *R. v. Pamajewon, R. v. Côté*,[54] *R. v. Adams*,[55] and *R. v. Delgamuukw*.

The second factor the court identified in determining integral Aboriginal practices concerns the nature of the claim being made. The court narrowed the nature of claim being put forward, as it often does when considering collective rights.[56] The chief justice wrote that to define integral Aboriginal rights one must identify the precise nature of the claim to determine whether the evidence provided supports its recognition. The correct characterization of a claim involves three considerations: 'the nature of the action which the applicant is claiming was done pursuant to an Aboriginal right, the nature of the governmental regulation, statute or action being impugned, and the tradition, custom or practice being relied upon to establish the right.'[57] The application of these steps in determining the precise nature of the claim being made was significant in all four cases, and the court's characterization of the claim in some instances changed the very question the people were attempting to litigate.[58]

For example, in the *Van der Peet* and *Smokehouse* cases, the court narrowed the consideration of the practice being claimed to a more precise articulation of the potential right. These two cases held that the most accurate characterization of the Aboriginal position was a claim for a right 'to exchange fish for money or other goods.'[59] Since the evidence in these cases did not support this more limited right, it was not necessary to consider a right to fish 'commercially' at a more general level. However, in *Gladstone* there was compelling evidence that the sale and exchange of fish was integral to the Nation's culture, and thus the court looked even further to determine whether there was an associated Aboriginal right to trade on a commercial basis. Indeed, the court held that such a right exists, and in so doing it held out a thin thread of hope for Aboriginal peoples seeking more encompassing rights. The *Gladstone* case demonstrates that precise rights to a practice may also be evidence of more general rights. This step-by-step approach to defining Aboriginal rights underlines the court's hesitancy to articulate them more broadly.

The third factor the court considered in the application of the 'integral to a distinctive culture' test concerns the centrality of the practice to the group claiming the right. The majority wrote that 'the claimant must demonstrate that the practice, tradition or custom was a central and significant part of the society's distinctive culture.'[60] This element of the court's test is based on a passage in *Sparrow*, where the Musqueam right to fish for food was stated to 'ha[ve] always constituted an integral part of their distinctive culture.'[61] Whether it was appropriate for the court in *Van der Peet* to develop its test for the definition of Aboriginal rights from these observations is debatable, since the Aboriginal right to fish for food in *Sparrow* was never open to serious question. Furthermore, the same paragraph of the *Sparrow* judgment contains an equally authoritative statement that the Musqueam 'always fished for reasons connected to their cultural and physical survival' and 'the right to do so may be exercised in a contemporary manner.'[62] Given that the idea of 'integral' in *Sparrow* included the contemporary exercise of rights necessary for physical and cultural survival, why did notions of survival and the contemporary exercise of rights not form part of the integral to a distinctive culture test in *Van der Peet*? It seems clear that Aboriginal rights should exist to ensure Indigenous peoples' physical and cultural survival, and not necessarily to preserve distinctive elements of pre-contact culture. The acceptance of these considerations would have strengthened Aboriginal peoples' interactions with other Canadians, and it would have been more consistent with the court's previous rulings. A conception of Aboriginal rights focused on protecting the physical and cultural survival of First Nations would recognize Aboriginal peoples as normative communities, with values, laws, cultures, languages, and traditions that interact and are recreated in their relationship with others. It would honour the contemporary legal generative capacity of Aboriginal groups in Canada.

The fourth factor the court articulated in determining whether an Aboriginal practice is integral to a distinctive culture is whether it has continuity with the activities that existed 'prior to the arrival of the Europeans.'[63] The focus on pre-contact practices restricts contemporary Aboriginal development. The rights of other Canadians are not limited to those practices that have continuity with their activities prior to their arrival in North America. Such a limitation would be perceived as the gravest form of injustice, and the two dissenting judgments criticize this part of the majority's test as 'freezing' Aboriginal rights, contrary to the admonition found within *Sparrow*.[64] Justice Claire L'Heureux-Dubé noted that defining Aboriginal rights by reference to pre-contact practices inappropriately crystallizes Aboriginal rights at an arbitrary date. She argued that this is contrary to the perspective of Aboriginal peoples, and overstates the impact of European influence on Aboriginal peoples.[65] Similarly, Justice Beverley McLachlin (now Chief Justice of Canada) stated that the majority's failure to recognize the distinction between rights and contemporary form 'freeze[s] [A]boriginal societies in their ancient modes and den[ies] to them the right to adapt, as all peoples must, to the changes in the society in which they live.'[66] These dissenting judgments implicitly recognize the inequity of creating non-Aboriginal rights following contact without extending this same entitlement to Aboriginal peoples.

After exploring the factors relevant to the application of the 'integral to a distinctive culture' test in some detail, the majority breezed through a list of six other considerations appropriate to defining Aboriginal rights. The chief justice wrote that, in defining Aboriginal rights, '[t]he courts must not undervalue the evidence presented by the [A]boriginal claimants' simply because it does not conform precisely with evidentiary standards in private litigation.[67] This is an important qualification, because certain evidence of pre-contact European practices will clearly be difficult or impossible to obtain.[68] The court eased a heavy evidentiary burden by this admonishment.

The court then stated that claims to Aboriginal rights are not general and universal, but relate to the specific history of the group claiming the right.[69] The court's failure to articulate general features of Aboriginal claims prevents their expansion. Of course, Aboriginal rights claims will usually be distinguishable from one another through particular histories of the claimant groups. But if claimants cannot rely on analogies from principles in other cases, Aboriginal peoples will have little opportunity to build a principled, protective jurisprudence.[70] Despite this disadvantage, the chief justice wrote that '[t]he fact that one group ... has an [A]boriginal right to do a particular thing will not be, without something more, sufficient to demonstrate that another [A]boriginal community has the same [A]boriginal right (562).' While there is a certain amount of truth to the statement that Aboriginal rights are fact and site specific, these reasons ignore a more global basis for Aboriginal rights. As explained in chapter 1, Aboriginal rights find their source in an overarching jurisprudential infrastructure of First Nations law. The court failed to recognize that one integral right possessed by all Aboriginal peoples is the right to organize their societies according to their traditions, customs, and laws.[71] The organization and laws of Aboriginal peoples should be universally protected as something that each group can successfully claim, even though their content will vary from group to group.

A seventh factor to consider in applying the integral test is that the practice being claimed as a right must be independently significant to the community, and not merely incidental to another tradition. Without providing justification or reasons, the chief justice wrote that '[i]ncidental practices, customs and traditions cannot qualify as [A]boriginal rights through a process of piggybacking on integral practices, customs and traditions.'[72] This assertion seems contrary to the court's earlier ruling in *R. v. Simon*, where incidental practices were given protection as Aboriginal rights.[73] It also suggests that, while the court is willing to protect independent rights in the abstract, it may be unwilling to preserve the place and means necessary to make the exercise of rights meaningful. It remains to be seen if and how the court will resolve this seeming contradiction.

The other three factors the court identified as important in determining Aboriginal rights involve the 'distinctive' nature of the Aboriginal practice in question. A distinctive practice is one that does not arise solely as a response to European influences, but can arise separately from the Aboriginal group's relationship to the land. Distinctiveness and the European influence on Aboriginal rights have been touched upon earlier in this chapter and will receive no further attention at this point. However, we should acknowledge the novelty of the idea that Aboriginal rights can arise not only from prior occupation of land, but from the prior social organization and distinctive cultures of Aboriginal people. Before these cases, it was uncertain whether Aboriginal rights arose solely through claims to Aboriginal title.[74] It is now clear that Aboriginal title need not be proved to sustain other Aboriginal rights. Section 35(1) of the constitution is emerging as the most relevant criterion in defining Aboriginal rights in Canada. In subsequent Supreme Court cases of *Adams* and *Côté* it was held that Aboriginal peoples in Quebec could claim food fishing rights even if they had not established Aboriginal title in the area in question.

Despite a few positive signs, the net effect of these ten factors is to circumscribe Aboriginal rights. They establish non-Aboriginal characterizations of aboriginality,[75] evidence,[76] and law[77] as the standards against which Aboriginal rights must be measured. Taken together, these factors compel the conformity of Aboriginal rights to Western formulations of law to secure recognition and affirmation in Canada's constitution. This creates problems for Aboriginal groups, since these norms are generally not sensitive to the '[A]boriginal perspective on the meaning of the rights at stake'[78] and consequently constrain the reception of Aboriginal legal viewpoints. As the Trickster demonstrates, rights need not be interpreted in such an inflexible and narrow manner.[79]

IV   Tahwahgi

Tahwahgi – Fall. The Couchiching Narrows, Orillia, Ontario. Nanabush has recently presided over the opening of the casino on the Chippewas of the Rama reservation. Confined for over a century, Anishinabek governance has escaped federalism's cells and now spills into the surrounding communities. Over one hundred thousand people travel to Rama and drop quarters in the casino's well. The woodland art of its outer walls encloses the interaction of mean tricks and kindness, help and neglect, charm and cunning. The rush to participate in self-government's outward flow has its periods of rest, too. Nanabush takes the three-minute walk to the lake. On the water the boats' sails hang loosely. For 4,000 years an Aboriginal weir raked these narrows to trap fish behind its wooden bars. Now behind the lake's shores the fingers of a new presence reach out. Nanabush looks back towards it, thinks about how he placed it perfectly. Buses disgorge their contents, cars and trains arrive every few minutes, the people of the reserve are also swept into its flow. Its grasp is extensive.

North of Rama, Chief Justice Antonio Lamer presides over the fate of two casinos on the Shawanaga and Eagle Lake reservations in the *Pamajewon* case. The communities have risked asking the court to rule that Aboriginal rights to self-government include high-stakes gambling. The rush into these communities is just beginning to build. The land is cleared for a new gaming hall and hotel, and signs on the highway announce the arrival of monster bingo. The chief justice takes a thirty-two-paragraph stroll around the place. With *Van der Peet* as a companion – a 'legal standard against which the appellants' claim must be measured'[80] – he explains the character of Aboriginal rights. Once again, he is given the task of deciding the character traits. The chief justice not only defines the character of an Aboriginal, he defines the character of an entire Aboriginal community. How is he going to do this? Can he identify the character of another culture? He consults his companion. *Van der Peet* has some words of advice: change the characterization of what the Aboriginal people are claiming. The chief justice agrees; that makes it easier. He confides: 'To characterize an applicant's claim correctly, a court should consider such factors as the nature of the action which the applicant is claiming was done pursuant to an [A]boriginal right, the nature of the governmental regulation, statute or action being impugned, and the tradition, custom or practice being relied upon to establish that right.'[81] The chief justice has provided three factors to consider in developing the correct characterization of a claim, but there is no mention of the standards by which these factors should be judged. What principles will guide judgments about the characterization of these factors? Should Aboriginal claims be characterized in a 'large, liberal and generous manner,'[82] with sensitivity to the 'Aboriginal perspective on the meaning of the rights at stake'?[83] Nope. No mention of such concerns here. With that issue out of the way, the chief justice provides his own characterization of what is being claimed.

He walks on. The people want him to see how the Band participates in deciding who lives where on the reserve, and under what conditions. He is invited to tour the Band Council office, read their governing by-laws, and see how the people depend on them. He declines. He stays out near the road. The chief justice turns his attention to the empty casino land, sees the monster being advertised. In the next breath, he states, 'when these factors are considered in this case it can be seen that the correct characterization of the appellants' claim is that they are claiming the right to participate in, and to regulate, high stakes gambling activity.'[84] His short promenade sidesteps claims about Aboriginal rights to self-government: '[t]he appellants themselves would have this Court characterize their claim as a broad right to manage the use of their respective reserve lands. To so characterize the appellants' claim would be to cast the Court's inquiry at a level of excessive generality.'[85]

This is a comfortable pace. One needs to get a little exercise, but there is no point in over-extending yourself. Chief Justice Lamer comes to rest on the assertion that '[t]he factors laid out in *Van der Peet* ... allow the Court to consider the appellants' claim at the appropriate level of specificity; the characterization put forward by the appellants would not allow the Court to do so.'[86] To consider that Aboriginal people would actually have a broad right to manage the use of their own lands would be to embrace too high a level of generality.

The chief justice is almost through with his visit. It is getting dark. But he has something to dispose of before he leaves; he must decide whether Shawanaga and Eagle Lake's 'participation in, and regulation of, gambling on reserve lands was an integral part of their distinctive culture.' The evidence, he determined, 'd[oes] not demonstrate that gambling, or that the regulation of gambling, was of central significance to the Ojibway people.' Prior to contact, informal gambling activities took place on a 'small scale.' The chief justice refers to a prior visitor: 'I also agree with the observation made by Flaherty Prov. Ct. J ... that "commercial lotteries such as bingo are a twentieth century phenomena and nothing of the kind existed amongst [A]boriginal peoples and was never part of the means by which these societies were traditionally sustained or socialized."'[87] Done. End of the trail. The claim is defeated since Anishinabek gambling, prior to contact, did not take place on a twentieth-century scale. It is hardly surprising that this standard of evidence could not be met. Not many activities in any society, prior to the twentieth century, took place on a twentieth-century scale. It is a good thing the rights of other Canadians do not depend on whether they were important to them two to three hundred years ago. Would non-Aboriginal Canadians be willing to have their fundamental rights defined by what was integral to European peoples' distinctive cultures prior to their arrival in North America?[88]

The door slams. The chief justice drives away. Self-government will serve more time in isolation, locked within federalism's cells. Few people will visit Shawanaga and Eagle Lake; even fewer will leave their money behind. The people of Shawanaga and Eagle Lake will not spend the rest of their lives, and that of their children's children, caught inside a casino.[89] The fresh October wind is brisk. Clear. Orange and yellow leaves dance in this breeze, and mimic the setting autumn sun. A walk to shore reveals Indian fishers pulling in their nets. Whitefish and trout will be served tonight. Lake Huron has witnessed this activity for centuries. No buses, trains, or cars crowding the life out of the community. No new presence; no grasping. Quiet settles back into the familiar rhythms of activity.

V   An Alternative Basis for the Constitutional Entrenchment of Aboriginal Rights

As the preceding account reveals, it is not clear why Aboriginal peoples must define their rights strictly by reference to the 'temporal roots of those rights in their historic presence – their ancestry – in North America.'[90] As Justice McLachlin noted in dissent, Aboriginal rights arise not from the moment of first contact with Europeans but from the laws and customs of the First Nations.[91] Even the majority judgment cited traditional laws and customs as important sources of Aboriginal rights.[92] If the Supreme Court's test to define Aboriginal rights relied more on the interaction between the common law and Aboriginal legal perspectives and less on cultural practices, that test would be more satisfactory, as is illustrated in Nanabush and the chief justice's visit to the casino.

Furthermore, finding that Aboriginal rights must be rooted in 'crucial elements' of pre-existing societies is, in the words of Justice McLachlin, too broad, too indeterminate, and too categorical a characterization of those rights.[93] The new test may be criticized as being too broad because 'integral is a wide concept, capable of embracing virtually everything that an [A]boriginal people customarily did.'[94] It may be too indeterminate because 'one encounters the problem that different people may entertain different ideas of what is distinctive, specific or central. To use such concepts as the markers of legal rights is to permit the determination of rights to be coloured by the subjective views of the decision maker.'[95] Finally, the 'integral to a distinctive culture' test may be too categorical because 'whether something is integral is an all or nothing test. Once it is concluded that a practice is integral to the people's culture, the right to pursue it obtains unlimited protection, subject only to the Crown's right to impose limits on the grounds of justification'[96]

An alternative basis for defining Aboriginal rights is the common law's recognition of the ancestral laws and customs 'of the [A]boriginal peoples who occupied land prior to European settlement.'[97] This basis for Aboriginal rights is to be preferred to that of the majority because it is more in line with the existing case law and the 'time honoured methodology of the common law.'[98] Under this methodology, the court would evaluate new situations by reference to what the law has recognized in the past. The chief justice did not take such an approach; rather, he engaged in a more theoretical approach to Aboriginal rights and reasoned from broad principles that find little or no support in past judgments. Madam Justice McLachlin's methodology and reasons, in contrast, follow a 'golden thread' of case law which defines the nature and incidents of Aboriginal rights by reference to the laws and customs of Indigenous people.[99] Her reasons led her to hold that section 35(1) has a twofold purpose: to protect the existing customary laws and rights of Aboriginal peoples, and to ensure that such customs and rights remain in the Aboriginal people until extinguished or surrendered by treaty. These two principles, according to Justice McLachlin, are supported by the common law and history, and 'may safely be said to be enshrined in s. 35(1) of the Constitution Act, 1982.'[100] Thus for Justice McLachlin, since Aboriginal rights rest on Aboriginal laws, section 35(1) must define them by reference to these pre-existing laws.

However, Chief Justice Lamer's test defines Aboriginal rights according to potentially stereotypical perceptions of Aboriginal characteristics rather than by their nature and source. This approach freezes the development of certain Aboriginal practices in the distant past. For example, under the chief justice's reasoning, Aboriginal hunting for the sale or exchange of furs may not be considered an Aboriginal right because some argue this practice developed solely as a result of European influence.[101] Such an understanding of Aboriginal rights cannot be correct. The idea that Aboriginal people do not have rights that developed solely in response to European influences is contrary to the history and the very possibility of the exploration and early development of many parts of North America.[102] This restriction of Aboriginal rights goes against the chief justice's own observation that the rights developed from the 'peculiar meeting of two vastly different legal cultures.'[103]

If Aboriginal rights developed through the meeting of two cultures, then surely those practices which resulted solely in response to European culture must be part of this legal regime. Otherwise, it is difficult to see how the law is 'intersocietal,' a description the chief justice himself employs.[104] The initial European presence in most parts of Canada would have been undermined if someone had told Aboriginal people that they had no rights to hunt and trade with the Hudson's Bay or North West Company because this practice developed solely through European culture. Europeans relied on the profit from the fur trade and would have been seriously handicapped in asserting sovereignty in North America if Aboriginal people had no rights to sell furs to them.[105] Furthermore, Aboriginal people themselves would have rebelled or refused to trade if anyone had seriously suggested that they had no rights to exchange or sell animals.[106] Such a policy would have been in direct conflict with the colonial policy in the settlement of Canada found in the Royal Proclamation: 'Trade with the said Indians shall be free and open to all.'[107] In short, Chief Justice Lamer's holding that practices arising from European influence cannot be Aboriginal rights ignores both history and the intersocietal nature of Aboriginal rights law.[108]

To take away the possibility that Aboriginal laws, traditions, and practices developed in response to the appearance of European cultures could continue to develop and be protected as rights is to take away the means to allow Aboriginal people to compete on the same basis, with equal power, with the settling peoples. Why should European laws, practices, and traditions, some of which originated solely though contact with Aboriginal peoples, be enabled to grow and develop from the moment of contact, while Aboriginal laws and practices, many of which also had their roots in the same moment of contact, are stopped in their progression? Such a holding is contrary to the chief justice's assertion that 'the essence of [A]boriginal rights is their bridging of [A]boriginal and non-[A]boriginal cultures.'[109] To accomplish this bridging of cultures and truly render the Aboriginal perspective of Aboriginal rights in terms 'cognizable to Canadian law,' as required by Chief Justice Lamer in the *Van der Peet* case, 'equal weight' must be placed on Aboriginal law.[110]

The downgrading of Aboriginal rights is even more apparent in the greater power given to Canadian governments to infringe Aboriginal rights in these cases. In *Gladstone*, the majority provided strong obiter dicta stating that Aboriginal rights must be capable of being limited and, as such, could be infringed by justifiable government legislation. This potentially widens the government's power to interfere with Aboriginal rights. Justifiable legislative objectives could include 'the pursuit of economic and regional fairness, and the recognition of the historic reliance upon, and participation in, the fishery by non-Aboriginal groups.'[111] This further potential for the infringement of Aboriginal rights must be considered in light of the fact that the government already enjoys a generous two-step opportunity to justify interference with Aboriginal rights, as outlined in *Sparrow*.[112] The concern that motivated the widening of permissible legislative infringement in *Gladstone* was the lack of any inherent limitation for Aboriginal people on the exercise of their rights. This concern is curious, from an Aboriginal perspective, because there are limitations on these rights – the laws and traditions of Aboriginal peoples.[113] As the Nanabush cases in the last two chapters illustrate, Aboriginal peoples have laws which dictate how a right may be exercised. Furthermore, non-Aboriginal peoples exercise exclusive rights all the time. In fact, exclusive rights are one of the distinguishing features of Western legal systems. Why should Aboriginal peoples fall outside the purview of central concepts of property law when they exercise exclusive rights? How can we explain the concern in assigning Aboriginal peoples exclusive rights when courts generally display no anxiety in allotting them to non-Aboriginal peoples?

The chief justice's failure to place equal weight on Aboriginal practices, customs, and traditions contradicts his stated purpose for section 35(1) of the constitution. The downgrading of Aboriginal practices severely constrains true reconciliation between the assertion of Crown sovereignty and the pre-existing rights of Aboriginal peoples. Reconciliation usually requires that each party to a relationship concede something to the other, and the majority's test does not require any relinquishment on the part of the Crown. It compels only Aboriginal peoples to give something up in reconciling the assertion of Crown sovereignty with pre-existing Aboriginal occupation. For example, the 'integral to a distinctive culture' test requires Aboriginal peoples to concede any protection for practices that may have developed solely as response to European cultures. Yet the adoption of new practices, traditions, and laws in response to new influences is integral to the survival of Aboriginal communities; reconciliation should not require a concession of those practices that enable them to survive as a contemporary community.[114] In limiting Aboriginal rights to integral practices not developed solely as a result of European influences the court denies these cultures the right to survive by adapting to new situations. This test appears to prevent Aboriginal peoples from competing on an equal footing within Canadian society and extinguishes their contemporary vigour as dynamic, competitive communities. Surely such a result conflicts with the 'noble purpose' the chief justice envisions for section 35(1) of the constitution.[115] Once again, the Trickster's engagement with the court can help identify whether the court has upheld such a noble purpose.

VI Peebon

Peebon – Winter. Frozen rights. Peebon's return always brings hardship, decay, and dissolution. His perpetual defeat of Neebin withers the plants, hardens the ground, and sends white beings through the skies. With his approach the animals sleep, and fish return to deep lakes to escape the rivers' congealing arteries. To the north, the ancient grandfathers retreat to their lodges. Their fires reflect on the sky – blue, white, and cold red – and illuminate the path of souls for those travelling to the land of the dead. It will be some time before the grandfathers' voices again accompany the clouds and let their fire fall across the earth. For now, they remain in their lodges, protect their fires, and await the return of Neebin. Peebon and Neebin's perpetual quest for supremacy continually enforces this cycle on the Anishinabek. While Peebon is in the ascendancy, Nanabush looks for ways to steal fire from the grandfathers, to bring it back to the Anishinabek and keep them warm.

Peebon's frigid sovereignty has wide dominion. Aboriginal practices that developed solely as a response to European culture are now frozen, courtesy of the 'integral test.' How can this result be reconciled with Chief Justice Antonio Lamer's own observation that Aboriginal rights developed from the 'peculiar meeting of two vastly different legal cultures'?[116] Nanabush stalks the land and looks for ways to steal fire. He approaches the common law warily. He might get burned. With suspicion that comes from experience, he knows the danger of trying to take something of value from that which can harm him greatly. Yet he is both brave and foolish, and so he tries. Nanabush reasons that if Aboriginal rights emerged through the meeting of two legal cultures, then they must be litigated by reference to the laws of both societies. The chief justice would appear to agree: '[T]he law of [A]boriginal rights is neither English or [A]boriginal in origin: it is a form of intersocietal law that evolved from long-standing practices linking the various communities.'[117] Despite this endorsement of Aboriginal law, Nanabush observes that the chief justice did not consult or apply Stólō, Nu-Chah-Nulth, Heiltsuk, or Ojibway law in defining Aboriginal rights under section 35(1) of the constitution.[118] While the court asserts that Aboriginal rights are based on traditional laws and customs 'passed down, and arising, from the pre-existing culture and customs of Aboriginal peoples,'[119] nowhere in these cases does the chief justice use the laws of the people charged, or the laws of any other Aboriginal people, to arrive at the standards through which he will define these rights.[120] The court does not use 'intersocietal' law in developing its test for Aboriginal rights.[121] In so observing, Nanabush has peered into the fire and found a branch sufficiently dense in its grain to keep a flame burning while he brings it home to his people.

Nanabush reaches in through the smoke and observes the chief justice engaged in an abstract, theoretical approach to defining Aboriginal rights. He did not fully reference the 'long-standing practices linking the various communities' in defining Aboriginal rights. Vacuous assertions about section 35(1) reconciling Crown sovereignty with the fact that Aboriginal peoples were here first may at the most elementary level qualify as an application of intersocietal law. However, the idea that reconciliation should take place *upon contact* finds no support in either Aboriginal or non-Aboriginal law. It is the chief justice's invention. Nanabush has firmly grasped the branch and taken it from the fire. The smoke is clearing. Nanabush then finds a confederate. Quoting from Madam Justice McLachlin's dissent in *Van der Peet*, he states: 'Aboriginal rights find their source not in a magic moment of European contact, but in the traditional laws and customs of the Aboriginal people in question ... One finds no mention in the text of s. 35(1) or in the jurisprudence of the moment of European contact as the definitive all-or-nothing time for establishing an Aboriginal right.'[122] Nanabush finds in this statement a more substantial basis upon which to define Aboriginal rights. He recalls that a 'morally and politically defensible conception of [A]boriginal rights will incorporate both legal perspectives.'[123] The development of the 'integral to a distinctive culture test' does not incorporate either legal perspective because neither the common law nor Aboriginal laws held that the 'moment of European contact' was the 'definitive' time for establishing an Aboriginal right.

It is now time for Nanabush to run home. The fires of his people are almost extinguished. What he has found may rekindle them. The common law's recognition of Aboriginal ancestral laws and customs, and of their continual evolution and interaction with the Crown, is a solid foundation for defining Aboriginal rights. It picks up a 'golden thread' running through the common law.[124] This methodology also fans the embers of Aboriginal law and encourages its development as a greater source of authority for Aboriginal and non-Aboriginal Canadians.[125] With this basis for defining Aboriginal rights the purpose of section 35(1) becomes truly 'intersocietal.' It also encourages the continued application of these laws: constitutional protection of the existing customary laws and rights of Aboriginal peoples ensures that such customs and rights remain in the Aboriginal people until extinguished or surrendered by treaty. Since Aboriginal rights rest on Aboriginal laws, section 35(1) must define these rights by reference to these pre-existing laws.

While Nanabush steals fire, Peebon's chilling pervasiveness continues to be felt. Nanabush's solitary actions may not be enough to permit a thaw. The Supreme Court of Canada's interpretations of Aboriginal rights remain restrictive and burdensome: the 'integral to a distinctive culture' test freezes the protection of practices that may have developed solely in response to European cultures. Yet the adoption of new practices, traditions, and laws in response to new influences is integral to the survival of any community. Reconciliation should not require Aboriginal peoples to concede those practices which allow them to survive as a contemporary community. However, the court's new test threatens Aboriginal cultures precisely on this point; they have no protection for practices devised in meeting challenges solely as a result of European influence.[126] Such a restriction is contrary to the chief justice's requirement that 'equal weight' be placed on Aboriginal law[127] by rendering it in terms 'cognizable to Canadian law.' The 'integral to a distinctive culture' test does not place equal weight on traditional Aboriginal law,[128] and it denies legal equality to Aboriginal peoples in their relationship with Canada.[129]

Peebon remains ascendant. His icy embrace chills. The dissolution and decay continue. Throughout the land Aboriginal practices are coldly suspended. It may be a long winter.

VII   Conclusion

The Supreme Court's 'integral to a distinctive culture' test does not extend protection to Aboriginal practices that developed solely as a result of European influence, even if those practices are crucial to their contemporary physical and cultural survival. Surely this result is less than a full recognition and affirmation of Aboriginal rights. Aboriginal peoples are entitled to expect legal protection for their continued existence as normative communities and nations within North America. Why entrench Aboriginal rights in the constitution if the societies they were meant to protect cannot survive? Canadian courts have not yet come to terms with the fact that, like others, Aboriginal people are at once traditional, modern, and postmodern. Physical and cultural survival depends as much on attracting legal protection for contemporary activities as it does on gaining recognition for traditional practices. The courts need to recognize that Aboriginal rights attach to Aboriginal activities whether the activities in question are making moccasins or marketing micro-chips. It is not the specific practice that is necessarily important to the definition of these rights; what counts in determining Aboriginal rights is whether and how these practices contribute to the survival of the group. The courts, however, seem to be operating under the assumption that protecting specific 'Aboriginal' activities satisfies the constitutional purpose for the entrenchment of Aboriginal rights, and *they* get to decide what is Aboriginal. They do not interpret Aboriginal in a 'large, liberal and generous manner,' with 'sensitivity to the [A]boriginal per-spective on the meaning of the rights at stake.'[130] Instead, they interpret Aboriginal in a partial and incomplete way.

The courts need to embrace a broader notion of Aboriginal rights. As I have tried to demonstrate, Aboriginal peoples of the Americas, by using their intellectual traditions to critique existing law, can assist in this venture. Our ideologies and approaches to law may yet yield impor-tant insights on the partiality of legal discourse. The Trickster's deploy-ment represents one such methodology and illustrates the relevance of First Nations inquiry in understanding the law. Indigenous traditions are not static; their strength lies in their ability to survive through the power of tribal memory and to renew themselves by incorporating new elements. By intermingling these approaches with the law, the Trickster and other traditions can speak as strongly to the continent's dominant legal institutions as they can to longstanding tribal relationships. Their vitality and authenticity points us beyond ourselves.[131] Their power lies not in how closely they adhere to their original form, but in how well they are able to develop and remain relevant under changing circumstances.[132]

Chapter Four

Nanabush Goes West: Title, Treaties, and the Trickster in British Columbia

'Ahnee. Ohoweti. Aan entootamaan?'
'Nahke piko.'
'Aan eshinihkaasoyan?'
'Nanabush nitishinihkaas.'
'Aanti wenciiyan?'
'Neyaashiinigming nitooncii, Keewatin nitooncii, Winnipeg nitooncii, Saskatoon nitooncii, Wetaskiwin nitooncii, Tswassen nitooncii, Gitsegukla nitooncii, Gingolx nitooncii ...'*

I   Noonkom Kaa-Kiishikaak (Today)

Nanabush travelled far from home. He has left the Great Lakes, crossed the prairies, and finds himself in a land of large trees, fast rivers, and broad ocean shores. To make the journey he has had to transform himself many times: badger, crow, old man, coyote, and now raven.[1] He marvels at the beauty of this place. It is 1872 in the newly formed province of British Columbia. The lower mainland is little more than a rough timber camp, with a few farms dotting the landscape.[2] It is still largely Aboriginal. A group of business and political leaders has gathered in New Westmin-

---

*'Hello. Over here, this way. What am I doing?'
'I don't know.'
'What is your name?'
'My name is Nanabush.'
'Where are you from?'
'I am from Nanash, I am from Keewatin, I am from Winnipeg, I am from Saskatoon, I am from Wetaskiwin, I am from Tswassen, I am from Gitsegukla, I am from Gingolx ...'

ister to discuss relations with the Indians. Raven wonders where the Indians are. He perches on the windowsill and listens in. The meeting is called to order. As the conversation dies, the small collection of farmers, merchants, and mill and cannery owners gives its attention to the convener. A civil servant strides to the front of the room and takes his place at the podium. He has been a surveyor and a trader, and has had some experience with the Indians. Raven thinks he is a curious man, rather dour, with his black suit and hat and long white beard.[3] The members of the group settle into their chairs and await his speech.

The speaker clears his throat and begins: 'Let us not talk of treaties with the Indians. It is nonsense.'[4] The crowd murmurs approval. Raven chokes out surprise. Not distracted, the man goes on: 'The absurd claim of the Indians of title to public land has never been acknowledged. On the contrary, it has been distinctly denied![5] As civilized people in the midst of savagery we have special entitlements in this emerging corner of the Empire. We carry the heritage and laws of Britannia with us, wherever we settle. The land in this province all belongs to the Queen.[6] True, there are less than 19,000 British citizens in the province, and the Chinese and Indians together outnumber us two to one.[7] But these Indians in our midst are bestial, not human. They are ugly and lazy.'[8] The crowd laughs, the speaker smiles. Raven marvels at how some tribes think they are better than others. The man resumes: 'The Indians are lawless and violent and must be brought under the laws of the country. Despite their condition, the law entitles them to the same civil rights as the rest of the population.[9] Nothing more. Why should they have special rights? The law does not make such distinctions. True, except with special permission, we have denied them the right to take up land as others can, through settlement and pre-emption.[10] But we have need of good land to encourage settlers to emigrate and build up this country.[11] We can't have Indians claiming their every fishing spot, village, camp site and trading post. There would be scarcely little left. And, yes, we have taken the provincial franchise away from them[12] – but this is for their own good. They do not know their own best interests.'[13] He scans the room, searching for disagreement. All is quiet. Raven too is silent; he wants to remember what has been said. He thinks this will be a good one to tell the people later; he cannot resist a good story. The speaker proceeds, 'And no one can fuss over our recent reductions to the size of their reserve land; it is of no real value to them. Its unproductive, uncultivated condition is utterly unprofitable to the public interests.[14] When we entered the dominion, all this was sanctioned. The Constitution by the terms of union permitted us to continue to treat the Indians as we always have. We will be honourable in following this law. We will act as good citizens. We have fulfilled our constitutional obligation and pursued a "policy as liberal as that hitherto pursued by the British Columbia government"[15] prior to its entrance into confederation. We are the founders of this great province. Let's not talk of treaties. What's past is past. We can only be just in our own time. We must be just today.' An enthusiastic chorus of hands and voices marks the end of the speech. Raven is amused. He will visit here again. They are his kind of people: capable of honesty and deception, charm and cunning, kindness and mean tricks. With this thought, he takes to the skies, circles the gathering. Across the clouds he hears the echoes: 'What's past is past. We can only be just in our time. We must be just today.' Raven catches these currents of time and decides to follow them. He wonders where they will lead.

II   Sovereignty's Alchemy: Transgressing the Law in Time and Space

British Columbia's legal history presents profound challenges for legislators, policy makers, and judges. Basic questions concerning title to land remain largely unresolved throughout the province, and decision makers struggle to make sense of the situation. The question of Aboriginal title in British Columbia has even found its way to the Supreme Court of Canada. In *Delgamuukw v. British Columbia*, the Supreme Court was asked to rule on the Gitksan and Wet'suwet'en[16] peoples' claim to Aboriginal title and self-government over approximately 58,000 square kilometres of land in the northwestern part of the province.[17] Both peoples have lived in this area as 'distinct people' for a 'long, long time prior to [British assertions of] sovereignty.'[18] For millennia, their histories have recorded their organization into Houses and Clans in which hereditary chiefs have been responsible for the allocation, administration, and control of traditional lands.[19] Within these Houses, chiefs pass on important histories, songs, crests, lands, ranks, and properties from one generation to the next.[20] The transfer of these legal, political, social, and economic entitlements is performed and witnessed through Feasts. Feasts substantiate the territories' relationships. A hosting House serves food, distributes gifts, announces the House's successors to the names of deceased chiefs, describes the territory, raises totem poles, and tells the oral history of the House. Chiefs from other Houses witness the actions of the Feast, and at the end of the proceedings they validate the decisions and declarations of the Host House. The Feast is thus an important 'institution through which the people [have] governed themselves,'[21] and it confirms the relationship between each House and its territories.[22] As the trial judge, Chief Justice MacEachern, observed: 'The spiritual connection of the Houses with their territory is most noticeably maintained in the feast hall, where, by telling and re-telling their stories, and by identifying their territories, and by providing food and other contributions to the feast from their territories, they remind themselves over and over again of the sacred connection that they have with their lands.'[23]

The first known European to contact the Gitksan and Wet'suwet'en peoples was William Brown, a Hudson's Bay Company trader who established a fort on Lake Babine in 1822. He described these people as 'men of property' and 'possessors of lands'[24] who regulated access to their territory through a 'structure of nobles or chiefs, commoners, kinship arrangements of some kind and priority relating to the trapping of beaver in the vicinity of the villages.'[25] Writing in his journal in 1823, Brown observed that the chiefs 'have certain tracts of country, which they claim an exclusive right to and will not allow any other person to hunt upon them.'[26] On this issue the trial judge in *Delgamuukw* accepted the evidence of Professor Arthur Ray, who said:

> When the Europeans first reached the middle and upper Skeena River area in the 1820's they discovered that the local natives were settled in a number of relatively large villages. The people subsisted largely off their fisheries which, with about two months of work per year, allowed them to meet most of their food needs. Summer villages were located beside their fisheries. Large game and fur bearers were hunted on surrounding, and sometimes, on more distant lands. Hunting territories were held by 'nobles' on behalf of the lineages they represented and these native leaders closely regulated the hunting of valued species. The various villages were linked into a regional exchange network. Indigenous commodities and European trade goods circulated within and between villages by feasting, trading and gambling activities.[27]

This evidence, among others, persuaded the trial judge that Aboriginal people had 'been present in parts of the territory, if not from time immemorial, at least for an uncertain, long time before the commencement of the historical period.'[28]

Despite finding an historic and contemporary Aboriginal presence in the areas claimed, MacEachern C.J., in a much criticized judgment,[29] dismissed the Gitksan and Wet'suwet'en's claims to ownership and jurisdiction. He held that '[A]boriginal rights, arising by operation of law, are non-proprietary rights of occupation for residence and [A]boriginal use which are extinguishable at the pleasure of the Sovereign.'[30] As Chief Justice Lamer observed on appeal, the trial judge 'was not satisfied that they owned the territory in its entirety in any sense that would be recognized by law.'[31] Chief Justice MacEachern's judgment rested upon the 'proposition ... that [A]boriginal rights are ... dependent upon the good will of the Sovereign' and 'existed at the pleasure of the Crown, and could be extinguished by unilateral act.'[32] Consequently, he held that '[A]boriginal rights to land had been extinguished [because] of certain colonial enactments which demonstrated an intention to manage Crown lands in a way that was inconsistent with [their continued existence].'[33] In his view, the law 'never recognized that the settlement of new lands depended upon the consent of the Indians.'[34] He therefore held that 'the Crown with full knowledge of the local situation fully intended to settle the colony and to grant titles and tenures unburdened by any [A]boriginal interests.'[35] Furthermore, he 'rejected the ... claim for a right of self-government, relying on both the sovereignty of the Crown at common law, and what he considered to be the relative paucity of evidence regarding an established governance structure' among the people.[36]

The Gitksan and Wet'suwet'en appealed this decision to the British Columbia Court of Appeal. In a 3:2 decision, the appellate court upheld the trial judge's rejection of Gitksan and Wet'suwet'en claims to ownership and jurisdiction, although it recognized lesser Aboriginal sustenance rights. In dealing with the claim to ownership, Macfarlane J.A., writing for the majority, stated: 'I think the trial judge properly applied correct legal principles in his consideration of the plaintiff's claim to ownership.'[37] Thus, the Court of Appeal left undisturbed Chief Justice MacEachern's finding that Aboriginal land rights were non-proprietary in nature and a burden on the Crown's underlying interest. Furthermore, in upholding the trial judge's decision concerning jurisdiction,[38] Justice Macfarlane wrote: 'I think that the trial judge was correct in his view that when the Crown imposed English law on all the inhabitants of the colony, and in particular, when British Columbia entered Confederation, the Indians became subject to the legislative authority in Canada. The division of governmental powers between Canada and the Provinces left no room for a third order of government.'[39]

Having failed to persuade the lower courts to recognize Aboriginal ownership and jurisdiction in their territories, the Gitksan and Wet'suwet'en appealed their case to the Supreme Court of Canada. In its decision, the Supreme Court did not substantially depart from the previous courts' reliance on assertions of British sovereignty in grounding its discussion of Aboriginal title. The court found that 'Aboriginal title is a burden on the Crown's underlying title.'[40] Furthermore, it did not specifically recognize or affirm Gitksan and Wet'suwet'en ownership or jurisdiction over their territories, although it set out a test to apply for proof of such claims in future cases.

Given British Columbia's legal history, the court's unreflective acceptance of the Crown's assertion of sovereignty over Aboriginal peoples in British Columbia raises many questions. The court's treatment of Crown sovereignty potentially undermines the very purpose of section 35(1) and perpetuates the historical injustice suffered by Aboriginal peoples at the hands of those who failed to respect their laws and cultures. This danger flows despite an extraordinarily progressive attempt to recognize and facilitate Indigenous legal pluralism within Canadian constitutional law. *Delgamuukw*'s continuation of Canada's imperial legacy in the face of its own promotion of respect for Aboriginal laws and customs impedes the development of Indigenous law in Canada. The dangers can be illustrated by analysing the Supreme Court's treatment of the following issues in *Delgamuukw*:

1 Do the pleadings preclude the Court from entertaining claims for [A]boriginal title and self government?
2 What is the ability of this Court to interfere with the factual findings made by the trial judge?
3 What is the content of [A]boriginal title, how is it protected by s. 35(1) of the *Constitution Act, 1982*, and what is required for its proof?
4 Has a claim to self-government been made out by the appellants?
5 Did the province have the power to extinguish [A]boriginal rights after 1871, either under its own jurisdiction or through the operation of s. 88 of the *Indian Act*?[41]

A   Pleadings

The common law emerged in a society characterized by a bewildering diversity of courts enforcing a variety of bodies of law:[42] courts of equity, market courts, manor courts, university courts, county courts, borough courts, ecclesiastical courts and aristocratic courts, among others.[43] The story of the common law is that of expansion at the expense of these other legal jurisdictions, through the use of writs. [44] The great English historian F.W. Maitland observed that writs were 'the means whereby justice became centralized, whereby the king's court drew away business from other courts.'[45] The common law in medieval England was a formulary system developed around a complex of writs that a litigant could obtain from the Chancery to initiate litigation in the Royal Courts.[46] Each writ gave rise to a specific manner of proceeding or form of action, with its own particularized rules and procedures.[47] These forms of actions were the procedural devices used to give expression to the theories of liability recognized by the common law.[48] Through their choice of writs litigants elected their remedies in advance of trial, and they could not subsequently amend their pleadings to conform to the proof needed for the case or to meet the court's choice of another theory of liability.[49] If litigants failed to select the proper writ for their action they could not succeed in their claim.[50] This uniformity allowed for the more centralized control of the entire common law structure,[51] and the sovereignty of the Crown expanded with the extension of the common law's jurisdiction.[52]

In many respects, the issues raised in the *Delgamuukw* case demonstrate that Canada, like England, contains a bewildering diversity of legal systems, a broad array of cultures, and various bodies of law. Between the Maritimes in the east and the mountains of the west are found the laws of the Mi'kmaq, Mohawk, Cree, Ojibway, Okanagan, Salish, Haida, Nisga'a, Gitksan, Wet'suwet'en, and other peoples. The story of the common law in Canada is that of attempted expansion at the expense of these Indigenous legal jurisdictions.[53] Contemporary pleadings perform a role similar to that of the ancient forms of action, as parties present written statements of factual and legal issues they believe the court can resolve. While today's pleadings are much more flexible than medieval forms of action,[54] if a party does not frame its case properly, the court may refuse to resolve the issue by declaring a defect in the pleadings. The discipline this uniformity imposes on litigants incidentally extends Crown sovereignty through the centralized control of access to justice. In effect, pleadings become a 'necessary passport to gain entry to the common law courts.'[55] Acquiring the appropriate visa is obligatory in disputing the justice of Crown dealings with Aboriginal peoples; the Crown does not recognize legal claims brought in any other way.[56] This frontier patrol of the border of the Canadian legal imagination[57] further extends Canadian sovereignty over Aboriginal territories.[58]

The problems inherent in the current system are apparent in *Delgamuukw*: the Supreme Court of Canada did not consider the specific merits of the Gitksan and Wet'suwet'en claims because of a defect in the pleadings. The Gitksan and Wet'suwet'en's pleadings 'originally advanced 51 individual claims on their own behalf and on behalf of their houses for "ownership" and "jurisdiction" over 133 distinct territories.'[59] The Court found that there were two changes in the pleadings from the trial to the appeal: claims for ownership and jurisdiction were replaced with claims for Aboriginal title and self-government; and the individual claims by each House were amalgamated into two communal claims, one advanced on behalf of each nation. The court held that the first change, concerning the substitution of Aboriginal title and self-government, was 'just and appropriate' in the circumstances because the trial judge allowed 'a de facto amendment to permit "a claim for [A]boriginal rights other than ownership and jurisdiction."'[60] It upheld the trial judge's ruling because 'it was made against the background of considerable legal uncertainty surrounding the nature and content of [A]boriginal rights.'[61] However, the court rejected the second change, concerning the amalgamation of individual claims into collective ones, because 'the collective claims were simply not in issue at trial.'[62] This finding seems rather formalistic and inflexible, given that the court attached considerable importance to the argument that these individual and collective claims are intertwined, for 'the territory claimed by each nation is merely the sum of the individual claims of each House.'[63] It appeared that the forms of action the Gitksan and Wet'suwet'en pleaded had to be exact, even though the court itself found considerable uncertainty in this area of law. The court's approach supports Maitland's observation that '[t]he forms of action we have buried, but they still rule us from their graves.'[64] The court 'reluctantly' concluded that the province had suffered some prejudice because the plaintiff's change denied the Crown 'the opportunity to know the appellants' case,'[65] and for this reason, it ordered a new trial.[66]

In order to evaluate the Supreme Court's conclusion concerning pleadings, it may be useful to consider the historical context of the Aboriginal peoples in British Columbia. Aboriginal peoples were a substantial majority of the population in the newly formed Province of British Columbia when it entered Confederation in 1871.[67] Despite their overwhelming numerical strength, they did not participate in the province's creation. Most Aboriginal people continued to live within their own governments on their lands, as they had done for centuries, and paid little regard to British assertions of sovereignty. In 1872, when Aboriginal peoples outnumbered the settler population approximately 4:1 in the province generally,[68] and more than 15:1 on the north coast,[69] one of the new province's first legislative acts was to exclude Indians from voting.[70] The provincial government also upheld the prejudicial laws enacted by the previous colonial govenment that denied Indians fee simple title to pre-empted lands taken up through settlement, a right freely granted to non-Aboriginal people in British Columbia.[71] Furthermore, this government did not acknowledge any legal interest of Aboriginal peoples over lands they traditionally used and occupied. The province surveyed extremely small and inadequate reserves for Indians,[72] and refused to recognize any broader Aboriginal title to land.[73] When Aboriginal peoples in British Columbia repeatedly tried to challenge this mistreatment, the province responded by further diminishing their land rights and political rights.[74] The federal government eventually followed suit by amending the Indian Act, so that it was virtually illegal to raise these matters before the courts.[75] The historical exclusion of Aboriginal peoples from democratic participation in British Columbia through the passage of these corrupt laws should be a paramount consideration in evaluating whether the court's treatment of pleadings in *Delgamuukw* is consistent with Canadian legal pluralism.

It is interesting to note that the result of the *Delgamuukw* case, which considers the wholesale territorial dispossession of two entire Aboriginal peoples, turns on the court's finding that *the province* suffered prejudice in framing the pleadings. By imposing these technical requirements on the form of a grievance, the courts, like the legislatures before them, make an assertion of sovereignty. By relying on a defect in the pleadings to refuse to consider the claim, this Crown Court announces that disputes will be resolved on the settlers' terms. There is something deeply troubling about allowing Crown assertions of sovereignty to drive the decision in a case that radically challenges these assertions and their effects. Given the imbalance in the parties' financial and political resources, and the century-long denial of Aboriginal land and political rights in British Columbia, this sleight of hand is remarkable. In effect, the court found that the Aboriginal peoples' passport papers were out of order. They were not permitted to cross the border separating Gitksan/Wet'suwet'en legal systems and the common law because they had not followed proper procedures. Sovereignty's extension is careful not to prejudice the Crown and non-Aboriginal law. As the discussion below will reveal, the court was much less concerned about the effect of its ruling on Aboriginal legal systems.

B   Listening for a Change – The Courts and Oral Tradition

In some societies, there is a propensity to doubt the reliability of oral traditions in drawing inferences from and conclusions about the past. This bias is evident in the way Aboriginal traditions have been treated in Canada. For example, in the late 1600s, Nicolas Perrot, a leading chronicler of Aboriginal history in the North American Great Lakes area, wrote about Aboriginal oral traditions in the most disparaging of terms: 'Among them there is no knowledge of letters or of the art of writing; and all their history of ancient times proves to be only confused and fabulous notions, which are so simple, so gross, and so ridiculous that they only deserve to be brought to light in order to show the ignorance and rudeness of these peoples.'[76] This wholesale dismissal of the utility of oral tradition was not confined to Perrot's century. Certain scholars in the twentieth century were equally dismissive of oral literacy. Robert Lowie, an influential American anthropologist, wrote that he could 'not attach to oral traditions any historical value whatsoever under any conditions whatsoever.'[77] Lowie had such a low opinion of oral tradition that he concluded that if 'primitive notions tally with ours, so much the better for them, not for ours.'[78] In the same vein, the noted English historian Hugh Trevor-Roper observed that it was inappropriate to write history based on oral traditions. He counselled his fellow historians that 'we should not amuse ourselves with the unrewarding gyrations of barbarous tribes in picturesque but irrelevant corners of the globe; tribes whose chief function in history, in my opinion, is to show to the present an image of the past from which, by history, it has escaped.'[79] Such views led Trevor-Roper to conclude that only people with written history should be studied: 'the rest is darkness ... and darkness is not the subject of history.'[80]

These contemptuous attitudes towards non-written history are pervasive and they have found expression in the context of courtroom practice and jurisprudential principle. Aboriginal people have been labelled by judges as, among other things, 'ignorant,'[81] 'primitive,'[82] 'untutored,'[83] 'savage,'[84] 'crude ... simple, uniformed and inferior people,'[85] who led lives that were 'nasty, brutish and short.'[86]

In *Delgamuukw* the Supreme Court of Canada partially acknowledged these biases against Aboriginal traditions and found that a 'special approach' was required in receiving and interpreting evidence from Aboriginal claimants that 'does not conform precisely with the evidentiary standards' generally applicable in private law cases.[87] The differential treatment of Aboriginal evidence was justified by the sui generis categorization of Aboriginal rights, which recognizes their unique source and nature.[88] The court reasoned that 'although the doctrine of [A]boriginal rights was a common law doctrine, [A]boriginal rights are truly *sui generis*, and demand a unique approach to the treatment of evidence which accords due weight to the perspective of [A]boriginal peoples.'[89] To apply this principle the court instructed judges to 'adapt the laws of evidence so that the [A]boriginal perspective on their practices, customs and traditions and on their relationship with the land, are given due weight.'[90] This approach allows a judicial decision maker to grant oral histories 'independent weight' and place them 'on an equal footing with the types of historical evidence that courts are familiar with.'[91] The court noted that these modifications to the rules of evidence were necessary to the litigation of Aboriginal rights. To do otherwise would 'impose an impossible burden of proof' on Aboriginal peoples and 'render nugatory' any rights they have, because most Aboriginal societies 'did not keep written records.'[92] The purported reconciliation of 'the perspective of [A]boriginal people' with 'the perspective of the common law' found in these new evidentiary standards is an important development in the court's articulation of principles to bridge the gap between Aboriginal and non-Aboriginal legal cultures.[93]

An examination of the elaboration of these principles in *Delgamuukw*, however, raises doubts about whether the court has really overcome the challenges nested in meshing these often-differing world-views. Has it departed from the bias against oral tradition in Canadian legal principle and practice? Despite the best of intentions, a further review of the court's analysis makes it clear that obstacles to placing Aboriginal oral tradition on the same footing with other types of evidence remain in place. After encouraging the accommodation of unique evidence from Aboriginal peoples, the court wrote that this reconciliation must not be done in a manner that 'strains the Canadian legal and constitutional structure.'[94] This caveat represents a substantial challenge for Aboriginal peoples. For various reasons explained below, it has the potential to subordinate Aboriginal tradition within the common law and constitutional regime. This does not place Aboriginal evidence on an equal footing in court. The Supreme Court's test for oral evidence privileges non-Aboriginal values and modes of historical interpretation, and it may foster a real or apprehended bias against Aboriginal litigants.

The court's caveat raises numerous problems for Aboriginal peoples. For example, the mere presentation of oral evidence often challenges some people's view of the core of the Canadian legal and constitutional structure. Aboriginal oral traditions may undermine the legitimacy of the country's legal system (an alternative view of the legitimacy of Canadian law will be developed in chapter 5), since in many parts of the country, certain oral traditions are most relevant to Aboriginal peoples because they keep alive memories of their unconscionable mistreatment at the hands of the British and Canadian legal systems. Their evidence records the 'fact' that the unjust extension of the common law and constitutional regimes often occurred through dishonesty and deception, and that the loss of Aboriginal land and jurisdiction happened against the will of the First Nations and without their consent.[95] These traditions include memories of government deception,[96] lies,[97] theft,[98] broken promises,[99] unequal and inhumane treatment,[100] suppression of language,[101] repression of religious freedoms,[102] restraint of trade and economic sanctions,[103] denial of legal rights,[104] suppression of political rights,[105] forced physical relocation,[106] and plunder and despoilation of traditional territories.[107] Oral traditions can be controversial because they frequently undermine the law's claim to legitimacy throughout Canada by shedding light on the illegality and/or unconstitutionality of Crown action.

Oral tradition may also be contentious on other grounds; it can, for instance, question the pretension of non-Aboriginal law's absolute pre-eminence throughout the country. However, my central purpose in this book is to demonstrate that Aboriginal law continues to exist as an important source of legal authority in Canada, even if it has been weakened through the unjust imposition of alien structures.[108] A number of Aboriginal groups assert that their law remains important in their lives, and that colonial legal structures have not extinguished their legal structures.[109] While they might acknowledge that the operation of their laws is encumbered by Canadian law, they also contend that their law stems from an alternative source of authority and does not depend upon Canadian executive, legislative, or judicial recognition.[110] To the extent that oral tradition encompasses these views, it presents a strong vision of legal pluralism that some courts have, at times, refused to implement.[111] The reception of oral traditions may compel the courts to endorse a breed of legal pluralism that might be seen as a challenge to the legal and constitutional structure of Canada. This tension is evident in *Delgamuukw.*

The oral evidence recited in *Delgamuukw* went beyond supporting the Gitksan and Wet'suwet'en's historic use and occupation of their territories. These histories contained a competing jurisprudential narrative that strained Canada's claim to exclusive jurisdiction over Gitksan and Wet'suwet'en lands.[112] The lower courts did not acknowledge the binary nature of this testimony because its subjective and evaluative elements caused the trial judge considerable difficulty. Some of the most striking evidence in this regard was the recitation of the Gitksan adaawk and Wet'suwet'en kungax, unwritten collections of important history, legends, laws, rituals, and traditions of Gitksan or Wet'suwet'en House organizations. They speak of these peoples' proprietary rights and responsibilities in the disputed territories and tell of the Indigenous legal regimes that govern relationships in their homelands. As sources of legal authority, the adaawk and kungax may be used to evaluate individual and collective actions. However, the judges in the lower courts saw the adaawk and kungax exclusively as testimony to be judged (and then only barely) and not as legal standards that would assist them in making their judgments. To use this evidence in a way that truly places equal weight on the Aboriginal perspective, the courts might have to accept the premise that Gitksan and Wet'suwet'en oral traditions are repositories of fact and law, and as such problematize Canada's claim to exclusive legal jurisdiction in these territories. Aboriginal traditions will necessarily strain Canada's legal system. While I argue throughout this book that Aboriginal legal systems can be accommodated within the courts and by the general polity, it may be difficult for some to overcome the fear that the recognition of Aboriginal legal structures would simply incapacitate Canada's legal system. This anxiety creates a challenge for courts applying *Delgamuukw*'s evidentiary standard.

The cultural basis of factual determinations presents another challenge for Aboriginal peoples trying to place their evidence on an equal footing with types with which the court is familiar. Even under the court's modified evidentiary standard, Aboriginal evidence must be received and evaluated by people within a structure and institution that has a very different ideological and cultural orientation from that of most Aboriginal peoples. This difference creates problems in evaluating what is factual across cultures. A leading historiographer of oral tradition, Jan Vansina, has observed that 'all messages are a part of a culture.'[113] In his seminal work on the subject, he wrote that messages 'are expressed in the language of a culture and conceived, as well as under-stood, in the substantive terms of a culture.'[114] He concluded that since culture shapes all messages, we must take culture into account when interpreting these messages. Since what constitutes a 'fact' is largely contingent on the language and culture out of which that information arises,[115] the people determining what is or is not 'fact' must work within the matrix of relationships they share with others.[116] The chal-lenge inherent in doing so represents one of the strongest objections to the thesis developed in this book: that Aboriginal and non-Aboriginal law can co-exist within the same legal space.

Since non-Aboriginal judges do not usually share the relationships of Aboriginal peoples, there is an enormous risk of non-recognition and misunderstanding when Aboriginal peoples submit their 'facts' to the judiciary for interpretation.[117] This problem is especially acute in litiga-tion because factual determinations are presented in an adversarial envi-ronment,[118] and those determinations can vary significantly between judicial interpreters according to the judge's language, cultural orien-tation, and experiences.[119] The potential for misunderstanding exists because each culture has somewhat different perceptions of space, time, historical truth, and causality.[120] The cultural specificity of what consti-tutes a fact in one culture may make it difficult for a person from a different culture to accept the same information as a fact.[121] Since vari-ations between groups help to encode facts with different meanings within each culture,[122] collective perceptions of these notions must be viewed through the lens of the culture that recorded them to be properly understood.

Judges who are called upon to evaluate the meaning, relevance, and weight of the evidence they receive must appreciate the cultural differ-ence in the intended meanings behind these messages if they are to draw appropriate inferences and conclusions.[123] Additionally, judges must master the implicit symbolic aspects of these messages to compre-hend their veracity and value. Every culture has its own shared imagery that conveys both meaning and emotion, found in metaphors, stock phrases, stereotypes, and other clichés.[124] The particular imagery of a culture as contained in these forms is essential to appreciation of 'the context of meaning' behind oral evidence.[125] Without this deeper knowledge, common law judges will have a difficult time understanding and acknowledging the meanings Aboriginal people give to the facts they present.[126] The evaluation of oral history evidence will be especially fraught with danger if the interpreters do not recognize the cultural foundation of knowledge, and acknowledge their own biases:[127] 'judges, like all other humans, operate from their own perspectives.'[128] Anthropologist Robin Ridington observed these problems in the factual underpinnings of the trial judge's decision in *Delgamuukw*:

> McEachern showed himself to be singularly blind to the unstated assumptions of his own culture. I suggest that a systemic and unacknowledged ethnocentric bias is, to use McEachern's own phrasing, 'fatal to the credibility and reliability' of his conclusions. From my experience evaluating texts about a variety of cultures, McEachern's decision ... reveals a sub-text of underlying but unexamined assumptions upon which the more logical edifice of the judgment is constructed. In *Delgamuukw*, Mr. Justice McEachern revealed a world view and an ideology appropriate to a culture of colonial expansion and domination. The judgment is well suited to be an apology for that culture. It is not well suited to find a place where [A]boriginal law and Canadian law can reach a just accommodation.[129]

Another problem Aboriginal people encounter in reconciling their evidence with Canadian constitutional and legal structures relates to the treatment of Aboriginal elders at the hands of lawyers and judges. Aboriginal Elders frequently have to endure questioning and procedures that are inconsistent with their status in their communities. The wisdom they have attained and the struggles they have endured in acquiring this knowledge demand that they be shown the highest honour and deepest respect. While presenting evidence in an adversarial setting is a harrowing experience for most people,[130] it can be especially troubling for Elders from certain groups, for whom such treatment is tantamount to discrediting their reputation and standing in the community. Apart from the tremendous strain placed on the individual enduring this experience, the process represents a major challenge to the culture more generally. To directly challenge or question Elders about what they know about the world, and how they know it, 'strains the legal and constitutional structure' of many Aboriginal communities. To treat Elders in this way is a substantial breach of one of the central protocols within many Aboriginal Nations, a fundamental violation of the legal order somewhat akin to requiring judges to comment on their decision after it is written. To subject Elders to intensive questioning demonstrates an ignorance and contempt for the knowledge they have preserved, and a disrespect and disdain for the structures of the culture they represent. Yet such behaviour is mandated by the Canadian legal system. Clearly, bridging Western and Aboriginal legal cultures is problematic on many levels. There is no simple and culturally acceptable way for Aboriginal peoples to place their traditions before the courts in the same way, and on the same footing, as the types of evidence courts are familiar with.[131]

Aboriginal peoples also lose some control over their own cultures when courts receive and interpret oral evidence. For millennia, Aboriginal peoples created, controlled, and changed their own worlds through the power of language, stories, and songs. Their words 'did not merely represent meaning, they possessed the power to change reality itself.'[132] Indigenous languages and cultures shaped First Nations legal, economic, and political structures, and the socio-cultural relationships upon which they were built. Many of these narratives were considered private property,[133] and restrictions on their presentation and interpretation helped to ensure that the authority to adjudicate and create meaning remained within Aboriginal societies. When another culture is allowed to authoritatively judge the factual authenticity and meaning of Aboriginal narratives, Aboriginal people lose some of their power of self-definition and determination.[134] Indigenous peoples experience this loss because the language and culture of Canadian law is not their own, and legal interpretation of their traditions and history is centralized and administered by non-Aboriginal people.[135] Aboriginal people barely participate in the administration of the court system, and they are certainly not in positions of control. The Supreme Court's progressive instruction that the laws of evidence be adapted to incorporate Aboriginal factual perspectives does not take into account the adverse costs of such a declaration. Despite the court's extraordinarily fair and generous intentions, its loosening of the evidentiary requirements with respect to oral histories may have the effect of diminishing Aboriginal control over First Nations cultures.

III   Onaako (Yesterday)

Raven has waited patiently, especially after travelling for such a long time. It is not like him to remain so still. He ponders the message of the New Westminister gathering, wonders about the Supreme Court's allegations in *Delgamuukw*. Eventually, he feels he has heard enough. He decides it is time to go and see some Indians. He heads north, follows the coast. He crawls on the wind, pulling himself along the spine of the guardians, who watchfully separate the valleys from the sea. Weeks later he comes to a beautiful river and flies up its valley. Raven looks around, finds it hard to believe that some people call this the 1800s. The Nass has not changed much since he was last here. When he approaches a village people watch him cautiously. He remembers these people, the Nisga'a. He helped them after the flood by bringing fire to the earth. He gave them law to govern themselves, the Ayuukhl.[136] Sometimes on seeing him they yell out 'Txeemsim, Txeemsim.'[137] Nanabush likes the recognition. Raven is popular here. He passes Gingolx and flies on to Sii Ayans. At the village he observes his figure carved in strange trees without branches, his characters sewn on the people's blankets. He must tell the Ojibway of this; they could learn something from these people. Raven decides to stay. He could get used to this treatment.

As Raven settles in, he finds the eagle, killer whale, and wolf are good companions.[138] He rediscovers the delicacies of salmon, steelhead, and oolichan. Raven gets comfortable, and watches the generations come and go. The people fish, trap, and trade. They laugh, cry, and wonder about the world around them. It is a rich world. There is rhythm to life here that feels as old as the world. But in time, he notices a change. One day he wakes up and sees that the Nisga'a are not what they once were. He feels weary. He is getting tired of the poverty, sickness, sadness, and suicide. Many people seem to have lost heart. The Indian Act has interfered with their traditional governance and land-holding systems.[139] Their Potlatch was outlawed, and their beautiful masks shipped to New York and Toronto.[140] Their totem poles were cut down and buried, or sent away.[141] Children were also shipped, and sometimes buried, stolen from parents and sent to residential schools.[142] When these schools closed, the children continued to go, but now as part of the child welfare or criminal justice systems.[143] Every attempt to resist these indignities has been quashed. When the Nisga'a assert title, their reserves are 'cut off' and made smaller.[144] When they try to go to court, land claims are all but outlawed.[145] With no vote, they have no political remedies; with no access to court, they have no legal remedies. Raven gets bored. He wants to see if he can discover the cause of these problems. He decides to head back south, hoping he can figure out what is wrong.

A   Content, Protection, and Proof of Aboriginal Title

In *Delgamuukw,* the Supreme Court of Canada boldly announced: '*Because it does not make sense* to speak of a burden on the underlying title before that title existed, [A]boriginal title crystallized at the time sovereignty was asserted.'[146] Sovereignty is pretty powerful stuff. Its mere assertion by one nation is said to bring another's land rights to a 'definite and permanent form';[147] simply conjuring sovereignty is sufficient to change an ancient people's relationship with its land. A society under sovereignty's spell is ostensibly transformed. Use and occupation can be extinguished,[148] infringed,[149] or made subject to another's designs.[150] How can lands possessed by Aboriginal peoples for centuries be undermined by another nation's assertion of sovereignty? What alchemy transmutes the base of Aboriginal possession into the golden bedrock of Crown title?[151]

The key words that unlock sovereignty's power are ancient. Practitioners of its craft can summon a tradition that reaches deep into the past;[152] its channeling flows from Classical times[153] through the Renaissance.[154] Political and legal ascendancy are conveyed to those who can conjure fictions that vindicate their claims of authority.[155] In the thirteenth century, Pope Innocent IV invoked sovereignty's oaths in the Middle East during the Crusades when he wrote: '[I]s it licit to invade a land that infidels possess or which belongs to them? ... [T]he pope has jurisdiction over all men and power over them in law ... so that through this power which the pope possesses I believe that if a gentile, who has no law except the law of nature ... does something contrary to the law of nature, the pope can lawfully punish him ... [I]f the infidels do not obey, they ought to be compelled by the secular arm ...'[156] Such proclamations provided authority for asserting sovereignty over and launching war on non-Christian peoples outside Europe.[157] In the fourteenth century, papal bulls called up these same covenants as people sailed out from Portugal and Spain to cast their words on Africa and North America.[158] Such assertions enabled Iberia's kings and queens to 'discover and make conquests of lands beyond the then-known borders of western Christendom.'[159] To facilitate these purposes, in 1513 another manifestation of sovereignty's power was revealed in the Requerimiento, required to be read aloud to peoples over which Spain intended to exercise control:[160]

On the part of the king, Don Ferdinand, and Doña Juana, his daughter, queen of Castile and León, subduers of the barbarous nations, we their servants notify and make known to you ... Of all these nations God our lord gave charge to one man called St. Peter, that he should be lord and superior to all men in the world, that all should obey him ... Wherefore, as best we can, we ask and require you ... that you acknowledge the Church as the ruler and superior of the whole world, and the high priest called Pope, and in his name the king and queen ... But if you do not do this or if you maliciously delay in doing it, I certify to you that with the help of God we shall forcefully enter into your country and shall make war against you in all ways and manners that we can, and shall subject you to the yoke of obedience of the Church and of their highnesses; we shall take you and your wives and your children and shall make slaves of them, and as such shall sell and dispose of them as their highnesses may command; and we shall take away your goods and shall do to you all the harm and damage that we can ... and we protest that the deaths and losses which shall accrue from this are your fault, and not that of their highnesses, or ours, or of these soldiers who come with us ...[161]

Documents such as the Requerimiento, numerous papal bulls, and other proclamations mingled to create a cant of conquest justifying assertions of sovereignty to others' lands.[162] The British and Americans in the seventeenth,[163] eighteenth,[164] and nineteenth[165] centuries chanted these historic incantations to bring them forward into contemporary jurisprudence.[166] Imperial courts participated as well. In *St. Catherines Milling and Lumber Co. v. The Queen*, a case from Ontario, Lord Watson wrote: '... [T]he tenure of the Indians was a personal and usufructuary right, dependent on the good will of the Sovereign. The lands reserved are expressly stated to be "parts of Our dominions and territories" ... It appears ... to be sufficient for the purposes of this case that there has been all along vested in the Crown a substantial and paramount estate, underlying the Indian title, which became a plenum dominium whenever that title was surrendered or otherwise extinguished.'[167] Sovereignty's incantation is like magic; its mantra, 'Aboriginal title is a burden on the Crown's underlying title.'[168] This mere assertion is said to displace previous Indigenous titles by making them subject to, and a burden on, another people's 'higher' legal claims.[169] Contemporary Canadian jurisprudence has been susceptible to this artifice.[170] In considering Aboriginal title, the Supreme Court declared that the Crown gained 'underlying title' when 'it asserted sovereignty over the land in question.'[171] As in past centuries, sovereignty purports to herald the diminishment of another's possessions, and in this respect the decision echoes ancient discourses of conquest. Is this, as the court requires of its jurisprudence, 'a morally and politically defensible conception of [A]boriginal rights'?[172] Is the mere assertion of sovereignty an acceptable justification for the Crown's displacement of Indigenous law and title?

That a legal entitlement to land could be secured over another entitlement merely through raw assertion makes no sense. As Chief Justice Marshall of the United States Supreme Court once observed, it is an 'extravagant and absurd idea.'[173] This position is even less 'morally and politically defensible' when the assertion of entitlement has benefited the Crown to the detriment of the land's original inhabitants. It 'does not make sense' to speak of Aboriginal title as a 'burden' on the Crown's underlying title.[174] Aboriginal people also wonder how *Crown title* can be said to have 'crystallized at the time sovereignty was asserted.'[175] The court may as well speak of magic crystals being sprinkled on the land as a justification for the diminution of Aboriginal occupation and possession. Crown title simply makes no sense to Aboriginal people (and one suspects to many non-Aboriginal people).

In keeping with these observations, the Supreme Court recognized that in its past decisions 'there has never been a definitive statement ... on the *content* of [A]boriginal title.'[176] It also acknowledged that its terminology has not been 'particularly helpful'[177] and that 'the courts have been less than forthcoming.'[178] Recently, the Supreme Court has attempted to clear up this confusion by characterizing Aboriginal title as sui generis.[179] As described earlier, courts characterize Aboriginal title as sui generis in order to distinguish it from 'normal' proprietary interests.'[180] While many Aboriginal people would agree that a legal doctrine that diminishes Aboriginal rights in ancient territories is 'abnormal,' the court cast this difference in a more positive light. It held that Aboriginal title is 'sui generis in the sense that its characteristics cannot be completely explained by reference either to the common law rules of real property or to the rules of property found in [A]boriginal legal systems.'[181] This holding is consistent with the thesis developed in chapters 1 and 2 of this book, that Indigenous laws form a part of the laws of Canada: 'As with other [A]boriginal rights, [Aboriginal title] must be understood by reference to both common law and [A]boriginal perspectives.'[182] The Supreme Court found that '[t]he idea that [A]boriginal title is sui generis is the unifying principle underlying the various dimensions of that title.'[183]

While the court's delineation of Aboriginal rights as sui generis by reference to Aboriginal perspectives is preferable to a definition based solely on the common law, the problems in *Van der Peet*, identified in the last chapter, reassert themselves here. In *Delgamuukw*, the court again declared that sui generis Aboriginal perspectives must be reconciled with British assertions of sovereignty. This reconciliation requirement might not have been troubling had the court recognized that reconciliation could not diminish Aboriginal legal and political rights without Aboriginal authorization.[184] Reconciliation of the two legal systems might also have appeared more promising if Aboriginal sovereignty was explicitly recognized as the standard against which British assertions had to be measured. However, the Supreme Court did not take this path. It chose instead to find that the 'reconciliation of [A]boriginal prior occupation with the assertion of the sovereignty of the Crown'[185] displaces the fuller pre-existent rights of the land's original occupants. The court noted, '[b]ecause ... distinctive [A]boriginal societies exist within, and are a part of, a broader social, political and economic community, over which the Crown is sovereign, there are circumstances in which, in order to pursue objectives of compelling and substantial importance to that community as a whole (taking account of the fact that [A]boriginal societies are a part of that community), some limitation of those rights will be justifiable. Aboriginal rights are a necessary part of the reconciliation of [A]boriginal societies with the broader political community of which they are part; limits placed on those rights are, where the objectives furthered by those limits are of sufficient importance to the broader community as a whole, equally a necessary part of that reconciliation.'[186] The court's approach to reconciliation thus forcibly includes non-treaty Aboriginal peoples within Canadian society and subjects them to an alien sovereignty, even though most have never consented to such an arrangement.[187] This inclusion subordinates Aboriginal legal systems and limits the uses to which Aboriginal peoples can put their lands. The implications of this approach deeply undermine original Aboriginal entitlements – on grounds none other than self-assertion![188] The limitations placed on Aboriginal peoples without their consent are reminiscent of the sorcery that declared that there has been 'vested in the Crown a substantial and paramount estate, underlying the Indian title' and that 'the tenure of the Indians was ... dependent on the good will of the sovereign.'[189]

The Supreme Court's tautology is ultimately similar to the trial judge's finding that 'the authorities make it clear that such sovereignty exists not just against other "civilized" powers but extends to the natives themselves: ... none of them suggest that the Crown, upon asserting sovereignty, does not acquire title to the soil.'[190] At trial, McEachern J. characterized the effect of Crown sovereignty as 'being far more pervasive than the outcome of a battle or a war ever could be.'[191] He stated that the 'events of the last 200 years are far more significant than any military conquest or treaties would have been,'[192] and concluded that Aboriginal people 'became a conquered people, not by force of arms, for that was not necessary, but by an invading culture and a relentless energy with which they would not, or could not compete.'[193] The court's failure to explain or distance itself from the conventional justifications for the assertion of sovereignty demonstrates why reconciling Aboriginal perspectives with the common law is troubling for Aboriginal peoples. It requires them to accept the pretense that mere Crown assertions of sovereignty have displaced underlying Aboriginal title. In being asked to reconcile their perspectives with assertions of Crown sovereignty, Aboriginal peoples are being asked to accept the notion that they are conquered.[194] Until the Supreme Court develops a (persuasive) explanation for how the assertion of Crown sovereignty 'crystallized' Aboriginal title, such a reconciliation will remain impossible.[195]

Conjuring Crown assertions of sovereignty validates the appropriation of Aboriginal land for non-Aboriginal people. It sanctions the colonization of British Columbia and directs Aboriginal peoples to reconcile their perspectives with the diminution of their rights. The Supreme Court's invocation of Crown assertions, behind a cloak of sovereignty, endorses the infringement of Aboriginal rights in furtherance of legislative objectives that are 'compelling and substantial'[196] to the 'European colonizers.'[197] The court writes:

> In the wake of Gladstone, the range of legislative objectives that can justify the infringement of [A]boriginal title is fairly broad. Most of these objectives can be traced to the *reconciliation* of the prior occupation of North America by [A]boriginal peoples with the assertion of Crown sovereignty, which entails the recognition that 'distinctive [A]boriginal societies exist within, and are a part of, a broader social, political and economic community' ... In my opinion, the development of agriculture, forestry, mining, and hydroelectric power, the general economic development of the interior of British Columbia, protection of the environment or endangered species, the building of infrastructure and the settlement of foreign populations to support those aims, are the kinds of objectives that are consistent with this purpose and, in principle, can justify the infringement of [A]boriginal title.[198]

Words, as bare assertions, are pulled out of the air to justify a basic tenet of colonialism: the settlement of foreign populations to support the expansion of non-Indigenous societies. Colonization is not a pretty thing, when you look into it.[199] In reconciling Crown assertions of sovereignty with ancient rights stemming from Aboriginal occupation, the court labels colonization as an 'infringement' (as if the interference with another nation's independent legal rights were a minor imposition at the fringes of the parties' relationship). Labelling colonization 'Infringement' is an understatement of immense proportions. While these 'infringements' must be 'consistent with the special fiduciary relationship between the Crown and [A]boriginal peoples,'[200] the effect of the court's treatment is to make Aboriginal land rights subject to the 'colonizer's' objectives.[201] The assertion of sovereignty places Aboriginal people in a dependent, feudal relationship with the Crown.[202]

This dependent relationship, and the effects of sovereignty's assertion, are further illustrated by the Supreme Court's description of the content of Aboriginal title. It is, paradoxically, 'a right to the land itself'[203] held by the Crown 'for the use and benefit' of the Aboriginal group.[204] While Aboriginal peoples may use their title lands 'for a wide variety of purposes,'[205] the fact that this title is held by another places Aboriginal peoples in a position analogous to serfs, dependent on their lord to hold the land in their best interests.[206] Why should Her Majesty hold Aboriginal land, when Aboriginal peoples in British Columbia have not ceded this interest? Why should a legal fiction permit the Crown to dispossesses original inhabitants of their radical title when the legal fact of Aboriginal possession has not been refuted?[207]

Rather than engaging these questions, the *Delgamuukw* judgment simply asserts that Aboriginal title lands are held by the Crown. The court found, quoting from *R. v. Guerin*, that 'the same legal principles governed the [A]boriginal interest in reserve lands and lands held pursuant to [A]boriginal title.'[208] Aboriginal peoples will find little solace in the statement that '[t]he Indian interest in the land is the same in both cases.'[209] The similarity of reserve and title land restricts Aboriginal title because 'the nature of the Indian interest in reserve land' is 'held by Her Majesty for the use and benefit of the respective bands for which they are set apart ...'[210] While the court focuses on the similarity between title and reserves to demonstrate the 'breadth' of uses for 'any ... purpose for the general welfare of the band,'[211] its reasons ignore the fact that this similarity removes the underlying title from the land's original inhabitants and vests it in another. This dispossession demonstrates the feudal character of the Crown/Aboriginal relationship concerning land. Even though the content of Aboriginal title encompasses 'the broad notion of use and possession ... which incorporates a reference to the present-day needs of [A]boriginal communities,'[212] such use occurs within the context of the Crown's radical position as lord over the land. The Supreme Court's expansive description of the content of Aboriginal title 'for the general welfare of the band' is betrayed by the narrow constriction upon which it rests. It gives Aboriginal people broad rights over a limited, diminished interest in land.

While the court was careful to note that Aboriginal title is not 'restricted to those uses which are elements of a practice, custom or tradition integral to the distinctive culture of the [A]boriginal group claiming the right,'[213] it nonetheless restricted Aboriginal title in another, related way. The inherent limitation the court finds attached to Aboriginal lands again demonstrates the Crown's feudalistic relationship with Aboriginal peoples. The chief justice observed that the 'content of [A]boriginal title contains an inherent limit that lands held pursuant to title cannot be used in a manner that is irreconcilable with the nature of the claimants' attachment to those lands.'[214] This restriction significantly undermines Aboriginal title because it compels Aboriginal peoples to surrender their lands to the Crown if they want to use them for certain 'non-Aboriginal' purposes. While the court was anxious not to restrict Aboriginal land rights 'to those activities which have been traditionally carried out on it,'[215] it is difficult to read its inherent limits in any other way.[216] According to Chief Justice Lamer, the nature of the group's attachment to land 'is determined by reference to the activities that have taken place on the land and the uses to which the land has been put by the particular group.' This attachment to land reflects the 'special bond' that makes the land part of the group's distinctive culture.[217] As a result, if occupation of Aboriginal land is established by reference to certain activities, the group cannot use the land 'in such a fashion as to destroy its value for such a use;'[218] '[i]f [A]boriginal peoples wish to use their lands in a way that [A]boriginal title does not permit, then they must surrender those lands and convert them into non-title lands to do so.'[219]

The unspoken hex of sovereignty places the Crown in the position of receiving and redesignating Aboriginal lands if they are to be used in non-traditional ways. Why does the Crown assume this pre-eminent role?[220] The fact that Aboriginal peoples are required to 'alienate' or 'surrender' their lands to the Crown to use them for non-traditional purposes indicates that at some level the court, despite its claims to the contrary, is defining the content of Aboriginal title by reference to traditional activities. Such definition makes Aboriginal title an inferior interest.[221] Establishing title by reference to specific practices is potentially inconsistent with the court's later statement that '[A]boriginal title differs from other [A]boriginal rights ..., [which are defined] in terms of *activities.*'[222] If Aboriginal title confers a '*right to the land* itself,'[223] then the court's imposition of inherent limits in terms of activities may well confine Aboriginal peoples in a legal straight-jacket with respect to their land use and to the polity with which they deal with these interests.[224]

Finally, the Supreme Court's test for the proof of Aboriginal title also demonstrates that this interest in land is defined by reference to assertions of Crown sovereignty. Non-Aboriginal sovereignty permeates the criteria Aboriginal groups must satisfy 'to make out a claim for [A]boriginal title.'[225] For example, in order to establish Aboriginal title, '(i) the land must have been occupied prior to *sovereignty*, (ii) if present occupation is relied on as proof of occupation pre-*sovereignty*, there must be a continuity between present and pre-*sovereignty* occupation, and (iii) at *sovereignty*, that occupation must have been exclusive' (emphasis added).[226] Why should Aboriginal groups bear the burden of proving their title while the Crown is presumed to possess it through bare words? Could the Crown establish occupation of land prior to sovereignty? Could the Crown show continuity of occupation between present and pre-sovereignty occupation? Could the Crown show that at sovereignty its occupation was exclusive? The Supreme Court's mantra of Crown sovereignty is repeated over and over again, serving as the measuring rod for proof of Aboriginal title. This sceptre is waved at each stage of the court's test to ensure that proof of Aboriginal occupancy reconciles prior Aboriginal occupation of North America with the assertion of Crown sovereignty.[227] But the Crown is the subsequent claimant. Should it not have to prove its land claims?[228] The court's acceptance of assertions of Crown sovereignty ensures that the Crown is not held to the same strict legal standard as Aboriginal peoples in proving its claims. This double standard is deeply discriminatory and unjust; it holds Aboriginal people to a higher standard in proving title, a standard that the Crown itself could not meet. The Crown is not required to meet any tests of occupation and exclusivity at the time of sovereignty;[229] it gains title through mere assertion. Whatever the justification advanced in earlier days for relieving the Crown of this burden, an unjust and discriminatory doctrine of this kind can no longer be accepted.[230]

The Supreme Court's approach should be contrasted with statements made in 1888 by the Gitksan and Wet'suwet'en's neighbours, the Nisga'a, who said:

What we don't like about the Government is their saying this: 'We will give you this much land.' How can they give it when it is our own? We cannot understand it ... They have never fought and conquered our people and taken the land in that way, and yet they say now that they will give us so much land – our own land. These chiefs do not talk foolishly, they know the land is their own; our forefathers for generations and generations past had their land here all around us; chiefs have had their own hunting grounds, their salmon streams, and places where they got their berries; it has always been so. It is not only during the last four or five years that we have seen the land; we have always seen and owned it; it is no new thing, it has been ours for generations. If we had only seen it for twenty years and claimed it as our own, it would have been foolish, but it has been ours for thousands of years. If any strange person came here and saw the land for twenty years and claimed it, he would be foolish. We have always got our living from the land ...[231]

IV   Awahsinaako (Day Before Yesterday)

In hearing this statement, Raven remembers the land of the Nisga'a, and suddenly recalls why he is here. He looks for some action, hears a crowd's murmur, and swoops down to join them. It's a good day, he thinks, and wonders where he is. He hears a tune he has always loved, 'Get Back'; then he knows. It is the summer of 1969. The Liberal Association of Vancouver has gathered at the Seaforth Armories for dinner. Prime Minister Pierre Trudeau has fled Ottawa's humidity to address them. Raven is looking forward to hearing him. He has heard that this man talks of a 'Just Society.' Raven settles by an open door and listens. After the mandatory salmon and rice have been served the Prime Minister takes the floor. He starts slowly. He has some policy to discuss, a proposal really. 'We won't recognize [A]boriginal rights,' he says.[232] Heads nod agreement. 'We can go on adding bricks of discrimination around the ghetto in which Indians live, and at the same time helping them preserve certain cultural traits and certain ancestral rights. Or, we can say you are at a cross roads – the time is now to decide whether the Indians will be a race apart in Canada, or whether they will be Canadians of full status.' The room is attentive. Raven is curious; why cannot Indians be different, preserve their culture, and be full Canadians? The Prime Minister gathers momentum. 'It's inconceivable, I think, that in a given society one section of a society should have a treaty with the other section of society. We must all be equal under the laws and we must not sign treaties amongst ourselves.' The crowd absorbs his thought. Raven remembers that there really are no treaties in British Columbia anyway. This is interesting, he thinks, once you devastate a people and make them unequal, you then promise equality. Is this justice, he wonders? He strains to hear more. Trudeau continues, 'Indians should become Canadians as all other Canadians. This is the only basis on which I see our society can develop as equals. But [A]boriginal rights, this really means saying, "We were here before you. You came and cheated us, by giving us some worthless things in return for vast expanses of land, and we want to reopen this question. We want you to preserve our [A]boriginal rights and to restore them to us." And our answer – our answer is "no."' These are strong words. Raven is silent. He now sees how the promise of equality can become a pretext for eliminating different ways of evaluating life.

He listens to the explanation for such action: 'If we think of restoring [A]boriginal rights to the Indians, well what about the French, who were defeated at the Plains of Abraham? Shouldn't we restore rights to them?' Some in the crowd search their memory, wondering: 'Did the Indians in B.C. battle the English? Was there a conquest?' Recollection is vague, no similar military battles are recalled. Yet the Prime Minister goes on, 'And what about the Acadians who were deported – shouldn't we compensate for this? What about the Japanese Canadians who were so badly treated at the end or during the last war? What can we do to redeem the past?' The question hangs in the air. Some wonder if the Acadians and Japanese should not be compensated. Raven turns the question around, thinks of the compensation British Columbians have freely received, using Indian land all these years. As people are lost in thought, the Prime Minister raises his hand and points over the audience. His finger punctures the air. 'I can only say as President Kennedy said when he was asked about what he would do to compensate for the injustices that the Negroes had received in American society. We will be just in our time. That is all we can do. We will be just today.' He is finished. Ringing applause engulfs the room. Raven laughs. It is easy to ask others to forget the past when it is to your benefit. Raven knows who will win and who will lose by this strategy.

Over the next few weeks, Raven watches as the Indians clearly reject Trudeau's speech.[233] They do not want the government to repeal the Indian Act, despite its repression.[234] He loves this; he knew they were just like him, paradoxical. They want to retain the very legislation that colonized them because they say it recognizes their special status. This is exactly how Txeemsim would have planned it. Raven smiles to himself, thrusts out his chest, and puffs up feathers. But he notices that the Prime Minister's speech has served as a rallying point for many Aboriginal groups. They want change, but they do not trust the government to bring it about without abrogating their rights. He then sees his old friends the Nisga'a press their land claim before the courts in the *Calder* case.[235] When the Supreme Court of Canada recognizes Aboriginal title as a legal interest, he knows something is up. When the government starts to negotiate with the Nisga'a, he decides to hang around, to see where this leads. But things get bogged down. For sixteen years, the province does not come to the table. Raven realizes he has some time on his hands. He decides to look in on the Supreme Court again. He likes their style, even though it sometimes makes him jealous.

A   The Claim to Self-Government

The *Delgamuukw* decision contains a two-paragraph examination of self-government. Although it accepted assertions of Crown sovereignty as sufficient to ground Crown rights throughout its judgment, the Supreme Court did not extend to Aboriginal peoples equivalent treatment. Relying on its earlier judgment in *R. v. Pamajewon*, the court reasserted that Aboriginal 'rights to self-government, if they existed, cannot be framed in excessively general terms.'[236] The contrast in the court's treatment of Crown and Aboriginal sovereignty could not be more striking. The court was quite willing to frame Crown rights to self-government in the most excessive and general of terms; simple utterances were sufficient to grant the Crown the widest possible range of entitlements to other peoples' ancient rights. Yet detailed evidence concerning Gitksan and Wet'suwet'en sovereignty over specific people and territory (Houses, clans, chiefs, Feasts, crests, poles, laws, and so forth) was too broad to 'lay down the legal principles to guide future litigation.'[237] The court held that the self-government claim advanced in *Delgamuukw* was cast in such broad terms that it was not cognizable under section 35(1) of the Constitution Act, 1982.[238] Is the Crown's assertion of broad rights of Crown sovereignty any more cognizable, given its unexamined extension and unquestioned acceptance by the court in this case? Where, in this treatment, is 'equality before the law'?[239]

Since Aboriginal people in British Columbia were not conquered and never agreed to relinquish their governmental rights, Aboriginal sovereignty should be placed on a footing equal or superior to Crown

sovereignty. If the court's treatment of Crown sovereignty were subjected to the same standards required for evidence of Aboriginal self-
government, perhaps it could be said of Crown sovereignty, as the court
wrote of Aboriginal sovereignty: 'The broad nature of the claim at trial
also led to a failure by the parties to address many of the difficult conceptual issues which surround the recognition of [Crown] self-government ... We received little in the way of submissions that would help us
to grapple with these difficult and central issues. Without assistance
from the parties it would be imprudent for the Court to step into the
breach. In these circumstances the issue of [Crown] self-government
will fall to be determined at trial.'[240] But the court was unwilling to 'step
into the breach' to consider the conceptual issues surrounding Aboriginal self-government. This discrepancy in the respective treatment of
Crown and Aboriginal sovereignty requires further explanation by the
court. The implications of the assertion of Crown sovereignty need to be
more carefully scrutinized to assess the legality and justice of the non-
consensual colonization of British Columbia. As it stands, the unequal
treatment of Aboriginal and Crown sovereignty perpetuates historical
injustices and fails to respect the distinctive legal systems of pre-existing
Aboriginal societies in contemporary Canadian society.[241]

V   Wehhkac (A Long Time Ago)

Raven finds little of interest in the judgment this time; he questions his
jealousy. He is tiring of the Supreme Court. 'Predictable,' he thinks. So,
he returns to Vancouver. He finds a paper draped over an old man in
the park and scans the headlines. The Nisga'a have ratified the treaty
and it has been approved by Parliament and passed the Legislature. He
reads on. The Nisga'a Final Agreement is an attempt by the governments of Canada and British Columbia and the Nisga'a Tribal Council
to produce a 'just and equitable settlement' that 'will result in reconciliation and establish a new relationship among them.'[242] Raven sees that
the Agreement is an ambitious one, providing for collective Nisga'a
ownership of approximately 2,000 square kilometres of land in the Nass
Valley watershed in northwestern British Columbia. The proposed
treaty covers such diverse issues as land titles, minerals, water, forests,
fisheries, wildlife, governance, the administration of justice, fiscal relations (including taxation), cultural property, and dispute resolution.
Raven notes that the Agreement appears to have the broad support of
the people for which it was negotiated. Yet he wonders whether the

Nisga'a Final Agreement is consistent with the laws of the Ayuukhl Nisga'a, and whether it preserves Nisga'a lands, economies, and social structures.[243] He reads through a summary of the Agreement, making a tally of its potential dangers.

He sees that approximately 1,992 square kilometres of land which the Nisga'a will hold as a fee simple interest in the treaty can be alienated[244] and thus conceivably be unavailable for Nisga'a use or possession at some time in the future.[245] If any future Aboriginal rights are found to exist by the courts, they will be held by Canada; not the Nisga'a.[246] Raven observes that the structure of Nisga'a governance significantly departs from, and in most respects replaces, the traditional House (wilp) system of government.[247] Raven counts the cost of some important Nisga'a law-making authority being subject to certain provincial and federal laws through equivalency or paramountcy provisions in the Agreement.[248] He wonders about the effect of ultimately subjecting Nisga'a institutions or court decisions to the discipline of the British Columbia Supreme Court.[249] He pauses when he reads that individual Nisga'a taxation will be collected under general revenues,[250] and that disagreements in respect of the Agreement will be resolved in non-Nisga'a Canadian courts.[251] These and other provisions, he muses, could represent a substantial challenge to Nisga'a attempts to fashion their lives in terms consistent with the Ayuuhkl. Yet, as he reads about the Nisga'a reaction to the Agreement, Raven sees that the people seem happy.

Looking up from his reading, Raven notes that it is a surprisingly clear day for February. The sidewalks are still wet, but standing on Hastings Avenue he has warmth on his back not felt for months. Across the harbour he can see 'the lions' on the north-shore mountains. Despite lingering fog, the sun might prevail today. Up the hill, inside the Hotel Vancouver on Georgia Street, people are gathered for a conference on the Nisga'a treaty. Raven makes his way there. He wants to hear what people have to say about this Agreement. Inside, people from all walks of life are in attendance: students, politicians, academics, civil servants, lawyers, business people, and retired folk. The organizers have worked hard to attract a good cross-section of the public. Raven listens to the speakers and is agitated by what he hears. He still feels uneasy that the treaty provides that Nisga'a conduct will be judged largely by non-Nisga'a laws. He wonders aloud, 'Where is the room for interaction between laws? Don't they remember Txeemsim?' He is also astonished to see some deny to others the very political protections they themselves hold most dear. Raven decides to say something. He transforms himself into the persona of a well-known member of the media. He knew that one day he would get a chance to retell this story. It is his turn to speak.

Raven rises, grasps the podium, and surveys the audience. Then he bellows, 'Let's trash the treaty. Let's scrap any talk of special group rights in British Columbia. We can't countenance race-based entitlements that sanction apartheid in our midst.[252] We must ensure that all British Columbians have equal rights and responsibilities under the Canadian Constitution.[253] We can't build walls around communities based on race.'[254] Raven thinks to himself, 'will they recognize the special group I am speaking of; will they know who is benefiting from racialized entitlements?' He also decides there is no need to tell them about *Delgamuukw*. Besides, where did the Supreme Court get off saying that Aboriginal title is a constitutionalized proprietary interest?[255] As he loosens his grip on the stand and peers over the mike he can see that some cautiously approve of his approach while others are openly hostile. The mixed reception feels right to him. He shifts his stance: 'We must be vigilant against government attempts to erode our democratic rights without input or participation. Too much has been done in secret; the government has kept the average person in the dark.[256] So-called consultation concerning our rights has been a sham. So far, consultation has consisted of the government telling people what already has been negotiated and decided. Nothing changes as a result of public meetings. The government has worked behind closed doors. How about letting the public in on this deal?'[257] He considers his next move. He will not tell them about the Nisga'a Agreement-in-Principle's two-year availability or its months-long review by a special legislative committee.[258] Why complicate a good tale?

Raven studies the crowd again. This is a good audience; no consensus is forthcoming. The Trickster again wonders who they will see in his words, and to whom they will attribute wisdom and foolishness. He would love to know if they ascribe his views to the Nisga'a's opponents, or to some of the Nisga'a themselves. He launches into his final assault: 'How can we permit great changes to the structure of society without a referendum?[259] Racially based governments require a constitutional amendment because they are not envisioned in the Constitution. The people must have their say. Some people who live on Nisga'a lands might be considered second class citizens, subject to an alien government's laws but unable to effectively influence these laws. Do we want to live in a country that constitutionalizes the denial of people's rights because they are not members of the charter group? Do we want to limit and qualify some people's political participation by not recognizing certain fundamental rights?' He will let these points sink in, see which way people take them. Raven finishes, 'Mistakes have been made by focusing on the past. Why turn back the clock?'[260] Together we must work towards a better future for all Canadians.[261] What's past is past. We must be just today.' His remarks meet with polite and sparse clapping and some hissing. Raven loves it. His work is finished for the moment. Maashkooc. He must soon head for home, Ani-kiiwe, before the Ojibway begin to think Nanabush has deserted them.

A   Extinguishment of Aboriginal Rights

The creation of British Columbia, based as it was on a unilateral declaration of sovereignty by the Crown, has questionable legal consequences.[262] It radically altered the structure of Aboriginal societies without a referendum. It made non-Aboriginal people in the province members of a privileged charter group, and simultaneously demoted Aboriginal people to second-class citizens virtually unable to participate in or influence the development of laws. For Aboriginal peoples, the creation of British Columbia took place behind closed doors, without consultation, and it failed to consider their basic rights. These actions are contrary to fundamental principles of both Canadian and Aboriginal law.

Aboriginal peoples had their own governments and laws; the Crown purported to arbitrarily change these pre-existing orders by granting itself the power to extinguish or infringe them. In *Sparrow*, the Supreme Court held that prior to the enactment of the Constitution Act, 1982, the federal government could extinguish Aboriginal rights without the consent of the group claiming the right.[263] The final section of *Delgammuukw* confirms this power.[264] The *Delgamuukw* court noted that section 91(24) of the Constitution Act, 1867 vests in the federal government the exclusive power to legislate in relation to 'Indians and Lands reserved for Indians.' This power was interpreted as 'encompass[ing] within it the exclusive power to extinguish [A]boriginal rights, including [A]boriginal title.'[265] The court arrived at its conclusion without questioning whether extinguishment was 'a morally and politically defensible conception of [A]boriginal rights.'[266] It simply assumed that '[i]n a federal system such as Canada's, the need to determine whether [A]boriginal rights have been extinguished raises the question of which level of government has the right to do so.'[267] The question of extinguishment is kept within the bounds of Crown sovereignty by examining only the interplay between federal and provincial powers in the constitution.[268] By framing extinguishment in terms of a 'need,' the court implies that it deems the subordination of pre-existing governments as necessary to the construction of Canadian federalism. There is no critical examination of whether it is lawful, in the first place, for one nation to extinguish another's rights without their democratic participation or consent through a distant assertion of sovereignty. The court's formulation of this doctrine seemingly forestalls any questioning of the legitimacy of acts that extinguished Aboriginal rights after the Crown's assertion of sovereignty and before 1982.

The limited scope of the Supreme Court's inquiry is illustrated in the three questions it addresses concerning extinguishment: (1) whether the *province* had the jurisdiction to extinguish Aboriginal rights between 1871 and 1982;[269] (2) if the *province* was without jurisdiction in this period, whether it could extinguish title through laws of general application; and (3) whether a *provincial* law, which could not otherwise extinguish Aboriginal rights, could have that effect through referential incorporation. Looking solely at the province's role in extinguishment, the court answered each of these questions in the negative by holding that the provincial level of government had no power to extinguish Aboriginal rights. Nowhere did the court comment explicitly on the participation and rights of Aboriginal people in this matter.[270] Such comment would have been more consistent with Aboriginal peoples' status as interpretive legal communities, and more in harmony with the idea that it is they who would have to consent to any alteration of their legal status.[271]

For example, in addressing the first question, the court held that the province could not establish jurisdiction to extinguish Aboriginal title because section 109 of the Constitution Act, 1867 only gave British Columbia ownership of lands that belonged to the colony at the time of union in 1871. The court stated, '[a]lthough that provision [s. 109] vests underlying title in provincial Crowns, it qualifies provincial ownership by making it subject to "any Interest other than that of the Province in the same."'[272] Since Aboriginal title lands are an '[i]nterest other than that of the Province in the same,' the province cannot extinguish title to these lands: section 91(24) of the Act gives the federal government jurisdiction over this interest.[273] In addressing the second question, the court held that the province could not establish jurisdiction to extinguish Aboriginal title through laws of general application: 'provincial laws which single out Indians for special treatment are ultra vires, because they are in relation to Indians and therefore invade federal jurisdiction.'[274] Finally, in addressing the third question the court held that the province could not extinguish Aboriginal title through referential incorporation because section 88 of the Indian Act, which allows referential incorporation in some cases, 'does not evince the requisite clear and plain intent to extinguish [A]boriginal rights.'[275] One can see in this treatment the narrow bounds within which the court's discussion of extinguishment occurs. While the court in *Delgamuukw* found that the provinces cannot exercise powers of extinguishment over Aboriginal title, this result does not mean that the Crown's assertion of sovereignty cannot dispossess Aboriginal peoples of their ancient rights. Dispossession by assertion is still possible, provided it is done by the proper manifestation of the Crown, which, in this instance, is the federal government.[276]

These wide powers of extinguishment illustrate the problem posed by unimpeded assertions of Crown sovereignty for Aboriginal peoples and their law in British Columbia. 'Taking the perspective of the [A]boriginal people themselves on the meaning of the rights at stake,'[277] as the Supreme Court itself proposed in *R. v. Sparrow*, one might question whether the authority of an imposed, obstructionist, and unrepresentative government should be recognized as legally infringing or extinguishing any '[A]boriginal legislative or other jurisdiction'[278] that Aboriginal people possess. In these circumstances, is the assertion of British sovereignty over Aboriginal peoples in British Columbia, as *R. v. Van der Peet* asks, a 'morally and politically defensible conception of [A]boriginal rights'? Does the decision, as *R. v. Côté* cautions, 'perpetuate historical injustice suffered by [A]boriginal peoples at the hands of the colonizers'? Is *Delgamuukw v. The Queen* consistent with the Supreme Court's own standard of upholding the 'noble and prospective purpose of the Constitutional entrenchment of [A]boriginal and treaty rights in the Constitution'?[279] If assertions of sovereignty operate as they have done throughout western European legal thought, should we wonder, as the Australian High Court did in *Mabo v. Queensland*, whether such an unjust and discriminatory doctrine can continue to be accepted?[280] As will be discussed in the next chapter, any consideration of the extinguishment of Aboriginal rights should assess the legality and legitimacy of extinguishment through the prism of these questions.

Questioning Canada's Title to Land: The Rule of Law, Aboriginal Peoples, and Colonialism

My Aunt Irene lived in a blue clapboard bungalow on the top of an escarpment that overlooked the reserve. From her front window you could see down Sydney Bay Bluff road, across the 'prairie,' to the peninsula that gave Cape Croker its name. Framing 'the Cape' were the vast cerulean waters of Georgian Bay. From this perch you could watch the people of Neyaashiinigming come and go. Aunt Irene could tell you the family history of each resident that passed by her window, and she knew the stories that made sacred each place they lived. When I was a young boy we would sometimes visit her and she would tell me something about this world. I always enjoyed the soda she served me, but was a little confused by her. As a small boy who spent more time off the reserve than on it, I did not know what to make of the strange world she unfolded to me.

When I was older I began to appreciate the knowledge Aunt Irene carried a little more. I can remember visiting her house with Grandpa Josh (her brother), my mother, and sister, and listening to her reminiscences. Although I would see her on and off through the years, she was never really a big part of my life. Then one day when I was in graduate school I went to ask about the history of the reserve. I was with my mother and Aunt Norma. We spent a few hours there and, in her unforgettable way, Aunt Irene told us the history of our family as it related to Cape Croker. She knew the history of my great-great-great-grandfather and grandmother, and everyone down through their line until my generation. I was amazed. She was a living history book. I finally caught a glimpse of the world that had so perplexed me as a young boy. I realized that the discomfort I once felt owed more to my lack of familiarity with the people she would talk about than to any unusual behaviour on her part. Her stories now gave me great comfort, as I became aware that I fit into this world she described and was related to it in more ways than I knew.

Aunt Irene's chronicles were deeply insightful and revealing. Aside from relating our family's past, her narrative uncovered a legal history that had been largely hidden from view during my formal university studies. I graduated with so-called distinction from the University of Toronto, with a specialist designation in Canadian political science and history, and then spent three more years in a rigorous Canadian law school, but neither program introduced the kind of information she related. I had sought out Aunt Irene because of my earlier experience with her. I knew there was more to the story of Canada than I was being taught. In particular, I was trying to understand the Canadian foundations of law and governance, but most of the information I found concerned its non-Aboriginal origins. The framework Aunt Irene provided helped me make sense of the fragmentary written and archival material that I had been sorting through prior to that visit. Her wonderful narrative helped me to resolve the papered remnants of our history into something approaching a recognizable representation. I later triangulated her stories with those of my great-uncle Fred, 'Chick' (Walter Johnson), John Nadgiwon, Aunt Norma, and my mother to unearth the details of Anishinabek participation in the foundations of this country.[1]

In these conversations and readings I rediscovered the tremendous implications of the interaction of Canadian and Indigenous legal values for our understanding of the past and continued development of Canada. My ancestors had acted through seven generations to maintain their community ties and apply principles consistent with their ancient teachings. Their efforts, understood in conjunction with principles underlying the rule of law, raise important questions about the justice and validity of Canada's claims to underlying title to its territorial land base and to exclusive sovereignty throughout its so-called Dominion.

Canadian courts have not given sufficient attention to the impact of Aboriginal legal perspectives on the country's foundational legal doctrines, as evidenced in unreflective statements like those made in *R. v. Sparrow*: '[t]here was from the outset never any doubt that sovereignty and legislative power, and indeed the underlying title, to such lands [meaning Aboriginal lands] vested in the Crown.'[2] They have too often accepted uncritically Crown proclamations to the effect that sovereignty and underlying title to land throughout the country belongs solely to Canada despite the presence of an unextinguished prior and continuing legal order. The courts' articulation of the rule of law in other contexts, and Aboriginal viewpoints on this matter,[3] suggest that a closer examination of these assumptions are in order.

A faithful application of the rule of law to the Crown's assertion of title throughout Canada would suggest that Aboriginal peoples possess the very right claimed by the Crown. According to the Supreme Court of Canada, the rule of law consists of two interrelated legal principles: it precludes arbitrary state power and requires the maintenance of a positive legal order.[4] Canada's assumption of underlying title and sovereignty throughout its claimed territory violates both of these fundamental principles. It is an arbitrary exercise of power aimed at dismantling Indigenous systems of law and normative order. Canada substantially invalidated Aboriginal peoples' territorial rights in the absence of informed consent, or persuasive legal explanation.[5] Furthermore, Canada's declaration of exclusive sovereignty over Aboriginal peoples violates the second principle of the rule of law because, in the process of this declaration, the Crown suppressed Aboriginal governance and denied these groups indispensable elements of law and order.[6]

Significantly, as I discovered from my visits with Aunt Irene, the rule of law is not the only paradigm violated by the way in which Canada has dealt with Aboriginal rights. Aboriginal perspectives in most corners of the country,[7] including Neyaashiinigming, pose equally strong challenges to the Crown's supposed overarching sovereignty and underlying title.[8] For example, the actions of my ancestors, when placed beside the Court's formulation of the rule of law, similarly demonstrate the tenuous nature of the Crown's claims to assume governance over and a radical interest in Indigenous lands. Contrary to common assumptions, Aboriginal peoples have not been subject to a presumed overriding authority in land or governance. For example, the treaty process has been exposed as a deeply flawed means by which to acquire these interests. In almost every treaty negotiation one can detect dishonesty, trickery, deception, fraud, prevarication, and unconscionable behaviour on the part of the Crown.[9] In most treaties, there was no consensus or 'meeting of the minds' on the question of the Crown receiving sovereignty or underlying title to the land from Aboriginal peoples.[10] Moreover, in many parts of Canada the Crown has never negotiated with Aboriginal peoples to receive a transfer of any rights to land or governance.[11] The Crown has merely asserted such rights, and acted as if their unilateral declarations have legal meaning. Most Aboriginal peoples regard the Crown's assertions and actions in this regard as the gravest injustice ever perpetrated upon them. They contend that they cannot be dispossesed of their land or governing powers unless they agree to surrender these rights with adequate knowledge and informed consent.

This chapter examines how fundamental constitutional principles combined with Aboriginal legal perspectives could be used to challenge Canada's claim to underlying title and exclusive sovereignty in the country. Such a process is necessary if Canada is to abide by its most valued precepts as 'a free and democratic society'[12] and to respect the legal orders of Indigenous peoples. Legal scrutiny of Crown sovereignty and title could simultaneously enable the country to abandon the colonial treatment of Aboriginal peoples in contemporary Canada and would be consistent with Aboriginal scepticism where Crown assertions are concerned. One should not found a just country on stolen land and repressive government. Many people may believe that some persuasive justification for the displacement of Aboriginal peoples can be coherently articulated in law. That is not the case. Aboriginal peoples have by and large been illegally and illegitimately forced to relinquish or reduce their claims to land and government because of the arbitrary actions of non-Aboriginal governments.[13] This is an issue of justice that directly implicates the rule of law and Aboriginal legal values.

Some Canadians do not realize that the nation is built upon a deeply troubling relationship with the land's original owners and governors. Many people assume that since their experience of life in Canada is one of fairness and justice, most people must experience life in Canada in this same way.[14] However, Canada is a country that does not have an 'even' experience of justice.[15] Aboriginal peoples have often been denied the essential legal rights in property (title)[16] and contract law (treaties)[17] that lie at the heart of our private law ordering.[18] This should be of concern to all Canadians, because such a basic failure of the rule of law presents a threat to the very fabric of our fundamental principles of order. If the rule of law cannot be relied upon to overcome the political and economic exploitation of Aboriginal peoples, what assurances do we have that it will not be equally vulnerable in situations involving non-Aboriginal Canadians? As mentioned in chapter 2, Aboriginal peoples might function like the miner's canary. When the most vulnerable among us suffer from the toxins present in our legal environment, their suffering serves as an important warning about the health of the larger legal climate.

Admittedly, some might argue that the notion that Aboriginal peoples should enjoy the full benefits of the rule of law precipitates the very problem I am cautioning against. It may be said that recognition of underlying Aboriginal title to lands in Canada, and of co-extensive sovereign powers between Aboriginal peoples and the Crown, would work to undermine Canadian society. On this view, past wrongs cannot be fully addressed because too much in the present relies upon these prior violations and indiscretions.[19] I have no hesitancy in recognizing that a shift of this magnitude would cause significant disruption for many people. Many Canadians are being unjustly enriched through the failure of the rule of law for Aboriginal peoples, and they will not easily give up their accoutrements and power. The struggle over these endowments will not occur without causing significant strain on our institutions. The full application of the rule of law to Aboriginal peoples would necessarily change our political systems and national economy to thoroughly accommodate Aboriginal peoples within a new national framework. Nevertheless, seriously disrupting our socio-political relations is not the same thing as completely undermining those relations, especially when the correction of the injustice may ultimately set the entire society on the path to a more peaceful and productive future.

To draw on a biblical analogy,[20] a house built upon a foundation of sand is unstable, no matter how beautiful it may look or how many people may rely upon it. It would be better to lift the house and place it on a firmer foundation, even if this course of action would create some real challenges for its occupants. Ultimately, replacing the foundation would prolong the structure's life, creating benefits for its inhabitants for generations beyond what would be possible if the house collapsed because of its unsupported weight. Canada is built on a foundation of sand so long as the rule of law is not consistently applied to Aboriginal peoples. This country must be placed on a firmer legal foundation by extending the full benefits of legal ordering to its original inhabitants. While the recognition of underlying Aboriginal title and the affirmation of Aboriginal sovereignty would cause severe disruptions in the Canadian social and economic fabric, it would ultimately set us on a more stable, secure foundation and correct the imperfections of our present ordering. This chapter is written with the understanding that the 'rule of law' and sensitivity to the meaning of the Aboriginal perspective' should be more than hollow phrases used by those who want to govern others to accomplish their own purposes.[21] It is motivated by the very conservative notion that the consistent application of the rule of law and the inclusion of Aboriginal perspectives can provide an important bulwark against arbitrariness and oppression for all Canadians.

I   The Rule of Law in Canada

Aristotle observed that '[r]ightly constituted laws should be the final sovereign' in any just political community.[22] He argued that the rule of law (dikaiosyne) is preferable to personal rule because law better distributes and combines moral virtue and important legal customs to make the members of a state just and good (nomos). The sovereignty of law could be threatened if 'the law itself [had] a bias in favour of one class or another' or if the laws were made 'in accordance with wrong or perverted constitutions.'[23] Failure to question the Crown's assertions of underlying title and exclusive sovereignty while Aboriginal assertions are subjected to strict secrutiny appears to create a bias in the law in favour of non-Aboriginal groups. This approach is not consistent with the rule of law. It upholds personal rule to the detriment of Aboriginal peoples and to the advantage of non-Aboriginal people. As discussed in the previous two chapters, the courts' failure to interrogate Crown assertions results in the unjust distribution of legal entitlements[24] and perverts Canada's 'supreme law,' the constitution, which proclaims that 'Canada is founded upon principles that recognize the supremacy of God and the rule of law.'[25] Failure to question personal rule is not consistent with section 52(1) of the Constitution Act, 1982, which states that the constitution is 'the supreme law of Canada.'

Canadian courts do not respect the supremacy of the constitution's rule of law when they unquestioningly support notions of underlying Crown title and exclusive sovereignty in the face of contrary Aboriginal evidence. This uncritical acceptance of government assertions and actions is not typical of the courts' approach to constitutional questions. In the *Manitoba Language Reference*, a case involving the constitutionality of all the laws of Manitoba, the Supreme Court of Canada radically queried the actions of the Manitoba Crown and legislature. The court affirmed the supremacy of law over the government, and wrote: 'The rule of law, a fundamental principle of our Constitution, must mean at least two things. First, that the law is supreme over officials of the government as well as private individuals, and thereby preclusive of arbitrary power. Indeed, it is because of the supremacy of law over the government, as established in ... s. 52 of the Constitution Act, 1982, that this court must find the unconstitutional laws of Manitoba to be invalid and of no force or effect.'[26] The court characterized the province's action in not translating its laws into French, as required by Manitoba's terms of union, as a blunt exercise of arbitrary power. It therefore drew upon the paramountcy of law to declare the province's entire statutory code invalid.[27] This result demonstrates that the 'rule of law constitutes an implied limit on the legislative jurisdiction of Parliament and the provincial legislatures, and that legislation inconsistent with the rule of law will therefore be held to be ultra vires.'[28] The drastic nature of the remedy shows that the courts will refuse to sanction an exercise of arbitrary power.

The Crown's assertion of sovereignty, which deprives Aboriginal nations of underlying title and overriding self-government, is likewise a blunt exercise of arbitrary power. Democratic principles of consultation and consent, though available, were not followed in the First Nations' inclusion in the Dominion's federal structures.[29] All other governments entering into Confederation were included on principles of consultation and consent. Each had the opportunity to make known its views, to craft the terms under which it would join the union, and to send representatives of the people to these discussions. Aboriginal peoples, except perhaps for the Métis in Manitoba, were not recognized as participating in Confederation in this manner, and thus became subject to it through the arbitrary acts of others. This has resulted in negative implications for Indigenous communities and significantly contributed to the devastation of their territories and communities.[30]

As one author states, '[t]he very essence of arbitrariness is to have one's status redefined by the state without an adequate explanation of its reasons for doing so.'[31] Aboriginal peoples have had their status redefined by Canada without persuasively sound juridical reasons. What could be more arbitrary than one nation substantially invalidating a politically distinct peoples' rights without providing an elementarily persuasive legal explanation? The Supreme Court has not effectively articulated how, and by what legal right, assertions of Crown sovereignty grant underlying title to the Crown or displace Aboriginal governance. Doctrines of discovery,[32] terra nullius,[33] conquest,[34] and adverse possession[35] have all been discredited in the common law and in international legal systems as legitimate bases to dispossess Aboriginal peoples of their land.[36] Moreover, the Crown's claim to possess Aboriginal land is wholly unsubstantiated by the physical reality at the time of their so-called assertions of sovereignty.[37] Its supposed right to exercise unilateral dominion over Indigenous peoples does not accord with the factual circumstances at the time of contact.[38] These 'vague' and 'unintelligible' propositions 'do not make sense' under the rule of law because they are factually untrue and lack legal cohesion.[39] The Crown's assertion of sovereignty diminishing Aboriginal entitlements is therefore arbitrary in the sense that it has been made without coherent reasons. The assertion of Crown sovereignty over Aboriginal peoples in Canada thus violates the first principle of the rule of law and is unconstitutional.

The unquestioned assertion of Crown sovereignty also violates the second principle of the rule of law: the sustenance of normative legal order through the production and preservation of positive laws. As has been illustrated throughout this work, the predominant interpretation of Crown sovereignty has stifled Aboriginal peoples in the creation and maintenance of laws supportive of their normative orders. The Supreme Court, again in the *Manitoba Language Reference*, described this second aspect of the rule of law in the following terms:

> ... the rule of law requires the creation and maintenance of an actual order of positive laws which preserves and embodies the more general principle of normative order. Law and order are indispensable elements of civilized life ... As John Locke once said, 'A government without laws is, I suppose, a mystery in politics, inconceivable to human capacity and inconsistent with human society' (quoted by Lord Wilberforce in *Carl Zeiss-Stiftung v. Rayner & Keeler Ltd.*, [1966] 2 All E.R. 536 (H.L.) at p. 577). According to Wade and Philips, *Constitutional Administrative Law* (9th ed. 1977), at p. 89: '... the rule of law expresses a preference for law and order within a community rather than anarchy, warfare and constant strife. In this sense, the rule of law is a philosophical view of society which in the Western tradition is linked with basic democratic notions.'[40]

Failure to recognize and affirm the positive and customary laws of Aboriginal peoples, which preserve and embody the general principles of their ancient normative orders, has sustained near-anarchy and constant strife within Aboriginal communities. A vague familiarity with the encumbrances placed on Aboriginal governments is sufficient to appreciate this fact. Aboriginal communities have suffered greatly because their governments have been oppressed.[41] The Crown's suppression of Aboriginal governance denies these groups indispensable elements of law and order. It displaces Aboriginal peoples' 'purposive ordering of social relations providing a basis upon which an actual [contemporary, culturally appropriate and effective] order of positive laws can be brought into existence.'[42] Any supposed justification for the denial of Aboriginal community participation in Canadian sovereignty constitutes, in Locke's words, 'a mystery in politics, inconceivable to human capacity and inconsistent with human society.'[43] The repression of Aboriginal powers of governance is therefore contrary to the second principle of the rule of law: it destroys the normative orderliness within Aboriginal communities.

Despite the disorder imposed on Aboriginal peoples by the assertion of Crown sovereignty, some would argue that the second principle of the rule of law must also consider the potential 'chaos and anarchy' that would ensue if the Crown's assertion were held to be invalid and of no legal force and effect. The court would not tolerate a legal vacuum,[44] nor would it tolerate a province being without a valid and effectual legal system.[45] Since the constitution would not suffer a province without laws, temporary validity, force, and effect would be given to those rights, obligations, and other effects that have arisen under those laws until such time as the problem leading to the invalidity could be corrected.[46] In other words, despite the invalidity of Canada's laws (because their arbitrary, non-legal foundation violates the first principle of the rule of law), the second principle of the rule of law would require (1) that Aboriginal normative orders be facilitated by recognizing their powers of governance, and (2) that Canadian laws continue in effect until the parties correct the invalidity by grounding Crown title and sovereignty on a sound, substantiated legal foundation. Therefore, the next time the Supreme Court considers Aboriginal governance in Canada, the second principle of the rule of law would require a recognition of the rights of these communities to maintain and create law and order in their lives. It would further require that the court declare Canada's invalid laws operative until they can be fixed by the federal Crown, negotiating with First Nations to place Crown sovereignty in a workable, but proper, legal framework.[47]

II   Courts and the Questioning of Crown Sovereignty

In suggesting that the Supreme Court interrogate Crown assertions of sovereignty a central question remains: are the courts permitted to engage in such an inquiry? The answer is yes. In the groundbreaking *Calder* case, the Supreme Court of Canada held that Canadian courts are not prevented from 'reviewing the manner in which the Sovereign acquires new territory' in cases dealing with Aboriginal title.[48] The 'Act of State' doctrine, which deals with this issue, was examined by the court and found not to apply. Justice Hall gave two reasons why it was inappropriate to extend the Act of State doctrine to cases dealing with Aboriginal title. First, a finding that this doctrine applied to cases dealing with Aboriginal title would be unsupported by prior jurisprudence.[49] Second, the Act of State doctrine only deals with situations where a 'Sovereign, in dealings with another Sovereign (by treaty or conquest) acquires land.'[50] In Canada the Crown seldom acquired underlying title land by treaty or conquest, and therefore this doctrine would have no application.[51]

The courts are thus permitted to review the effects of the Crown assertion of sovereignty over Aboriginal peoples in Canada. In fact, such oversight of the proper conduct of the other branches of government is required by the independence of the court as an institution, and of the judiciary as individuals within this institution.[52] Judicial independence has been guaranteed for centuries and is a cornerstone of English and Canadian constitutionalism.[53] Canadian courts are separate and autonomous from the Crown and the legislature and do not function as the servants of the Queen or Parliament. They administer the rule of law, which is 'superior and antecedent not only to legislation and judicial decisions but also to the written constitution.'[54] As the British Columbia Court of Appeal noted in *BCGEU v. British Columbia (A.G.)*:

> It must be noted that judicial independence was won in England after centuries of struggle with the executive and legislative branches of government. It was finally established in 1701 by the *Act of Settlement* ... when tenure for the judges was established.
>
> As Sir William Holdsworth, the distinguished British legal historian has said in a *History of English Law*:
>
>> The judiciary has separate and autonomous power just as truly as the King or Parliament; and in the exercise of these powers, its members are not more in the position of servants than the King or Parliament in the exercise of their powers ... The judges have powers of this nature, being entrusted with the maintenance of the Supremacy of law, they are and have long been regarded as a separate and independent part of the constitution.[55]

Judicial independence and the supremacy of law ensures that courts are free to question the actions of the other branches of government as required when an action is brought before them.[56] Presumably, this means that the courts would be permitted to scrutinize unilateral Crown assertions of sovereignty and find them invalid if those assertions failed to comply with the rule of law.[57] The court, as an independent body, would not be disallowed from finding that the laws of Canada or any province relating to Aboriginal lands and governance are beyond the reach of the Crown or Parliament, if they do not comply with the rule of law as expressed in the constitution's principles or provisions.[58] To be more specific, if the court found that the Crown did not comply with the law in gaining underlying title and overriding sovereignty in Canada it would have to hold that assertions to such title and sovereignty were 'of no legal force or effect' until the parties created a supportable legal framework.[59]

Readers may question whether, despite the institutional possibility, individual judges would ever declare invalid the unilateral exercise of Crown sovereignty over Aboriginal peoples in any part of the country. There would be an enormous temptation to do everything possible to avoid such an outcome, given the stakes involved. After all, it may be asked, who would respect the law and the judiciary if they arrived at this conclusion? It could be argued that too many people throughout Canada would be displaced and subject to immense suffering. Most Canadians would consider a decision to this effect unreasonable, impractical, unrealistic, unsound, and indicative of a lack of knowledge of the law or history of Aboriginal rights. Since few people would understand the court's justification for such a decision, the administration of justice might also be brought into disrepute.

Yet, doesn't this line of inquiry look at the issue only from one side? Aboriginal people and others puzzled by the wide effect of Crown assertions might develop a greater respect for the judiciary if the courts ruled according to principles of law. They would consider such a conclusion reasonable, practical, realistic, sensible, and demonstrative of an understanding of the law and history of Aboriginal rights. They would see that a rejection of Crown assertions to sovereignty could help reduce the suffering of Aboriginal peoples arising from their alienation from their own land and organizing institutions. Such a decision could even enhance the reputation of the administration of justice, as the court would be seen to be applying the law in accordance with its highest principles. The courts' questioning of unilateral Crown assertions of sovereignty would be a substantial development of Canada's legal order. It would highlight the guarantee to every Canadian of an impartial and independent judiciary, which has been described as 'the most important benefit of civilization.'[60]

Regardless of the challenges a judge may encounter in questioning assertions of Crown sovereignty, his or her decision cannot be based on a numeric tally of public opinion.[61] The judiciary is independent.[62]

Conclusions must be legally expressed. They must be coherent and internally inconsistent. It is not appropriate for judges to use their power in any other way. While most judges would no doubt struggle with a ruling that suspends the negative effects on Aboriginal peoples of assertions of Crown sovereignty, if reason led to such a conclusion and they chose to rule otherwise, the very integrity of the Canadian legal fabric would be undermined.[63] If the judiciary is to take the constitution, the rule of law, and its own office seriously, judicial independence mandates 'impartial and disinterested umpires.'[64] Any judge who reviewed the assertion of sovereignty over Aboriginal peoples would be expected to do so in an impartial manner,[65] without bias or a predisposition as to the result.[66] The fair and equitable application of law demands strict adherence to this standard.[67]

III   Oral Traditions, the Constitution, and the Rule of Law

How can the exclusive authority Canada has accorded to itself to extinguish or diminish the distinct rights of Aboriginal peoples, without allowing their participation in such decisions, be justified constitutionally? In order to be legally valid and politically legitimate, Canada's claim must be congruent with broader constitutional principles. In the *Quebec Secession Reference*, the Supreme Court of Canada identified some of these principles in ruling that a unilateral declaration of sovereignty by Quebec would be unconstitutional.[68] The court observed that in the Canadian 'constitutional tradition, legality and legitimacy are linked.'[69] Any consideration of the diminishment of Aboriginal rights should therefore review these broader legal principles to assess the legitimacy of the Crown's assertion of sovereignty in Canada. Indeed, the entrenchment of Aboriginal rights in the constitution underscores the need for this wide examination. As the Supreme Court observed in the leading case of *R. v. Sparrow:* 'Section 35 calls for a just settlement for [A]boriginal peoples. It renounces the old rules of the game under which the Courts established courts of law and denied those courts the authority to question sovereign claims made by the Crown.'[70]

When courts question sovereign claims made by the Crown, they must look at the entirety of the Canadian constitutional law framework. As the court counselled in the *Quebec Secession Reference*, their review must take into account an oral tradition 'behind the written word,' 'an historical lineage stretching back through the ages, which aids in the consideration of the underlying constitutional principles.'[71] The legality and legitimacy of the law dealing with Aboriginal peoples depend on these 'fundamental and organizing principles,'[72] which 'are the vital unstated assumptions upon which the text is based.'[73] The unstated precepts that 'inform and sustain the [Canadian] constitutional text' in relation to Aboriginal peoples are two-pronged. They can be drawn from the oral traditions of Aboriginal peoples throughout this country,[74] and they can be sourced in the unwritten traditions of the West.[75] The courts should examine how Aboriginal oral traditions, laws, and perspectives could inform and sustain Canada's constitutional text,[76] just as they have explored the influences of Western law on the constitution. Comparing the Supreme Court's principles in the *Quebec Secession Reference* with Aboriginal reflections on Canadian constitutionalism, like those told to me by my Aunt Irene, demonstrates the potential interaction of the two traditions.

In the *Quebec Secession Reference*, the Supreme Court of Canada identified the fundamental traditions influencing the interpretation of Canada's constitutional text as federalism, democracy, constitutionalism and the rule of law, and the protection of minorities.[77] The court described these precepts as 'underlying constitutional principles' that 'may in certain circumstances give rise to substantive legal obligations which constitute substantive limitations upon government action.'[78] What can these four constitutional principles, considered together,[79] tell us about the legality and legitimacy of the extinguishment of Aboriginal rights prior to 1982, and their justifiable infringement subsequent to 1982? A brief examination of each doctrine reveals that Aboriginal peoples can interrogate and overturn assertions of Crown sovereignty that permit the unilateral extinguishment and diminishment of Aboriginal rights.

A   Federalism

The first principle the Supreme Court considered in the *Quebec Secession Reference* was federalism. The court wrote that the federal system is only partially complete 'according to the precise terms of the *Constitution Act, 1867*'[80] because the 'federal government retained sweeping powers that threatened to undermine the autonomy of the provinces.'[81] A simple reading of the Constitution Act, 1867 would seem to confirm the notion that the federal government secured the paramount legislative authority over the provinces in Canada.[82] The court observed that the structure of the document was unbalanced: since 'the written provisions of the Constitution do not provide the entire picture' of the Canadian federal structure, the courts have had to 'control the limits of the respective sovereignties.'[83] This interpretation was necessary to facilitate 'democratic participation by distributing power to the government thought to be most suited to achieving the particular societal objective,' with regard to the diversity of the component parts of Confederation.[84] It limited the power of the federal government relative to provincial governments and resulted in a more appropriate sharing of political power between the two orders.[85] Provincial power has been significantly strengthened under this interpretation.[86]

Applying these principles to the treatment of Aboriginal peoples, would it not also be possible to regard the federal system as only partially complete?[87] It could similarly be argued that the 'federal government retained sweeping powers' relative to Aboriginal peoples 'which threatened to undermine the autonomy' of these groups.[88] Furthermore, since the 'written provisions of the Constitution does [sic] not provide the entire picture' in relation to Aboriginal peoples, the courts could also 'control the limits of the respective sovereignties' by distributing power to the Aboriginal government 'thought to be most suited to achieving [a] particular societal objective.' If the courts can draw on unwritten principles of federalism to fill in the 'gaps in the express terms of the constitutional text'[89] to strengthen provincial powers, could they not apply the same principles to facilitate 'the pursuit of collective goals by [the] cultural and linguistic minorities'[90] that comprise Aboriginal nations? Following the court's reasoning, the principle of federalism could be applied to question assertions of sovereignty that purportedly diminish Aboriginal powers. Federal power over Aboriginal peoples would thereby be circumscribed, allowing Aboriginal people to function as an equal integral part of the federal structure in Canada.

Significantly, Anishinabek traditions would be consistent with principles of Canadian federalism and they provide clues as to how this system could be rebalanced to incorporate Anishinabek interests. Anishinabek law contains 'an historical lineage stretching back through the ages, which aids in the consideration of the underlying constitutional principles'[91] in Crown/Aboriginal relations. Some of the stories told by Aunt Irene illustrate this legal genealogy. For instance, in 1763, the generation of my great-great-great-grandparents, First Nations leaders in the Great Lakes and upper Ohio river valley were invited to attend a conference at Niagara with William Johnson, the Crown's chief representative for Indian Affairs, to discuss principles that would govern their relationship.[92] This was the first such meeting of Anishinabek peoples with representatives of the Crown, who had previously been their enemies on the battlefield.[93] The gathering was thus significant in setting the framework by which the parties would relate to one another. Through participation and consent, the Anishinabek and the Crown representatives created a pattern to follow in 'constituting' their relations. The principles agreed to at this inaugural meeting therefore provide pointed guidance for those concerned with Aboriginal peoples' place within Canadian federalism. Those principles include, among others, the recognition of Aboriginal governance,[94] free trade, open migration, respect for Aboriginal land holdings, affirmation of Aboriginal permission and consent in treaty matters, criminal justice protections, military assistance,[95] respect for hunting and fishing rights, and adherence to principles of peace and friendship.[96] The principles elaborated at Niagara have never been entirely abrogated and they underpin Canada's legal structure. Other treaty nations can point to similar promises recognizing their place in Canada's political structures,[97] as such meetings generally involved the negotiation of principles to govern their relationship with the Crown. These agreements have formed the implied term and condition of subsequent treaties[98] and could inform contemporary interpretations of Canada's federal relationship with First Nations throughout the country.

The treaty at Niagara,[99] negotiated through July and August of 1764, was at the time regarded as 'the most widely representative gathering of American Indians ever assembled,'[100] as approximately two thousand chiefs and representatives were in attendance.[101] At least twenty-four nations[102] had gathered with 'representative nations as far east as Nova Scotia, and as far west as the Mississippi, and as far north as Hudson Bay.'[103] The assembled nations included peoples from the great western and eastern Indian confederacies of the day: the Algonquins, Chippewas (Anishinabek), Crees, Fox, Hurons, Pawnees, Menominees, Nippisings, Odawas, Sacs, Toughkamiwons, Potawatomies, Cannesandagas, Caughnawagas, Cayugas, Conoys, Mohicans, Mohawks, Nanticokes, Onondagas, and Senacas.[104] Aboriginal people throughout the Great Lakes and northern, eastern, and western colonial regions travelled for months and weeks to attend this meeting.[105]

When everyone was assembled,[106] Sir William Johnson presented 'the terms of what he hoped would prove a Pax Britannica for North America.'[107] On behalf of the Crown he read the terms of the Royal Proclamation, gave gifts,[108] and presented two different wampum belts to the gathered Indians. In turn, Aboriginal representatives accepted the belts, made speeches, and promised peace to establish a state of mutual respect between the parties.[109] One belt Johnson passed, the Gus Wen Tah or Two-Row wampum, has been described as follows: 'There is a bed of white wampum which symbolizes the purity of the agreement. There are two rows of purple, and those two rows have the spirit of your ancestors and mine. There are three beads of wampum separating the two rows and they symbolize peace, friendship and respect. These two rows will symbolize two paths or two vessels, travelling down the same river together. One, a birch bark canoe, will be for the Indian people, their laws, their customs and their ways. The other, a ship, will be for the white people and their laws, their customs and their ways. We shall each travel the river together, side by side, but in our own boat. Neither of us will try to steer the other's vessel.'[110] The two-row wampum has important implications for federalism because it reflects a conception of governance that recognizes the simultaneous interaction and separation of settler and First Nations societies. An agreement to this effect was first struck by the Haudonosaunee upon contact with Europeans; the principles it represents were renewed by them in 1764 and received for the first time by the Anishinabek in the same year.[111] The two-row wampum belt illustrates a First Nation/Crown relationship founded on peace, friendship, and respect; neither nation will interfere with the internal affairs of the other. The belt contemplates interaction and sharing between First Nations and the Crown, as demonstrated by the three rows of white beads. But it also envisions separation and autonomy between the two governments, as represented by the two parallel rows of purple beads. The twin principles of separation and integration are a recurring theme in Crown–First Nations relations, and they are consistent with a notion of Canadian federalism that respects the need to distribute power to the government thought to be best suited to achieving the particular societal objective, having regard to the diversity of the component parts of Confederation.[112]

The second belt Sir William Johnson presented, which was accepted by the assembled group, also displays themes consistent with Canadian federalism. After referencing the two-row wampum,[113] Thomas Anderson, a Superintendent of Indian Affairs in 1845, described the second belt as follows: 'On the other wampum belt is marked at one end a hieroglyphic denoting Quebec on this continent, on the other, is a ship with its bow towards Quebec; betwixt those two objects are wove 24 Indians, one holding the cable of the vessel with his right, and so on, until the figure on the extreme left rests his foot on the land at Quebec. Their traditional account of this is, that at the time it was delivered to them (1764) Sir William Johnson promised, in the name of the Government, that those Tribes should continue to receive presents as long as the sun would shine ... and if ever the ship came across the Great salt lake without a full cargo, these tribes should pull lustily at the cable until they brought her over full of presents.'[114] The principles found in this belt similarly envision a political relationship that incorporates autonomy and integration. The Indians and Crown are clearly separate from one another, yet they are connected in important physical ways. The offer of mutual support and assistance (the cable can be pulled from either end) that also respects the independent nature of each party is a powerful archetype for Canada's federal relationships. Sir William Johnson himself, in introducing this belt at Niagara in 1764, captured the mutuality and diversity embedded in this agreement:

> Brothers of the Western Nations, Sachems, Chiefs and Warriors; You have now been here for several days, during which time we have frequently met to renew and Strengthen our Engagements and you have made so many Promises of your Friendship and Attachment to the English that there now remains for us only to exchange the great Belt of the Covenant Chain that we may not forget our mutual Engagements.
>
> I now therefore present you the great Belt by which I bind all your Western Nations together with the English, and I desire that you will take fast hold of the same, and never let it slip, to which end I desire that after you have shewn this belt to all Nations you will fix one end of it to the Chipeweighs at St. Mary's whilst the other end remains at my house, and moreover I desire that you will never listen to any news which comes to any other Quarter. If you do it, it may shake the Belt.[115]

The principles symbolized in this belt, together with Johnson's speech and the two-row wampum, are important because they testify to the foundational treaty of alliance and peace between First Nations and the Crown in Canada. Through the exchange of promises, presents, and wampum the parties agreed to subsequently adhere to principles that incorporated two jurisprudential worlds. While these principles find partial expression in the written text of the constitution and the Royal Proclamation, they are given much fuller exposition through the oral and documentary law and history that underlies Canada's constitutional text.[116] Recognition of the Indigenous lineage in Canada's constitutionalism would contribute to working out the legality and legitimacy of Canadian law, consistent with the principles in the *Quebec Secession Reference*.

B Democracy

The second principle considered by the Supreme Court in the *Quebec Secession Reference* was democracy. The court held that 'democracy has always informed the design of our constitutional structure, and continues to act as an essential interpretive consideration to this day.'[117] According to the court, democracy 'can best be understood as a sort of baseline against which the framers of our Constitution, and subsequently, our elected representatives under it, have always operated.'[118] The court's notion of democracy[119] embraces ideas of majority rule, the promotion of self-government and the accommodation of cultural and group identities, the popular franchise, and the consent of the governed. Despite the promises made at Niagara, Canada has rarely followed through with these principles in its dealings with Aboriginal peoples.

Applying the Supreme Court's framework, Canada's unilateral attempts to extinguish Aboriginal rights and repeated denials of the legal right to question this treatment undermine majority rule. Aboriginal peoples were in the majority in most parts of the country at the time their rights were purportedly extinguished, and they were later denied the political and legal means to challenge the Crown's actions.[120] Furthermore, as discussed in the last chapter, the Crown's assumption of overarching sovereignty does not promote community self-government, nor does it accommodate Aboriginal identities. Aboriginal governments were overlaid by elected Indian Act governments, and Aboriginal individuals were subjected to ruthless assimilation policies.[121] Finally, denial of underlying Aboriginal title and the equality of Aboriginal sovereignty does not secure the consent of the governed. Aboriginal peoples in every province and community have consistently resisted the unilateral extinguishment and diminishment of their rights by the Crown.[122] In fact, as Aunt Irene told me, the lives of my great-great-grandparents were strongly influenced by their attempts to resist the contraction of their participation with the land and those who were newly settling on it. Their efforts, and those of others like them, should become more visible in Canada's constitutional structure. Otherwise, Canada will continue to fail to abide by and apply the democratic ideals underlying its constitution.

My great-great-grandparents lived during a time of unparalleled transition in Anishinabek communities, and their response to these changes contains important lessons for Canadian democracy. They maintained a belief in and practice of consent and participation in government, despite the arrival of hundreds of thousands of settlers who strained their traditional economic, social, and spiritual relationships. Peter Kegedonce Jones, my great-great-grandfather, was chief of the Nawash band in this period and his behaviour exemplified this strong democratic tradition.[123] In 1837, when he was twenty years of age, Peter attended school at Beaverton, Ontario, on the shores of Lake Simcoe, two hours north of Toronto. While he was in school the Rebellion of Upper Canada took place, led by William Lyon Mackenzie. Peter became involved in the Rebellion and his participation was recounted by his grandson: 'I can still recollect hearing him tell me the story of his experiences at this time – how he was recruited as one of Mackenzie's supporters, given a blanket, a musket, powder horn and shot, and after months of weary waiting, was finally taken with others, to the vicinity of Toronto and York, as it was then called. Here they waited, but never had the chance to get into action.'[124] Oral tradition recalls with pride Peter's association with a cause that sought to extend citizen involvement in Canadian politics in community with other Canadians.

Peter's partner, Margaret, also exemplified ideals consistent with Canada's democratic principles. She was born around 1820 in the place now known as Alberta, the child of an Ojibway mother and a Scottish father. Her father, Joseph McLeod, was a fur trader in the Northwest in the early 1800s. When his fur trading days were over, he deserted his Native family and returned to Scotland to live on the Isle of Skye. Margaret's Anishinabek mother, Teresa Riel, raised her daughter in the traditional Ojibway manner. The family eventually migrated from the prairies and settled at La Cloche, on the north shore of Lake Huron. When they heard that Peter was taking people into his community, the McLeods moved from La Cloche to settle at Nawash.[125] Margaret married Peter in the 1840s, when she was in her early twenties.

Margaret developed skills throughout her life that indicate the importance accorded by Anishinabek people to participation in public affairs. She was a midwife and medicine woman who possessed a vast knowledge of herbal remedies for curing various ailments. She would selflessly spend her time gathering the natural harvest of flora, fauna, herbs, and roots from the shores of the lakes, the grasslands, and the forest for the benefit of the community.[126] Margaret shared these medicines and her healing skills freely, without thought of payment or monetary reward. She was also a teacher and educator who spoke three languages: Ojibway, French, and English. French was spoken in the home, Ojibway in the community, and English when she went off the reserve. As Margaret grew older she became a repository of the traditions, myths, parables, fables, allegories, legends, and stories of our people,[127] and thus greatly assisted in the maintenance of community values and the ancient ethics of participation. In fact, many of the stories recounted in these pages echo her words and themes. They contain strong messages about the importance of participation and consent – principles that are central to democratic thought and could be considered an integral part of Canada's unwritten constitutional heritage.

Unless Aboriginal peoples and perspectives are included in Canada's governing institutions, the country will not create a legitimate framework or legal foundation upon which to build an appropriate political relationship. Despite the strong democratic traditions characteristic of many First Nations, Canadian courts and politicians have not identified and implemented a system that reflects the legal heritage and aspirations of Aboriginal peoples. The political exclusion of Aboriginal people represents a failure of democracy. As the Supreme Court observed in the *Quebec Secession Reference*,

> It is the law that creates the framework within which the 'sovereign will' is to be ascertained and implemented. To be accorded legitimacy, democratic institutions must rest, ultimately, on a legal foundation. That is, they must allow for the participation of, and accountability to, the people, through public institutions created under the Constitution. Equally, however, a system of government cannot survive through adherence to the law alone. A political system must also possess legitimacy, and in our political culture, that requires an interaction between the rule of law and the democratic principle. The system must be capable of reflecting the aspirations of the people. But there is more. Our law's claim to legitimacy also rests on an appeal to moral values, many of which are embedded in our constitutional structure.[128]

The court here suggests that the Canadian constitution must create a 'framework' and a 'legal foundation' for people's participation in federal structures. Aboriginal peoples throughout Canada have never received an unencumbered opportunity to participate as traditional or effective governments within the federal structure. They have not been a part of the Canadian 'framework,' and thus have been virtually prevented from officially promoting and implementing normative values consistent with their vision of Canadian democracy. Legally, their exclusion is most telling when it includes the Crown's extinguishment and infringement of Aboriginal rights without requisite participation or consent. Morally, the exclusion from democratic participation is most repugnant when the assumption of extinguishment and infringement leads to forced integration, assimilation, and cultural eradication. Though such labelling may not be completely consistent with usage in international law and treaties, for many Aboriginal peoples, extinguishment is reminiscent of genocide.[129] The principle of democracy, from both the Canadian Supreme Court and Aboriginal legal perspectives, cannot sanction such treatment.

C   The Rule of Law

The third principle examined by the Supreme Court in the *Quebec Secession Reference* is the rule of law. While this principle has been discussed in some detail above, it is worth observing that the rule of law must be placed beside federalism and democracy when considering the dispossession Aboriginal people face as a result of the Crown's assertion of underlying title and overarching sovereignty. In the *Quebec Secession Reference*, the court observed that 'at its most basic level, the rule of law vouchsafes to the citizens and residents of the country a stable, predictable and ordered society in which to conduct their affairs.'[130] The unilateral extinguishment of Aboriginal rights before 1982, coupled with the infringement of those rights since 1982, does not ensure a predictable and ordered society: it severely disrupts Aboriginal nations and causes deeply rooted resentment of the federal government.[131] This resentment translates into strained, adversarial relations, periodic blockades, and endless litigation. It tears apart the fabric of Aboriginal communities[132] and leads to instability within the larger population by reducing investment, creating social tension, and causing uncertainty.[133] The consequences of this resentment could further escalate and lead to dissension and violence if left unattended. If relations between Aboriginal peoples and others ever degenerate to the point of frequent, chronic violence, the legal doctrines allowing for non-consensual Crown derogation from Aboriginal rights might be one of the underlying causes of such distress. Such a situation would be partially attributable to the failure of the Canadian state to fully extend the rule of law to Aboriginal peoples.

The failure of the Crown and the courts to protect Aboriginal peoples from arbitrary power has already affected First Nations in at least three profound ways. First, there were few safeguards to protect the fundamental human rights and individual freedoms of Aboriginal peoples throughout most of Canada's history.[134] As a result, their individual and collective lives were unduly 'susceptible to government interference.'[135] Governmental interference is evidenced through the suppression of Aboriginal institutions of government,[136] the denial of land,[137] the forced taking of children,[138] the criminalization of economic pursuits,[139] and the negation of the rights of religious freedom,[140] association,[141] due process,[142] and equality.[143] A second manifestation of the lack of protection for Aboriginal peoples under the rule of law is that the parties to the creation of Canada did not ensure that, as a vulnerable group, Aboriginal peoples were 'endowed with institutions and rights necessary to maintain and promote their identities against the assimilative pressures of the majority.'[144] This lack of cultural protection led to further vulnerability and violence, as Aboriginal peoples were not extended the institutional means to resist the violation of their rights. A final consequence of the failure to extend the rule of law to Aboriginal peoples is that the political organization of Canada did not 'provide for a division of political power'[145] that would prevent the provincial and federal governments from usurping the powers of Aboriginal governments. Non-Aboriginal governments usurped Aboriginal authority 'simply by exercising their legislative power to allocate additional political power to [themselves] unilaterally.'[146] Consequently, these governments have been unjustly enriched at the expense of Aboriginal peoples. These various transgressions of the rule of law illustrate the problems of founding a country without incorporating the legal perspectives and ideas of all of its inhabitants. They do not produce a stable, ordered, and predictable society. For all these reasons, the courts must not sanction the continued violation of the rule of law with respect to Aboriginal peoples.

Perhaps nothing is more illustrative of Canada's violation of the rule of law with respect to Aboriginal peoples than the Indian Act, first passed in 1876.[147] My great-grandfather, Charles Kegedonce Jones, was the first chief of the Chippewas of the Nawash elected under the Indian Act's provisions. He worked for over fifty years in this position and struggled to make it relevant to the values and activities of the people he served. The Act imposed a normative structure on Aboriginal communities that was largely inconsistent with their own legal and political systems. Charles found it difficult to integrate the statute's authoritarian proscriptions with the consensual approach to governance found within

Anishinabek political and legal thought. His successes in responding to community needs were most often achieved in spite of the Indian Act, and he had to take great steps to preserve the rule of law at Cape Croker, which that statute undermined.

For example, Charles had to overcome threats to Anishinabek normative order and the rule of law in the areas of property law, governance, family relations, education, freedom to contract, and religious freedom. The Indian Act contained provisions that forcibly prohibited or restricted Anishinabek order in all these areas. While Charles and his councils did the best they could to maintain their means of subsistence (for example through Band resolutions dealing with sales of timber on our lands,[148] the lease and pasture of farm land,[149] the acquisition of seeds for cultivation,[150] the purchase of livestock,[151] and the harvesting of their fisheries)[152] the Indian Act's provisions largely prevented them from making the rule of law effective within their community.[153] The Indian Act is an affront to the rule of law throughout Canada. It stands as evidence of the arbitrary nature of Canada's political order relative to Aboriginal peoples. It must be repealed and replaced by a document that facilitates the recreation of normative order in Aboriginal communities.

The rule of law has also suffered in the community's relations with its non-Native neighbours. Charles's father Peter had signed two treaties in 1854[154] and 1857[155] that promised many material goods and services in return for non-Native people settling on Anishinabek territory. In fact, Peter's signature was the first one on the 1857 treaty. These treaties covered over 500,000 acres of prime land in southwestern Ontario, extending east from Goderich on Lake Huron to Arthur in central-southwestern Ontario, and then north to Owen Sound on Lake Huron. Anishinabek people felt (and still feel) deeply for their lands, and making the decision to share them with others was not easy. Yet Peter and his people signed the treaty as an exercise of governance, to obtain promises that would perennially compensate for their loss. The promises secured for sharing the land included, among others, increasing capital payments through trust funds deposits and payments, perpetual medical assistance, the provision of education, the building of infastructure (such as roads, public buildings, and docks), housing, hunting, fishing, and timber rights. The Anishinabek were told 'that from the sale of the land [they] would soon have a large income, would all be able to ride in carriages, roll in wealth and fare sumptuously every day.'[156] The government's promises were not fulfilled, despite Anishinabek adherence to the treaty's terms. Among other problems there were issues with reserve size,[157] non-native settlement,[158] the development of agricultural lots,[159] the building of schools,[160] the provision of funds,[161] and official sanction for acts undertaken by the Band Council.[162]

Charles and others of his generation repeatedly petitioned Canada to respect the rule of law and adhere to its treaty promises. Canada did not respond to these appeals, and to this day it has not lived up to its commitments. The Nawash have even had to pursue litigation to compel the government to abide by its covenants. The violation of basic legal principles of offer, agreement, and consideration does not bode well for the rule of law in Canada. While Canadians enjoy the material wealth and political benefits that derive from access to such a large piece of land, the Anishinabek are criticized for wanting to enjoy the contemporary benefits that flow from their side of the bargain. Canadians are quite happy to uphold the right for non-Native people to perpetually live on treaty lands but often blanche when Native people assert perpetual rights to housing, education, medical care, or federal transfers of money. The rule of law should not sanction such uneven and arbitrary applications of normative order. The principles embedded in the *Quebec Secession Reference* direct us otherwise.

D   The Protection of Minorities

Fourth, and finally, in considering the legality and legitimacy of constitutional principles that relate to the diminishment of Aboriginal rights it should be recalled that the Supreme Court in the *Quebec Secession Reference* held that 'the protection of minority rights is itself an independent principle underlying our constitutional order.'[163] To return to the arguments made at the beginning of this chapter, Aboriginal title and sovereignty must not be unilaterally subject to Crown title and sovereignty because this would fail to protect Aboriginal peoples from the majority in Canada. Aunt Irene's stories, and those of countless thousands of Elders throughout this country, must be incorporated into our understanding of Canadian constitutionalism. Failure to abide by their views would, in the words of the *Quebec Secession Reference*, defeat the 'promise' of section 35, which 'recognized not only the ancient occupation of land by [A]boriginal peoples, but their contributions to the building of Canada, and the special commitments made to them by successive governments.'[164] The Crown's claim that it can define and adjudge Aboriginal rights on its authority alone does not seem consistent with the court's observation that 'the protection of minority rights was clearly an essential consideration in the design of our constitutional structure.'[165] One wonders how Canadians would respond if the positions were reversed and Aboriginal peoples were vested with the exclusive power to interpret and circumscribe non-Aboriginal rights. They would likely want to be protected in such circumstances and insist on the application of principles similar to those outlined in this chapter. The courts, in one of their roles, are a counter-majoritarian body; they should be ever-mindful of the challenges faced by peoples in a minority situation in Canada and act to protect their rights from unfair occlusion.

The courts must combine the principles of federalism, democracy, the rule of law, and the protection of minorities to assess the legality and legitimacy of Canada's assertions with respect to Aboriginal peoples. If the courts agree with the conclusions suggested in this chapter, then Canada's laws should be declared invalid, though enforceable, by the application of the rule of law until the parties resolve this situation through negotiation, participation and consent. Until this negotiation occurs, Aboriginal peoples will continue to protest the unjust application of Canadian law to their societies. If the relationship between Crown and Aboriginal sovereignties is not resolved through law and negotiation, Aboriginal peoples may one day claim a right to be released from a situation that denies them the fundamental guarantees of a free and democratic society. They may claim they are not subject to Canada's jurisdiction, because Canada's claims over them are not legal or legitimate. As both an Anishinabek and Canadian citizen, I look forward to the day when Aboriginal peoples will be able to claim the benefits of the rule of law – both their own and Canada's. I sincerely hope that the day will never come when rights to live according to Canadian constitutionalism are unalterably withdrawn, and Aboriginal peoples must rely on a declaration of external self-determination to sustain their communities.

IV Conclusion: The Rule of Law and Self-Determination

This chapter has illustrated that the Crown's assertion and the courts' acceptance of a subsequent claimant's non-consensual assertion of rights over another legal ordering is not consistent with the law's highest principles. Any judicial or other sanction of the colonization, subjugation, domination, and exploitation of Aboriginal peoples in Canada is not a 'morally and politically morally defensible conception of [A]boriginal rights.'[166] It 'perpetuat[es] historical injustice suffered by [A]boriginal peoples at the hands of [the] colonizers;'[167] it is illegitimate and illegal. In the absence of negotiation and reconciliation, this treatment may ultimately result in a claim of a legal right to self-determination for those who suffer such abuses. Ideally, Aboriginal self-determination should receive negotiated expression within Canada through an appropriate extension of the rule of law in matters of federalism, democracy, and minority protection. Otherwise, we might properly regard the Crown's treatment of Aboriginal peoples as 'colonial rule' that leads   to their 'subjugation, domination and exploitation' and blocks their 'meaningful exercise of self-determination.'[168]

Under international law, people who are prevented from exercising self-determination within a nation state may have a right of 'external self-determination:' a right to secede from the country in which they live. In commenting on the implications of obstructing self-determination, the Supreme Court in the *Quebec Secession Reference* observed that external self-determination can be claimed in three circumstances: 'the international law right to self-determination only generates, at best, a right to external self-determination in situations of former colonies; where a people is oppressed, as for example under foreign military occupation; or where a definable group is denied meaningful access to government to pursue their political, economic, social and cultural development. In all three situations, the people in question are entitled to a right to external self-determination because they have been denied the ability to exert internally their right to self-determination.'[169] Aboriginal peoples may have an argument for self-determination on the authority of these principles if the Crown's assertions of sovereignty are not tempered in ways suggested in this chapter. If negotiated settlement does not occur, and the principles outlined in the *Quebec Secession Reference* are not extended to them, Aboriginal peoples may be able to argue that they are colonial peoples with a right to external self-determination. They could say in such circumstances that they are 'inherently distinct from the colonialist Power and the occupant Power and that their "territorial integrity," all but destroyed by the colonialist or occupying Power, should be fully restored.'[170] Furthermore, Aboriginal peoples may be able to claim the legal right to self-determination by arguing that Canada's diminishment and extinguishment of their rights has not 'promote[d] ... [the] realization of the principle[s] of equal rights and self-determination of peoples ... bearing in mind that subjection of peoples to alien subjugation, domination and exploitation constitutes a violation of the principle [of friendly relations], as well as a denial of fundamental human rights, and is contrary to the [Charter of the United Nations].'[171] Finally, Aboriginal people may claim the right to self-determination because the unilateral extinguishment of their rights prior to 1982, and the rules forbidding them to question this injustice, means the Canadian government does not represent 'the whole people belonging to the territory without distinction of any kind.'[172]

If Aboriginal peoples were able to show the force of any one of the arguments developed in this chapter or to establish that they are entitled to the legal right of self-determination, this could take them a great distance in undoing the 'spell' of Crown sovereignty under which they currently function. Even in the absence of an appropriate response from Canada, Aboriginal peoples could use international law principles to work towards eliminating the injustice of unilateral assertions of Crown sovereignty. Each party needs to explore these issues more fully and to negotiate and reconcile their differences through joint effort. Aboriginal perspectives underlying the Canadian constitutional framework need to be brought to light. Adherence to the rule of law requires that the parties develop a conception of participation and citizenship in Canada that respects and includes Aboriginal peoples and their laws more explicitly in its framework.

Chapter Six

'Landed' Citizenship:
An Indigenous Declaration of
Interdependence

My grandfather was born in 1901 on the western shores of Georgian Bay, at the Cape Croker Indian resere. Generations before him were born on the same soil. Our births, lives, and deaths on this site have brought us into citizenship with the land. We participate in its renewal, have responsibility for its continuation, and grieve for its losses. As citizens with this land, we also feel the presence of our ancestors and strive with them to ensure that the relationships of our polity are respected. Our loyalties, allegiance, and affection are related to the land. The water, wind, sun, and stars are part of this federation; the fish, birds, plants, and animals share the same union. Our teachings and stories form the constitution of this relationship and direct and nourish the obligations it requires. As we have seen, the Chippewas of the Nawash have struggled to sustain their citizenship in the face of the diversity and pluralism that have become part of the land. This has not been an easy task. Our codes have been disinterred, disregarded, and repressed. To redirect this trajectory I have tried to suggest how Anishinabek jurisprudence might be reinscribed on the earth consistent with land-centred conceptions of citizenship. This might be accomplished through the incorporation of Indigenous law in formal legal reasons, the interaction of customary Indigenous law with less formal administrative and political structures, the critique of judicial doctrines from the perspective of Indigenous legal values and traditions, and the comparison of Indigenous legal perspectives with Canadian constitutionalism. One further change, however, is required to fully reinscribe Anishinabek laws and invóke a citizenship with the land.

I   Relocating Citizenship

More than thirty years have passed since Harold Cardinal wrote an influential book entitled *The Unjust Society*. In it he described the troubling situation Indians found themselves in during the late 1960s.[1] Written in response to the Trudeau government's plan to eliminate Indian rights, *The Unjust Society* outlined the denial of Indian citizenship.[2] Cardinal's message captured the feelings of Aboriginal people everywhere. He chronicled a disturbing tale of how Indians had been marginalized in Canada through bureaucratic neglect, political indifference, and societal ignorance. He labelled Canada's treatment of Indians as 'cultural genocide'[3] and in the process, publicized the absence of Indian rights. Aside from identifying the problems, he outlined thoughtful solutions to overcome the threats to our underlying citizenship, organized around the central theme of Indian control of Indian affairs. Cardinal called for action to protect special Aboriginal connections with the land, advocating the strengthening of Indian organizations,[4] the abolition of the Department of Indian Affairs,[5] educational reform,[6] restructured social institutions,[7] broad-based economic development,[8] and the 'immediate recognition of all Indian rights for the re-establishment, review and renewal of all existing Indian treaties.'[9] His ideas resonated throughout Indian country and parallel proposals became the mainstay of Indian political discourse for the next three decades.[10] Cardinal articulated a revolutionary message in a potentially transformative time.

The massive, five-volume Report of the Royal Commission on Aboriginal Peoples released in 1996[11] effectively recounts the same story and proposes the same solutions. Despite some notable achievements in the intervening years, such as constitutional recognition and affirmation of Aboriginal rights, Indigenous citizenship with the land is increasingly tenuous. Aboriginal people continue to suffer, their rights are being abrogated, and the solution is Aboriginal control of Aboriginal affairs. Like Cardinal, though more expansively, the commission recommended a series of legislative and policy goals including the strengthening of Aboriginal nations,[12] the abolition of the Department of Indian Affairs,[13] educational reform,[14] restructured social institutions,[15] broad-based economic development,[16] and the immediate recognition of all Aboriginal rights for the re-establishment, review, renewal, and creation of treaties.[17] Same story, same solutions. A revolutionary message in a reactionary time.

If Cardinal's message went largely unheeded over thirty years ago, why repeat it now? Does the call for Aboriginal control of Aboriginal affairs stand a greater chance at the turn of the twenty-first century than it did in the late 1960s? While there are hopeful signs on the horizon,[18] there is also cause for concern.[19] Despite the wisdom of the message, reaction to the commission has so far been as feeble as the response to Cardinal. In the meantime, Aboriginal citizenship with the land is being slowly diminished. The disenfranchisement of our people (and our spirits) from the land, water, animals, and trees continues at an alarming rate. The legal values of our societies remain hidden. We need a new story, new solutions. We no longer require a revolutionary message in a tranformative time; we need a transformative message in a reactionary time.

To preserve and extend our participation with the land, and our association with those who now live on it, it is time to talk of Aboriginal control of Canadian affairs. Various sites of power in Canada must be permeated with Aboriginal people, institutions, and ideologies, consistent with the principles outlined by the Supreme Court in the *Quebec Secession Reference*. Aboriginal people must work individually and as groups beyond their communities to enlarge and increase their influence over matters that are important to them. We need an Aboriginal prime minister, Supreme Court judge, and numerous Indigenous CEOs. We need people with steady employment, good health, and entrepreneurial skills. They should be joined by Indian scientists, doctors, lawyers, and educators; by Aboriginal union leaders, social activists, and conservative thinkers.[20] We need these people to incorporate Indigenous ideologies and perspectives into their actions, including ideas about the federalism we should enjoy with the earth. These people could either join compatible existing groups or form new political organizations, research institutions, and corporate enterprises to expand Aboriginal influence. They should stand beside reserve-based teachers such as Aboriginal Elders, chiefs, grandmothers, aunties, hunters, fishers, and medicine people as bearers and transmitters of culture. For too long the burden of cultural transmission has been borne by reservation-based teachers and leaders. While their knowledge will always remain vitally important in the expansion of ideas, Aboriginal people in different settings within Canada must shoulder some of this responsibility. Aboriginal people must transmit and use their culture in matters beyond 'Aboriginal' affairs. Aboriginal law must become relevant to other Canadians. Aboriginal citizenship must be extended to encompass people from around the world who have come to live on our land.

After all, this is *our* country. As holders of a prior but continued Indigenous citizenship, Aboriginal people have an ongoing stewardship and a legal obligation to participate in its changes. We have lived here for centuries, and will live here for centuries more. We will continue to influence the land's resource utilization, govern its human relation-ships, participate in trade, and be involved in all of its relations – as we have done for millennia. Fuller citizenship requires that these responsi-bilities be undertaken in concert with other Canadians, as well as on our own, in our own communities. Aboriginal control of Aboriginal affairs is a good message, and it has to be strengthened – but it can also be limit-ing. If pursued single-mindedly, it is not consistent with holistic notions of citizenship that must include the land, and all the beings upon it. When we speak of Aboriginal control of Aboriginal affairs, Canadians obviously feel they have little stake in that message,[21] other than what 'they' think 'we' take from 'them' in the process.[22] Canada's stake in Aboriginal peoples, and in the land, has to be raised at radical, liberal, and conservative levels.

II The World of Citizenship

The Anishinabek world is bigger than the First Nation, reserve, or settle-ment. Approximately half of the Anishinabek population lives outside these boundaries,[23] certainly our traditional lands and relationships extend beyond them. Even if the reserve is where we live, national and international forces influence the most 'remote' or seemingly local time-honoured practice. In fact, an autonomous Aboriginal nation would encounter a geography, history, economics, and politics that requires participation with Canada and the world to secure its objec-tives. Aboriginal control of Canadian affairs is an important means by which to influence and participate with our lands. Without this power, we are excluded from significant decision-making structures that have the potential to destroy our lands. This is a flawed notion of citizenship. Canadians must participate with us, and in the wider view of polity that sustained our relations for thousands of years.

The notion of citizenship in Western democracies is widely con-tested.[24] In Canada, different rights and responsibilities are asserted under its banner, making it difficult to determine the precise contours of citizenship in the Canadian community.[25] Some correlate citizenship with the possession of civil, political, and social rights.[26] From this view-point, citizenship involves the enjoyment of such rights as freedom from arbitrary government actions, the right to the franchise and representa-tion in public affairs, and the right to certain minimum standards of living. This perspective places great emphasis on the formal rules and procedures of the law in creating and sustaining citizenship. Citizenship for some is thus a matter of legal status and can be discovered in the common law and constitutional texts. On this view, the law creates and sustains membership in Canada by providing a system that treats everyone as a full and equal member of society. If any of these rights were withheld or violated, people would be marginalized or unable to participate in the community.[27] A rights-oriented view of citizenship addresses these concerns and has a powerful hold on our national institutions and ideologies.[28] While insufficient to express our fullest aspirations of citizenship towards one another, there is much value in such an approach.[29]

In the post-war period, however, pointed criticism has been made of the rights-oriented conception of citizenship. Some have observed that this model relies too heavily on a person's legal status and does not readily promote self-reliance and personal responsibility. Rights-based notions of citizenship have been said to foster passivity and dependency in public life because they do not cultivate the reciprocal obligations between people that build the larger institutions of the community.[30] Those who take this stance contend that the characterization of citizenship in terms of protection from or claims against the state facilitates a 'retreat from citizenship and a particular "clientalization" of the citizen's role.'[31] I agree; the dependency and passivity generated by a rights-oriented approach requires us to demand much more of the concept of citizenship.

These deficiencies have led some to devise a second theory of citizenship, one that involves more than just a passive entitlement to certain rights and requires the positive acceptance of responsibility for the health and well-being of the community.[32] This idea of citizenship places a greater emphasis on cooperation, self-restraint, and public spiritedness outside the formal bonds of the state. It encourages and celebrates those who are willing to freely engage or defer their own self-interest for the good of others, without being compelled to do so. This activity-based form of citizenship has been described as a 'need': a moral obligation to concern and associate ourselves with the perils and problems of 'strangers' in our society.[33] This view of citizenship suggests that if people passively rely on the state for their entitlements and status, and do not contribute to society in some other way, the bonds of community upon which a state depends can weaken or be forever broken. To counter this danger, an activity-based citizenship requires some kind of social space that permits people to freely come together for their own purposes and to pursue goals that may not be officially pursued by the state.[34] This kind of citizenship requires a degree of toleration for activities, associations, and institutions that are not formally sponsored or promoted by the First Nation, provinces, Parliament, or the judiciary.[35] Such activities indirectly depend on the restraint of individuals, courts, and legislatures in not prohibiting or usurping the roles of these groups.[36] It permits the formation of relationships and identities on grounds that do not depend on command-and-control operatives found within rights-oriented conceptions of the law. This too is an attractive notion of citizenship. It is to be praised because it treasures activity-based participation in society and does not eclipse interpretations of citizenship that lie outside a narrow, legalistic formulation.

While both of these theories of citizenship seem to capture many of our expectations of Canadian society, in the context of my call for Aboriginal control of Canadian affairs, they are insufficient in themselves. An exclusive focus on these particualr conceptions could prevent an appreciation of citizenship's more richly shaded hues. Citizenship must also take into account the varied self-perceptions people hold within communities,[37] and these views must sometimes mingle to create common understandings and a larger vision of who we are as fellow citizens.[38] The creation of this vision of citizenship must be a concern of the state, and not just of private organizations and associations. Citizenship in the state must begin to develop an interactive reciprocity on certain matters of vital concern and address the more subjective elements of who people 'feel they are' in relation to others in society.[39] This is not to say that each party must always incorporate the self-understandings of the other. In fact, freedom of conscience, belief, and association exist to protect against such impositions. Most opinions, beliefs, and convictions would remain the subjects of argument and disagreement, as they lie outside the realm of fundamental and first-order organizing principles that prescribe how we understand our union as citizens. Other opinions, beliefs, and convictions might even change for one or both parties as they develop the mechanisms for incorporating the varied understandings that this conception of citizenship contemplates.

The importance of interchange is mentioned only to highlight the fact that sometimes in the life of a country the adoption and implementation of others' allegiances, relationships, and responsibilities are necessary for the creation of a larger socio-legal-political community. This is one reason why I have emphasized throughout this book the constitutionally mandated, intersocietal pluralism that lies at the heart of Canada's legal traditions. The conjunction of legal values creates an important site for the mutual reception, modification, or acceptance of parties' understandings of who they are in their relationship to land and to each other. It serves as a single example of how these considerations could be extended to other institutions in our society. Without such intercourse on matters central to the self-preservation of identity and place in the world, parties are left with the options of coercion or separation to settle their differences. In order to engage the fraternal ties of citizenship to which this third theory aspires, it is crucial that certain understandings be developed and sponsored by the state so that some groups do not feel excluded, despite possessing common rights and sharing reciprocal participatory institutions with other members of the community.[40] Such exclusion can cause people to feel oppressed – imprisoned by others' views and actions – in a false, distorted, and reduced mode of being.[41]

Currently, Aboriginal peoples often feel oppressed.[42] They struggle to fully identify themselves as citizens in Canada because they rarely see their primary perspectives and interests mirrored in the law, the expressed goals of the state, or the prevailing associations in society. Their failure to fully identify with Canada is not wholly a problem of legal status or degree of participation with others, although these are obviously contributing factors. Aboriginal exclusion from more holistic notions of citizenship runs even deeper. Current conceptions of citizenship are deficient both because they fail to give socio-cultural recognition to Aboriginal peoples' primary relationships and loyalties *and* because non-Aboriginal Canadians have not considered or made many of these allegiances, relationships, and obligations their own. Aboriginal control of Canadians' affairs would begin to reverse these two failings. Aboriginal control of Canadian affairs would nourish Aboriginal peoples' own view of their place in the world and assist other Canadians in adjusting their views and activities to take into account Aboriginal peoples, institutions, and ideologies.

III   Changes in the Land

If we pursue this third notion of citizenship, what will the new narrative sound like? How will its constituent stories be arranged? How does this new narrative relate to the former? What is lost, and what is gained? The development of another narrative may severely undermine those who have invested their aspirations and energies in ideas represented by Cardinal or the commission, even if the message is complimentary. Some have expended a tremendous amount of time and effort developing messages of an exclusive citizenship and measured separatism for Indians, through a form of self-government. But that approach, while appropriate, helpful, and deserving of recognition, is not rich enough to encompass the wide variety of relationships we need to negotiate in order to live with the hybridity, displacement, and positive potential of our widening circles.[43] The extension of Aboriginal citizenship into Canadian affairs is a developing reality because of our increasingly complex social, economic, and political relations. Intercultural forces of education, urbanization, politics, and intermarriage draw Indigenous people into closer relationship with non-Aboriginal Canadian society.[44] The impulse behind the call for this refocused narrative lies in the changing dynamics of the Indian population. Since 1961, our populations have quadrupled,[45] rates of urban residency have climbed to 50 per cent of the total Aboriginal population,[46] and one in every two Aboriginal people marries a non-Aboriginal person.[47] Moreover, our health has improved,[48] and incomes have increased.[49] While these indicators hide continuing individual and collective pain, numerous Aboriginal people frequently interact with Canadians in significant ways.

I have taught at four of Canada's larger universities in the past eight years, and my experience in each of them indicates that an increasing number of Aboriginal people are graduating from these institutions prepared to contribute at the First Nations, provincial, national, and in some cases at the international level. Over 150,000 Aboriginal people now have or are currently enrolled in post-secondary education.[50] That is a significant development, since in 1969 there were fewer than eight hundred Aboriginal post-secondary graduates.[51] When 150,000 is measured against our overall population of approximately a million people, it becomes apparent that Aboriginal citizenship is expanding – and that Aboriginal control of Aboriginal affairs, while necessary, is not enough to reflect our cultural participation within Canada. I have directly supervised and watched graduate a hundred Aboriginal law students, and have spoken to and visited with hundreds more. I have seen them find employment as entrepreneurs, managers, lawyers, teachers, politicians, researchers, and public servants. In the wider university setting I have witnessed a similar phenomenon. In May 1997, I was present at the graduation of the top medical student at the University of British Columbia, an Ojibway woman. A few months earlier, I served as an external reviewer of the Native Indian Teacher Education program at UBC and discovered that some of the province's most respected educators, and a good number of its principals, graduated from this program. Aboriginal success is also evident in UBC's programs in forestry, business, health, engineering, and arts. These deep changes, which can be statistically and anecdotally proven, indicate that Aboriginal narratives on citizenship must be transformed.

At the same time, I have witnessed the struggles some of these Aboriginal students experience. Racism,[52] cultural alienation, family tragedy, poor academic preparation, insensitive teachers, and unresponsive curricula conspire to rob many Aboriginal people of the benefits education can bring. Furthermore, I know that many people who could be participating are not, some out of choice, but most because of the colonial pathologies that continue to resonate within our communities. The backdrop of these and other continued challenges may generate a cool reaction to assertions of Aboriginal control of Canadian affairs. I anticipate that the account I am suggesting will meet with some resistance.

For example, it may be thought that I am advocating assimilation. I am not. Assimilation implies a loss of political control, culture, and difference. As I have tried to illustrate throughout this book, Aboriginal control of Canadian affairs has the potential to facilitate the acquisition of political control, the continued development of culture, and respect for difference because it could change contemporary notions of Canadian citizenship.[53] As chronicled in chapter 2, citizenship under Aboriginal influence may generate a greater attentiveness to the land uses and cultural practices preferred by many Aboriginal peoples. Canadian notions of citizenship might not only develop to include greater scope for people's involvement in sustenance activities, they might also reduce the tolerance for land uses that extirpate these pursuits. Recognition of the importance of these objectives could thus shield Aboriginal peoples from assimilation by ensuring sufficient space for the pursuit of preferred Aboriginal activities. Moreover, Canadian citizenship under Aboriginal influence may expand to recognize the land as a party to Confederation in its own right. Many Aboriginal groups have well-developed notions about how to recognize the land as citizen. In the Anishinabek language, the land is animate and perceived as having rights and obligations in its relations with humankind. Aboriginal peoples may be able to persuade other Canadians to consider the adverse impact of their activities on the land itself, as an entity in its own right.[54] Aboriginal values and traditions could help reframe the relationships within our polity. Aboriginal peoples would resist assimilation through such recognition because their values where the land is concerned could be entrenched in Canada's governing ideas and institutions. They could help to reconfigure Canada in an important way.

IV   Living Tradition

Tradition can be the dead faith of living people, or the living faith of dead people.[55] If Indigenous traditions are not regarded as useful in tackling contemporary concerns and recognized as applying in current circumstances, then they are nothing but the dead faith of living people. On the other hand, if our people, institutions, and ideologies have relevance beyond our boundaries, this marks the living faith of our ancestors – the living traditions of dead people. Aboriginal peoples can resist assimilation by applying their traditions to answer the questions they encounter in the multifaceted, pluralistic world they now inhabit. This has been the consistent theme of this book.

When my great-great-grandfather placed his name and totemic symbol on a treaty that surrendered 500,000 acres in southern Ontario, he did not assent to assimilation.[56] He sought control in Canada amidst changing cultural circumstances. He knew that Chippewa/Anishinabek culture could benefit from the promises of non-Aboriginal education, employment, housing, and medicine. These were pledged to us in return for our allowing other people to participate in citizenship with the land. We have fulfilled our part of the agreement: other people enjoy the land. It is now time for Aboriginal peoples to reap the fruits of promises related to Canadian affairs. This is not to extinguish Aboriginal culture through its interaction with Canada; it is to enrich it by allowing for its development and application to our current needs. There is contemporary worth in Indigenous traditions that consider all the constituent parts of the land to be related. While I regard this knowledge as imperfect and incomplete, it is also insightful and wise. There is much to be gained by applying this knowledge within Aboriginal communities and within Canada as a whole. Our intellectual, emotional, social, physical, and spiritual insights can simultaneously be compared, contrasted, rejected, embraced, and intermingled with those of others. In fact, this process has been operative since before the time that Indigenous peoples first encountered others on their shores.

Concerns about assimilation may not be the only grounds on which some may object to a narrative of Aboriginal control of Canadian affairs. Participation within Canada may not sound or appear to be 'Aboriginal.' It may be argued that this notion violates sacred treaties and compromises traditional cultural values.[57] Yet, it should be asked: what does it mean to be Aboriginal or traditional? Aboriginal practices and traditions are not 'frozen,' as I have argued throughout this book. Aboriginal identity is constantly undergoing renegotiation. We are traditional, modern, and postmodern people. Our values *and* identities are constructed and reconstructed through local, national, and sometimes international experiences. As discussed in chapter 3, the meaning of Aboriginal is not confined to some pristine moment prior to the arrival of Europeans in North America. Similarly, the notion of Canadian, or any other cultural identifier, is not static.[58] As Edward Said observed about identity and culture:

> No one today is purely *one* thing. Labels like Indian, or woman, or Muslim or American are not more than starting-points, which if followed into actual experience for only a moment are quickly left behind. Imperialism consolidated the mixture of cultures and identities on a global scale. But its worst and most paradoxical gift was to allow people to believe they were only, mainly, exclusively, white, or Black, or Western, or Oriental. Just as human beings make their own history, they also make their cultures and ethnic identities. No one can deny the persisting continuities of long traditions, sustained habitations, national languages and cultural geographies, but there seems no reason except fear and prejudice to keep insisting on their separation and distinctiveness, as if that was all human life was about.[59]

As Said implies, the formation of culture and identity is contingent on our interactions with others. This insight makes it difficult to argue that Aboriginal control of Canadian affairs is not 'Aboriginal.' Aboriginal values and identity develop in response to their own and other culture's practices, customs, and traditions.[60] 'Aboriginality' is extended by Aboriginal control of both Canadian and Aboriginal affairs. Since important aspects of Aboriginal identity are influenced by Canada, Aboriginal control of Canadian affairs is one way to assert more control over what it means to be Aboriginal. Such assertions may even shape what it means to be Canadian.

Some, however, may not be impressed with this fluid notion of what it means to be Aboriginal. It may be objected that I have gone too far, that the idea that Aboriginal citizenship could include non-Aboriginal people inappropriately stretches tradition. For example, it might be claimed that Aboriginal control of Canadian affairs violates sacred cultural traditions such as the two-row wampum belt. The Gus Wen Tah, as will be recalled, was first adhered to by the Anishinabek in 1764, when the British made an alliance with the Indians of the upper Great

Lakes.[61] The belt consists of three parallel rows of white beads, separated by two rows of purple. To some, the belt suggests a separate nation-to-nation relationship between First Nations and the Crown that prohibits Aboriginal participation in Canadian affairs. This interpretation flows from a focus on the purple rows. One purple row symbolizes the British going down a river, politically navigating their ship of state, while the other represents the Indians going down a river of their own, similarly controlling their ship of state. Some have said 'these two rows never come together in that belt, and it is easy to see what that means. It means that we have two different paths, two different people.'[62] This reading of the belt centres on the autonomy of each party; the parallel purple lines are thought to signify that neither party was to interfere in the political organization of the other. In this symbolism is rooted the idea of Aboriginal control of Aboriginal affairs. In fact, according to this description Aboriginal control of Canadian affairs seems to violate a fundamental tenet of the Gus Wen Tah.

In considering the potential of the Gus Wen Tah for embracing a notion of citizenship that includes non-Aboriginal people, two important observations must be made. First, the Gus Wen Tah contains more than two rows of beads. The three rows of white beads represent a counterbalancing message that signifies the importance of sharing and interdependence. These white rows, referred to as the bed of the agreement,[63] stand for peace, friendship, and respect. When these principles are read together with those depicted in the purple rows, it becomes clear that ideas of citizenship must also be rooted in notions of mutuality and interconnectedness. The ecology of contemporary politics teaches us that the rivers on which we sail our ships of state share the same waters. There is no river or boat that is not linked in a fundamental way to the others; that is, there is no land or government in the world today that is not connected to and influenced by others. This is one reason for developing a narrative of Aboriginal citizenship that speaks more strongly to relationships that exist beyond 'Aboriginal affairs.' Tradition, in this case represented by the Gus Wen Tah, can support such an interpretation.

In weighing the Gus Wen Tah's potential to encompass Aboriginal control of Canadian affairs reference must be had to other belts exchanged in the same period. The Gus Wen Tah cannot be read in isolation from these other instruments, for they clarify the meaning of the two-row wampum. Just as one should not interpret a treaty solely according to its written words, the Gus Wen Tah should not be read solely on the basis of its woven characters. As will be remembered, the Gus Wen Tah was one of two belts exchanged at Niagara in 1764; the other belt emphasized the interdependence of the Indians of the Great Lakes and the nascent settler population. A ship was woven into one end of the belt, with its bow facing towards Quebec; at the other end of the belt is an image of Michilimackinac, a place in the centre of the Great Lakes regarded as the heart of the Chippewa/Anishinabek homelands. Between these two images were woven twenty-four Indians holding one another's hands, with the person furthest to the right holding the cable of the ship, while the one on the extreme left has his foot resting on the land at Quebec. Representatives of the twenty-two First Nations assembled at Niagara in 1764 touched this 'Belt of Peace' as a symbol of friendship and as a pledge to become 'united.'[64] This belt portrays the connection between Aboriginal and non-Aboriginal peoples and the lands they occupied. In fact, in this belt the Indians are holding on to the ship, pulling it towards them so that they can receive and participate in the benefits from the non-Indigenous population. Aboriginal tradition can thus support a notion of citizenship that encourages autonomy and at same time unifies and connects us to one another, and to the lands we rely on.

V   Aboriginal Citizenship and the Dominion of Canada

Concerns about Aboriginal control of Canadian affairs will of course extend beyond borders of Indian reserves, Inuit lands, and Métis settlements. The idea may also cause concern among the broader Canadian public. The radical approach to Aboriginal control of Canadian affairs will raise concerns about the potentially wrenching effects of this kind of action. If Aboriginal people are going to participate in Canadian and global politics, a great deal of change within the country will be required. Assertive and aggressive demands for control may bring to mind ethnic and racial strife in other countries. However, even more conciliatory liberal or conservative approaches could create difficulties, as some within the current establishment will not be prepared to cede or share any power. They must, however, learn to share. The chairs, corridors, and halls of Canadian legislatures, universities, courts, law societies, unions, and corporate boards of directors have been sluggish in responding to the influx of Aboriginal people. To my knowledge, although this needs to be supplemented with further research, there are approximately ten Aboriginal legislators, twenty tenured Aboriginal professors, eighteen Aboriginal judges, one law society bencher, no national Aboriginal union executives, and no Aboriginal members of boards of directors in Canada's twenty-five largest corporations. These levels of representation must change if Canada is ever to enjoy an inclusive citizenship.

Such a change would not require the granting of any special numeric weight to Aboriginal peoples. If Aboriginal peoples, who make up 5 per cent of the general population, were to enjoy proportionate participation in national institutions, there could potentially be over fifty Aboriginal legislators, 1,700 tenured Aboriginal professors, 100 Aboriginal judges, and hundreds of Aboriginal union and corporate executives. As argued throughout this book, participation at this level could result in real changes to the way land in Canada is treated and allocated. There is no doubt that the exercise of Aboriginal participation in decision-making power would have a significant impact on Canadian affairs. While I appreciate that not all Aboriginal peoples would adhere to the notions of citizenship outlined in this chapter, my experience and knowledge convinces me that their participation would promote many of the ideas developed here.[65] Many of these people would help to reformulate ideas about the place of land in our conceptions of citizenship; some, if not all, would work to incorporate and advance the philosophies and values described herein, because such ideas and experiences have a central place in many Aboriginal communities.[66] Aboriginal participation even at a level proportionate to the Aboriginal population in Canada would have an unparalleled effect on the functioning of our society, and on our conceptions of citizenship.

The broader Canadian public might yet question the equity and fairness of Aboriginal control of Canadian affairs. If Aboriginal peoples represent approximately 5 per cent of Canada's population and have exclusive control of land on their reserves, why should they be granted any interest and influence over land use outside of those reserves? It may be argued that Aboriginal peoples cannot expect to both control their own affairs and exercise significant influence over the affairs of others. It may appear as if Aboriginal peoples would enjoy rights in Canada that others do not possess. One response to this concern may rest on the legal status of Aboriginal peoples under Canadian constitutional and property law. Simply put, Aboriginal peoples may not have surrendered their rights over land outside their reserves. In those areas of the country where Aboriginal peoples never entered into agreements with the Crown, they maintain a relationship with land outside their reserves that flows from their pre-existing use and occupation of that land.[67] Furthermore, even where Aboriginal peoples entered into treaties with the Crown, the oral history and text of these agreements often contains guarantees of Aboriginal land use outside reservation boundaries for numerous livelihood purposes.[68] Many Aboriginal peoples have thus never consented to sever all relations with the land outside of their reservations. On equitable and legal principles, Canadian law may support the notion that Aboriginal peoples have a right to influence decisions made outside their reserves, on their traditional lands, even if they have control over their own affairs.

Another response to concerns about the fairness of Aboriginal peoples having exclusive control over their own lands and being allowed as well to participate in the control of lands outside their boundaries involves the recognition that federalism and the rule of law should operate to encourage the simultaneous integration and separation of communities.[69] An exclusive focus on Aboriginal control of Aboriginal affairs does not facilitate or strengthen the relationships Aboriginal peoples have with others. Aboriginal control of Aboriginal affairs focuses on autonomy to the exclusion of interdependence. The concurrent assertion of Aboriginal control of Canadian affairs rebalances interdependence with autonomy. Non-Aboriginal Canadians have long enjoyed both autonomy and interdependence through their participation in provincial and national communities that attempt to represent their local, national, and international concerns. Aboriginal peoples have never fully participated with other Canadians in this way. At the local level their position has been largely ignored; at the national level their interests have been repressed by centuries-long colonial control; at the international level they have been barely visible. Thus, to assert that Aboriginal peoples should control Canadian affairs is, at some levels, to claim for Aboriginal peoples the right to enjoy the same privilege as other Canadians, and to participate as citizens with appropriate federal structures and representation. There is no unfairness in such a claim; in fact, it would be unfair to prevent Aboriginal peoples from participating in Canada's federal structures in the same way as other regional and national communities do. Viewed in this light, it may hardly seem transformative to speak of Aboriginal control of Canadian affairs, given the well-entrenched notions about federalism in Canada. Sadly, however, this discourse is ground-breaking when dealing with Aboriginal peoples. Their historical treatment and recent narratives have focused ideas of citizenship on principles that facilitate autonomy to the exclusion of other, more interdependent models of citizenship.[70]

VI   Aboriginal Citizenship and Social Cohesion

Even if Aboriginal peoples have rights concerning land outside of their reservations by virtue of the application of legal rights and the principles of federalism, non-Aboriginal people may question the fairness of Aboriginal peoples qualifying for citizenship in their political system, when they cannot qualify as citizens in Aboriginal peoples' systems. Other institutions of federalism guarantee mobility rights between various jurisdictions;[71] membership in other federal structures is not restricted by ethnicity. In response, many Aboriginal peoples would argue that their circumstances are different, and that ethnic restrictions on citizenship are essential to the existence and survival of the group.[72] While I believe that restrictions on Aboriginal citizenship are necessary to maintain the social and political integrity of the group, I must admit I am troubled by conceptions of Aboriginal citizenship that depend on blood or genealogy. Nothing in blood or descent alone makes an Aboriginal person substantially different from any other person.[73] Despite the best of intentions, exclusion from citizenship on the basis of blood or ancestry can lead to racism and more subtle forms of discrimination that destroy human dignity.

While I do not favour limits on citizenship on racialized grounds, it may be appropriate to establish rigorous citizenship requirements on other grounds to protect and nurture these communities. Aboriginal peoples are much more than kin-based groups. They have social, political, legal, economic, and spiritual ideologies and institutions that are transmitted through their cultural systems. As was argued in chapters 1 and 2, these systems do not depend exclusively on ethnicity; they can be learned and adopted by others with some effort. Aboriginal peoples should consider implementing laws consistent with these traditions to extend citizenship in Aboriginal communities to non-Aboriginal people provided that they meet certain standards that allow for the reproduction of these communities' values. The extension of citizenship would respect the autonomy of Aboriginal communities while at the same time recognizing our interdependence as human beings.

Ultimately, however, a narrative of Aboriginal control of Canadian affairs does not conclude with a greater representation of Aboriginal people within existing Canadian institutions. Control in Canada is not exercised merely through people and institutions. Both are governed by deep-seated, global, and national tenets that animate and direct the acceptable bounds within which people and institutions can exercise power. Aboriginal notions of citizenship with the land are not currently included among these accredited ideologies. Attempts to assert Aboriginal control of Canadian affairs will encounter a matrix of power that works to exclude notions of 'land as citizen.' This resistance will be especially evident when the economic implications of Aboriginal control are understood. In some cases, the application of Indigenous traditions, especially in the legal sphere, might require that Aboriginal people share the wealth from the land with other Canadians; in other instances, it may mean that a proposed use would have to be modified or terminated. A reorientation of this magnitude is not likely to occur without substantial opposition from those who currently benefit from the prevailing ideologies allocating power. To surmount this challenge, Aboriginal peoples must employ many complementary discourses of control. Aboriginal control of Canadian affairs must join prevailing narratives of Aboriginal control of Aboriginal affairs in preserving and extending citizenship with the land.[74]

Recently, in a book called *Citizenship in Diverse Societies*, Will Kymlicka and Wayne Norman suggested that any description of citizenship must concern itself with more than rights, civic participation, and identity. They argue that citizenship should also include a conception of social cohesion, which promotes social stability, political unity, and civil peace.[75] Many people are worried that the proliferation of rights, the multiplication of community allegiances, and the strengthening of people's diverse identities are destructive of citizenship as a whole. Societal unity is important to citizenship because it allows people to build societies that are greater than the sum of their individual rights, associations, and identities. It facilitates the empathy, common concern, and compassion essential to the functioning of any civil society. It encourages the removal of barriers that restrict sharing and exchange, and thereby assists in the free flow of goods, services, affluence, and assistance. Social cohesion addresses an ideal of citizenship that applies 'not [just] at the individual level, but at the level of the political community as a whole.'[76]

In the context of Aboriginal citizenship, Professors Kymlicka and Norman's addition is appropriate. Some may worry about the potential of Aboriginal control of Canadian affairs to undermine civic peace. There may be genuine concern that social cohesion in Canada would be threatened by the recognition of Aboriginal rights, the flourishing of Native organizations, and the strengthening of Aboriginal identities.[77] Blockades, burning docks, insolvent churches, and sporadic confrontations, after all, are often blamed on the recognition of differentiated notions of Aboriginal citizenship.[78] While some may argue that these conflicts stem from the historic non-recognition of Aboriginal participation in government, those worried about differentiated Aboriginal citizenship maintain that the affirmation of 'special rights' unnecessarily fans the embers of social strife. Whatever position is taken on the causes of Aboriginal/non-Aboriginal discord, it is both distressing and disheartening to witness the continued conflict. The distrust, suspicion, animosity, and hostility that sometimes erupts between Aboriginal and non-Aboriginal Canadians cannot be good for either group over the long term. Surely, any relevant conception of citizenship must address the issues of cohesion, unity, and peace.

This same concern about the potential of Aboriginal rights to undermine 'peace, friendship and respect' also finds expression in the academic literature. Two books published by high-profile Canadian political scientists demonstrate apprehensions about Aboriginal control of Aboriginal affairs, although they take different approaches. In *First Nations? Second Thoughts*, University of Calgary Professor Tom Flanagan largely rejects the separate treatment of Aboriginal peoples in matters of land and governance because of the potential threat posed by such treatment to individual choice, representative government, a free market economy, and progress in human affairs.[79] His thesis seems to be that the bonds of unity in Canada will be eroded if, as a country, Canada follows what he terms the 'aboriginal orthodoxy' (which stresses Aboriginal rights, treaties, economies, identity, sovereignty, nationality, and governance). For Professor Flanagan the pursuit of these aspects of Aboriginal citizenship is problematic because it would 'redefine Canada as an association of racial communities rather than a polity whose members are individual human beings,' 'encourage Aboriginal peoples to see others ... as having caused their misfortune,' and 'encourage Aboriginal people to withdraw into themselves.'[80] Clearly, Professor Flanagan sees problems with concepts of Aboriginal citizenship that accentuate group rights, reinforce Aboriginal organizations, and emphasize Aboriginal identity. While certain elements of his argument may seem to overstep the mark if one is concerned about fostering civic peace,[81] his emphasis on concerns of stability and peace is worthy of attention.

Alan Cairns, for his part, sees problems with elements of a transforming narrative of Aboriginal citizenship on other grounds. In *Citizens Plus: Aboriginal Peoples and the Canadian State*, Professor Cairns wonders 'what will hold us together?' if aspects of Aboriginal citizenship are stressed to the exclusion of their relationships with other Canadians.[82] Cairns is not as concerned as Flanagan with the fact that Aboriginal peoples stress group rights, develop diverse organizations, and nurture strong identities; rather, his worry is that these elements of citizenship could override a shared sense of 'interdependence' within Canada if we do not simultaneously highlight social cohesion. In making such observations Cairns follows Adeno Addis, who observed that 'the task of political and legal theory in the late twentieth century must be one of imaging institutions and vocabularies that will affirm multiplicity while cultivating solidarity.'[83] For all of these reasons we must consider social cohesion as an element of citizenship when we catalogue Canada's relationship with Aboriginal peoples. Our common welfare seems to depend on our interest in one another, and thus requires that we move beyond status, association, and identity in defining the contours of citizenship. In this regard, Cairn's observation at the end of his book is insightful: 'the members of Aboriginal nations will continue to have rights and duties vis-à-vis federal and provincial governments, the obvious vehicle of which is citizenship. Further, a common citizenship will facilitate the coming and going of Aboriginal individuals and families across self-government nations. Our practical task ... is to enhance the compatibility between Aboriginal nationhood and Canadian citizenship.'[84]

Canada is somewhat unique among Western nations in constitutionally embracing a theory of differentiated citizenship. Aboriginal control of Aboriginal affairs is important to the flourishing of Aboriginal communities. However, this notion of citizenship presents certain challenges to social cohesion, political stability, and civic peace. The question this book has addressed is whether it is possible to facilitate Aboriginal control of Aboriginal affairs while simultaneously encouraging Aboriginal control of Canadian affairs. Ultimately, it may be instructive to return to the insights of Kymlicka and Norman. They argue 'that it is clearly unhelpful to talk as if there is a zero-sum relationship between minority rights and citizenship; as if every gain in the direction of accommodating diversity comes at the expense of promoting citizenship.'[85] This observation is certainly applicable to Aboriginal peoples in the Canadian context (although the 'minorities' label is inappropriate).[86] The accommodation of Aboriginal conceptions of citizenship does not come at the expense of promoting more general Canadian citizenship. It is true that unique concerns arise when a country recognizes Indigenous rights and departs from more universalized and common notions of citizenship. However, with reasoned exchange and shared relationships, fears about the accommodation of difference can be overcome in such a way that promotes, rather than sacrifices, citizenship. In fact, as Kymlicka and Norman remind us, 'refusal to grant recognition and autonomy to such groups [like Aboriginal peoples] is often likely to provoke even more resentment and hostility from members of national minorities, alienating them further from their identity as citizens of the larger state.'[87] I would add: refusal to recognize the interdependent nature of Aboriginal/non-Aboriginal relationships is also likely to provoke resentment and hostility from each group, alienating them further from their identity as citizens with the land.

The simultaneous call for Aboriginal control of Aboriginal affairs and Aboriginal control of Canadian affairs could actually enhance citizenship. When Aboriginal peoples no longer feel that the survival of their languages, cultures, and distinctive practices is threatened, they may become more willing to embrace their relationships with others in this country. Likewise, when non-Aboriginal Canadians no longer worry that their resources, rights, and livelihoods will be taken from them if they recognize a differentiated Aboriginal citizenship, the rights secured through such recognition may encourage their mutual reinforcement. Of course, there is no guarantee that feelings of interdependence will flourish under such protection. Nevertheless, the stronger rooting of all peoples' rights, associations, and identities within the soil of the Canadian political economy is a necessary, if not a sufficient, condition for the enjoyment of stronger bonds of national unity.

VII Conclusion

There is a 'special bond' between Aboriginal peoples and the lands they have traditionally occupied.[88] These bonds should be reflected in the discourses of Aboriginal citizenship. To speak only of Aboriginal control of Aboriginal affairs would disenfranchise most Aboriginal peoples from their traditional lands. Measured separatism would separate many from places they hold dear. Why should an artificial line drawn around my reservation bar me from a relationship with the vast areas my ancestors revered? The marking of such boundaries could prevent the acknowledgment and strengthening of continued Aboriginal reliance, participation, and citizenship with the lands they use outside the lines. As expressed in my experience at Philosopher's Walk, insisting on these boundaries could conceal legal relationships, rights, and obligations Indigenous to this land. Aboriginal peoples still honour the places made meaningful by an earlier generation's encounters. They still travel through these places and rely on them for food, water, medicine, memories, friends, and work. They still remember the stories and laws that guide their conduct towards these lands. Many are hesitant to relinquish their relationship with this territory in the name of Aboriginal self-government merely because non-Aboriginal people now live and rely on this land. Aboriginal control of Canadian affairs would simultaneously recognize the meaningful participation of Aboriginal people with one another and with their non-Aboriginal neighbours. It entails a deeper commitment to preserve and extend the special relationship Aboriginal peoples have with the land. Under Aboriginal control age-old territorial citizenships and legal obligations would not be abandoned merely because non-Aboriginal people are now necessary to preserve the land's ancient relations.

In 1976 my grandfather died, on the same shores he had been born on seventy-five years earlier. He did not live his whole life there, however; his life's experiences were not bounded by the artificial borders of a colonial department's Indian reserve. As a young boy, he hunted with his father in traditional territories recently converted into rich, fertile farmlands. As a young man, he worked in Wiarton, Owen Sound, Windsor, and Detroit as a plasterer and labourer. He also fished in the waters of Georgian Bay and Lake Huron (and, in later years, taught his grandson to fish). He then went on to Hollywood, acted in hundreds of films, and married a non-Aboriginal Californian. As a middle-aged man, he came back to the reserve when Pearl Harbor was bombed, but worked off-reserve as a labourer and hunted off-reserve to support his family. He received an honorary doctorate from the University of Kentucky in recognition of his knowledge of plants and medicines throughout the 1.5 million acres of land his grandfather had treatied over. Everywhere he went, including California, he always found people with whom he could speak Ojibway. During the last twenty-five years of his life, he lived alternately on the reserve with my grandmother in their old cabin, on our hunting grounds north of the reserve, and with some of his eight children, who lived off-reserve in non-Aboriginal towns throughout the traditional territory. Conceptions of Aboriginal citizenship must be enriched to reflect this full range of legal relationships with the land. Aboriginal culture is not static and, at least in Anishinabek Ontario, it develops and re-develops through a wider variety of interactions than is recognized in conventional narratives of citizenship. Narratives of Aboriginal legal and political participation should be transformed to reflect this fact.

Afterword:
Philosopher's Walk – The Return

In 1998 I came full circle in my professional life. I returned to the University of Toronto as a professor in the law school. Philosopher's Walk still sat heavily on its ancient spirits. It seemed abandoned, though hundreds of people crossed it every day. I arrived in the late summer. I walked its length, and watched as the sun eventually gave way to the snow, which later surrendered to spring rains. Trees filled their naked arms with leaves once again, but the earlier presence of the Walk remained silent. Or so I thought.

It was May, at the end of my first school year back at U of T. I was working late when I heard a heartbeat. It was strong and steady, audible above the traffic's din. A deep, low pulse echoed from the Walk and spilled out into the city night. I was intrigued. I threw on a sweater and made my way down the stairs from my office to discover its source. I passed the frozen faces of presidents, judges, and deans, and the dead oak panels supporting the portraits of a generation of the school's graduates. As I moved out into the parking lot, between towered sleeping pillars, I became certain of what I heard.

When I rounded the corner and looked over the Walk I saw what I had expected. A huge drum sat on the Walk surrounded by four singers, their long black hair braided, calling out into the night. Heads down, they pounded out the song of the earth, mimicking its pulse and rhythm. They were there from the Native Friendship Centre, singing for a friend who had died. Life was returning to the Walk.

This experience brought a new awareness. Over the next few months I began to notice the small changes that had taken place since my time as a student there. The Gus Wen Tah hung outside the Bora Laskin Law Library. A group of Aboriginal students had placed it there a few years earlier to remind classmates of their constitutional obligations.[1] Its two purple and three white rows stood as a testament to how peoples should treat one another as they gathered to this place. I reflected on how appropriate it was that the first thing students would see, before they ever walked inside the library and set their eyes on a case book, was a law that predated the reception of the common law in Canada. With the placement of that wampum, Philosopher's Walk began to stir.

When the students returned, I began to notice who they were. They came from across Canada and around the world and their intelligence and diversity was unmistakable. Among this body of able young people were members of Canada's First Nations and Métis populations. Though their numbers were still small, Philosopher's Walk had once again becoming a gathering place for Aboriginal people. They no longer came to fish or hunt, but they did bring gifts. Sometimes it was tobacco or sweet-grass; I watched small bundles pass silently between them in return for the help they gave one another. More often their offerings were their hearts and minds, as they struggled to make sense of a legal system that displaced their laws and yet maintain a sense of hope. I came to know their pasts, varied and similar. Middle class and poor, children of residential schools and any-where-in-Canada high schools. They were synchronously ordinary and exceptional, yet each one gave something unique to the restoration of Philosopher's Walk.

Others joined in the subtle transformation of the place. I taught fifty and sixty non-Aboriginal people at a time as we grappled to understand the issues identified in this book. Before even entering my class many had recognized the pain and injustice faced by Aboriginal peoples as a result of inequitable laws and policies. After studying the technicalities and details of the law they offered great insights into its flaws and made excellent suggestions about its reform. They were thoughtful, meticulous, and inspiring. Even faculty interest in Aboriginal legal issues was strong. What a change from ten years earlier, when it seemed to me that few at the law school knew or cared about the place of Aboriginal peoples and law in Canada.

To add to the changes I saw around me, one spring day I heard a rustle outside my office window. Momentarily distracted, I glanced through the glass, but went on with my work. Then I saw movement out of the corner of my eye. My attention focused, I stood up and lingered at the window-sill, searching for the cause of the disturbance. I studied the parking lot three storeys below, and scanned the tree a few feet from my wall. Nothing. Then from under the air-conditioner, sitting just above my windowpane, a blur. I watched as a small black body cast itself into the air, unfurled its wings, and glided to the pavement below. Over the next few minutes I followed the bird's movements, as it darted back and forth between my window and the world around it. Each time it landed in front of me there were small pieces of wood and paper in its beak that were then stuffed into the tiny space under the air conditioner.

Over the next few weeks my office felt like a nursery. First there was a settling in as eggs were laid and tended and safety and comfort were established in this unaccustomed surrounding. Next, came the sound of new life as the eggs hatched and hungry young mouths needed feeding. Then came the time of movement. The scratching and bumping against the underside of the metal casement would have driven me crazy had I not been so refreshed by the thought of their tenacity. They had picked what seemed a most unlikely spot to continue their place in the world: an old, austere building in the middle of a noisy, concrete tangle.

When the day came that the nest was deserted, and the office finally quiet again, I reflected on what had happened. Here was a lesson to linger on. I knew that this home would one day be filled again. That was important. I thought it significant that the nest was safe and separate from potentially dangerous influences, as life was passed from one generation to the next. It was absolutely necessary that the birds were as free as possible from direct outside influence as they undertook the task of rearing their young. Yet I also found it instructive to contemplate why the nest alone was not big enough or sufficient to ensure that the young would eventually grow to be healthy and strong. The parents constantly interacted with both these few twigs under the air-conditioner and their larger territory to maintain the lives of their young and themselves. They needed not only control of their own small slat of wood to survive, but also access to the wider world. They would be nothing without the water, bugs, worms, trees, pavement, and garden outside the nest. Their independence and interdependence was held in fine balance, and crucial to their sustenance through time.

Philosopher's Walk never seemed more alive to me as I reflected on this experience and the others that had occurred during my last year at U of T. Here was the reproduction of a pattern of life in the area that once seemed to me to be forever silenced. While the stream is still buried, Indigenous routines and customs that once blanketed the region are again discernable. The law school and its physical structure have not succeeded in extinguishing these previous forms. The trees, birds, and peoples that used to frequent these gentle hills can still be found here.

In them one hears echoes of the land's ancient voices. While it requires an attuned ear, even in the law school you can hear the resonance of the land's previous legal relationships. The spirit power of Philosopher's Walk is returning; its voice can sometimes be heard for miles.

Notes

Preface

1 'Listening for a Change: The Courts and Oral Tradition (2001) 39 *Osgoode Hall Law Journal* 1; 'Uncertain Citizens: The Supreme Court and Aboriginal Peoples' (2001) 80 *Canadian Bar Review* 15; 'Sovereignty's Alchemy: An Analysis of *Delgamuukw v. The Queen*' (1999) 37 *Osgoode Hall Law Journal* 537; 'Reliving the Present: Title, Treaties and the Trickster in British Columbia' (1999) 120 *BC Studies* 99; 'Frozen Rights in Canada: Constitutional Interpretation and the Trickster' (1997) 22 *American Indian Law Review* 37; 'Living between Water and Rocks: First Nations, the Environment and Democracy' (1997) 47 *University of Toronto Law Journal* 417; 'The Trickster: Integral to a Distinctive Culture' (1997) 47 *Constitutional Forum* 29; 'With or Without You: First Nations' Law (in Canada)' (1996) 41 *McGill Law Journal* 630–5; 'Because it does not make sense: Sovereignty Power in *R. v. Delgamuukw*,' in Diane Kirkby, ed., *Law, History and Colonialism: Empire's Reach* (Manchester: Manchester University Press, 2001); 'Landed Citizenship: Narratives of Aboriginal Political Participation,' in *Will Kymlicka, ed., Citizenship in Diverse Societies* (Oxford: Oxford University Press, 2000); repr. in Alan Cairns, ed., *Citizenship, Diversity and Pluralism* (Montreal: McGill-Queen's, 1999).

Introduction

1 Angus Gunn and Ira Nishisato, 'Holwood and Wymilwood' (1993–4) *Nexus* 20.
2 Ibid.
3 For a discussion of how architecture can commodify place, see Sharon

Zukin, *Landscapes of Power: From Detroit to Disney World* (Berkeley: University of California Press, 1991), at 43–8.

4 Meaning 'at the river.'

5 Meaning 'back burnt grounds.' Donald B. Smith, *Sacred Feathers* (Toronto: University of Toronto Press, 1987), at 18.

6 My feelings in this regard are similar to those described by Tony Hiss when viewing a two-acre farm landscape in Flushing, New York: 'My sense of community and connection is stretched in several different directions at once, so that "now" seems to be a time that began many generations ago and has no foreseeable ending, and even "we" seems to involve the land itself and the people living on it.' Tony Hiss, *The Experience of Place* (New York: Random House, 1990), at 107.

7 For a description of the Ojibway's use of this area, see Peter Schmalz, *The History of the Ojibway of Southern Ontario* (Toronto: University of Toronto Press, 1990).

8 My reserve is the Chippewas of the Nawash on the Bruce Peninsula. Our people now locate themselves at this place, three hours from Toronto (see Chapter 2). For its history, see John Borrows, 'A Genealogy of Law: Inherent Sovereignty and First Nations Self-Government' (1992) 30 *Osgoode Hall Law Journal* 291.

9 Smith, *Sacred Feathers*, at 11.

10 Ibid.

11 Law supports the markets and structures of land use. For a discussion of how capitalism continually eradicates and reshapes place, see Zukin, *Landscapes of Power*, especially Chapter 1, 'Market, Place and Landscape.'

12 For a chronicle of this history see Sidney Harring, *White Man's Law: Native People in Nineteenth-Century Jurisprudence* (Toronto: University of Toronto Press, 1998).

Chapter 1

1 Edward Benton-Banai, *The Mishomis Book: The Voice of the Ojibway* (Hayward, WI: Indian Country Communications, 1988), at 93.

2 Alan McMillan, *Native Peoples and Cultures of Canada* (Toronto: Douglas & McIntyre, 1988), at 1. For more detailed statistical information about First Nations, see Marlite A. Reddy, *Statistical Record of Native North Americans* (Washington, DC: Gale Research, 1993). A fascinating historical statistical survey of First Nations peoples in North America is Russell Thornton, *American Indian Holocaust and Survival: A Population History since 1492* (Norman: University of Oklahoma Press, 1987).

3 'Aboriginal' in Canadian law includes Indian, Inuit, and Métis people: see
s. 35(2) of the Constitution Act, 1982 (Canada), enacted as Schedule B to
the Canada Act, 1982 (U.K.) 1982, c. 11.

4 A good historic overview of Aboriginal peoples in northern North America
is found in Olive P. Dickason, *Canada's First Nations: A History of Founding
Peoples from Earliest Times* (Toronto: McClelland and Stewart, 1992). For a
description of the contemporary vitality of First Nations in Canada, see
Boyce Richardson, *People of Terra Nullius: Betrayal and Rebirth in Aboriginal
Canada* (Toronto: Douglas and McIntyre, 1993).

5 An overview of the distinctiveness of First Nations in different regions in Canada is found in R. Bruce Morrison and C. Roderik Wilson, eds., *Native Peoples:
The Canadian Experience*, 2nd ed. (Toronto: McClelland and Stewart, 1992).

6 For an excellent textual and pictorial representation of the pre-contact geo-
graphical spaces that First Nations peoples occupied in Canada, see Cole
Harris and Geoffrey Matthews, eds., *Historical Atlas of Canada*, vol. 1, *From the
Beginning to 1800* (Toronto: University of Toronto Press, 1987).

7 A representative description of one culture's (Gitksan and Wet'su'wet'en)
societal conventions is found in Gisday Wa and Delgam Uukw, *The Spirit in
the Land* (Gabriola Island, BC: Reflections Press, 1992).

8 'The body of rules, whether proceeding from formal enactment or from cus-
tom, which a particular state or community recognizes as binding on its
members or subjects.' *Oxford English Dictionary*, 2nd ed. (Oxford: Clarendon
Press, 1989) at 712. Articles commenting on First Nations law include
Bradford Morse and Gordon Woodman, eds., *Indigenous Law and the State*
(Providence, RI: Foris, 1988); Michael Coyle, 'Traditional Indian Justice in
Ontario: A Role for the Present?' (1986) 24 *Osgoode Hall Law Journal* 605. For
a contrary view, see Roger F. McDonnell, 'Contextualizing the Investigation
of Customary Law in Contemporary Native Communities' (1992) 34 *Canadian Journal of Criminology* 299; *Delgamuukw v. British Columbia* (1991), 79
D.L.R. (4th) 185 (B.C.S.C.) at 455: 'What the Gitksan and Wet'suwet'en witness[es] describe as law is really a most uncertain and highly flexible set of
customs which are frequently not followed by the Indians themselves.' But
see also Michael Asch, 'Errors in *Delgamuukw*: An Anthropological Perspective' in Frank Cassidy, ed., *Aboriginal Title in British Columbia: Delgamuukw v.
The Queen* (Lantzville, BC: Oolichan Press, 1991), at 221. For a fuller description of Wet'suwet'en law, see Antonia Mills, *Eagle Down is Our Law: Witsuwit'en Law, Feasts and Land Claims* (Vancouver: UBC Press, 1994).

9 For cases involving the reception of First Nations' law into Canadian law, see
Connolly v. Woolrich (1867), 17 R.J.R.Q. 75 (Que.S.C.), affirmed as *Johnstone v.
Connelly* (1869), 17 R.J.R.Q. 266 (Que.Q.B.); *R. v. Nan-e-quis-a Ka* (1899), 1

Territories Law Reports 211 (N.W.T.S.C.); *R. v. Bear's Shin Bone* (1899), 3 C.C.C. 329 (N.W.T.S.C.); *Re Noah Estate* (1961), 32 D.L.R. (2d) 686 (N.W.T.T.C.); *Re Deborah* (1972), 28 D.L.R. (3rd) 483 (N.W.T.C.A.); *Mitchell v. Dennis*, [1984] 2 C.N.L.R. 91 (B.C.S.C.); *Casimel v. I.C.B.C.*, [1992] 1 C.N.L.R. 84 (B.C.S.C.); *Vielle v. Vielle*, [1993] 1 C.N.L.R. 165 (Alta. Q.B.).

10 For a useful discussion of how courts apply these different European sources of law in First Nations' jurisprudence, see Sabastien Grammond, 'Aboriginal Treaties and Canadian Law' (1994) 20 *Queen's Law Journal* 57.

11 An informative collection of essays that explores the 'cultural creation of legal meaning' has been edited by Robert Post: *Law and the Order of Culture* (Los Angeles: University of California Press, 1991).

12 Robert M. Cover, 'Foreword: Nomos and Narrative' (1983) 97 *Harvard Law Review* 11.

13 In Canadian case law First Nations cultures and Aboriginal rights are often undifferentiated from the cultures and rights of general Canadian populations. In *Jack and Charlie v. The Queen* (1986), 21 D.L.R. (4th) 641 (S.C.C.) at 651, the court inappropriately expected that Coast Salish people could use frozen deer meat for their religious ceremonies, because the practice was regarded as being akin to a sacrament. In *Pawis v. The Queen* (1979), 102 D.L.R. (3d) 602 (F.C.T.D.) at 607, the court erroneously treated promises to preserve Ojibway culture and associated treaty rights as 'tantamount to a contract' between private individuals. This allowed the court to defeat all arguments that the treaty recognized cultural differences.

14 Many examples can also be found of the courts treating First Nations cultures as inferior to non-Native cultures. See, for instance, *R. v. Syliboy*, [1929] 1 D.L.R. 307 (N.S.Co.Ct.) at 313, where Patterson J. held that the Mik'maq were 'uncivilized' peoples and consequently incapable of exercising sovereignty. For an excellent discussion of how common law and international legal doctrines have treated First Nations as inferior, and thus permitted their dispossession, see Robert A. Williams, Jr, *The American Indian in Western Legal Thought: The Discourses of Conquest* (New York: Oxford University Press, 1990).

15 Jeremy Webber, 'Relations of Force and Relations of Justice: The Emergence of Normative Community Between Colonists and Aboriginal Peoples' (1995) 33 *Osgoode Hall Law Journal* 623.

16 The courts can approach the interpretation of Aboriginal rights as a search for consistency because: 'Judges have, by the nature of their office, a particular concern with the normative structure of a community through time. The very means by which they justify their decisions require that they reflect upon the substance of previous judgements, that they care about consistency

over time and across contemporaneous judgements, and that they take seriously the law's claim to be a framework of justice ...' Jeremy Webber, 'The
Jurisprudence of Regret: The Search for Standards of Justice in Mabo'
(1995) 17 *Sydney Law Review* 5 at 27–8.

17 However, if the courts decided to base their decisions on inconsistency, one
could argue that Aboriginal rights would prevail. The general principle that
the common law will recognize a customary title only if it is consistent with
the common law is subject to an exception in favour of traditional Native
title. *Mabo v. Queensland (No. 2)* (1992), 107 A.L.R. 1 at 43, per Brennan J.
Therefore, in the case of inconsistency between First Nations and British law,
the courts would apply a sui generis 'conflict of laws' test that would 'resolve
ambiguity in the favour of the Indians.' *Nowegijick v. The Queen* (1983), 144
D.L.R. (3d) 193; *Jones v. Meehan*, 175 U.S. 1 (1899). However, it is the position of this book that there is a great deal more consistency between Canadian law and First Nations law than the courts have previously recognized.
Decisions do not always have to rely on the fact that First Nations laws are
received in the law as an exception to the general rule; they can be received
in the same manner as other sources of law. This would result in Aboriginal
law applying in many more circumstances, as courts can find that First
Nations' laws are often compatible with the common law.

18 Brian Slattery, 'Understanding Aboriginal Rights' (1987) 66 *Canadian Bar
Review* 727 at 733; Brian Slattery, 'Making Sense of Aboriginal Rights' (2000)
79 *Canadian Bar Review* 196 at 200–4.

19 Ibid.

20 Jack Woodward, preface to *Native Law* (Scarborough, Ont.: Carswell, 1990).
See also *Native Communications Society of B.C. v. M.N.R.*, [1986] 3 F.C. 471
(C.A.). For a supporting argument, see Brian Slattery, 'The Independence of
Canada' (1983) *Supreme Court Law Review* 369.

21 'One must not be asked to drop all Western legal thought at the door in
identifying aboriginal rights and characterizing their content and implications. They are unique. That does not mean that useful comparison and
analogy is impossible. After all, these rights receive their recognition and
protections through the common law ...' *Delgamuukw v. British Columbia*
(1993), 104 D.L.R. (4th) 470 at 572 (B.C.C.A.), per Wallace J.A.

22 For example, First Nations laws form a part of the 'laws of Canada.' The fact
that pre-existing Aboriginal rights form a part of the laws of Canada was recognized by the Supreme Court of Canada in *R. v. Roberts*, [1989] 2 C.N.L.R.
146 (S.C.C.) at 156.

23 The recognition of legal pluralism has similarly been encouraged by other
authors: Sally Engle Merry, 'Law and Colonialism' (1991) 25 *Law and Society*

Review 889; J. Griffiths, 'What Is Legal Pluralism?' (1986) 24 *Journal of Legal Pluralism and Unofficial Law* 1; G. Teubner, 'Rethinking Legal Pluralism' (1992) 13 *Cardozo Law Review* 1443; Peter Fitzpatrick, 'Law and Societies' (1984) 22 *Osgoode Hall Law Journal* 115; W. Pue, 'Wrestling with Law: (Geographical) Specificity vs. (Legal) Abstraction' (1990) 11 *Urban Geography* 566; Harry W. Arthurs, *Without the Law* (Toronto: University of Toronto Press, 1985); Brian Slattery, 'Rights, Communities and Tradition' (1991) 41 *University of Toronto Law Journal* 447.

24 For a discussion of the continuing existence of First Nations rights despite much colonial interference, see Royal Commission on Aboriginal Peoples, *Partners in Confederation: Aboriginal Peoples, Self-Government, and the Constitution* (Ottawa: Supply and Services, 1993).

25 First Nations rights continued to exist despite intrusive interference on the part of the government. This was confirmed in *R. v. Sparrow*, [1990] 1 S.C.R. 1075 at 1097: 'That the right is controlled in great detail does not mean that the right is thereby extinguished.'

26 Chief Blaine Favel of the Federated Saskatchewan Indian Nations wrote about the continued existence of dispute resolution in First Nations, 'First Nations Perspectives on the Split in Jurisdiction,' in Richard Gosse, James Youngblood Henderson, and Roger Carter, eds., *Continuing Poundmaker and Riel's Quest: Presentations Made at a Conference on Aboriginal People and Justice* (Saskatoon: Purich Publishing, 1994) at 137.

27 *Connolly v. Woolrich* at 79.

28 *R. v. Guerin*, [1984] 2 S.C.R. 335 at 376–7 (S.C.C.).

29 See *Calder v. A.G.B.C.* (1973), 34 D.L.R. (3d) 145 at 208 (S.C.C.); *Delgamuukw v. British Columbia* at 520–39 (B.C.C.A.); *United States v. Santa Fe Pacific Ry. Co.*, 314 U.S. 339 at 354 (U.S.S.C., 1941); *R. v. Sparrow* at 1092–3.

30 See *Re Beaulieu's Petition* (1969), 67 W.W.R. 669 (N.W.T.Terr.Ct.); *Tucktoo v. Kitchooalik*, [1972] 5 W.W.R. 203 (N.W.T.C.A.), affirming [1972] 3 W.W.R. 194; *Re Wah-Shee* (1975), 21 R.F.L. 156 (N.W.T.S.C.). Custom is an exception to the general principle that the common law is homogeneous and universal and gives rise to rights that prevail over those that flow from the common law generally. See *Hammerton v. Honey* (1876), 24 W.R. 603; *Lockwood v. Wood*, [1844] 6 Q.B. 50 at 64 (Ex.Ct.); *New Windsor Corp. v. Mellor*, [1975] 1 Ch. 380 at 387 (C.A.); *Champneys v. Buchan* (1857), 4 Drew. 104.

31 *Delgamuukw v. British Columbia* at 644 (B.C.C.A.), per Lambert J.A.: 'all aboriginal rights are sui generis.'

32 *A.G. Canada v. Giroux* (1916), 30 D.L.R. 123 (S.C.C.); *Western Industrial Contractors Ltd. v. Sarcee Developments Ltd.* (1979), 98 D.L.R. (3d) 424 (S.C.C.); *Miller v. The King*, [1950] 1 D.L.R. 513 (S.C.C.).

33 The Australia High Court has also recognized that the common law draws on Aboriginal legal sources. *Mabo v. Queensland (No. 2)* at 42. For discussion of this case see M.A. Stephenson and Suri Ratnapala, eds., *Mabo: A Judicial Revolution* (St. Lucia, Queensland: University of Queensland Press, 1993); Richard H. Barlett, *The Mabo Decision: Commentary and Text* (Toronto: Butterworths, 1993). The *Mabo* decision was subsequently confirmed through legislation (see Native Title Act 1993 (Aus.), 1993, No. 110).

34 *Casimel v. I.C.B.C.*, [1994] 2 C.N.L.R. 22 at 32 (B.C.C.A.), per Lambert J.A.

35 Ibid. at 30.

36 *Delgamuukw v. British Columbia*, [1997] 3 S.C.R. 1010 (land); *R. v. Sioui*, [1990] 1 S.C.R. 1025 (governance); *R. v. Gladstone*, [1996] 2 S.C.R. 723 and *Mitchell v. Canada (M.N.R.)*, [1999] 1 C.N.L.R. 112 (F.C.A.) (trade); *R. v. Nan-e-quis-a Ka* (1899), 1 Territories Law Reports 211 (N.W.T.S.C.), *R. v. Bear's Shin Bone* (1899), 3 C.C.C. 329 (N.W.T.S.C.) (marriage); *Re Tagornak Adoption Petition*, [1984] 1 C.N.L.R. 185 (N.W.T.S.C.) and *B.C. Birth Registration No. 1994-09-040399*, [1998] 4 C.N.L.R. 7 (B.C.S.C.) (adoption); *Re Noah Estate* (1961), 32 D.L.R. (2d) 686 (N.W.T.T.C.) (death).

37 See Joseph H. Smith, ed., 'The Mohegan Indians *v.* Connecticut,' in *Appeals to the Privy Council from the American Plantations* (New York: Octagon Books, 1965), 442; *Sheldon v. Ramsay* (1852), 9 U.C.R. 105 at 133–4; *British Columbia (A.G.) v. Canada (A.G.)*, [1906] A.C. 552 at 554–5 (J.C.P.C.), applied in *Delgamuukw v. British Columbia* (B.C.S.C.); *Sero v. Gault* (1921), 50 O.L.R. 27 at 31–3; *Tee-Hit-Ton Indians v. United States*, 348 U.S. 272 (U.S.S.C. 1955); *Isaac et al. v. Davey* (1974), 51 D.L.R. (3d) 170 at 180 (C.A.), affirmed 77 D.L.R. (3d) 481 (S.C.C.); *Milirrpum v. Nabalco Pty. Ltd.* (1971), [1972–1973] A.L.R. 65 (N.T.Sp.Ct.); *Delgamuukw v. British Columbia* at 577 (B.C.C.A.), per Wallace J.A. During the period of Canadian law's disregard of First Nations rights, First Nations laws continued because of the strength, principles, and practices of Aboriginal communities. See e.g. Douglas Cole and Ira Chaikin, *An Iron Hand Upon the People: The Law against the Potlatch on the Northwest Coast* (Vancouver: Douglas & McIntyre, 1990); Katherine Pettipas, *Severing the Ties That Bind: Government Repression of Indigenous Religious Ceremonies on the Prairies* (Winnipeg: University of Manitoba Press, 1994). In this period, First Nations were able to preserve their laws and rights in spite of the common law.

38 *Sheldon v. Ramsay* at 123.

39 The contested origins of legal principles in Aboriginal rights jurisprudence are described in Kent McNeil, *Common Law Aboriginal Title* (Oxford: Clarendon Press, 1989); Bruce Clark, *Native Liberty, Crown Sovereignty: The Existing Aboriginal Right of Self-Government in Canada* (Montreal: McGill-Queen's University Press, 1990).

40 Case law from British Columbia has held that in the case of conflict between Aboriginal laws and Canadian laws, the latter will prevail. See *Delgamuukw v. British Columbia* at 453 (B.C.S.C.); *R. v. Williams*, [1995] 2 C.N.L.R. 299 (B.C.C.A.).

41 See *St. Catherines Milling and Lumber Co. v. The Queen* (1888), 14 App. Cas. 46 at 54–5 (P.C.); *Smith et al. v. The Queen* (1983), 147 D.L.R. (3d) 237 (S.C.C.); *A.G. Quebec v. A.G. Canada* (1920), 56 D.L.R. 373 at 378–9 (J.C.P.C.) (Star Chrome case).

42 *St. Catherines Milling and Lumber Co. v. The Queen* at 55.

43 *R. v. Sparrow* at 1103. For an excellent critique of these conclusions, see Michael Asch and Patrick Macklem, 'Aboriginal Rights and Canadian Sovereignty: An Essay on *R. v. Sparrow*' (1991) 29 *Alberta Law Review* 498.

44 *Jones v. Fraser* (1886), 2 C.N.L.C. 203 (S.C.C.); *Robb v. Robb* (1891), 3 C.N.L.C. 613; *Smith v. Young* (1898), 3 C.N.L.C. 656; *R. v. Williams* (1921), 4 C.N.L.C. 421; *Logan v. Styres* (1959), 20 D.L.R. (2d) 416 (Ont. H.C.).

45 *St. Catherines Milling and Lumber Co. v. The Queen.*

46 See Peter Kulchyski, *Unjust Relations: Aboriginal Rights in Canadian Courts* (Toronto: Oxford University Press, 1994); Paula Mallea, *Aboriginal Law: Apartheid in Canada?* (Brandon, MB: Bearpaw Publishing, 1994); Thomas Berger, *A Long and Terrible Shadow: White Values and Native Rights in the Americas, 1492–1992* (Toronto: Douglas and McIntyre, 1991).

47 See Royal Commission on Aboriginal Peoples, *The High Arctic Relocation*, vols. 1, 2 (Ottawa: Supply and Services, 1994); Geoffrey S. Lester, 'Aboriginal Land Rights: Some Remarks Upon the Ontario Lands Case (1885–1888)' (1988) 13 *Queen's Law Journal* 132; Paul Chartrand, 'Aboriginal Rights: The Dispossession of the Métis' (1991) 29 *Osgoode Hall Law Journal* 457; Kent McNeil, 'A Question of Title: Has the Common Law Been Misapplied to Dispossess the Aboriginal?' (1990) 16 *Monash University Law Review* 91.

48 See John Borrows, 'Negotiating Treaties and Land Claims: The Impact of Diversity within First Nations Property Interests' (1992) 12 *Windsor Yearbook of Access to Justice* 179; Sid Harring, 'The Liberal Treatment of Indians: Native People in Nineteenth Century Ontario Law' (1992) 56 *Saskatchewan Law Review* 297.

49 See Georges Erasmus and Joe Sanders, 'Canadian History: An Aboriginal Perspective,' in Diane Engelstad and John Bird, eds., *Nation to Nation: Aboriginal Sovereignty and the Future of Canada* (Concord, ON: Anansi Press, 1992), at 3– 11; Cassidy, ed., *Aboriginal Self-Determination*; Boyce Richardson, ed., *DrumBeat: Anger and Renewal in Indian Country* (Toronto: Summerhill Press, 1989).

50 For articles assessing the effect of judicial interpretation on different aspects of First Nations rights, see Michael Asch and Catherine Bell, 'Definition and

Interpretation of Fact in Canadian Aboriginal Title Litigation: An Analysis of *Delgamuukw*' (1993–4) 19 *Queen's Law Journal* 503; Patrick Macklem, 'First Nations Self-Government and the Borders of the Canadian Legal Imagination' (1991) 36 *McGill Law Journal* 382; Bruce Ryder, 'The Demise and Rise of the Classical Paradigm in Canadian Federalism: Promoting Autonomy for the Provinces and First Nations' (1991) 36 *McGill Law Journal* 308; Mary-Ellen Turpel, 'Home/Land' (1991) 10 *Canadian Journal of Family Law* 17; Leslie Hall Pinder, *The Carriers of No: After the Land Claims Trial* (Vancouver: Lazara Press, 1991); Robin Ridington, 'Cultures in Conflict: The Problem of Discourse,' in W.H. New, ed., *Native Writers and Canadian Writing* (Vancouver: UBC Press, 1990) at 273; Joan Ryan and Bernard Ominayak, 'The Cultural Effects of Judicial Bias,' in Kathleen Mahoney and Sheilah Martin, eds., *Equality and Judicial Neutrality* (Toronto: Carswell, 1989), at 346; Louise Mandell, 'Native Culture on Trial' in Mahoney and Martin, ibid., at 358.

51 In *Paul v. Canadian Pacific Ltd.*, [1988] 2 S.C.R. 654 (S.C.C.), the court held, at 673, that '*it would be inconsistent* to hold that possession through the Crown could be claimed in order to divest the Indians of an interest which the Crown holds for their benefit' (emphasis added).

52 Even an interest in land as great as a fee simple grant of land may be compatible with Aboriginal laws and title. See *Delgamuukw v. British Columbia* at 532 (B.C.C.A.), per Macfarlane J.A.

53 Ibid.

54 *R. v. Guerin* at 382.

55 *Mitchell v. M.N.R.*, [2001] 3 C.N.L.R. 122 at 148.

56 For a discussion of the shared nature of Aboriginal/non-Aboriginal sovereignty see Mr Justice Binnie's dissent in *Mitchell* at 163–77, though he disagrees with the majority on the issue of potential incompatability in the dispute under examination in that case.

57 The case of *R. v. Howard*, [1994] 2 S.C.R. 299, however, indicates a potential retreat from principles of liberal interpretation in First Nations jurisprudence. For a critique of that case, see Joel Bakan, Bruce Ryder, David Schneiderman, and Margot Young, 'Developments in Constitutional Law: The 1993–1994 Term' (1995) 6 *Supreme Court Law Review* 67 at 83–9.

58 Dickson C.J.C. considered the conflict arising in *Guerin*, and wrote that 'the Crown ... should have returned to the Band to explain what had occurred and seek the Band's counsel on how to proceed.' *R. v. Guerin* at 388. Wilson J. stated the point more strongly by noting that in case of conflict between Aboriginal and non-Aboriginal interests, the Crown's right would yield to the Indians' interest: 'The Bands do not have the fee in the lands; their interest is a limited one. But it is an interest which cannot be derogated from or

interfered with by the Crown's utilization of the land for purposes incompatible with the Indian title unless, of course, the Indians agree.' Ibid. at 349.

59 See *Ross v. Registrar of Motor Vehicles*, [1975] 1 S.C.R. 5; *Multiple Access Ltd. v. McCutcheon*, [1982] 2 S.C.R. 161; *Bank of Montreal v. Hall*, [1990] 1 S.C.R. 121; *Husky Oil v. M.N.R.*, [1995] 3 S.C.R. 453.

60 *R. v. Guerin* at 382. The phrase 'sui generis' seems to have first been used in a student note published in July 1984, commenting on a U.S. case. The note was published a few months before the *Guerin* decision was released. See Kimberly T. Ellwanger, 'Money Damages for the Breach of the Federal-Indian Trust Relationship After Mitchell II' (1983–4), 59 *Washington Law Review* 675 at 687. See also Richard Bartlett, 'The Fiduciary Obligation of the Crown to the Indians' (1989) 53 Saskatchewan Law Review 301 at 317.

61 *Funk and Wagnall's Standard College Dictionary* (Toronto: Fitzhenry and Whiteside, 1978) at 1339.

62 This is why, as Judson J. observed, the characterization of Aboriginal title as a personal and usufructuary right 'was not helpful in determining the nature of Indian title.' *Calder v. A.G.B.C.* at 156.

63 The use of the phrase 'other common law rights' recognizes the fact that Aboriginal rights, while maintaining their own, independent existence, are a part of Canadian common law. See *R. v. Roberts* (S.C.C.).

64 *R. v. Van der Peet*, [1996] 2 S.C.R. 507 at 534–5.

65 *Delgamuukw v. British Columbia* at 649 (B.C.C.A.), per Lambert J.A. (dissenting). See also cases consolidated under *Western Australia v. Commonwealth of Australia* (1995), 128 A.L.R. 1 (H.C.).

66 *Delgamuukw v. British Columbia* (B.C.C.A.).

67 The unique nature of Aboriginal land rights was highlighted by the Supreme Court of Canada in *Paul v. Canadian Pacific Ltd.* at 678 [505 in DLR].

68 As recognized by the Supreme Court of Canada in *R. v. Van der Peet* at 545, Aboriginal rights are based in the traditional laws and customs of the pre-existing societies of Aboriginal peoples.

69 Ibid. at 539. See also Brian Slattery, 'The Organic Constitution: Aboriginal Peoples and the Evolution of Canada' (1996) 34 Osgoode Hall Law Journal 101.

70 See Jeremy Webber, 'Relations of Force and Relations of Justice: The Emergence of Normative Community Between Colonists and Aboriginal Peoples' (1995) 35 *Osgoode Hall Law Journal* 263.

71 For a further discussion of Indigenous difference in Canadian constitutional thought, see Patrick Macklem, *Indigenous Difference and the Constitution of Canada* (Toronto: University of Toronto Press, 2001).

72 *R. v. Guerin* at 376.

73 *Calder v. A.G.B.C.* at 156 (emphasis added).

74 *R. v. Van der Peet* at 538 (S.C.C.).

75 Ibid. at 546.

76 Ibid.

77 *Van der Peet*, ibid., citing Mark Walters, 'British Imperial Constitutional Law and Aboriginal Rights: A Comment on *Delgamuukw v. B.C.*' (1992) 17 Queen's Law Journal 350 at 412–13 (emphasis omitted).

78 *R. v. Van der Peet* at 545.

79 *Delgamuukw v. British Columbia*, [1997] 3 S.C.R. 1010 at 1082 (S.C.C.).

80 Ibid. at 1081.

81 *Johnson v. McIntosh*, 21 U.S. (8 Wheat) 542 at 570 (U.S.S.C. 1823), quoted in *R. v. Guerin* at 378 (S.C.C.).

82 *Campbell v. Hall* (1774), 1 Cowp. 204 at 208–9.

83 *R. v. Guerin* at 336 (S.C.C.).

84 *Mitchell* at 122.

85 Ibid at 130.

86 Ibid.

87 This is not to suggest, however, that the courts will always find that Aboriginal law has survived the Crown's assertions. As expressed by McLachlin C.J.C., Aboriginal interests and laws may not survive as rights when (1) they were incompatible with the Crown's assertion of sovereignty, (2) they were surrendered voluntarily via the treaty process, or (3) the government extinguished them.' Ibid at 130. Nevertheless, despite this potential for invalidating Aboriginal laws under the common law, McLachlin C.J.C. declined to rule on the issue of whether 'sovereign incompatability' under her first category is a necessary component of defining rights protected with Canada's constitution. Ibid. at 148. Furthermore, it is worth observing that the surrender of Aboriginal laws and customs through the treaty-making process, or their extinguishment through government action, has never received judicial comment. When one also remembers that as a result of their constitutionalization Aboriginal rights (including the exercise of Aboriginal laws) cannot be unilaterally abrogated by any government, there are good reasons to give a broad reading to the Chief Justice's assertion that '[b]arring one of these exceptions, the practices, customs and traditions that defined the various aboriginal societies as distinctive cultures continued as part of the law of Canada.'

88 *R. v. Delgamuukw*, [1997] 3 S.C.R. 1010 (S.C.C.) at 1081.

89 *R. v. Van der Peet.*

90 The importance of culture to the survival of Aboriginal peoples as Aboriginal peoples may be seen in the statement made by Leroy Little Bear, 'What's

Einstein Got to Do With It?' in Gosse, Youngblood Henderson, and Carter, *Continuing Poundmaker and Riel's Quest* at 70–1. Note also the statements made in the opening address of the plaintiffs in *Delgamuukw v. British Columbia* (S.C.C.), repr., [1988] 1 C.N.L.R. 14 at 36: 'If one culture refuses to recognize another's facts in the other culture's terms, then the very possibility of dialogue between the two is drastically undermined. The challenge for this court in understanding the nature of Gitskan and Wet'suwet'en validation of facts and in accepting Gitskan and Wet'suwet'en history as real, is part of the court's task in treating Gitskan and Wet'suwet'en societies as equals.'

91 The High Court of Australia has recognized that the laws of Indigenous peoples are implicit in other rights protected by the common law. See *Mabo v. Queensland*, at 43–4.

92 *R. v. Roberts* (S.C.C.).

93 *R. v. Sparrow* at 1099.

94 That is not to say that courts will be able to reference a unified First Nations law which will apply in the same way, across different First Nations. Obviously, First Nations will have their own specific laws that are factually particular to their territories.

95 The recognition of the authenticity of Aboriginal laws, and their compatibility with Canadian law, has been assisted by recognition and affirmation of Aboriginal rights in the Canadian constitution: 'The existing aboriginal and treaty rights of the aboriginal peoples of Canada are hereby recognized and affirmed.' Constitution Act, 1982, being Schedule B of the Canada Act 1982 (U.K.), 1982, c. 11, s. 35(1).

96 Barry Lopez, *Crow and Weasel* (San Francisco: North Point Press, 1990), at 48.

97 See E. Adamson Hoebel, *The Law of Primitive Man* (New York: Atheneum, 1974); Karl N. Llewellyn and E. Adamson Hoebel, *The Cheyenne Way: Conflict and Case Law in Primitive Jurisprudence* (Norman: University of Oklahoma Press, 1941); Max Gluckman, *Politics, Law and Ritual in Primitive Society* (Chicago: Aldine Publishing, 1965).

98 For a sampling of these stories see George Blondin, *When the World Was New: Stories of the Sahtu Dene* (Yellowknife: Outcrop, 1990); Jack Funk and Gordon Lobe, eds., ... *And They Told Us Their Stories: A Book of Indian Stories* (Saskatoon: Saskatoon District Tribal Council, 1991); Peter Knudston and David Suzuki, *Wisdom of the Elders* (Toronto: Stoddart, 1993); Steve Wall and Harvey Arden, *Wisdom Keepers: Meetings with Native American Spiritual Elders* (Hillsboro, OR: Beyond Words, 1990).

99 Our common law is comprised of custom and long-used ways of doing things. Chief Justice Tom Tso, 'The Process of Decision Making in Tribal Courts' (1989) 31 *Arizona Law Review* 225.

100 Hugh Brody, *Maps and Dreams: Indians and the British Columbia Frontier* (Vancouver: Douglas and McIntyre, 1988), esp. chapters 3 and 5; G. Copway or Kah-ge-ga-gah-bowh, *The Traditional History and Characteristic Sketches of the Ojibway Nation* (1850; repr. Toronto: Coles, 1972), at 95–7; Basil Johnston, 'One Generation from Extinction,' in Daniel David Moses and Terry Goldie, eds., *An Anthology of Canadian Literature in English* (Toronto: Oxford University Press, 1992), at 99; Tom Porter, 'Traditions of the Constitution of the Six Nations,' in Leroy Little Bear, Menno Boldt, and J. Anthony Long, eds., *Pathways to Self-Determination: Canadian Indians and the Canadian State* (Toronto: University of Toronto Press, 1984), at 14.

101 *In Re Certified Question II: Navajo Nation v. MacDonald* (1989), 16 *Indian Law Reporter* 6086 (Navajo Supreme Court); edited version appears in David Getches, Charles Wilkinson and Robert Williams, Jr, *Federal Indian Law*, 4th ed. (Minneapolis: West Publishing, 1998).

102 Ibid.

103 Ibid.

104 Nancy L. Cook, 'Outside the Tradition: Literature as Legal Scholarship' (1994) 63 *University of Cincinnati Law Review* 95 at 116–39; Robert M. Cover, 'The Folktales of Justice: Tales of Jurisdiction' (1985) 14 *Capital University Law Review* 179 at 182; Valerie Karno, 'Bringing Fiction to Justice: Including Individual Narrative in Judicial Opinions' (1990) 2 *Hastings Women's Law Journal* 77 at 79; Thomas Ross, 'The Richmond Narratives' (1989) 68 *Texas Law Review* 381 at 385–6.

105 See Brian Simpson, 'The Common Law and Legal Theory,' in William Twining, ed., *Legal Theory and Common Law* (Oxford: Basil Blackwell, 1986), 19 at 22.

106 One theory of the common law is that law comes into being through declaration and established immemorial usage. See Sir Matthew Hale, *The History of the Common Law of England*, 5th ed. (Chicago: University of Chicago Press, 1974), at 12, 39–43; William Blackstone, *Commentaries on the Laws of England*, vol. 1, ed. S.G. Tucker (New York: W.E. Dean, 1845), at 68–70.

107 For a discussion of how stories and customs develop into law, see Carleton Kemp Allen, *Law in the Making*, 7th ed. (Oxford: Clarendon Press, 1964); Alan Watson, 'An Approach to Customary Law' (1984) University of Illinois Law Review 561; Gluckman, *Politics, Law and Ritual*; Harold J. Berman, *Law and Revolution: The Formation of the Western Legal Tradition: The Folklaw* (Cambridge: Harvard University Press, 1983), at 52–84.

108 For a theoretical examination of how law in 'primitive' societies fulfils these functions, see Wesley N. Hohfeld, *Fundamental Legal Conceptions, as Applied in Judicial Reasoning and Other Legal Essays*, ed. Walter W. Cook (New Haven:

Yale University Press, 1964); Max Radin, 'A Restatement of Hohfeld' (1938) 51 *Harvard Law Review* 1145; William Seagle, *The Quest for Law* (New York: Knopf, 1941).

109 For a discussion of the importance of the integrity of principles in legal systems, see Ronald Dworkin, *Law's Empire* (London: Fontana, 1986) at 176–84 and 219–24; Ronald Dworkin, *Taking Rights Seriously* (Cambridge: Harvard University Press, 1977).

110 For a discussion of the attributes decisions must possess in order to be considered 'legal' see Leopold Pospisil, *Anthropology of Law* (New York: Harper and Row, 1971), 30–51.

111 For an argument that oral traditions and the customary systems based on them are not like the common law, see generally E.P. Thompson, *Whigs and Hunters* (London: Allen Press, 1975), E.P. Thompson, *Customs in Common* (London: Merlin Press, 1991).

112 William Bright, *American Indian Linguistics and Literature* (New York: Mouton, 1984).

113 See Jane Dickson-Gilmore, 'Finding the Ways of the Ancestors: Customary Change and Invention of Tradition in the Development of Separate Legal Systems' (1992) 34 *Canadian Journal of Criminology* 479.

114 I say 'purportedly' because the common law is forever being reinterpreted to fit the demands placed on it today.

115 Perhaps not ironically, I cannot find anything written about this. However, cautions against inappropriately writing oral history are something I hear all the time when discussing this issue with Indigenous peoples.

116 Royal Commission on Aboriginal Peoples, *Report of the Royal Commission on Aboriginal People*, Volume 1, *Looking Forward, Looking Back* at 33, cited in *Delgamuukw v. British Columbia* at 1068 (S.C.C.).

117 Though I recognize that even common law cases change from telling to telling because of the different facts and issues the judge decides to highlight.

118 See Penny Petrone, *Native Literature in Canada: From Oral Tradition to the Present* (Toronto: Oxford University Press, 1990) at 17.

119 'When contact with the white man is established, a new set of problems arises and requires a logical cultural explanation to restore the world to order. Hence old myths are altered and new ones are generated to explain the process of cultural change.' Frances M.P. Robinson, introduction to *Visitors Who Never Left*, ed. Chief Kenneth B. Harris (Vancouver: UBC Press, 1974), at xv.

120 See Gloria Valencia-Weber, 'Tribal Courts: Custom and Innovative Law' (1994) 24 New Mexico Law Review 227 at 229.

121 *Delgamuukw v. British Columbia* at 1068 (S.C.C.), quoting from *Report of the*

Royal Commission on Aboriginal People, Volume 1, *Looking Forward, Looking Back* (Ottawa: Minister of Supply and Services Canada, 1996).

122 Words quoted from *Delgamuukw v. British Columbia* at 1068 (S.C.C.), paraphrasing Clay McLeod, 'The Oral Histories of Canada's Northern Peoples, Anglo-Canadian Evidence Law, and Canada's Fiduciary Duty to First Nations: Breaking Down the Barriers of the Past' (1992) 30 *Alberta Law Review* 1276.

123 I am also providing an example of First Nations legal narrative to make 'concrete' these legal principles. Furthermore, the cases presented use 'bits of the past to unsettle the present and deprive it of peace of mind.' Martha Minow, 'Stories in Law,' in Peter Brooks and Paul Gewirtz, eds., *Law's Stories: Narrative and Rhetoric in the Law* (New Haven, CT: Yale University Press, 1996), 24–36 at 33. They demonstrate how current environmental practices are out of line with ancient North American jurisprudential principles.

124 For a description of the development of the case method as a tool to study law, see Russell Weaver, 'Langdell's Legacy: Living with the Case Method' (1991) 36 *Villanova Law Review* 517. A critique of the 'supposed' endeavour to establish an objective theory of law by using the case method can be found in Karl Llewellyn, 'Some Realism about Legal Realism: Responding to Dean Pound' (1931) 44 *Harvard Law Review* 1222, particularly at 1222–3; Felix Cohen, 'Transcendental Knowledge and the Functional Approach' (1935) 35 *Columbia Law Review* 809.

125 Our home has been called the Cape Croker Indian Reserve by the Department of Indian and Northern Affairs. It is located on the Bruce Peninsula on the western shores of Georgian Bay in southern Ontario.

126 See Katherine T. Bartlett, 'Tradition, Change and the Idea of Progress in Feminist Legal Thought' (1995) *Wisconsin Law Review* 303 at 331: 'the strength of a tradition is not how closely it adheres to its original form but how well it is able to develop and remain relevant under changing circumstances.' See also Jaroslav Pelikan, *The Vindication of Tradition* (New Haven: Yale University Press, 1984), at 54: 'It is, then, a mark of authentic and living tradition that it points us beyond itself.'

127 *Nanabush the Trickster v. Deer, Wolf et al.* (Time Immemorial), 0002 Ojibway Cases (1st) 3 (Anishinabe Supreme Court). George G.E. Laidlaw wrote the judgment of John York, John Nadjiwon concurring [oral testimony, 1992], Justice Windigo dissenting. See George E. Laidlaw, 'Ojibway Myths and Tales' Twenty-Seventh Annual Archeological Report 86 (Ontario: Ministry of Education, 1915).

128 *Crow, Owl and Deer et al. v. Anishinabek* (Time Immemorial), 0001 Ojibway

Cases (1st) 1 (Anishnabe Supreme Court). Judgment written by Basil Johnston, *Ojibway Heritage* (Toronto: McClelland and Stewart, 1976) at 56, John Nadjiwon concurring.

129 *The Rest of the Forest v. The Birch Tree* (Time Immemorial), 0002 Ojibway Cases (1st) 2 (Anishnabe Supreme Court), judgment of Patronella Johnston, *Tales of Nokomis* (Toronto: Stoddart, 1975). See also Dorothy M. Reid, ed., *Tales of Nanabozho* (Toronto: Oxford University Press, 1963), at 47.

130 Other First Nations also have laws, expressed as stories, that guide their interpretation of environmental justice. See Robert A. Williams, Jr, 'Large Binocular Telescopes, Red Squirrel Pinatas, and Apache Sacred Mountains: Decolonizing Environmental Law in a Multicultural World' (1994) 95 *West Virginia Law Review* 1133 at 1135.

131 See James Boyd White, *Justice as Translation* (Chicago: University of Chicago Press, 1990).

132 Ibid. at xiii and 80.

133 The notion that law can be retranslated and contingently detached from its colonial context assists decision makers in recognizing the inherent pluralism that exists in Canadian law. Recognition of the pluralism of Canadian law also enables First Nations to employ its legal forms and symbols as simultaneous acts of accommodation and resistance. See Sally Engel Merry, 'Resistance and the Cultural Power of Law' (1995) 29 *Law and Society Review* 11 at 22–3.

134 Beverly McLachlin, in Rebecca Johnson, John McEvoy, Thomas Kuttner, and Wade MacLauchlan, eds., *Gerard v. La Forest at the Supreme Court of Canada, 1985–1997* (Ottawa: Canadian Historical Association, 2000).

135 Francis Jennings et al., eds., *The History and Culture of Iroquois Diplomacy* (Syracuse, NY: Syracuse University Press, 1985); Robert S. Allen, *His Majesty's Indian Allies: British Indian Policy in the Defence of Canada, 1774–1815* (Toronto: Dundurn Press, 1993); Richard White, *The Middle Ground: Indians, Empires and Republics in the Great Lakes Region, 1650–1815* (Cambridge: Cambridge University Press, 1991).

136 See Julian T. Inglis, ed., *Traditional Environmental Knowledge: Concepts and Cases* (Ottawa: Canadian Museum of Nature, 1993); Thom Alcoze, 'Our Common Future: Native Land Use and Sustainable Development,' in *The Guelph Seminars on Sustainable Development* (Guelph, ON: University of Guelph, 1990), reproduced in Elaine L. Hughes, ed., *Environmental Law and Policy* (Toronto: Emond Montgomery, 1993), 568. See also Heino Lilles, 'A Plea for More Human Values in Our Justice System' (1992) 17 *Queen's Law Journal* 328.

137 For an example of First Nations law being applied to environmental prob-

lems, see Randy Kapashesit and Murray Klippenstein, 'Aboriginal Group
Rights and Environmental Protection' (1991) 36 *McGill Law Journal* 925.

138 A similar situation is occuring in Australia, where the court has shown a will-
ingness to adjust its rules to accommodate the needs of Aboriginal appli-
cants. See *Milpurrurru v. Indofurn Pty. Ltd.* (1994), 130 A.L.R. 659 (Aust.
F.C.). For comment, see Kamal Puri, 'Cultural Ownership and Intellectual
Property Rights Post-*Mabo*: Putting Ideas into Action' (1995) 9 *Intellectual
Property Journal* 293.

139 See Donald Auger, 'Crime and Control in Three Nish-nawbe-Aski Nation
Communities' (1992) 34 Canadian Journal of Criminology 317; Obo-
nasawin-Irwin Consulting Inc., *Future Aboriginal Community Justice Project
Development Needs* (Brantford, ON: O.I. Consulting, 1992); Samuel Stevens,
'Northwest Territories Community Justice of the Peace Program,' in Royal
Commission on Aboriginal Peoples, *Aboriginal Peoples and the Justice System: A
Report of the National Roundtable on Aboriginal Justice Issues* (Ottawa: Supply
and Services, 1993), at 385; Muskrat Dam First Nation, *Anishinaabe Justice in
Muskrat Dam: A Study of Past and Present Practices* (Waterloo, ON: Fund for
Dispute Resolution, 1994).

140 See Michael Jackson, 'Locking Up Natives in Canada' (1989) 23 University
of British Columbia Law Review 205; Leonard Mandamin et al., 'The Criminal Code and Aboriginal People' (1992) (Special Edition) *University of British Columbia Law Review* 5 at 21–7; Rupert Ross, 'Leaving Our White Eyes
Behind: The Sentencing of Native Accused' [1989] 3 C.N.L.R. 1; Sharon
Moyer and Lee Axon, *An Implimentation Evaluation of the Native Community
Council Project of the Aboriginal Legal Services of Toronto* (Toronto: Ministry of
the Attorney General, 1993); Solicitor General Canada, Corrections
Branch, *Community Holistic Healing: Hollow Water First Nation* (Ottawa: Solici-
tor General, 1993); *R. v. Gladue*, [1999] 1 S.C.R. 688; *R. v. Wells*, [2000] 1
S.C.R. 207.

141 For a detailed analysis of the use of First Nations law to resolve cross-cul-
tural disputes, see Michael Jackson, 'In Search of the Pathways to Justice:
Alternative Dispute Resolution in Aboriginal Communities' (1992) (Special
Edition) *University of British Columbia Law Review* at 41; Kent Roach, *Due Pro-
cess and Victims' Rights: The New Law and Politics of Criminal Justice* (Toronto:
University of Toronto Press, 1999).

.142 Leading cases dealing with sentencing circles are: *R. v. Moses* (1992), 71
C.C.C. (3d) 347 (Y.Terr.Ct.); *R. v. Webb*, [1993] 1 C.N.L.R. 148 (Y.Terr.Ct.); *R.
v. Cheekinew* (1993), 80 C.C.C. (3d) 143 (Sask. Q.B.); *R. v. Morin* (1993), 114
Sask. R. 2 (Sask. Q.B.), reversed (1995) 101 C.C.C. (3d) 124 (Sask. C.A.).

143 For a discussion of how traditional principles of First Nations are preserved

in their interaction with contemporary Western legal concepts, see John Borrows, 'Contemporary Traditional Equality: The Effect of the Charter on First Nations Politics' (1994) 43 *University of New Brunswick Law Journal* 19.

144 *R. v. Morin* at 5 (Sask. Q.B.). Although the Court of Appeal overturned the lower court's decision, it stated that 'sanctions other than imprisonment' could be available for 'all' offenders. *R. v. Morin* at 139 (Sask. C.A.).

145 There will, no doubt, be resistance to applying Aboriginal legal principles outside of disputes involving Aboriginal peoples. See *R. v. Willcocks* (1995), 22 O.R. (3d) 552 (Gen. Div.), where a Jamaican Canadian in Toronto's Black community was denied access to an alternative justice program similar to Aboriginal initiatives.

146 See Mark Dockstator, 'Towards An Understanding of First Nations Self-Government' (D.Jur.Thesis, Osgoode Hall Law School, 1994); James Dumont, 'Justice and Aboriginal People,' in *Aboriginal Peoples and the Justice System: Report of the National Roundtable on Aboriginal Issues* (Ottawa: Supply and Services, 1993), at 42; Clare Brant, 'Native Ethics and Rules of Behaviour' (1990) 35 *Canadian Journal of Psychiatry* 534; Benton-Banai, *The Mishomis Book*.

147 T.S. Eliot, 'Tradition and the Individual Talent,' in *Selected Essays* (London: Faber, 1953) at 3–4.

148 Jo Carillo, 'Surface and Depth: Some Methodological Problems with Bringing Native American-centred Histories to Light' (1993) 20 *New York University Review of Law and Social Change 405*.

149 M.B. Hooker, *Legal Pluralism* (Oxford: Clarendon Press, 1975).

150 For a critical analysis of the difficulty one judge experienced in trying to understand law from another culture, see Robin Ridington, 'Fieldwork in Courtroom 53: A Witness to Delgamuukw,' in Cassidy, *Aboriginal Title in British Columbia* at 208; Pinder, *The Carriers of No*; Julie Cruickshank, 'Invention of Anthropology in British Columbia's Supreme Court: Oral Tradition as Evidence in *Delgamuukw v. BC*' (1992) 95 *BC Studies* 25.

151 See Aviam Soifer, 'Objects in the Mirror are Closer Than They Appear' (1994) 28 *Georgia Law Review* 533, esp. at 552.

152 A good description of how the predominant culture's power works against new forms of legal analysis is found in Richard Delgado, 'Rodrigo's Final Chronicle: Cultural Power, the Law Reviews, and the Attack on Narrative Jurisprudence' (1995) 68 *Southern California Law Review* 545, esp. at 569–70, 572.

153 See Austin Sarat and Roger Berkowitz, 'Disorderly Differences: Recognition, Accommodation, and American Law' (1994) 6 *Yale Journal of Law and the Humanities* 285, esp. at 296.

154 See Robert A. Williams Jr., 'Sovereignty, Racism, Human Rights: Indian Self-Determination and the Postmodern World Legal System' (1995) 2 *Review of Constitutional Studies* 146, esp. at 174.

155 For an explanation of how Western legal principles rhetorically invert the laws of subcultures within a state, see Peter Fitzpatrick, *The Mythology of Modern Law* (New York: Routledge, 1992), esp. at 80–1.

156 For an excellent article exploring how Indigenous law and identity was treated as inferior to American law see Jo Carillo, 'Identity as Idiom: Mashpee Reconsidered' (1995) 28 *Indiana Law Review* 517, esp. at 526–31.

157 Chief Justice Robert Yazzie, Navajo Judicial Branch, 'Healing as Justice: The American Experience' [Spring 1995] *Justice as Healing: A Newsletter on Aboriginal Concepts of Justice* 7. This newsletter is edited by James (Sakej) Youngblood Henderson and is produced by the Native Law Centre in Saskatoon.

158 For example, I anticipate that some will accuse me of romanticizing First Nations law or idealizing practices within First Nations legal institutions. I will be the first to admit that not all Anishinabe people follow the environmental law outlined in the *Deer, Wolf* case, or in their other laws. Some people have forgotten or disregard these laws, and our communities have accordingly suffered. This disregard has often been the result of colonialism, but sometimes it has occurred through dissent. However, there is a degree of deviation in any society's observance of its laws, and that does not mean those laws are non-existent. See Ronald Dworkin, *A Matter of Principle* (Cambridge: Harvard University Press, 1985), at 24–5. It merely demonstrates that the formation and observance of all law is fluid and contingent on a variety of social, political, and economic factors. For a description of the conditional nature of law in general subject areas, see David Kairys, ed., *The Politics of Law: A Progressive Critique*, rev. ed. (New York: Pantheon Books, 1990).

159 For an exceptional discussion of how arguments of equality and difference can work to dispossess First Nations of rights, and how normative notions of distributive justice can be applied to successfully mediate First Nations difference, see Patrick Macklem, 'Distributing Sovereignty: Indian Nations and Equality of Peoples' (1993) 45 *Stanford Law Review* 1311.

160 An example of how Indigenous law can be applied along with other laws is revealed in a statement of judges from the international community who investigated the claims of Native Hawaiian people: 'The tribunal considers that it is applying the law as fully and honestly as it knows. It refuses, however, to define law in a formalistic or colonial manner. It is guided [by concepts of law drawn from Indigenous, international and domestic] laws ... Law is a great river that draws from these sources as tributary rivers, and the

Tribunal will apply law in this spirit. We have found indigenous understanding of law to be an indispensable and powerful background for this verdict, and we believe that law experience and wisdom of indigenous peoples generally is helping ... nations to develop a more useful and equitable sense of law.' Ka Ho'okolokolonui Kanaka Maoli, People's International Tribunal, Hawaii (1993), 'Interim Report: Kanaka Maoli Nation, Plaintiff *v.* United States of America, Defendant' (12–21 August 1993, typescript), quoted in Merry, 'Resistance and the Cultural Power of Law,' at 22.

161 See Hoebel, *The Law of Primitive Man,* at 30–45, where he writes about methods and techniques of reliable ethnography to discern Aboriginal law. See generally Edward Hedican, *Applied Anthropology in Canada: Understanding Aboriginal Issues* (Toronto: University of Toronto Press, 1995).

162 For an examination of how courts use recorded precedent to discover First Nations law in the Navajo Nation, see Daniel Lowery, 'Developing a Tribal Common Law Jurisprudence: The Navajo Experience' (1993) 18 *American Indian Law Review* 379 at 394. See also Philmer Bluehouse and James Zion, 'Hozhooji Naat'aanii: The Navajo Justice and Harmony Ceremony' (1993) 10 *Mediation Quarterly* 329; James Wallingford, 'The Role of Tradition in the Navajo Judiciary: Re-emergence and Revival' (1994) 19 *Oklahoma City University Law Review* 141; Christine Zuni, 'The Southwest Intertribal Court of Appeals' (1994) 24 *New Mexico Law Review* 304.

163 The treatises, of course, would have to be specific to the Nation at trial.

164 The Supreme Court of Canada ruled that judicial notice of historical facts concerning First Nations could be introduced even if they were not part of the record at lower courts. *R. v. Sioui,* [1990] 1 S.C.R. 1025 at 1050. See also *R. v. White and Bob* (1964), 50 D.L.R. (2d) 613 at 629 (B.C.C.A.), affirmed (1965), 52 D.L.R. (2d) 481n (S.C.C.); *Monarch Steamship Co. Ltd. v. Karlshamns Oljefabriker (A/B),* [1949] A.C. 196 at 234; *Read v. Bishops of Lincoln,* [1892] A.C. 644 at 652–4 (P.C.).

165 The Navajo Nation Court in the United States has developed useful and culturally sensitive rules to qualify expert witnesses in First Nations law; see *In Re Estate of Belone v. Yazzie* (1987), 5 *Navajo Reporter* 161 at 166–7.

166 These are people who can 'reconcile [their] paper knowledge with the vast knowledge that is held by [their] elders – "the keepers of the tribal encyclopedia."' The Honorable Robert Yazzie, Chief Justice of the Navajo Supreme Court, 'Life Comes From It: Navajo Justice Concepts' (1994) 24 *New Mexico Law Review* 175 at 190.

167 For example, there are over three hundred First Nations people with law degrees in Canada today, with varying degrees of expertise in cross-cultural knowledge and interpretation.

168 Patricia Monture-Okanee, 'Alternative Dispute Resolution: A Bridge to Aboriginal Experience?' in C. Morris and Andrew Pirie, eds., *Qualifications for Dispute Resolution: Perspectives on the Debate* (Victoria: University of Victoria Centre for Dispute Resolution, 1994), at 131.

169 Alternatively, some First Nations lawyers will regard their talents best used in other places, and may not even want to work in this field. For a discussion of this issue, see Sam Deloria and Robert Laurence, 'What's an Indian? A Conversation about Law School Admissions, Indian Tribal Sovereignty and Affirmative Action' (1991) 44 *Arkansas Law Review* 1107.

170 Jürgen Habermas, 'Address: Multiculturalism and the Liberal State' (1995) 47 *Stanford Law Review* 849 at 850.

171 For an insightful article on the burdens of learning and applying both First Nations and non-Native law, see Frank Pommersheim, 'Liberation, Dreams and Hard Work: An Essay on Tribal Court Jurisprudence' (1992) *Wisconsin Law Review* 411, esp. at 450–5.

172 See Mark Suchman, 'Invention and Ritual: Notes on the Interrelation of Magic and Intellectual Property in Preliterate Societies' (1989) 89 *Columbia Law Review* 1264.

173 In 1995 the Saskatchewan Federated Indian College approached the University of Saskatchewan and the College of Law to begin a discussion to determine the feasibility of having 'traditional' First Nations Cree law taught in a degree program. Harold Cardinal, Sakej Henderson, Georges Sioui, Patricia Monture-Okanee, Maria Campbell, and myself were all present at a meeting with representatives of the university to agree to further pursue the institutionalized communication of First Nations law by First Nations elders and other knowledgable people.

174 [T]his is a movement which not only uses law as a mode of resistance but also challenges the legitimacy of nation-state law as the sole or even primary source of law ... [T]his movement attempts to redefine some aspects of law while accepting its symbolic power, seizing the concept of justice and deploying it as separate from state law.' Merry, 'Resistance and the Cultural Power of Law,' at 22–3.

175 Glen Morris, Director of the Fourth World Centre for the Study of Indigenous Law and Politics, University of Colorado at Denver, quoted in Ulla Hasager et al., *Ka Ho'okololonui Kanaka Maoli: The People's International Tribunal Hawai'i MANA'O* (Honolulu: Honolulu Publishing, 1993), at 9.

176 As the *Nanabush v. Deer, Wolf* case suggests, if First Nations laws are not honoured and respected, they may eventually no longer be practised on Canadian lands. Just as the deer left the Anishinabek and practised their ways with the protection of the crows, First Nations may decide to practise

their laws through the protection of others. When First Nations laws are no longer available to Canadian law, Canadians will not enjoy the substantial benefits that these laws can contribute to society. Thus, in applying the holding of the *Deer, Wolf* case to the question of the acceptance of First Nations law in Canada, it is clear that while First Nations law can have an independent existence without being received into Canadian law, Canadian law cannot be truly independent until it more fully receives non-colonial sources of law. Depending on the acceptance of the principles presented in this article, as First Nations our laws will, in the end, be exercised with or without Canada.

177 It is, then, up to First Nations communities, and those people who have a bridging knowledge of both Aboriginal and Canadian law, to decide if and how they will utilize these principles within First Nations. The fact that First Nations legal interpreters can facilitate the reception of First Nations laws into Canadian law should be not taken to mean that they will be qualified to practise First Nations law within the communities. There are other considerations within First Nations cultures that may work against the use of 'lawyers' advocating and interpreting the law within. A helpful discussion of this issue is found in Frank Pommersheim, 'The Contextual Legitimacy of Adjudication in Tribal Courts and the Role of the Bar as an Interpretive Community' (1988) 18 *New Mexico Law Review* 49 at 68. This debate has not yet begun in Canada; however, the use of people to interpret First Nations law does not necessarily damage the internal workings of Aboriginal legal systems when they are not consciously trying to invoke a principle for reception into Canadian law.

178 In fact, the abandonment of traditional laws can lead to loss of Native rights more generally: see *Mabo v. Queensland* at 43.

179 Bartlett, 'Tradition, Change and the Idea of Progress,' at 330.

180 Since state and Indigenous law interact in the everyday life of First Nation peoples, it is important that each system be responsive to the values of the other: see generally Maria Teresa Sierra, 'Indian Rights and Customary Law in Mexico: A Study of the Nahuas in the Siera de Puebla' (1995) 29 *Law and Society Review* 227.

181 See Roderick A. MacDonald, 'Recognizing and Legitimating Aboriginal Justice: Implications for a Reconstruction of Non-Aboriginal Legal Systems in Canada,' in Royal Commission on Aboriginal Peoples, *Aboriginal Peoples and the Justice System: A Report of the National Roundtable on Aboriginal Justice Issues* (Ottawa: Supply and Services, 1993), at 232.

182 Benton-Banai, *The Mishomis Book*, at 91–3.

Chapter 2

1 Letter from Dr D.W. Larson, Professor of Botany and Director of the Cliff Ecology Research Group at the University of Guelph, to Ed Philips, Minister of Municipal Affairs (24 October 1994) (on file with author). Eight-thousand-year-old tree stumps are found underwater less than one kilometre away from the northern tip of Hay Island, which will be described subsequently.

2 Diving in this area this past summer I found fire pits twenty to twenty-five feet from shore in some five feet of water.

3 Anishinabek, translated, means 'the good beings.' The Anishinabek have also been called Ojibway or Chippewa Nation. Our Nation surrounds the Great Lakes, and its people can be found in Michigan, Wisconsin, Minnesota, North Dakota, Manitoba, and Ontario.

4 Neyaashinigmiing, translated, means 'narrow neck of land.' Neyaashinigmiing is also known as the Cape Croker Indian reserve. This Indian reservation is composed of 15,000 acres on the western portion of Lake Huron.

5 Kookoominiising, translated, means Owl Island.

6 For a political history of our use of this area, see John Borrows, 'A Genealogy of Law: Inherent Sovereignty and First Nations Self-Government' (1992) 30 *Osgoode Hall Law Journal* 291.

7 Details about our interactions with the land and water are found in John Borrows, 'Negotiating Treaties and Land Claims: The Impact of Diversity within First Nations Property Interests' 12 *Windsor Yearbook of Access to Justice* 179.

8 Oral tradition, recounted at meeting between Cape Croker and Cuesta Planning Consultants (17 May 1993).

9 W.R.J. Armstrong, Consulting Planner, *Planning Report, Hay Island, Albemarle Township* (1992) at 2 (on file with author). The soils of the Island are predominantly heavy clays at the base of the bluff, with sandy and silty soils elsewhere.

10 See Patrick Macklem, 'First Nations Self-Government and the Borders of the Canadian Legal Imagination' (1991) 36 *McGill Law Journal* 382.

11 The Chippewas of Neyaashinigming would probably suffer the same fate, caught between jurisdictions, even if they were located in the United States. For example, U.S. environmental law sometimes treats tribes as states. See The Safe Drinking Water Act, 42 U.S.C. s. 300j–11(a)(1) (1988); The Clean Water Act, 33 U.S.C. S. 1377(e)(1988). At other times tribes are almost completely subsumed under federal plenary power. *United States v. Sandoval*, 231 U.S. 28 (U.S.S.C. 1913); *Morton v. Mancari*, 417 U.S. 535 (1974); *Delaware*

Tribal Business Committee v. Weeks, 430 U.S. 73 at 84 (1977). Furthermore, the U.S.S.C. has complicated this jurisdictional maze, placing Indigenous peoples between the competing jurisdictions of federal and state governments for different purposes. See e.g., *Oklahoma State Tax Comm'r v. Citizens Band of Potawatomi Indian Tribe of Oklahoma*, 498 U.S. 505 (1991); *Brendale v. Confederated Tribes and Bands of the Yakima Nation*, 492 U.S. 408 (1989). This constriction between jurisdictions occurs despite the idea that Indian Nations are supposed to be the 'Third Sovereign.' Charles Wilkinson, *American Indians, Time and the Law: Native Societies in a Modern Constitutional Democracy* (New Haven, CT: Yale University Press, 1987), at 53–86.

12 A similar situation is noted in the United States: see Kevin Worthen and Wayne Farnsworth, 'Who Will Control the Future of Indian Gaming? "A Few Pages of History Are Worth a Volume of Logic"' (1996) *Brigham Young University Law Review* 407 at 410.

13 The Indian Act, R.S.C. 1985, c. I-5, gives the Minister of Indian Affairs, not the Indigenous community, final authority and discretion over all aspects of Indian life. It virtually controls all official legal interactions on Indian reservations in Canada. The Indian Act is an extremely paternalistic termination era-like legislation designed to 'protect,' 'assimilate,' and 'civilize' Indians. It was designed to 'continue until there is not a single Indian in Canada that has not been absorbed into the body politic.' J.R. Miller, *Skyscrapers Hide the Heavens: A History of Indian-White Relations in Canada* (Toronto: University of Toronto Press, 1989), at 207. A description of the Act's purposes is found in J.R. Tobias, 'Protection, Civilization and Assimilation: An Outline History of Canada's Indian Policy,' in J.R. Miller, ed., *Sweet Promises: A Reader on Indian-White Relations in Canada* (Toronto: University of Toronto Press, 1991), at 127.

14 The Indian Act is completely inadequate in addressing environmental planning issues. For example, the Act's permit and licensing scheme relative to waste disposal and timber removal seems to encourage utilization rather than prevention. For example, the maximum fine for violation of these environmental standards is a mere one hundred dollars. It is foreseeable that people would treat these penalties as extremely inexpensive licences enabling them to exploit the reserve's environment without great cost. See Indian Reserve Waste Disposal Regulation, C.R.C. 1978, c. 960 and Indian Timber Regulations, C.R.C. c. 961, amended SOR/93–244, in Shin Imai, *The 1997 Annotated Indian Act* (Scarborough, ON: Carswell, 1996), at 208–17.

15 For example, Indians cannot directly raise environmental issues off reserves even where they have a strong legal interest, if the government has not for-

mally accepted that interest. See the Canadian Environmental Assessment Act, S.C. 1992, c. 37, s. 48, paras. 1(e) and 6. This prohibits Indians from formally questioning most activities which affect their extended environments, such as hunting and fishing off reserve, and the performance of heritage and cultural rights off reserve.

16 For example, the applicable legislation in this case, Planning Act, S.O. 1983, c. 1, contained no provisions for the notice or participation of First Nations in any municipal, environmental, or land-use decision.

17 For an examination of unequal allocations of space in a U.S. urban context, see Richard Thompson Ford, 'The Boundaries of Race: Political Geography in Legal Analysis' (1994) 107 *Harvard Law Review* 1843.

18 Ronen Shamir, 'Suspended in Space: Bedouins under the Law of Israel' (1996) *Journal of Law and Society* 231 at 234.

19 For examples of how zoning and property rights inappropriately bound and constrain the integrity of natural environments in forest, rural, and 'wilderness' lands, and how this might be overcome, see Reed Noss and Allen Cooperrider, *Biodiversity* (Washington: Island Press, 1994), at 129–77; William Alverson et al., 'Zoning for Diversity,' in *Wild Forests: Conservation Biology and Public Policy* (Washington, DC: Island Press, 1994), at 160–78.

20 See introduction.

21 For example, at common law there is a persistent line of cases which assumes away Indigenous environmental cultivation and settlement prior to the arrival of the colonists. See e.g., *Delgamuukw v. British Columbia* (1991), 79 D.L.R. (4th) 185 (B.C.S.C.). See also *Mabo v. Queensland (No. 2)* (1992), 107 A.L.R. 65 for a recitation of this line of cases, and its subsequent overturning in Australia.

22 See Douglas W. Allen, 'Homesteading and Property Rights: or How the West Was Really Won' (1991) 34 *Journal of Law and Economics* 1; Fred S. McChesney, 'Government as Definer of Property Rights: Indian Lands, Ethnic Externalities and Bureaucratic Budgets' (1990) 19 *Journal of Legal Studies* 297; Terry Anderson and Peter Hill, 'The Race for Property Rights' (1990) 33 *Journal of Law and Economics* 177.

23 A notable exception in this regard is airshed emission or watershed-effluent charges, levied by government agencies against known polluters. This pollution tax system attempts to reduce the total pollution in an airshed or watershed. For an evaluation of their effectiveness, see generally G. Bruce Doern, ed., *The Environmental Imperative: Market Approaches to the Greening of Canada* (Toronto: C.D. Howe Institute, 1990); Robert Hahn and Gordon Hester, 'Marketable Permits: Lessons for Theory and Practice' (1989) 16 *Ecology Law Quarterly* 361; David Hoskins, 'Acid Rain, Emissions Trading and the Clean

Air Act Amendments of 1989' (1990) 15 *Columbia Journal of Environmental Law* 329; Brennan Van Dyke, 'Emissions Trading to Reduce Acid Deposition' (1991) 100 *Yale Law Journal* 2707.

24 William Cronon's excellent study of the physical and economic development of Chicago demonstrates that the area's settlement depended on the exploitation of natural ecosystems, and a denial of any connection of this ecosystem to humans. William Cronon, *Nature's Metropolis: Chicago and the Great West* (New York: W.W. Norton, 1991), at 205–6.

25 James [Sakej] Henderson explained that the fracture between ecology, Indigenous peoples, and North American law occurs 'because of the discontinuity in the colonist's mind between the experience of place and language available to describe it ... Colonial writers and artists in Canada have viewed the landscape as negative in their wilderness and civilization dichotomy called the wascousta syndrome. Canadian society has incorporated this negative view into moral and legal coordinates of savage and human, colonized and colonists. This gothic view of the Aboriginal landscape and its inhabitants was viewed as either an unconsciousness or chaos or a kind of existence that is cruel and meaningless.' Sakej Henderson, 'Mikmaw Tenure in Atlantic Canada' (1995) 18 *Dalhousie Law Journal* 196.

26 See Andrew Goudie, *The Human Impact on the Natural Environment*, 4th ed. (Cambridge, MA: MIT Press, 1994) for a discussion of how human activities have degraded vegetation, animals, soil, water, geomorphology, and climate. See Sharon Zukin, *Landscapes of Power: From Detroit to Disneyland* (Berkeley: University of California Press, 1991) for an excellent description of how the globalization of production, and the international transfer of capital has reduced citizens' autonomy in constructing their landscapes.

27 See Jane Jacobs, *The Death and Life of Great American Cities* (New York: Modern Library, 1992); Jane Jacobs, *The Economy of Cities* (New York: Random House, 1988).

28 See Tony Hiss, *The Experience of Place* (New York: Random House, 1990), at 103–25; Jorge Hardoy and David Satterthwaite, eds., *Small and Intermediate Cities: Their Role in Regional and Natural Development in the Third World* (Boulder, CO: Westview Press, 1995).

29 M. Patricia Marchak, *Logging the Globe* (Montreal: McGill-Queen's University Press, 1995).

30 K.A. Kohn, ed., *Balancing on the Brink of Extinction: The Endangered Species Act and Lessons for the Future* (Washington, DC: Island Press, 1991); James A. Burnett et al., *On the Brink: Endangered Species in Canada* (Saskatoon: Western Producer Prairie Books, 1989).

31 For a detailed discussion and statistical tabulation of these trends, see Lester

R. Brown et al. and Worldwatch Institute, *Vital Signs: The Trends That Are Shaping Our Future* (New York: W.W. Norton, 1995) and World Resources Institute, *UNEP and UNDP's Biannual World Resources* report (New York: Oxford University Press, 1996).

32 Stanford University human biologist Peter Vitousek has estimated that humankind is currently 'appropriating' 40 per cent of the products of terrestrial photosynthesis and channelling this biological production through their economies. See Peter Vitousek et al., 'Human Appropriation of the Products of Photosynthesis' (1986) 34 *Bioscience* 368.

33 An excellent historical example of how an alignment of interests, institutions, and ideas can coalesce to exploit the environment for the benefit of certain groups is found in Cronon, *Nature's Metropolis*.

34 Economics is, without a doubt, an extremely significant reason for environmental degradation. Economic reformations are also critical to enhancing our settlements. For an overview of the literature suggesting an integration of economics and ecology see D. Rapport, 'The Interface of Economics and Ecology,' in Ann-Mari Jansson, ed., *Integration of Economy and Ecology: An Outlook for the Eighties* (Stockholm: Asko Laboratory, University of Stockholm, 1984); M. Jacobs, *The Green Economy: Environment, Sustainable Development and the Politics of the Future* (Vancouver: UBC Press, 1991); Joseph Seneca and Michael Taussig, *Environmental Economics*, 3rd ed. (Englewood Cliffs, NJ: Prentice-Hall, 1984). For a discussion of some of the limitations of an economic analysis of the environment see Mark Sagoff, *The Economy of the Earth: Philosophy, Law and the Environment* (Cambridge: Cambridge University Press, 1988).

35 The idea that humans are part of the earth's ecosystems is the foundational premise in Mathis Wackernagel and William Rees, *Our Ecological Footprint: Reducing Human Impact on the Earth* (Gabriola Island, BC: New Society Publishers, 1996).

36 Ibid. at 4. See also Aldo Leopold, *Sand County Almanac and Sketches Here and There* (New York: Oxford University Press, 1949) at 220.

37 G.H. Brundtland and World Commission on Environment and Development, *Our Common Future* (Oxford: World Commission on Environment and Development, 1987).

38 Ibid. at 43.

39 While the numerous definitions of sustainability make it difficult to 'pin down' this concept's meaning, the aspiration for sustainability signals an approach to planning our settlements that is more fully sensitive to the interaction of human activities and the natural environment. For different definitions of sustainable development see Richard Stren et al., eds., *Sustainable*

Cities: Urbanization and the Environment in International Perspective (London: J. Kingsley Publishers, 1992) (focusing on urban sustainability); Herman Daly, 'Sustainable Development: From Concept and Theory towards Operational Principles,' in *Steady State Economics*, 2nd ed. (Washington, DC: Island Press, 1991) at 1 (focusing on the purposeful vagueness of sustainability definitions); P. Christenson, 'Increasing Returns and Ecological Sustainability,' in Robert Costanza, ed., *Ecological Economics: The Science and Management of Sustainability* (New York: Columbia University Press, 1991) (focusing on economic sustainability). For an example of the effect the concept of sustainable development has had on the design and governance of settlements, see Virginia Maclaren, *Sustainable Urban Development in Canada*, vol. 1, *Summary Report* (Toronto: Icurr Press, 1992).

40 For an explanation of why the integration of natural and human activities (particularly economics) can be a problem in creating healthier natural environments, see William Rees, 'Economics, Ecology, and the Limits of Conventional Analysis' (1991) 40–1 *Journal of the Air and Waste Management Association* 1.

41 'Indigenous' can be a problematic term because it is not always clear which groups should be included within its meaning. Inclusion could be determined legally, culturally, or racially, through self-identification, or through any combination of the foregoing. See James Frideres, 'Who Is a Native?' in *Native Peoples in Canada: Contemporary Conflicts*, 4th ed. (Scarborough, ON: Prentice-Hall, 1993), at 24–46. In this paper Indigenous refers to groups of organized societies who can trace their ancestry in North America to a period pre-dating the arrival of colonial (usually European) settlers.

42 Brundtland, *Our Common Future*, at 114–16.

43 For other examples of how First Nations thought may assist in overcoming our democratic and environmental problems, see A.L. Booth, and H.M. Jacobs, 'Ties That Bind: Native American Beliefs as a Foundation for Environmental Consciousness' (1990) 12 *Environmental Ethics* 27; John Ragsdale, 'Law and Environment in Modern America and Among the Hopi Indians: A Comparison of Values' (1986) 10 *Harvard Environmental Law Review* 417.

44 For descriptions of how Indigenous peoples have contributed their knowledge to improve environments, see Eugene N. Anderson, *Ecologies of the Heart: Emotion, Belief and the Environment* (New York: Oxford University Press, 1996).

45 See Roy Rappaport, *Pigs For Ancestors: A Ritual Ecology of a New Guinea People*, 2nd ed. (New Haven, CT: Yale University Press, 1984); J. Donald Hughes, *American Indian Ecology* (El Paso: Texas Western University Press, 1983); Hugh Brody, *Maps and Dreams: Indians and the British Columbia Frontier* (Vancouver: Douglas and McIntyre, 1988). Janis Alcorn, *Huastec Mayan Ethnobotany* (Aus-

tin: University of Texas Press, 1984); Billie DeWalt, 'Using Indigenous Knowledge to Improve Agricultural and Natural Resource Management' (1994) 53 *Human Organization* 123–31; Raymond Firth, *We, The Tikopia* (Boston: Beacon Press, 1936); Robin Riddington, *Little Bit Know Something* (Vancouver: Douglas and McIntyre, 1990); Chris Vescey and Robert Venables, eds., *American Indian Environments: Ecological Issues in Native American History* (Syracuse, NY: Syracuse University Press, 1980). For a contrary view see Robert Edgerton, *Sick Societies: Challenging the Myth of Primitive Harmony* (Toronto: Maxwell Macmillan, 1992); Martin Lewis, *Green Delusions: An Environmental Critique of Radical Environmentalism* (Durham, NC: Duke University Press, 1992).

46 See Eugene Anderson, *Ecologies of the Heart: Emotion, Belief and the Environment* (New York: Oxford University Press, 1996) at 26.

47 Jane Jacobs, *The Death and Life of Great American Cities* (New York: Modern Library, 1992), at 16–7.

48 Indigenous ideas regarding the environment comprise a field of knowledge with its own disciplinary integrity. Through both observation and contemplation Indigenous peoples devised empirically testable methods for checking the impact of certain practices. This methodology also has its limitations. Indigenous insights regarding the environment, while valuable, are partial and must be pooled with information from other disciplines to answer the pressing questions we face.

49 Shepard Kresh III, *The Ecological Indian: Myth and History* (New York: W.W. Norton, 1999).

50 Peoples, as well as lands, can become colonized. Colonialism is not just a process of physical settlement but a 'mode of discourse with supporting institutions, vocabulary, scholarship, imagery, doctrines, even ... bureaucracies and styles.' Edward Said, *Orientalism* (New York: Vintage Books, 1978). As peoples accept and reproduce this discourse, they can become colonized. For an interesting description of how subtly displacing the discourse of colonialism can be, even in a supposedly objective field like mathematics, see Alan J. Bishop, 'Western Mathematics: The Secret Weapon of Cultural Imperialism' (1990) 32 Race and Class 51–65. For a survey of writing in this field, see Bill Ashcroft, Gareth Griffiths, and Helen Tiffin, eds., *The Post-Colonial Studies Reader* (New York: Routledge, 1996).

51 For example, Alaskan Natives have contributed to the degradation of their forest resources. See Frank Cassidy and Norman Dale, *After Native Claims: The Implications of Comprehensive Claims Settlements for Natural Resources in British Columbia* (Lantzville, BC: Oolichan Books and Institute for Research on Public Policy, 1988), at 104–7.

52 Ronald J. Rychlak, 'People as Part of Nature: Reviewing the Law of the Mother,' (1994) 13 *Stanford Environmental Law Journal* 451.

53 However, there is an argument that Indigenous environmental ideas have been partially integrated with broader North American ideologies; some say that the American environmental movement 'was shaped by the influence of prominent Plains' Indians individuals at the turn of the century.' See Gudrun Dahl, 'Environmentalism, Nature and Otherness: Some Perspectives on Our Relations with Small Scale Producers in the Third World,' in Gudrun Dahl, ed., *Green Arguments and Local Subsistence* (Stockholm: Stockholm Studies in Anthropology, 1993) at 6, citing O.D. Schwartz, 'Plains Indian Influences on the American Environmental Movement: Ernest Thompson Seton and Ohiyesa,' in Paul A. Olsen, ed., *The Struggle for the Land: Indigenous Insight and Industrial Empire in the Semi-arid World* (Lincoln: University of Nebraska Press, 1990).

54 Some observers have characterized people's alienation from the natural environment, through suppressing their participation in its use, as 'environmental racism.' Environmental racism can refer to any 'policy, practice or directive that disadvantages (whether intended or unintended) individuals, groups, or communities based on race or color' (but see *Washington v. Davis*, 426 U.S. 229 (1976) where intent was held necessary to discrimination). Under this definition, environmental racism is suffered by Indigenous peoples in both the United States and Canada. Robert Bullard, 'The Threat of Environmental Racism' (1993) 7 *Natural Resources and the Environment* 23 at 24. Race has long been used to exploit the environment; see Williamson Chang, 'The Wasteland in the Western Exploitation of Race and the Environment' (1992) 63 University of Colorado Law Review 849; Robert Bullard, *Dumping in Dixie: Race, Class and Environmental Quality* (Boulder, CO: Westview Press, 1990); Rick Whaley and Walter Bresette, *Walleye Warriors: An Effective Alliance against Racism and for the Earth* (Philadelphia: New Society Publishers, 1994).

55 This observation was first made by Felix Cohen, *Handbook of Federal Indian Law* (Washington, DC: U.S. Government Printing Office, 1942), introduction.

56 For example, the cancers caused by uranium pollution on the Serpent River Reserve west of Espanola, Ontario, alerted other non-Native communities in the area to the injuries they would face if they did not react. See Claudia Notzke, *Aboriginal People and Natural Resources in Canada* (North York, ON: Captus Press, 1993), at 305–7; *Uranium* (Ottawa: National Film Board of Canada, 1985).

57 Ironically, the denial of Indigenous participation has led to large loopholes that could pose a danger to surrounding non-Native communities. For example, in the United States some Indian reserves have sited nuclear waste in their lands to produce greater revenues. This poses a threat to surround-

ing state and local authorities, and there are few opportunities for these external communities to participate in tribal decisions. Nation-to-nation cooperation and harmonization of Indian, federal, state, and provincial law may create incentives to deter these activities within First Nations. For contrasting opinions on the appropriateness of Indigenous control over nuclear waste siting see Nancy B. Collins and Andrea Hall, 'Nuclear Waste in Indian Country: A Paradoxical Trade' (1994) 12 *Law and Inequality Journal* 267; Kevin Gover and Jana Walker, 'Escaping Environmental Paternalism: One Tribe's Approach to Developing a Commercial Waste Project in Indian Country' (1992) 63 *University of Colorado Law Review* 933.

58 The 'law and community' literature explores how law shapes social life in places far removed from the formal domain of courts. See Austin Sarat and Thomas Kearns, *Law in Everyday Life* (Ann Arbor: University of Michigan Press, 1993); Robert Ellickson, *Order without Law: How Neighbors Settle Disputes* (Cambridge: Harvard University Press, 1991); Carol Greenhouse et al., *Law and Community in Three American Towns* (Ithaca, NY: Cornell University Press, 1994); John Conley and William O'Barr, *Rules versus Relationships: The Ethnography of Legal Discourse* (Chicago: University of Chicago Press, 1990); Robert Post, ed., *Law and the Order of Culture* (Berkeley: University of California Press, 1991).

59 See Alan Hunt, 'Law, Community, and Everyday Life: Yngvesson's Virtuous Citizens and Disruptive Subjects' (1996) 21 *Law and Social Inquiry* 179.

60 Similar and supporting examples of the suppression of Indigenous participation in shaping their environment are found in Joe Carillo, 'Identity as Idiom: Mashpee Reconsidered' (1995) 28 *Indiana Law Review* 517 at 544–51; Charles Wilkinson, 'Home Dance, the Hopi, and the Black Mesa: Conquest and Endurance in the American Southwest' (1996) *Brigham Young University Law Review* 449–82; Winona LaDuke, 'A Society Based on Conquest Cannot be Sustained: Native Peoples and the Environmental Crisis,' in Richard Hofrichter, ed., *Toxic Struggles: The Theory and Practice of Environmental Justice* (Philadelphia: New Society Publishers, 1993), at 98–106.

61 For a similar argument in another context, see Sakej Henderson, 'Mikmaw Tenure in Atlantic Canada' (1995) 18 *Dalhousie Law Journal* 196 at 207.

62 Anderson, *Ecologies of the Heart*, at 17, 33.

63 For further descriptions of a methodology that allows for the bringing of racial and minority perspectives to legal writing, see Robin D. Barnes, 'Race Consciousness: The Thematic Content of Racial Distinctiveness in Critical Race Scholarship' (1990) 103 *Harvard Law Review* 1864; Derrick Bell, 'Racial Reflections: Dialogues in the Direction of Liberation' (1990) 37 *U.C.L.A. Law Review* 1037; Angela Harris, 'Race and Essentialism in Feminist Legal

Theory' (1990) 42 *Stanford Law Review* 581; Mari Matsuda, 'Looking to the Bottom: Critical Legal Studies and Reparations' (1987) 22 *Harvard Civil Rights-Civil Liberties Law Review* 323; Mari Matsuda, 'Affirmative Action and Legal Knowledge: Planting Seeds in Plowed Up Ground' (1988) 11 *Harvard Women's Law Journal* 1; Patricia Monture, *Ka-Nin-Geh-A-Sa-Nonh-Ya-Gah* (1986) 2 *Canadian Journal of Women and the Law* 159; Robert A. Williams, Jr, 'Taking Rights Aggressively: The Perils and Promise of Critical Legal Theory for People of Color' (1987) 5 *Law and Inequality Journal* 103.

64 See John Borrows, 'Constitutional Law from a First Nations Perspective: Self Government and the Royal Proclamation' (1994) 28 *University of British Columbia Law Review* 1.

65 *Canada: Indian Treaties and Surrenders*, 1891 ed., repr., vol. 1 (Toronto: Coles, 1993), at 113.

66 *R. v. Jones and Nadjiwon*, [1993] 3 Can. Native Law R. 182 (Ont. Prov. Div.).

67 John Borrows, 'A Genealogy of Law: Inherent Sovereignty and First Nations Self-Government' (1992) 30 *Osgoode Hall Law Journal* 291 at 319–36. My great-great grandfather, Peter Kegedonce Jones, was the lead signature on this treaty.

68 The Indian agent had great control over Indian land transactions and this sale raises large issues of conflict of interest and violations of the government's fiduciary duty to the Indians. Letter from Chief Ralph Akiwenzie, Chippewas of Nawash, and Chief Richard Kahgee, Chippewas of Saugeen, to Judith Coward, Plans Administration Branch, Ministry of Municipal Affairs (17 December 1992) (on file with author).

69 *Canada: Indian Treaties and Surrenders* 416A & B, vol. 3 at 267–9.

70 The validity of the surrender and sale of Hay Island has been called into question by the Joint Council of Neyaashinigmiing and Saugeen and is still the subject of an outstanding land claim. The Chippewas of the Saugeen are a neighbouring reservation of Anishinabek people who have the same history and legal interests in the area as Neyaashinigmiing.

71 An Official Plan is a planning document which contains goals, objectives, and policies to manage and direct physical change of a geographic district. It is developed by land-use planners in consultation with politicians and affected citizens.

72 *County of Bruce Planning and Economic Development Report*, No. 21–92 (24 June 1992).

73 Letter from Brenda Elliot, minister, to Chief Ralph Akiwenzie (14 September 1995) (on file with author). Save for noting that the developer must complete a Schedule C Class EA process, the development is presently slated to go ahead.

74 As such, Neyaashinigmiing is requesting a hearing before the Ontario Municipal Board in order to make environmental impacts known. Letter from Ralph Akiwenzie, Chief of the Chippewas of the Nawash, to Al Leach, Minister of Municipal Affairs (3 November 1995) (on file with author).

75 Chief Akiwenzie coincidentally noticed a small advertisement in the paper for meeting about development on Hay Island. Had this small announcement been missed, even today we may still not have known about the proposal.

76 However, even after the Nawash became aware of the proposed development, they were only invited to one meeting with the proponents and received one follow-up letter from them. Correspondence of W.D. Scott, Cuesta Planning Consultants, to Darlene Johnston, legal counsel to the joint councils (13 September 1993) (on file with author). Such interaction and limited participation between the parties is hardly conducive to the sharing of meaningful information relative to environmental planning for the project.

77 In fact, the number of houses proposed for the Hay Island development would represent approximately half the houses currently on the reserve. For environmental planning purposes, you cannot increase the population of a remote and environmentally sensitive area by one-third and not address the impact of these numbers.

78 *County of Bruce Planning and Economic Development Report*; Armstrong, *Planning Report*, at 9.

79 Letter from Chief Ralph Akiwenzie, Chippewas of Nawash, and Chief Richard Kahgee, Chippewas of Saugeen, to Judith Coward, Plans Administration Branch, Ministry of Municipal Affairs (17 December 1992). However, there were informal talks about mainland access with one individual on the reserve. This person held reserve land under a certificate of possession (a ticket of permission to occupy) across from the Island and did not disclose these talks to the Band Council. For judicial discussion of an individual's legal interest in individual land holdings on Canadian Indian reservations see *Boyer v. Canada* (1986), 26 D.L.R. (4th) 284, leave to appeal to S.C.C. refused (1986), 72 N.R. 365.

80 Letter from Chief Ralph Akiwenzie, Chippewas of Nawash, and Chief Richard Kahgee, Chippewas of Saugeen, to Judith Coward, Plans Administration Branch, Ministry of Municipal Affairs (17 December 1992) at 2.

81 Armstong, *Planning Report*, at 9.

82 Letter of Ralph Akiwenzie, Chief of Chippewas of the Nawash, to planner, Chris Laforest, County of Bruce Planning and Economic Development (24 July 1992) (on file with author).

83 See *Boyer v. Canada*. I should also disclose that the Mr Jones referred to in the above circumstances is my uncle, and that I have no financial interest in any of these events.

84 Conversation with Darlene Johnston, Chippewa Land Claims Researcher (12 April 1996).

85 See Stewart Elgie, 'Injunctions, Ancient Forests and Irreparable Harm: A Comment on *Western Canada Wilderness Committee v. A.G. British Columbia*' (1991) 25 *University of British Columbia Law Review* 387; Andrew Roman, 'From Judicial Economy to Access to Justice: Standing and Class Actions,' in Canadian Bar Association, *Environmental Law: An Environmental Primer* (Toronto: Canadian Bar Association, 1991).

86 Canadian federal authority over 'Indians, and Lands reserved for the Indians' stems from s. 91(24) of the Constitution Act, 1867 (U.K.), 30 & 31 Vict., c. 3, and from a fiduciary obligation to uphold the honour of the Crown in dealing with Indians. *R. v. Sparrow*, [1990] 1 S.C.R. 1075 U.S. federal authority over 'Indian Tribes' arises from the constitution's Commerce and Treaty Provision in Article I, section 8, clause 3, and through a judicially created 'plenary power' (see *U.S. v. Sandoval*, 231 U.S. 28 (1913); *Morton v. Mancari*, 417 U.S. 535 (1974); *U.S. v. Wheeler*, 435 U.S. 313, 319 (1978)).

87 Stephen Crawford, PhD (Zoology), also expressed a similar concern. Letter of Stephen Crawford to Ed Philips, Minister of Municipal Affairs (10 November 1994) (on file with author).

88 Peter Schmalz, PhD, The Saugeen-Ojibway Fishery: Historic Use And Contemporary Practice (1990) (on file with author).

89 *If Only You Would Ask Us.* Videotape. (Toronto: McClean-Hunter, 1993) (Interview with Wilmer Nadjiwon, elder).

90 For a history of Great Lakes Anishinabe fisheries and a description of their fishery practices, see R. Doherty, *Disputed Waters: Native Americans and the Great Lakes Fishery* (Lexington: University of Kentucky Press, 1990); Charles Cleland, 'The Inland Shore Fishery of the North Great Lakes: Its Development and Importance in Pre-History' (1982) 47 *American Antiquity* 761–85; Tim E. Holtzkamm et al., 'Rainy River Sturgeon: An Ojibway Resource in the Fur Trade Economy,' in Kerry Abel and Jean Friesen, eds., *Aboriginal Resource Use in Canada: Historical and Legal Aspects* (Winnipeg: University of Manitoba Press, 1991), at 119.

91 For example, on 16 August 1996 the people of Neyaashinigmiing imposed a moratorium on all fishing for food or trade because of the scarcity of all species within their waters. The moratorium will be lifted when there is evidence of increased stocks. See Chippewas of the Nawash, Band Council Motion No. 355.

92 Successful examples of the integration of Indigenous knowledge regarding water quality and fish habitat can be found. See Evelyn Pinkerton, ed., *Co-operative Management of Local Fisheries* (Vancouver: UBC Press, 1989), 1–73, 137–291.

93 See Richard Yarnell, *Aboriginal Relationships Between Culture and Plant Life in the Upper Great Lakes Region* (Ann Arbor: University of Michigan Press, 1964); Charles Cleland, *The Prehistoric Animal Ecology and Ethnozoology of the Upper Great Lakes Region* (Ann Arbor: University of Michigan Press, 1966); Charles Bishop, *The Northern Ojibwa and the Fur Trade: An Historical and Ecological Study* (Toronto: Holt Rinehart and Winston, 1974).

94 See Basil Johnston, *Ojibway Heritage* (Toronto: McClelland and Stewart, 1976), at 71.

95 Harold Hickerson, *The Chippewa and their Neighbours: A Study in Ethnohistory* (New York: Holt Rinehart and Winston, 1970).

96 For a commentary which discusses the Indigenous 'sense of place,' see James Anaya, 'Native Land Claims in the United States: The Un-Atoned-for Spirit of Place' (1994) 18 *Cultural Survival Quarterly* 52.

97 See Johnston, *Ojibway Heritage*, at 43.

98 See Archives of Ontario (AO), Manuscript (MS) 108, Cape Croker Reserve Records, Box 103.

99 The Hay Island plan also failed to consider the importance of the two open areas on the island to the deer population, and how the resort's location would subject these fields to heavy use. The deer of Hay Island interact with the deer at Neyaashiinigming by swimming across the water in summer or, more likely, crossing the ice in winter. The proposed development did not consider the increased pressure the use of this open space would place on the two deer populations by creating a situation of greater competition between them. Some people in our community know much about the deer behaviour and migration patterns. Their participation in the settlement's design could have been very valuable in creating a more sustainable future for the deer, for the Anishinabek, and for future Hay Island residents, who would enjoy the presence of wildlife in their midst.

In order to use and conserve animal resources more efficiently the Anishinabek seasonally hunt in different locations according to where they find adequate numbers of deer. This practice allows the people of Neyaashiinigming to reduce pressure on a population by leaving certain hunting grounds fallow from year to year. Many Anishinabek hunting grounds are only used every third year, depending on the size of the animal population. Baron De Lahontan, *New Voyages to North American*, vol. 1 (New York: Burt Franklin, 1905), 210, 319, 481–3. This rotational movement and use of hunting grounds can settle 'into well established patterns, an annual round' (Doherty, *Disputed Waters* at 11–12), which enables the Anishinabek to keep track of deer populations over a large area. Had they been able to participate in the Hay Island proposal, the Anishinabek could have provided important information about the abundance or scarcity of deer in different traditional hunting sites located at some distance from the island. Informed decisions could then have been made about the particular impact of the Hay Island proposal on the overall health and numbers of deer in the area. Since this consultation did not occur, an important opportunity to enhance understanding about animal populations in the environment has been lost.

100 In the winter of 1995, our forester took Nation lawyer Darlene Johnston and myself to the west shores of the reserve and showed us a fascinating discovery. There, along the top of a long serpentine shaped hill, just below the bluff, were indentations regularly spaced at twenty-foot intervals – a burial ground!

101 After all, it was the oral tradition within our community that maintained the memory of these sites. Oral tradition from my great aunt Irene holds that before contact people would visit Neyaashiinigming from as far away as Lake Superior. They would come to be healed in the bays. Those who did not respond were buried below the bluffs in the surrounding area.

102 Cemeteries Act (Revised) R.S.O., c. C.4., s. 71(1)(a), 72. A similar result is found in U.S. law. See *Newman v. State of Florida*, 174 So. 2d 479, 483 (Fla. Dist. Ct. App. 1965), where a college student found a skull in the Everglades. The skull was that of a Seminole Indian who had died two years earlier. The student was charged with maliciously disturbing the contents of a grave. The court concluded that the burial did not come under the protection of the cemetery laws because it was in an unmarked grave, even though this was the Seminole custom. For information and discussion of the (mis)treatment of Indigenous burial sites in the United States, see the Native American Graves Protection and Repatriation Act, 25 U.S.C. at 3001, et seq. P.L. 101–601; Margaret Bowman, 'The Reburial of Native American Skeletal Remains: Approaches to the Resolution of a Conflict' (1989) 13 Harvard Environmental Law Journal 147; Jack Trope and Walter Echo Hawk, '*Native American Graves Protection and Repatriation Act*: Background and Legal History' (1992) 24 *Arizona State Law Journal* 35.

103 Finally, the suppression of Neyaashiinigming's participation in the Hay Island proposal also prevented other important public policy issues from being canvassed. For example, Hay Island is currently the subject of a land claim, and any development may be premature and prejudice both the land claim and the resort. What happens if the land claim is ruled as valid, and

the development has already begun? Could the developer be forced to consider selling the site to the government, in trust, for the Chippewa, and thus forfeit sunk costs expended on preliminary development activities? Would the commencement of the development negatively affect the remedies a judge would be willing to give the reserve? Might the land no longer be regarded as returnable if there are significant financial interests on it? The social and cultural consequences of placing such a development beside a reserve while these issues remain outstanding need to be considered in any full environmental planning exercise. Without such consideration, both the reserve and the owners of Hay Island could stand to lose a great deal in social and economic environmental terms.

104 The same jurisdictional problem exists in the United States. See Judith V. Royster and Rory Snow Arrow Fausett, 'Control of the Reservation Environment: Tribal Primacy, Federal Delegation, and the Limits of State Intrusion' (1989) 64 *Washington Law Review* 581; Charles Wilkinson, 'Cross-Jurisdictional Conflicts: Analysis of Legitimate State Interests on Federal and Indian Lands' (1982) 2 U.C.L.A. *Journal of Environmental Law and Policy* 145.

105 However, there are similarities between First Nations and municipalities for other purposes. See Kevin Worthen, 'Two Sides of the Same Coin: The Potential Normative Power of American Cities and Indian Tribes' (1991) 44 *Vanderbilt Law Review* 1273; *Otineka Development Corp. v. The Queen*, [1994] 2 C.N.L.R. 83 (T.C.C.) (Indian bands/tribes are like municipalities for tax exemption purposes).

106 For further discussion of provincial relations with Indigenous peoples, see J. Anthony Long and Menno Boldt, eds., *Governments in Conflict: Provinces and Indian Nations in Canada* (Toronto: University of Toronto Press, 1988); David Hawkes, ed., *Aboriginal Peoples and Government Responsibility: Exploring Federal and Provincial Roles* (Ottawa: Carleton University Press, 1989). For a thoughtful article which suggests that provinces may have obligations to Indigenous peoples in any event, see Leonard Rotman, 'Provincial Fiduciary Obligations to First Nations: The Nexus between Governmental Power and Responsibility' (1994) 32 *Osgoode Hall Law Journal* 736.

107 Menno Boldt, *Surviving as Indians: The Challenge of Self-Government* (Toronto: University of Toronto Press, 1993), at 111.

108 The confrontational use of blockades and direct action is briefly described by Peter Blue Cloud, 'Resistance at Oka,' in Peter Naboy, ed., *Native American Testimony: A Chronicle of Indian-White Relations from Prophecy to the Present, 1492–1992* (New York: Viking Press, 1992).

109 For an example of a more successful inclusion of Indigenous peoples in environmental decision making, see Wendy Espeland, 'Legally Mediated

Identity: *The National Environmental Policy Act* and the Bureaucratic Construction of Interests' (1994) 28 *Law and Society Review* 1149.

110 When environmental costs are not internalized, resource exploitation is described as being analogous to a drug addiction. Resource extraction in a local economy usually continues long after such use is sustainable and reduces the carrying capacity of the resource. Subsidies are then given to these dependent communities, which further reduces net wealth. Eventually, the resource is depleted, the community searches for other resource extractive industries, and the cycle of dependence is played over again. See William Freudenburg, 'Addictive Economies: Extractive Industries and Vulnerable Localities in a Changing World Economy' (1992) 57 *Rural Sociology* 305. For a more optimistic view, see Thomas Michael Power, 'Thinking about Natural Resource Dependent Economies: Moving beyond the Folk Economics of the Rear View Mirror,' in Richard Knight and Sarah Bates, eds., *A New Century for Natural Resources Management* (Washington, DC: Island Press, 1995), at 235–53.

111 Some have argued that people will always devalue the future in comparison to the present. See George Ainslie, *Picoeconomics: The Strategic Interaction of Successive Motivational States with the Person* (Cambridge: Cambridge University Press, 1993). Such future discounting is problematic for sustainability. David Pearce and R. Kerry Turner, *Economics of Natural Resources and the Environment* (Brighton: Harvester Wheatsheaf, 1990) at 129, 158, 211. Some however have written that any predisposition to sacrifice the future to the present can be overcome; see Barry S. Gower, 'What Do We Owe Future Generations?' in David Cooper and Joy Palmer, eds., *The Environment in Question: Ethics and Global Issues* (New York: Routledge, 1992).

112 A classic popular recital of the denial of Native Americans' land rights is Dee Brown, *Bury My Heart at Wounded Knee* (Toronto: Bantam Books, 1970).

113 Laurence A. French, ed., *The Winds of Injustice: American Indians and the U.S. Government* (New York: Garland Publishers, 1994).

114 The isolation of citizens from their governments has led to serious questions about the capacity of republican democracy to sustain its legitimacy. Jean Bethke Elshtain, *Democracy on Trial* (Don Mills, ON: Anansi, 1995); Jonathan Raush, *Demosclerosis: The Silent Killer of American Government* (New York: Times Books, 1994).

115 Arguments about the removal of citizens from the political process and their replacement with artificial structures can be found in Joel Bakan, *Just Words: Constitutional Rights and Social Wrongs* (Toronto: University of Toronto Press, 1997), esp. at chap. 6; Alan Hutchinson, *Waiting for Coraf: A Critique of Law and Rights* (Toronto: University of Toronto Press, 1995), at chap. 5.

116 For concerns about U.S. constitutional discourse, see Glenn H. Reynolds, 'Prenumbral Reasoning on the Right' (1992) 140 *University of Pennsylvania Law Review* 1333 at 1346–8. For Canadian constitutional concerns see, generally, 'The Quebec Referendum and Its Aftermath' (1996) 7 *Constitutional Forum*. For First Nations constitutional concerns, see John R. Wunder, *Retained by the People: The History of American Indians and the Bill of Rights* (New York: Oxford University Press, 1994); Andrew Orkin, *Sovereign Injustice: Forcible Inclusion of the James Bay Crees and Cree Territory into a Sovereign Quebec* (Fullict, QC: Grand Council of the Crees, 1996).

117 The subordination of citizens to special interests groups in the United States has been described in Mancur Olson, *The Rise and Decline of Nations: Economic Growth, Stagflation and Social Rigidities* (New Haven, CT: Yale University Press, 1982); Raush, *Demosclerosis* at 17–20, 64–97. An account of how Indigenous peoples in the United States were subject to special interest groups is found in Russel Barsh and James Youngblood Henderson, *The Road: Indian Tribes and Political Liberty* (Berkeley: University of California Press, 1980), at 31–136. For a series of essays discussing the domination of Indigenous peoples by special interest groups in Canada, see Ian Getty and Antoine Lussier, eds., *As Long as the Sun Shines and the Water Flows: A Reader in Canadian Native Studies* (Vancouver: UBC Press, 1990), at 29–190.

118 In the 1980s, of thirty-two democratic countries surveyed, voter turnout for elections in both the United States and Canada ranked in the lower bottom quarter. Jerome H. Black, 'Reforming the Context of the Voting Process in Canada: Lessons from Other Democracies,' in Herman Bakvis, ed., *Voter Turnout in Canada* (Toronto: Dundurn Press, 1991), at 61. For a discussion of First Nations voter turnout in Canada, see Robert A. Milen, ed., *Aboriginal Peoples and Electoral Reform in Canada* (Ottawa: Dundurn Press, 1991).

119 See Christopher Lasch, *The Revolt of Elites and the Betrayal of Democracy* (New York: W.W. Norton, 1995). In Canada see André Blais and Elisabeth Gidengil, *Making Representative Democracy Work* (Toronto: Dundurn Press, 1991), at 34–41.

120 For an excellent article linking the decline of citizen participation with the degrading of our social and natural environments, see Gerald Frug, 'The City as a Legal Concept' (1980) 93 *Harvard Law Review* 1059. It should also be noted that for many lower income groups, there was little or no decline or loss of participation in their environments: their class or racial status obstructed their participation from the outset.

121 See e.g., 'Overview,' in David Butler and Austin Ranney, eds., *Referendums: A Comparative Study of Practice and Theory* (Washington, DC: American Enterprise Institute for Public Policy Research, 1978).

122 The progressives of an earlier generation called for the creation of direct democracy. See Joseph P. Zimmerman, *Participatory Democracy: Populism Revived* (New York: Praeger, 1986). Direct democracy as it is advocated today usually refers to instruments such as the referendum, initiative, and recall. Referendums are votes to approve or disapprove of issues or laws passed by legislatures. See David MacDonald, 'Referendums and Federal General Elections in Canada,' in Michael Cassidy, ed., *Democratic Rights and Electoral Reform in Canada* (Ottawa: Dundurn Press, 1991), at 301. The recall is a device whereby elected officials are subject to the review and discharge of the electors whose votes put them in office. Peter McCormick, 'Provision for the Recall of Elected Officials: Parameters and Prospects,' in ibid. at 269. An initiative is a law written by the populace. For descriptions of the contemporary use of instruments of direct democracy, see Thomas Cronin, *Direct Democracy: The Politics of Initiative, Referendum and Recall* (Cambridge: Harvard University Press, 1989); Patrick Boyer, *Lawmaking by the People: Referendums and Plebiscites in Canada* (Toronto: Butterworths, 1982); A. Stewart, *The Initiative, Referendum and Recall: Theory and Applications* (Monticello, IL: Vance Bibliographies, 1983); Laura Tallian, *Direct Democracy: An Historical Analysis of the Initiative, Referendum and Recall Process* (Los Angeles: Los Angeles Peoples Lobby, 1977).

123 The theory is that people may be more likely to be satisfied with their governments and abide by their laws if they feel that they are responsible for creating them. Nevil Johnson, 'Types of Referendum,' in Austin Ranney, ed., *The Referendum Device: A Conference* (Washington, DC: American Institute for Public Policy Research, 1981), at 26. Furthermore, supporters of direct democracy state that it will 'produce an open educated debate on issues which otherwise might have been inadequately addressed.' Speech to the U.S. Senate by Senator Mark Hatfield, Cong. Rec., vol. 25, no. 11 (5 February 1979), as quoted in Everett D. Ladd, *The American Polity: The People and Their Government* (New York: W.W. Norton, 1985), at 102.

124 See R.P. Fairfield, ed., *The Federalist Papers* No. 10 (Garden City, NJ: Anchor Books, Doubleday & Co., 1966), at 20 (James Madison). Madison also noted, 'If a majority be united by a common interest, the rights of the minority will be insecure.' Ibid. No. 51 at 323. This caused him to conclude that the administration of government 'in person' leads to faction, injustice, and oppression.

125 See, e.g., Douglas Hasio, 'Invisible Cities: The Constitutional Status of Direct Democracy in a Democratic Republic' (1992) 41 *Duke Law Journal* 1267 at 1270; Julian Eule, 'Judicial Review of Direct Democracy' (1990) 99

Yale Law Journal 1503; Glenn H. Reynolds, 'Is Democracy Like Sex?' (1995) 48 *Vanderbilt Law Review* 1635 at 1648–54.

126 Derrick Bell, 'The Referendum: Democracy's Barrier to Racial Equality' (1978) 54 *Washington Law Review* 1 at 13. Moreover, direct democracy itself may be as open to manipulation by elected officials as representative legislative processes. The often simple 'Yes' and 'No' answers found in most direct ballots do not necessarily reveal the popular interest behind the votes. Furthermore, if during a campaign there are highly contested positions with complex and overlapping interests there is ample room for legislators to place their own interpretation on the results of a vote. For arguments about the difficulty of judging a majority's will, see William Riker, *Liberalism against Populism: A Confrontation between the Theory of Democracy and the Theory of Social Change* (San Francisco: W.H. Freeman, 1982); J. Coleman and John Freejohn, 'Democracy and Social Choice' (1986) 97 Ethics 11.

127 For an interesting call for the extension of rights to the environment, which could be read to include voting rights, see Christopher Stone, 'Should Trees Have Standing?' (1972) 45 *Southern California Law Review* 450; Lawrence Tribe, 'Ways Not to Think about Plastic Trees: New Foundations for Environmental Law' (1974) 83 *Yale Law Journal* 1315. For a criticism of the view that 'things' in the environment have rights, see P.S. Elder, 'Legal Rights for Nature: The Wrong Answer to the Right(s) Question' (1984) 22 *Osgoode Hall Law Journal* 309.

128 Other minority communities could also contribute important knowledge concerning improved settlements.

129 For one model of how an Indigenous group successfully integrated political and ecological activities within its own territory, see Paul Nissenbaum and Paul Shardle, 'Building a System for Land-Use Planning: A Case Study for the Puyallup Tribe,' in Stephen Cornell and Joseph Kalt, eds., *What Can Tribes Do? Strategies and Institutions in American Indian Economic Development* (Los Angeles: American Indian Studies Center, 1992), at 135–78.

130 This occurred in Ontario's 1994 Planning Act, S.O. 1983, c. 1. However, the Planning Act is now being rewritten by the new government in Ontario, and the provision relating to First Nations has been removed.

131 For empirical research regarding the importance of procedure in democracies see Tom Tyler, 'Multiculturalism and the Viability of Democratic Societies' (paper presented to the Law and Society Summer Workshop, 1996) (unpublished, on file with author). A list of some of the substantive elements of democracy is found in 'Special Issue: Approaching Democracy: A New Legal Order for Europe' (1991) 58 *University of Chicago Law Review* 439.

132 Incorporation of Aboriginal ideas and institutions into the existing regime, while helpful, could not fully accommodate the different orientations Indigenous peoples have to the land. For a discussion of these differences, see Sakej Henderson, 'Mikmaw Tenure in Atlantic Canada' (1995) 18 *Dalhousie Law Journal* at 216–36. Aboriginal visions of land and entitlements within their Indigenous federation were unlike the European legal notion of property. The Aboriginal vision of property was of ecological space that creates our consciousness, not an ideological construct or a fungible resource. Ibid. at 217.

133 For a discussion of how the integration of different discourses can occur see James Bond White, *Justice as Translation* (Chicago: Chicago University Press, 1990), at 3–21. For Indigenous peoples it is important that integration does not become assimilation in order that our cultures can survive. White's proposal concerning the integration of language is healthy because he assumes both that culture will retain something and that it will change in response to encounters with another culture.

134 Ibid. at 1.

135 An Aboriginal world-view is a spatial consciousness rather than a material consciousness. See Henderson, 'Mikmaw Tenure in Atlantic Canada,' at 219.

136 John Nadjiwon was a friend of my grandfather. They used to go hunting together and over the years my grandfather shared many stories with him. John told me these stories in this context, and I pass them along in the same way to acknowledge the influence of my grandfather in their continuation.

137 *Nanabush the Trickster v. Ducks, Mudhen and Geese* 0004 Ojibway Cases (1st) 3 (Anishinabe Supreme Court) (Time Immemorial). G.E. Laidlaw wrote the judgment of John York, Alec Philemon and Rose Holliday concurring, Justice Windigo dissenting. See Laidlaw, 'Ojibway Myths and Tales'; Richard Dorson, *Bloodstoppers and Bearwalkers* (Cambridge: Harvard University Press, 1952), at 49.

138 For a discussion of the problems of defining resources as 'natural,' because some interceding human agency is required to define them as such, see William Cronon, *Changes in the Land: Indians, Colonists and the Ecology of New England* (New York: Hill and Wang, 1983), at 165.

139 The mudhen escaped too, but in the commotion Nanabush stepped on its feet. This duck is now called the Diver, and it still has red eyes today because of the smoke from Nanabush's lodge.

140 Other members of the body are left as watchmen in different tellings of this story.

141 The blood touched some leaves, which ever after became known as red willows. When red willows are mixed with tobacco and burned, it is said they provide a better smoke.

142 See Christopher Vescey, *Traditional Ojibway Religion and its Historical Changes* (Philadelphia: American Philosophical Society, 1983) at 145.

143 Edward Benton-Banai, *The Mishomis Book: The Voice of the Ojibway* (Hayward, Wis.: Indian Country Communications, 1998), at 56. Personal care is a law Nanabush learned from the raccoon, and taught to the Anishinabe. For the incident which teaches respect and thanks for gifts from the earth, see the 'Legend of the Three Sisters,' in Gerald Haltiner, *Stories the Red People Told* (Aspena, MI: G. Haltiner, 1951), at 16.

144 *Bears, Bees et al. v. Rabbits* 0003 Ojibway Cases (1st) 30 (Anishinabe Supreme Court) (Time Immemorial). Judgment appears in Johnston, *Ojibway Heritage*, at 44; Louise J. Walker, concurring, *Legends of Green Sky Hill* (Grand Rapids, MI: Eerdmans, 1959), at 27. Basil Johnston lives at Neyaashinigmiing.

145 See the earlier holding of *Nanabush v. Deer, Wolf, et al.*

146 I have been asked, usually by non-lawyers, why do you let your audience down by telling this allegory which gives a simple answer to environmental questions that could be better resolved, in a more sophisticated way, through a number of other disciplinary approaches? I respond that I agree that the question could be effectively answered through other approaches. However, I also note that I am not aware of any widespread common law principles in either Canada or the United States which directly raise or protect the environment in the way these cases suggest. I use Anishinabe law to illustrate the importance of these principles because the common law does not do so.

147 See Henderson, 'Mikmaw Tenure in Atlantic Canada,' at 220–21. This paper argues that the structure of North American legal language, used to describe our settlements and democracy, should recognize the shared space of Indigenous and non-Indigenous peoples. This may assist in the creation of a 'tradition of responsible action.'

148 I would like to thank Matthew Kirchner for bringing this point to my attention.

149 Supporting arguments concerning the application of restorative principles in environmental law are found in Diane Saxe, 'Reflections on Environmental Restoration' (1992) 2 *Journal of Environmental Law and Policy* 77.

150 As will be recalled, Anishinabe law on this point was also drawn from *Nanabush v. Deer, Wolf, et al.*

151 My family is the Otter totem. It is the medicine clan and it is our responsibility to guard and share these powers. A description of the Anishinabe clan

system is found in Verna Ruth Landes, *The Ojibway Woman* (New York: W.W. Norton, 1971).

152 This experience was so memorable to me because it reminded me of a story my great-great-great-great-great grandmother has passed down to us. It is now recorded as 'Jewel Weed' in Verna Patronella Johnson, *Tales of Nikomis* (Don Mills, ON: Musson Book Co., 1975), at 14–17.

Chapter 3

1 Penny Petrone, *Native Literature in Canada: From Oral Traditions to the Present* (Toronto: Oxford University Press, 1990), at 16.

2 Lenore Keeshig-Tobias, quoted in Hartmut Lutz, *Contemporary Challenges: Conversations with Canadian Native Authors* (Saskatoon: Fifth House, 1991), at 85.

3 Gerald Vizenor, *The People Named the Chippewa: Narrative Histories* (Minneapolis: University of Minnesota Press, 1984), at 4.

4 For a composite Trickster Story, see Thomas King, 'The One about Coyote Going West,' in Thomas King, ed., *All My Relations: An Anthology of Canadian Native Fiction* (Toronto: McClelland & Stewart, 1990).

5 Daniel David Moses, 'The Trickster Theatre of Tomson Highway' (1987) 60 *Canadian Fiction Magazine* 88.

6 See Barbara Babcock Adams, 'A Tolerated Margin of Mess: The Trickster and His Tales Reconsidered' (1975) 11 *Journal of Folklore Institute* 147; Henry Rowe Schoolcraft, 'Historical and Methodological Perspectives,' in Andrew Wiget, ed., *Critical Essays on Native American Literature* (Boston: G.K. Hall, 1985) at 21; John Borrows, 'Constitutional Law From a First Nations Perspective: Self-Government and the Royal Proclamation' (1994) 28 *University of British Columbia Law Review* 1 at 6–10; Gerald Vizenor, *The Trickster of Liberty: Tribal Heirs to a Wild Baronage* (Minneapolis: University of Minnesota Press, 1988).

7 For a series of articles that examines the similarities and differences between jurisprudence and stories, see Peter Brooks and Paul Gewirtz, *Law's Stories: Narrative and Rhetoric in the Law* (New Haven: Yale University Press, 1996).

8 See James Boyd White, *Justice as Translation* (Chicago: University of Chicago Press, 1990), at 255: 'To attempt to translate puts you in a place between texts, between languages.'

9 See Jürgen Habermas, *Justification and Application: Remarks on Discourse Ethics* (Cambridge, MA: MIT Press, 1993).

10 For further discussion on the use of this methodology, see Charles Taylor,

Philosophy and the Human Sciences (Cambridge: Cambridge University Press, 1985), at 116–33; Charles Taylor, 'The Politics of Recognition,' in Amy Gutman and Charles Taylor, eds., *Multiculturalism and the Politics of Recognition* (Princeton: Princeton University Press, 1992); Borrows, 'Constitutional Law From a First Nations Perspective,' at 1–10.

11 For a discussion of how racialized perspectives can create alternative legal interpretations, see Richard Devlin, 'We Can't Go on Together with Suspicious Minds: Judical Bias and Racialized Perspective in *R. v. R.D.S.*' (1995) 18 *Dalhousie Law Review* 408.

12 In this sense the Trickster's methodology has similarities with objectives often associated with critical race theory. See 'Introduction' in Mari Matsuda, Charles Lawrence, and Richard Delgado, eds., *Words That Wound: Critical Race Theory, Assaultive Speech, and the First Amendment* (Boulder, CO: Westview Press, 1993), 4–7; Richard Delgado and Jean Stephanic, *Failed Revolutions: Social Reform and the Limits of Legal Imagination* (Boulder, CO: Westview Press, 1994).

13 In *R. v. Van der Peet*, [1996] 2 S.C.R. 507, the accused was charged under s. 61(1) of the Fisheries Act, R.S.C. 1970, c. F-14, with selling salmon caught under the authority of an Indian food fishing licence, contrary to s. 27(5) of the British Columbia Fishery (General) Regulations, SOR/84–248, which prohibited the sale or barter of fish caught under such a licence.

14 [1996] 2 S.C.R. 723. In *Gladstone*, the accused was charged under s. 61(1) of the Fisheries Act with attempting to sell herring spawn on kelp caught under the authority of an Indian food fish licence, contrary to the same regulations used to charge Van der Peet, and of attempting to sell herring spawn on kelp caught without a licence, contrary to s. 20(3) of the Pacific Herring Fishery Regulations, SOR/83–324.

15 [1996] 2 S.C.R. 672. In *Smokehouse*, the accused was an incorporated company which owned and operated a food processing plant. It was charged under s. 61(1) of the Fisheries Act with selling and purchasing fish not caught under the authority of a commercial fishing licence, contrary to s. 4(5) of the British Columbia (General) Regulations, and of selling and purchasing fish contrary to s. 27(5) of these same regulations.

16 [1996] 2 S.C.R. 821. In *Pamajewon*, the accused were charged under ss. 201(1) and 206(1) of the Criminal Code with the offence of keeping a common gaming house and conducting a scheme for the purposes of determining the winners of property.

17 Douglas Sanders, 'The Indian Lobby,' in Keith Banting and Richard Simeon, eds., *And No One Cheered: Federalism, Democracy and the Constitution Act* (Toronto: Methuen, 1983), at 301–32.

18 See Rights of the Aboriginal Peoples of Canada, Part II, Constitution Act,
1982, Schedule B to Canada Act 1982 (U.K.); Canadian Charter of Rights
and Freedoms, Part I, Constitution Act, 1982, Schedule B to Canada Act
1982 (U.K.). Aboriginal rights were placed outside of the Canadian Charter
to shield collective Aboriginal rights from erosion due to its individualist orientation. See William Pentney, 'The Rights of the Aboriginal Peoples of Canada and the Constitution Act 1982, Part I: The Interpretive Prism of s. 25'
(1988) 22 *University of British Columbia Law Review* 21. Section 25 of the Constitution Act, 1982 reflects this concern:

> The guarantee in this Charter of certain rights and freedoms shall not
> be construed so as to abrogate or derogate from any Aboriginal, treaty
> or other rights or freedoms that pertain to the Aboriginal peoples of
> Canada including
> (a) any rights or freedoms that have been recognized by the Royal
> Proclamation of October 7, 1763; and
> (b) any rights or freedoms that now exist by way of land claims agree-
> ments or may be so acquired ...

For judicial interpretation confirming this protection, see *R. v. Stienhuaer,*
[1985] 3 C.N.L.R. 187 at 191 (Alta. Q.B.); *Augustine and Augustine v. R.; Barlow v. R.,* [1987] 1 C.N.L.R. 20 at 44 (N.B.C.A.). For an excellent article discussing the problems of imposing individual rights on Canadian Aboriginal
peoples see Mary Ellen Turpel, 'Aboriginal Peoples and the Canadian Charter: Interpretive Monopolies, Cultural Differences' (1989–90) 6 *Canadian
Human Rights Yearbook* 3.

19 Bryan Schwartz, 'Unstarted Business: Two Approaches to Defining s. 35 –
What's in the Box, and What Kind of Box?' in *First Principles, Second Thoughts*
(Montreal: Institute for Research on Public Policy, 1986), at chap. 24.

20 For an analysis of the First Ministers Conferences mandated by s. 37 of the
constitution see Kathy Brock, 'The Politics of Aboriginal Self-Government: A
Canadian Paradox' (1991) 34 *Canadian Public Administration* 272. For suggestions building upon the Charlottetown Accord, see Peter Hogg and Mary
Ellen Turpel, 'Implementing Aboriginal Self-Government: Constitutional
and Jurisdictional Issues' (1995) 74 *Canadian Bar Review* 187.

21 The most recent example of the wider view of Aboriginal rights that can
emerge from the political process is found in the final report of the Royal
Commission on Aboriginal Peoples, *Report of the Royal Commission on Aboriginal People, Vols. 1–6* (Ottawa: Minister of Supply and Services Canada, 1996).
This report summarizes and extends many ideas for protecting and improving Aboriginal rights within Canada.

22 Previous cases which held that Aboriginal rights should be given a large, liberal, and generous interpretation include *Jones v. Meehan*, 175 U.S. 1 (1899) at 10–11; *Nowegijick v. The Queen* (1983), 144 O.L.R. (4th) 193 at 198; *R. v. Simon* (1985), 24 D.L.R. (4th) 390 at 435 (S.C.C.); *R. v. Sioui*, [1990] 1 S.C.R. 1025.

23 R.S.C. 1985, c. C-46.

24 The Supreme Court of Canada wear these robes as a symbol of respect for the judicial office.

25 *R. v. Van der Peet*, 534, per Lamer C.J.C.

26 Ibid. at 535.

27 Ibid. at 537.

28 Ibid. at 538.

29 Ibid. at 539.

30 Ibid. at 543.

31 See *Johnson v. McIntosh*, 21 U.S. (8 Wheat) 542 (U.S.S.C. 1823) at 572–4 and *Worcester v. Georgia*, 31 U.S. (6 Pet.) 515 at 542–3 & 559 (1832). See also *R. v. Sparrow*, [1990] 1 S.C.R. 1075 at 1103: 'there was from the outset, never any doubt, that sovereignty and legislative power, and indeed the underlying title, to such lands vested in the Crown.'

32 *Sparrow*, at 1099.

33 *Van der Peet*, at 549, per Lamer C.J.C.

34 Ibid. at 548.

35 Ibid. at 553–4.

36 See Daniel Francis, *The Imaginary Indian: The Image of the Indian in Canadian Culture* (Vancouver: Arsenal Pulp Press, 1992).

37 *Van der Peet*, at 555, per Lamer C.J.C.

38 Ibid. at 555.

39 Ibid.

40 Ibid. at 562.

41 Ibid. at 536.

42 Ibid. The articulation of this second purpose, reconciliation, as a reason for the entrenchment of s. 35(1) in the constitution was unexpected because it was not formerly a part of Aboriginal rights jurisprudence.

43 Ibid. at 538. The justification for this reason drew strongly from early U.S. jurisprudence in the Marshall cases. For commentary on the Marshall cases see Rennard Strickland, 'A Tale of Two Marshalls: The Cherokee Cases and the Cruel Irony of Supreme Court Victories' (1994) 47 *Oklahoma Law Review* 111; Philip Frickey, 'Marshalling the Past and Present: Colonialism, Constitutionalism and Interpretation in Federal Indian Law' (1993) 107 *Harvard Law Review* 381.

44 It is ironic that this assertion of British sovereignty should form one of the principle bases and underlying purposes for the existence of Aboriginal rights. At its most simple level, one might have thought that the assertion of British sovereignty was the last thing that would inform the constitutionalized protection of Aboriginal rights, since it is almost always British sovereignty that most severely threatens these rights. For criticism of the law's artificial and self-serving acceptance of the Crown claims of sovereignty see Brian Slattery, 'Understanding Aboriginal Rights' (1987) 66 *Canadian Bar Review* 727 at 730.

45 *Van der Peet*, at 548, per Lamer C.J.C.

46 Ibid. at 549.

47 Ibid. at 553–5.

48 Or to put the question affirmatively, in recognizing Aboriginal rights, one must ask 'whether or not a practice, tradition or custom is a defining feature of the culture in question' prior to European influences: ibid. at 554.

49 For a discussion of the court's limited understanding of Aboriginal culture see Turpel, 'Aboriginal Peoples and the Canadian Charter.'

50 *Sparrow*, at 1112. For an excellent commentary on this case see Michael Asch and Patrick Macklem, 'Aboriginal Rights and Canadian Sovereignty: An Essay on *R. v. Sparrow*' (1991) 29 *Alberta Law Review* 498. For a comparison with U.S. law see Matthew D. Wells, 'Sparrow and Lone Wolf: Honoring Tribal Rights in Canada and the United States' (1991) 66 *Washington Law Review* 1119.

51 *Van der Peet*, at 550, per Lamer C.J.C.

52 For an elaboration of the difficulties encountered in articulating Aboriginal world-views before common law courts see Robin Ridington, 'Cultures in Conflict: The Problem of Discourse,' in W.H. New, ed., *Native Writers and Canadian Writing* (Vancouver: UBC Press, 1990); Leslie Hall Pinder, *The Carriers of No: After the Land Claims Trial* (Vancouver: Lazara Press, 1991); Ryan and Ominayak, 'The Cultural Effects of Judicial Bias;' Louise Mandell, 'Native Culture on Trial,' in Mahoney and Martin, eds., *Equality and Judicial Neutrality*, 358; Michael Jackson, 'The Case in Context,' in Don Monet and Ardythe Wilson, eds., *Colonialism on Trial: Indigenous Land Rights and the Gitksan and Wet'suwet'en Sovereignty Case* (Philadelphia: New Society, 1992), x–xi.

53 In dissent, Madam Justice L'Heureux-Dubé stated 'I do not think it appropriate to qualify this proposition by stating that the perspective of the common law matters as much as the perspective of the native when defining Aboriginal rights.' *Van der Peet*, at 589.

54 (1996), 138 D.L.R. (4th) 385. In the *Coté* case, the issues were whether an

Aboriginal right to fish must be necessarily incidental to a claim of Aboriginal title and whether s. 35(1) protections outlined in *Van der Peet* extended to areas included within the former colonial regime of New France. The court held that 'Aboriginal rights may exist independently of Aboriginal title' (para. 38) and that s. 35(1) 'would fail to achieve its noble purpose if ... it only protected those defining features [of Aboriginal societies] which were fortunate enough to receive the protection of European colonizers' (para. 52). Thus, Aboriginal rights could extend to areas within the former colonial regime of New France.

55 (1996), 138 D.L.R. (4th). The *Adams* case also addressed the issue of whether Aboriginal rights are inherently based in claims to land, or whether claims to land are simply one manifestation of a broader concept of Aboriginal rights. The court held that 'Aboriginal rights do not exist solely where a claim to Aboriginal title has been made out' at para. 26. It stated that the *Van der Peet* test does not require that an Aboriginal group satisfy a further hurdle of demonstrating that their connection to land where the activity was taking place was of central significance to their distinctive culture.

56 For a discussion of the willingness of courts to alter the nature of claims to collective rights see Leon Trackman, 'Native Cultures in a Rights Empire: Ending the Dominion' (1997) 45 *Buffalo Law Review* 189 at 196–212.

57 *Van der Peet*, at 552, per Lamer C.J.C.

58 For a perceptive article that discusses the law's recharacterization of Aboriginal claims because of its inability to directly address colonialism see Mary Ellen Turpel, 'Home/Land' (1991) 10 *Canadian Journal of Family Law* 17 at 34.

59 *Van der Peet*, at 563, per Lamer C.J.C.; *Smokehouse* (para. 21), per Lamer C.J.C.

60 *Van der Peet*, at 554, per Lamer C.J.C.

61 *Sparrow*, at 1099.

62 Ibid.

63 *Van der Peet*, at 555.

64 '[T]he phrase existing Aboriginal rights must be interpreted flexibly so as to permit their evolution over time' *Sparrow*, at 1093.

65 *Van der Peet*, at 596–7, per L'Heureux-Dubé J.

66 Ibid. at 632, per McLachlin J.

67 Ibid. at 559, per Lamer C.J.C.

68 For evidentiary problems in Aboriginal rights litigation, see Michael Asch and Catherine Bell, 'Definition and Interpretation of Fact in Canadian Aboriginal Title Litigation: An Analysis of *Delgamuukw*' (1993–4) 19 *Queen's Law Journal* 503; Clay McLeod, 'The Oral Histories of Canada's Northern Peoples, Anglo-Canadian Evidence Law, and Canada's Duty to First Nations: Breaking Down the Barriers of the Past' (1992) 30 *Alberta Law Review* 1276

69 *Van der Peet* at 562.

70 The court took a similar approach in *R. v. Marshall*, [1999] 3 S.C.R. 456; see also John Borrows, 'Domesticating Doctrines: Aboriginal Peoples after the Royal Commission' (2000) 46 *McGill Law Journal* 571.

71 The court does not recognize that Aboriginal laws are universally protected Aboriginal rights even though they note that traditional laws form the basis of Aboriginal rights in an earlier part of the judgment. *Van der Peet*, at 547, per Lamer C.J.C.

72 Ibid. at 560.

73 In *Simon*, the Aboriginal accused had a right to carry a gun in closed season on his hunting grounds because its possession was reasonably incidental to his protected treaty right to hunt in all seasons.

74 For the inappropriateness of applying the 'integral' test to Aboriginal title see Kent McNeil, 'The Meaning of Aboriginal Title,' in Michael Asch, ed., *Aboriginal and Treaty Rights in Canada: Essays on Law, Equality and Respect for Difference* (Vancouver: UBC Press, 1997), 135–54.

75 For accounts that problematize non-Aboriginal accounts of aboriginality see Ghislain Otis, 'Opposing Aboriginality to Modernity: The Doctrine of Aboriginal Rights in Canada' (1997) 12 *British Journal of Canadian Studies* 1; Gillian Cowlishaw, 'Did the Earth Move for You? The Anti-Mabo Debate' (1995) 6 *Australian Journal of Anthropology* 32.

76 Commentary on non-Aboriginal interpretations of Aboriginal evidence is found in Geoff Sherrott, 'The Court's Treatment of the Evidence in *Delgamuukw v. B.C.*' (1992) 56 *Saskatchewan Law Review* 441; Louis Assier-Andrieu, 'Anthropology as the Eye of the Law' (1993) 33 *Journal of Legal Pluralism* 179; Marlee Kline, 'The Colour of Law: Ideological Representations of First Nations in Legal Discourse' (1994) 3 *Social and Legal Studies* 451.

77 For a critique of the application of non-Aboriginal characterizations of Aboriginal law, see Don Monet and Ardythe Wilson, *Colonialism on Trial: Indigenous Land Rights and the Gitksan and Wet'suwet'en Sovereignty Case* (Philadelphia: New Society, 1992).

78 *Sparrow*, at 1112.

79 See John Borrows, 'Contemporary Traditional Equality: The Effect of the Charter on First Nations Policies' (1994) 43 *University of New Brunswick Law Journal* 19.

80 *Pamajewon* at 832, per Lamer C.J.C.

81 Ibid. at 833, quoting from *Van der Peet* at 552.

82 *R. v. Sioui* at 1038.

83 *Sparrow* at 1112.

84 *Pamajewon* at 833.

85 Ibid. at 834.

86 Ibid.

87 Ibid. at 835.

88 Unfortunately, some Canadians may know exactly what it is like to have fundamental rights defined by what was integral to European culture prior to its arrival in North America. People disadvantaged on the basis of sex, class, race, and so forth, may well feel their rights depend on what was defining European culture 200–300 years ago.

89 An Anishinabe writer has described this experience in an excellent novel: Louise Erdrich, *The Bingo Palace* (New York: Harper Collins, 1994). U.S. statute and case law dealing with Indian gaming is found in Naomi Mezey, 'The Distribution of Wealth, Sovereignty and Culture Through Indian Gaming' (1996) 48 *Stanford Law Review* 711.

90 *Van der Peet*, at 539, per Lamer C.J.C.

91 Ibid. at 634, per McLachlin J.

92 Ibid. at 545, per Lamer C.J.C.

93 Ibid. at 638–40, per McLachlin J.

94 Ibid. at 638.

95 Ibid. at 639.

96 Ibid. at 639.

97 Ibid. at 642.

98 Ibid. at 641.

99 Ibid. at 643.

100 Ibid. at 648.

101 Arthur J. Ray, *Indians in the Fur Trade: Their Role as Trappers, Hunters and Middlemen in the Lands Southwest of Hudson Bay, 1660–1870* (Toronto: University of Toronto Press, 1974), at 51–7.

102 Richard White, *The Middle Ground: Indians, Empires, and Republics in the Great Lakes Region, 1650–1815* (Cambridge: Cambridge University Press, 1991); J.R. Miller, *Skyscrapers Hide the Heavens: A History of Indian-White Relations in Canada* (Toronto: University of Toronto Press, 1989), at 23–82; Olive P. Dickason, *Canada's First Nations: A History of the Founding Peoples from Earliest Times* (Toronto: McClelland and Stewart, 1992), at 86–215; *Report of the Royal Commission on Aboriginal People*, Volume 1, *Looking Forward, Looking Back*, at 99–137.

103 *Van der Peet*, at 547.

104 Ibid.

105 See generally Harold Adams Innis, *The Fur Trade in Canada: An Introduction to Canadian Economic History* (Toronto: University of Toronto Press, 1962).

106 In fact, Indians did rebel on those occasions where they were told they had no rights to occupy and use their lands. See Francis Jennings, *The Ambiguous Iroquois Empire* (New York: W.W. Norton, 1984); Cornelius Jaenen, *Friend and Foe: Aspects of French-Amerindian Cultural Contact in the Sixteenth and Seventeenth Centuries* (New York: Columbia University Press, 1976); Leslie F.S. Upton, UBC Press, 1979).

107 The Royal Proclamation of 7 October 1763, R.S.C. 1985, App. II, No. 1. See also Borrows, 'Constitutional Law From a First Nations Perspective.'

108 A holding that denies the protection of Aboriginal practices that developed solely as a result of European contact would also violate Canada's fiduciary obligation towards Aboriginal peoples to maintain the honour of the Crown in dealings with Aboriginal peoples. For discussion of this doctrine see Leonard Rotman, *Parallel Paths: Fiduciary Doctrine and the Crown-Native Relationship in Canada* (Toronto: University of Toronto Press, 1996); David Elliot, 'Aboriginal Peoples in Canada and the United States and the Scope of the Fiduciary Relationship' (1996) 24 *Manitoba Law Journal* 137; Peter W. Hutchins, David Schulze and Carol Hilling, 'When Do Fiduciary Obligations to Aboriginal Peoples Arise?' (1995) 59 *Saskatchewan Law Review* 97.

109 *Van der Peet* at 547.

110 Ibid. at 554–5.

111 *Gladstone* at 775, per Lamer C.J.C, *Delgamuukw*, at 1111.

112 Under the *Sparrow* test for infringement, first the Aboriginal group must demonstrate a prima facie interference with their rights because legislation is unreasonable, causes undue hardship, or denies the preferred means of exercising rights. If the group passes this test the court may still hold that interference is justified if the Crown can show a valid legislative objective for infringing the law and demonstrate that the honour of the Crown was preserved in the enactment.

113 However, the Supreme Court of Canada has recently narrowed the bounds in which First Nations laws can apply. See *R. v. Nikal* (1996), 133 D.L.R. (4th) 658; *R. v. Lewis* (1996), 133 D.L.R. (4th) 700.

114 A discussion about the importance of the continued interaction of state law and customary Indigenous law is found in Maria Teresa Sierra, 'Indian Rights and Customary Law in Mexico: A Study of the Nahuas in the Sierra De Pueblo' (1995) 29 *Law and Society Review* 227.

115 *Côté* at 406.

116 *Van der Peet* at 547.

117 Ibid.

118 These communities have laws relating to selling fish and gambling that the

court could receive and consider in developing its sui generis Aboriginal rights jurisprudence. These laws 'may be helpful by way of analogy' in defining and interpreting Aboriginal rights. See *R. v. Simon* at 404.

119 *Van der Peet* at 546.

120 For an excellent discussion of the persistence of customary tribal law, see Valencia-Weber, 'Tribal Courts.'

121 The diverse sources of law in Canada, including Aboriginal law, are examined in Patrick Glenn, 'The Common Law in Canada' (1995) 74 *Canadian Bar Review* 261.

122 *Van der Peet* at 634, per McLachlin J.

123 Ibid. at 547, per Lamer C.J.C.

124 Ibid. at 643, per McLachlin J.

125 For supporting argument see, Sakej Henderson, 'First Nations Legal Inheritances: The Mikmaq Model' (1996) 23 *Manitoba Law Journal* 1; Henderson, 'Micmaw Tenure in Atlantic Canada' (1995) 18 *Dalhousie Law Journal* 1; James Youngblood Henderson, Margjorie Benson, and Isobel Findlay, *Aboriginal Tenure in the Constitution of Canada* (Scarborough, ON: Carswell, 2000), at 397–426.

126 If reconciliation is to be used to define Aboriginal rights at all, a better approach to reconciliation would have made 1982 the effective date for the definition of rights. The Constitution Act recognized and affirmed those rights which were existing in 1982, *not* at the date when Europeans asserted sovereignty in what is now Canada.

127 *Van der Peet* at 554–5.

128 The downgrading of Aboriginal rights is even more apparent in the greater power given to Canadian governments to infringe Aboriginal rights in these cases. For further comment see Kent McNeil, 'How Can Infringements of the Constitutional Rights of the Aboriginal Peoples Be Justified?' (1997) 8 *Constitutional Forum* 33.

129 For an argument that develops the equality of peoples as central to reconciling Crown/Aboriginal relationships see Patrick Macklem, 'Normative Dimensions of an Aboriginal Right to Self-Government' (1995) *Queen's Law Journal* 173; Macklem, 'Distributing Sovereignty: Indian Nations and Equality of Peoples' (1993) 45 *Stanford Law Review* 1311.

130 *Sparrow* at 1112; *Pamajewon* at 833.

131 Jaroslav Pelikan, *The Vindication of Tradition* (New Haven, CT: Yale University Press, 1984), at 54.

132 Katherine Bartlett, 'Tradition, Change and Progress in Feminist Legal Thought' (1995) *Wisconsin Law Review* 303.

Chapter 4

1 First Nations across Canada know the Trickster by these different names. Nanabush has various persona in different cultures. The First Nations people of the coastal Northwest know him as Raven; he is Glooscap to the Mi'kmaq of the Maritimes; and is known as Coyote, Crow, Wisakedjak, Badger, or Old Man among other First Nations people in North America.

2 For a description of the lower mainland in this period see Cole Harris, *The Resettlement of British Columbia: Essays on Colonialism and Geographical Change* (Vancouver: UBC Press, 1997), at 68–102.

3 The Nisga'a impression of the first surveyors in their territory is recorded in a video interview by Bill Cameron with Alvin McKay in *C.B.C. Journal Native Series* 1 (Toronto: Canadian Broadcasting Corporation, 1990).

4 For this view by one British Columbian in this period, see British Columbia, *Papers Connected with the Indian Land Question, 1850–1875* (Victoria: Government Printer, 1875), appendix at 11.

5 Ibid.

6 See Proclamation 2, issued by Governor James Douglas on 14 February 1959: 'All the lands in British Columbia, and Mines and Minerals therein, belong to the Crown in fee.' British Columbia, *List of Proclamations for 1858 ... 1864* (New Westminster: Government Printing Office, n.d.). This statute was based on jurisprudence like *Campbell v. Hall* and earlier statutes such as An Act for Extending the Jurisdiction of the Courts, 1803, 43 Geo. III, c. 138 and an Act for Regulating the Fur Trade and Establishing a Criminal and Civil Jurisdiction Within Certain Parts of North America, 1821, 1 & 2 Geo. IV, c. 66. Both these acts were repealed and replaced by the Imperial Act to Provide for the Government of British Columbia, 2 August 1858.

7 In fact ten years after union, in 1881, after a considerable period of growth in their population, there were only 19,069 'white' people in the province. See Harris, *The Resettlement of British Columbia* at 140. This is based on extrapolations from figures in his research. There would be significantly fewer than 19,000 'white' people in the province, and substantially more than 30,000 Aboriginal and Chinese people. 'White' is a word the settlers used to describe themselves.

8 These sentiments parallel the views of Joseph Trutch, a policy adviser to the British Columbia government between 1864 and 1871. Trutch's prejudices towards the Indians are found in Robin Fisher, 'Joseph Trutch and Indian Land Policy' 12 (Winter 1971–72) BC Studies at 3, quoted in Paul Tennant, *Aboriginal Peoples and Politics: Indian Land Question in British Columbia, 1849–1989* (Vancouver: UBC Press, 1990), at 39.

9 Expressions of this view are found in Joseph Trutch's communication. See ibid. They are also found in George Stewart, *Canada Administration of the Earl of Dufferin* (Toronto: Rose-Belford, 1878), at 492–3.

10 British Columbia, An Ordinance to Define the Law Regulating Acquisition of Land in British Columbia, 31 March 1866. Enforcement of this provision is found in British Columbia, *Papers Connected With the Indian Land Question 1850–1875*, at 49.

11 British Columbia, *Papers Connected with the Indian Land Question, 1850–1875*, at 33.

12 Qualification and Registration of Voters Act, 1872, s. 13.

13 British Columbia, *Papers Connected with the Indian Land Question, 1850–1875*, at 42.

14 Ibid.

15 British Columbia, *Sessional Papers*, 1871 at 12. See also Robin Fisher, *Contact and Conflict: Indian European Relations in British Columbia* (Vancouver: UBC Press, 1992), at 161. For Trutch's role in these negotiations see Tennant, *Aboriginal Peoples and Politics*, at 43–5.

16 The Wet'suwet'en are an Athabaskan-speaking people, and the Gitksan are associated with the Tsimshian language group. Their territories are located in or near villages sites on the Skeena, Babine and Bulkley Rivers. See Gisday Wa and Delgam Uukw, *The Spirit in the Land* (Gabriola Island, BC: Reflections Press, 1992), at 1–20.

17 Hereditary Chief Alice Jeffery summarized their action: 'The Gitksan people feel we have absolute title and ownership to our land.' Alice Jeffery, 'Remove Not the Landmark,' in Frank Cassidy, ed., *Aboriginal Title in British Columbia* (Lantzville, BC: Oolichan Books, 1991), 58 at 61.

18 *Delgamuukw* (1991), 79 D.L.R. (4th) 185 at 278, 282 (B.C.S.C.).

19 For a description of these histories see *Delgamuukw*, [1997] 3 S.C.R. 1010 at 1071–2 (S.C.C.).

20 See Antonio Mills, *Eagle Down in Our Law: Witsuwit'en Law, Feasts and Land Claims* (Vancouver: UBC Press, 1994).

21 *Delgamuukw* at 608 (B.C.C.A.), per Lambert J.A.

22 Ibid.

23 *Delgamuukw* at 233 (B.C.S.C.).

24 Arthur Ray, Court document Tr. 202, p. 13387, Report, Ex. 960, p. 27. See also Arthur Ray, 'Fur Trade History and the Gitksan and Wet'suwet'en Comprehensive Claim: Men of Property and the Exercise of Title,' in K. Abel and F. Friesen, *Aboriginal Resource Use in Canada* (Winnipeg: University of Manitoba Press, 1991), 301.

25 *Delgamuukw* at 281 (B.C.S.C.).

26 Arthur Ray, Trial document Ex. 964–5, p. 1(87).

27 *Delgamuukw* at 278–9 (B.C.S.C.).

28 Ibid. at 281.

29 See Dara Culhane, *The Pleasure of the Crown* (Vancouver: Talon Books, 1998); and Don Monet and Ardythe Wilson, eds, *Colonialism on Trial: Indigenous Land Rights and the Gitksan and Wet'suwit'en Sovereignty Case* (Philadelphia: New Society, 1992); Leslie Hall Pinder, *The Carriers of No: After the Land Claims Trial* (Vancouver: Lagara Press, 1991); Cassidy, ed., *Aboriginal Title in British Columbia*; Michael Asch and Cathy Bell, 'Challenging Assumptions: The Impact of Precedent in Aboriginal Rights Litigation,' in Asch, *Aboriginal and Treaty Rights in Canada* at 1; Julie Cruickshank, 'Invention of Anthropology' in British Columbia's Supreme Court: Oral Tradition as Evidence in *Delgamuukw v. B.C.* (1992) 95 *BC Studies* 25; Robin Fisher, 'Judging History: Reflections on the Reasons for Judgment in *Delgamuukw v. B.C.*' (1992) 95 B.C. Studies 43; Joel Fortune, 'Construing *Delgamuukw*: Legal Arguments, Historical Argumentation and the Philosophy of History' (1992) 51 *University of Toronto Faculty of Law Review* 80; Mark Walters, 'British Imperial Constitutional Law and Aboriginal Rights: A Comment on *Delgamuukw v. B.C.*' (1992) 17 *Queen's Law Journal* 350; Natalie Oman, 'Sharing Horizons: A Paradigm for Political Accommodation in Intercultural Settings (PhD thesis, McGill University, 1997).

30 *Delgamuukw* at 416 (B.C.S.C.).

31 *Delgamuukw* at 1034 (S.C.C.).

32 Ibid. at 1033, 1037.

33 Ibid. at 1038.

34 Ibid. at 1037.

35 Ibid. at 1038.

36 Ibid. at 1035. Satsan (Herb George), former speaker for the Office of the Hereditary Chiefs, wrote: 'We view this judgment for what it is – a denial and a huge misunderstanding and ignorance of the First Nations across this country. It is a failure to recognize the First Nations of this country for what they are and who they are – the First Nations of this land – the owners of this land.' Satsan, 'The Fire Within Us,' in Cassidy, ed., *Aboriginal Title in British Columbia*, 53 at 56. By relying on assertions of British sovereignty to diminish and dispossess Gitksan and Wet'suwet'en rights to land, MacEachern C.J. continued a trend imbricated in the very bedrock of Western European legal thought. His reasons for judgment employed ancient discursive practices that recognized prior Aboriginal presence on the land but denied this fact any attendant legal protection. Paul Tennant, a leading political scientist of Aboriginal issues, observed that 'the major political and historical significance of the *Delgamuukw* judgment is that it embodies the white traditional

views ... based squarely on the cognitive framework and belief systems that underlie and maintain the traditional white views.' Paul Tennant, 'The Place of Delgamuukw in British Columbia History and Politics – And Vice Versa,' in Cassidy, ed., *Aboriginal Title in British Columbia*, 73 at 81–2.

37 *Delgamuukw* at 498 (B.C.S.C.).

38 For commentary on the jurisdictional aspect of this judgment see Bob Freedman, 'The Space for Aboriginal Self-Government in British Columbia: The Effect of the Decision of the British Columbia Court of Appeal in *Delgamuukw v. British Columbia*' (1994) 28 *University of British Columbia Law Review* 49.

39 *Delgamuukw* at 520 (B.C.C.A.).

40 *Delgamuukw* at 1098 (S.C.C.).

41 Ibid. at 1061, per Lamer C.J.C.

42 See Patrick Glenn, 'The Common Law in Canada' (1995) 74 *Canadian Bar Review* 261 at 265, 276; Sir Matthew Hale, *The History of the Common Law of England* at 39–43. The cultural diversity in the development of the United Kingdom is nicely detailed in Norman Davies, *The Isles: A History* (New York: Oxford University Press, 1999).

43 See John H. Baker, *An Introduction to English Legal History*, 3rd ed. (London: Butterworths, 1996).

44 See Frederic W. Maitland and Francis C. Montague, *A Sketch of English Legal History* (London: G.P. Putnam and Sons, 1915), at 1–130.

45 See Frederic W. Maitland, *The Forms of Action at Common Law* (Cambridge: Cambridge University Press, 1948), at 11.

46 See Maitland and Montague, *A Sketch of English Legal History*, at 100–1.

47 See M.P. Furmston, ed., *Cheshire, Fifoot and Furmston's Law of Contract*, 11th ed. (London: Butterworths, 1986), at 2.

48 Henry Campbell Black, *Black's Law Dictionary*, 5th ed. (St Paul, MN: West Publishing, 1979), at 587.

49 Ibid.

50 See Albert K.R. Kiralfy, ed., *Potter's Historical Introduction to English Law and its Institutions* (London: Street and Maxwell, 1962), at 293–7.

51 See Margaret H. Ogilvie, *Historical Introduction to Legal Studies* (Carswell: Toronto, 1982), at 70, 101, 106–7.

52 See Stroud F.C. Milsom, *Historical Foundations of the Common Law*, 2nd ed. (Toronto: Butterworths, 1981), at 11–36.

53 See e.g. Sakej Henderson, 'Mikmaw Tenure in Atlantic Canada' (1995) 18 *Dalhousie Law Journal* 196.

54 The forms of action were abolished in the following Acts: The Real Property Limitation Act, 1833, 3 & 4 Will. IV, c. 27, s. 36; Common Law Procedure Act, 1852, 15 & 16 Vict., c. 76; Judicature Act, 1873, 36 & 37 Vict., c. 66.

55 Ogilvie, *Historical Introduction to Legal Studies*, at 70.

56 In this regard Macfarlane J.A. quoted A.V. Dicey who wrote: 'There is no person or body or persons who can, under the English Constitution, make rules which override or derogate from an Act of Parliament, or which (to express the same things in other words) will be enforced by the courts in contravention of an Act of Parliament.' Albert Venn Dicey in *Law of the Constitution*, 10th ed. (London: Macmillan, 1959), at 40, quoted in *Delgamuukw* at 520 (B.C.C.A.), per Macfarlane J.A.

57 See Patrick Macklem, 'First Nations Self-Government and the Borders of the Canadian Legal Imagination' (1991) 36 *McGill Law Journal* 382.

58 It should be remembered that the Gitksan and Wet'suwet'en voluntarily submitted themselves to the court's process when they drafted their pleadings and filed their statement of claim. As a result, some may assert that they could not take issue with consolidation of the common law's jurisdiction at the expense of Indigenous legal systems. However, it should also be noted that in framing their case they were 'seeking recognition of the societies (native and non-native) as equals and contemporaries.' Gisday Wa and Delgam Uukw, *The Spirit in the Land*, at 21. In their opening statement, at 8–9, the chiefs expressed their position as follows: 'In your legal system, how will you deal with the idea that the chiefs own the land? The attempts to extinguish our system have been unsuccessful. Gisday Wa has not been extinguished ... The purpose of this case, is to find a process to place the Gitksan and Wet'suwet'en ownership and jurisdiction within the context of Canada. We do not seek a decision as to whether our system might continue or not. It will continue.

59 *Delgamuukw* at 1061 (S.C.C.), per Lamer C.J.C.

60 Ibid. at 1062.

61 Ibid.

62 Ibid. at 1063.

63 Ibid.

64 Maitland, *The Forms of Action*, at 2.

65 *Delgamuukw* at 1063 (S.C.C.), per Lamer C.J.C.

66 As a result, everything else the court wrote after this point in the judgment can be regarded as obiter dicta, 'words of an opinion entirely unnecessary for the decision of the case ... Such are not binding as precedent.' *Black's Law Dictionary* at 967.

67 Aboriginal peoples were still in the majority in the province ten years later. See Harris, *The Resettlement of British Columbia*, at 140.

68 Projected from Wilson Duff's figures. See Wilson Duff, *The Indian History of British Columbia*, vol. 1, *The Impact of the White Man* (Victoria: Provincial Museum of British Columbia, 1964), at 42–5.

69 Harris, *The Resettlement of British Columbia*, at 138. The proportional representation of Aboriginal to non-Aboriginal people was even greater in Gitksan and Wet'suwet'en territory prior to Confederation. There was no land alienation prior to 1871, and while some miners, missionaries, and traders lived among them in small numbers at this time, it was not until the early 1900s that the first farmers settled there. See *Delgamuukw* at 343 (B.C.S.C.).

70 See An Act to Amend 'The Qualification and Registration of Voters Amendment Act, 1871,' 1872 (B.C.), 35–38 Vict., No. 39, s. 13.

71 See An Ordinance to further define the law regulating the acquisition of Land in British Columbia, 1866 (B.C.), 29 Vict., No. 24, s. 1, which provided: 'The right conferred ... on British Subjects or aliens ... of pre-empting and holding land in fee simple unoccupied and unsurveyed and unreserved Crown lands in British Columbia, shall not (without the special permission of the Governor first had in writing) extend or be deemed to have been conferred on ... any Aborigines of this Colony or the Territories neighbouring thereto.' A further amendment passed by the Legislative Council on 22 April 1870 extended the denial to 'any of the Aborigines of this Continent.'

72 The major policy maker for Indian affairs in British Columbia from 1864 until after union in 1871 was Joseph Trutch, who stated, concerning Indian reserves:

> The Indians regard these extensive tracts of land as their individual property; but of by far the greater portion thereof they make no use whatever and are not likely to do so; and thus the land, much of which is either rich pasture or available for cultivation and greatly desired for immediate settlement, remains in an unproductive condition – is of no real value to the Indians and utterly unprofitable to the public interests.
>
> I am therefore of the opinion that these reserves should, in almost every case, be very materially reduced.

British Columbia, *Papers Connected with the Indian Land Question, 1850–1875*, at 42.

73 Joseph Trutch, in denying Aboriginal title in British Columbia observed: 'The title of the Indians in the fee of the public lands, or any portion thereof, has never been acknowledged by Government, but, on the contrary, is distinctly denied.' 'Report to the Government on the Subject of Indian Reserves,' in ibid., appendix at 11.

74 See Tennant, *Aboriginal Peoples and Politics*, at 96–114.

75 Section 141 of the Indian Act was amended to read: 'Every person who, without the consent of the Superintendent General expressed in writing,

receives, obtains, solicits or requests from any Indian any payment or contribution or promise of any payment or contribution for the purpose of raising a fund or providing money for the prosecution of any claim which the tribe or band of Indians to which such Indian belongs, or of which he is a member, has or is represented to have for the recovery of any claim or money for the benefit of said tribe or band, shall be guilty of an offence and liable upon summary conviction for each such offence to a penalty ...' For commentary see Brian Titley, *A Narrow Vision: Duncan Campbell Scott and the Administration of Indian Affairs in Canada* (Vancouver: UBC Press, 1986), at 59.

76 Nicolas Perrot, 'Memoir on the Manners, Customs, and Religion of the Savages of North America,' in Emma Blair, ed., *The Indian Tribes of the Upper Mississippi Valley and Region of the Great Lakes*, vol. 1 (Cleveland: Arthur H. Clark, 1911), at 31.

77 Robert Lowie, 'Oral Tradition and History' (1915) 17 *American Anthropologist* 597 at 598. One of Lowie's main objections to oral tradition was that the actions and events remembered within societies with these traditions did not often deal with significant items. For example, he was critical of the Assiniboine Indians' failure to remember the introduction of the horse among them after the arrival of Europeans. In response to his criticism it may be observed that all history is selective in what it records as being significant. 'Selection is inevitable, and with the recognition of this comes the possibility of new doubts about its objectivity.' Ronald F. Atkinson, *Knowledge and Explanation in History* (London: Macmillan Press, 1978), at 69. It is possible that at first the Assiniboine did not view the coming of the Europeans and the horse as very significant and thus did not select this event as worthy of recording in their traditions.

78 Robert Lowie, 'Oral Tradition and History' (1917) 30 *Journal of American Folklore* 161 at 163.

79 Hugh Trevor-Roper, *The Rise of Christian Europe* (London: Thames and Hudson, 1965), at 9.

80 Ibid.

81 *Beecher v. Wetherby*, 95 U.S. 517 at 525 (U.S.S.C., 1877).

82 *Calder v. A.G.B.C.* (1971), 13 D.L.R. (3d) 64 at 66 (B.C.C.A.). Chief Justice Davey was upbraided for this comment by Justice Hall of the Supreme Court of Canada, who wrote, 'in so saying this in 1970, he was assessing the Indian culture of 1858 by the same standards Europeans applied to the Indians of North America two or more centuries before.' *Calder v. A.G.B.C.* at 170 (S.C.C.).

83 *R. v. Syliboy*, [1929] 1 D.L.R. 307 at 315 (N.S.Co.Ct.). In reference to this label Chief Justice Dickson observed that 'such language is no longer accept-

able in Canadian law and, indeed, is inconsistent with a growing sensitivity to native rights in Canada.' *R. v. Simon* (1985), 24 D.L.R. (4th) 390 (S.C.C.).

84 *Johnson v. McIntosh,* 21 U.S. (8 Wheat) 542 (U.S.S.C. 1823); *Ex Parte Crow Dog,* 109 U.S. 556 (U.S.S.C., 1913), (U.S.S.C.).

85 *United States v. Sandoval,* 231 U.S.

86 *Delgamuukw* Part 2 (B.C.S.C.) at 13, per McEachern J.

87 *Delgamuukw* at 1065 (S.C.C.), per Lamer C.J.C., quoting *Van der Peet* at 558–9. It should also be noted that the Supreme Court, in other circumstances, has also affirmed the importance of not mechanically applying the so-called exception to hearsay evidence when circumstantial probability warrants its admission. See *R. v. Khan,* [1990] 2 S.C.R. 531; *R. v. Smith,* [1992] 2 S.C.R. 915. The Supreme Court has also extolled the virtues of oral history more generally, and even written that this history contains 'unwritten norms' that 'stretch back through the ages' and 'inform and sustain' Canada's highest legal document, the Canadian constitution. See *Reference Re Secession of Quebec,* [1998] 2 S.C.R. 217 at 240, 248, 249.

88 *Delgamuukw* at 1066 (S.C.C.), per Lamer C.J.C. For commentary on the sui generis nature of Aboriginal rights see John Borrows and Len Rotman, 'The Sui Generis Nature of Aboriginal Rights: Does It Make a Difference?' (1997) 36 *Alberta Law Review* 9.

89 *Delgamuukw* (S.C.C.).

90 Ibid. at 1067 (S.C.C.), per Lamer C.J.C.

91 Ibid. at 1069. It should be noted that the court's adaptation of evidentiary standards finds parallels elsewhere in the jurisprudence. The *Delgamuukw* case has been criticized by many in the business community for the new 'uncertain' evidentiary standards it creates. But in the mid-eighteenth century the courts drastically changed the rules of evidence to receive commercial and merchant customs and evidence for virtually the first time. It is interesting and somewhat ironic to note that the foundation of law protecting commercial transactions was as revolutionary in its time as the *Delgamuukw* case may appear to business today. See Ogilvie, *Historical Introduction to Legal Studies,* at 345.

92 Ibid., quoting from *R. v. Simon* at 407.

93 *Delgamuukw* at 1065 (S.C.C.).

94 Ibid. at 1066.

95 There are many accounts of the mistreatment Aboriginal peoples have endured at the hands of colonial governments. A good overview is found in *Report of the Royal Commission on Aboriginal People,* volume 1, *Looking Forward, Looking Back* at 245–591.

96 Aboriginal peoples remember that civil servants charged with protecting

their rights often deceived them in very costly ways. For an example, see the facts of *R. v. Guerin*, [1984] 2 S.C.R. 688. For an excellent study of deception in Canadian/Aboriginal relations see Sally Weaver, *Making Canadian Indian Policy: The Hidden Agenda, 1968–1970* (Toronto: University of Toronto Press, 1981).

97　Harold Cardinal, *The Unjust Society: The Tragedy of Canada's Indians* (Edmonton: Hurtig, 1969), at 27–50.

98　Many Aboriginal people remember the theft of their masks, totem poles, button blankets, carvings, medicine bundles, land, and their ancestors' bones. For a non-Aboriginal account that cites many Aboriginal sources see generally Ronald Wright, *Stolen Continents: The New World through Indian Eyes* (Toronto: Penguin Books, 1992).

99　See Paul Chartrand, 'Aboriginal Rights: The Dispossession of the Métis' (1991) 29 *Osgoode Hall Law Journal* 357; almost every major Indian treaty also has unfulfilled promises. See Royal Commission on Aboriginal People, *Report of the Royal Commission on Aboriginal People*, volume 2, *Restructuring the Relationship* (Ottawa: Supply and Services, 1996), esp. chapter 2. Specific examples of the courts permitting the Crown to break its promises are found in *Attorney General of Ontario v. Attorney General of Canada: Re Indian Claims*, [1897] A.C. 199 at 213; *R. v. Sikyea* (1964), 43 D.L.R. (2d) 150.

100　Aboriginal people who fought in the wars received disturbingly unequal treatment when they returned home. See Fred Gaffen, *Forgotten Soldiers* (Penticton, BC: Theytus Books, 1985). Aboriginal peoples have also been treated unequally and inhumanely in Canada's criminal law system. See Royal Commission on Aboriginal People, *Bridging the Cultural Divide: A Report on Aboriginal People and Criminal Justice in Canada* (Ottawa: Supply and Services, 1996). The Supreme Court of Canada has commented about the current 'crisis' this treatment has spawned: *R. v. Gladue*, [1999] 1 S.C.R. 688.

101　David A. Nock, *A Victorian Missionary and Canadian Indian Policy: Cultural Synthesis vs. Cultural Replacement* (Waterloo: Wilfrid Laurier University Press, 1988), at 40, 78; George Manuel and Michael Posluns, *The Fourth World* (Don Mills, ON: Collier-Macmillan, 1974), at 67. For personal anecdotes that keep alive the effect of this treatment see Celia Haig-Brown, *Resistance and Renewal: Surviving the Indian Residential School* (Vancouver: Tillicum Library, 1988), at 1–2.

102　See Katherine Pettipas, *Severing the Ties that Bind: Government Repression of Indigenous Religious Ceremonies on the Prairies* (Winnipeg: University of Manitoba Press, 1994).

103　For a history of restraint on trade encountered on the prairies see Sarah Carter, *Lost Harvests: Prairie Indian Reserve Farmers and Government Policy*

(Montreal: McGill-Queen's University Press, 1990). For a history of the sanctions Aboriginal peoples suffered in the west coast fishing trade see Diane Newell, *Tangled Webs of History: Indians and the Law in Canada's Pacific Coast Fisheries* (Toronto: University of Toronto Press, 1993).

104 In 1927, the federal government made it illegal to raise money to pursue land claims without government approval. See Indian Act, R.S.C. 1927, c. 98, s. 149. For commentary, see Tennant, *Aboriginal People and Politics*, at 111–13.

105 The federal government attempted to forcibly replace the Haudenosaunee Confederacy Council at Six Nations with an elected band council, and the courts later upheld this action. See *Logan v. Styres* (1959), 20 D.L.R. (2d) 416 (Ont. H.C.). The federal government similarly suppressed west coast political structures by outlawing the potlatch. For a description and commentary, see Douglas Cole and Ira Chaikin, *An Iron Hand Upon the People: The Law against the Potlach on the Northwest Coast* (Vancouver: Douglas and MacIntyre, 1990).

106 Whole communities suffered resettlement. For an example, see Royal Commission on Aboriginal Peoples, *The High Arctic Relocation: A Report on the 1953–1955 Relocation* (Ottawa: Supply and Services, 1994). For information about further relocations see *Report of the Royal Commission on Aboriginal People*, volume 1, *Looking Forward, Looking Back*, chap. 11 at 411–543. Individuals were also forcibly relocated through residential schools and provincial child welfare regimes. See A.C. Hamilton and C.M. Sinclair, *The Justice System and Aboriginal People: Report of the Aboriginal Justice Inquiry in Manitoba*, vol. 1 (Winnipeg: Queen's Printer, 1991), at 509–20.

107 Irene Spry, 'The Tragedy of the Loss of the Commons in Western Canada,' in Getty and Lussier, *As Long as the Sun Shines*, at 203. John Goddard, *Last Stand of the Lubicon Cree* (Vancouver: Douglas and McIntyre, 1991).

108 For a discussion of how the imposition of non-Aboriginal structures has weakened but not destroyed Aboriginal authority, see John Borrows, 'A Genealogy of Law: Inherent Sovereignty and First Nataions Self-Government' (1992) 30 *Osgoode Hall Law Journal* 291.

109 For a sample of this opinion, see Grand Chief Michael Mitchell, 'An Unbroken Assertion of Sovereignty,' in Boyce Richardson, *DrumBeat: Anger and Renewal in Indian Country* (Toronto: Summerhill Press, 1989) at 105–36; Frank Cassidy, ed., *Aboriginal Self-Determination* (Lantzville, BC: Oolichan Books, 1991), at 33–62; Ovide Mercredi and Mary Ellen Turpel, *In the Rapids: Navigating the Future of First Nations* (Toronto: Viking Books, 1993), at 13–36.

110 In this they have some support from the Supreme Court of Canada, who

termed Indigenous laws 'pre-existing,' which has its source prior to the assertion of British sovereignty. *Delgamuukw* at 1082, 1092 (S.C.C.).

111 Though the court has accepted a weaker version of Indigenous legal plural-ism: see *Van der Peet* at 538, 545–7; *Delgamuukw* at 1082, 1092, 1099–1100, 1105–6 (S.C.C.).

112 Mills, *Eagle Down is Our Law.*

113 Jan Vansina, *Oral Tradition as History* (Madison: University of Wisconsin Press, 1985), at 124.

114 Ibid.

115 Ludwig Wittgenstein, *Philosophical Investigations*, 2nd ed., trans. G.E.M. Anscombe (Oxford: Basil Blackwell, 1967), at paras. 154–5. He wrote that meaning and understanding of a fact is 'know[ing] how to go on.' If you do not have an understanding of 'how to go on' in a culture that is different from your own, you do not know the facts of that culture.

116 Martin Heidegger, *Being and Time*, trans. John Macquarrie and Edward Rob-inson (New York: Harper and Row, 1962) at 157.

117 See Richard Rorty, 'On Ethnocentrism: A Reply to Clifford Geertz' (1986) 25 Michigan Quarterly Review 525; Abdullahi Ahmed An-Na'im, 'Problems of Universal Cultural Legitimacy for Human Rights,' in Abdullahi Ahmed An-Na'im and Francis Deng, eds., *Human Rights in Africa: Cross-Cultural Per-spectives* (Washington, DC: Brookings Institute, 1990), 331.

118 For the special challenges of presenting history in an adversarial courtroom environment see Donald J. Bourgeois, 'The Role of the Historian in the Lit-igation Process' (1986) 67 *Canadian Historical Review* 2; G.M. Dickinson and R.D. Gidney, 'History and Advocacy: Some Reflections on the Historian's Role in Litigation' (1987) 68 *Canadian Historical Review* 576; Vansina, *Oral Tradition as History*, at 102–3.

119 Richard Devlin, 'Judging and Diversity: Justice or Just Us?' (1996) 20 *Provin-cial Court Judges Journal* 4.

120 For example, in spatial terms, early Christians visualized the Garden of Eden as being in Mesopotamia and thus attempted to explain all human migration as somehow stemming from this point. But many Ojibway people trace their origin to Michilimackinac Island in the Great Lakes and refer-ence their migrations from this place. Temporally speaking, Christianity, Islam, and Judaism have tended to view time as being linear, progressing, and 'marching on.' Other cultures such as the Maya, Ainu, or Cree have thought of time as being cyclical and repetitive. Causality or change can also differ between groups. See Vansina, *Oral Tradition as History*, at 125–33.

121 Vasina has written that 'Historical truth is also a notion that is culture spe-cific.' Ibid. at 129.

122 See Charles Taylor, *Philosophy and the Human Sciences* (Cambridge: Cambridge University Press), at 119, 121; Vasina, *Oral Tradition as History*, at 124.

123 A leading enthnohistorian wrote: 'Historical records can be interpreted only when the cultural values of both the observer and the observed are understood by the historian. In the study of modern Western history, the experience of everyday life may suffice to supply such knowledge. Yet this implicit approach does not provide an adequate basis for understanding the behavior of people in earlier times or in cultures radically different from our own.' Bruce Trigger, *Natives and Newcomers: Canada's Heroic Age Reconsidered* (Montreal: McGill-Queen's University Press, 1985) at 168.

124 Vansina, *Oral Tradition as History*, at 124.

125 Ibid. at 137.

126 See Louise Mandell, 'Native Culture on Trial'; Joan Ryan and Bernard Ominayak, 'The Cultural Effects of Judicial Bias,' in Kathleen Mahoney and Sheilah Martin, eds., *Equity and Judicial Neutrality* (Toronto: Carswell, 1989); Robin Ridington, 'Cultures in Conflict: The Problem of Discourse,' in Witt. New, ed., *Native Writers and Canadian Writing* (Vancouver: UBC Press, 1990).

127 For further commentary on the historical and cultural assumptions of Chief Justice McEachern's decision in *Delgamuukw* see Fortune, 'Construing *Delgamuukw*'; Asch and Bell, 'Definition and Interpretation of Fact'; Fisher, 'Judging History'; Sherrott, 'The Court's Treatment of the Evidence.'

128 *R.D.S. v. The Queen* (1997), 10 C.R. (5th) 1 (S.C.C.), per L'Heureux-Dubé J. and McLachlin JJ. at para. 35.

129 Ridington, 'Fieldwork in Courtroom 53,' in Frank Cassidy, ed., *Aboriginal Title in British Columbia:* Delgamuukw v. The Queen (Lantzville, BC: Oolichan Books, 1992), at 211–12.

130 For one historian's description of his 'ordeal' in court, see Arthur Ray, 'Creating the Image of the Savage in Defence of the Crown' (1990) 6 *Native Studies Review* 13.

131 *Delgamuukw* at 1065, 1068 (S.C.C.). See also Clay McLeod, 'The Oral Histories of Canada's Northern Peoples, Anglo-Canadian Evidence Law, and Canada Fiduciary Duties to First Nations: Breaking Down the Barriers of the Past' (1992) 30 *Alberta Law Review* 1276 at 1279.

132 Penny Petrone, *Native Literature in Canada: From Oral Traditions to the Present* (Toronto: Oxford University Press, 1990), at 9–12.

133 Ibid.

134 One lawyer has commented on this process as follows: 'What counts as fact? What can sustain us? With more and more sophisticated technologies we

have destroyed the stories. In court cases, we word search transcripts to reassemble the evidence; it doesn't resemble anything that was said by anyone. We cut the words, even our written words, away from the environment, and hold them up as pieces of meaning, hacked up pieces of meaning. As lawyers we don't have to take any responsibility to construct a world. We only have to destroy another's construction. We say no. We are civilized, well-heeled, comfortable carriers of no. We thrive on it. Other races die.' Pinder, *The Carriers of No*, at 10.

135 There are only sixteen Aboriginal judges in Canada, none of whom sit on an appellate court. For an explanation of the importance of Aboriginal control over traditional knowledge and culture, see Gordon Christie, 'Aboriginal Rights, Aboriginal Culture and Protection' (1998) 36 *Osgoode Hall Law Journal* 447.

136 Alex Rose, ed., *Nisga'a: People of the Nass River* (Vancouver: Douglas and McIntyre, 1993), at 15.

137 This is the Trickster's name in Nisga'a territory.

138 These are the clans of the Nisga'a, along with the Raven.

139 An Act to amend certain Laws respecting Indians and to extend certain Laws relating to matters connected with Indians to the Provinces of Manitoba and British Columbia, S.C. 1974, c. 21.

140 Indian Act, R.S.C. 1886, c. 46, s. 114. For commentary, see Cole and Chaikin, *An Iron Hand upon the People*.

141 Totem poles were cut down and used in the community as foundations for a building constructed by the non-Nisga'a.

142 See 'Residential Schools: Chapter 10,' in *Report of the Royal Commission on Aboriginal People*, volume 1, *Looking Forward, Looking Back*, at 333–408.

143 This point is also made in A.C. Hamilton and C.M. Sinclair, *The Justice System and Aboriginal People: Report of the Aboriginal Justice Inquiries in Manitoba*, Vol. 1 (Winnipeg: Queen's Printer, 1991), at 509–33.

144 British Columbia Indians Land Settlement Act, 1 July 1920, R.S.C.; Order in Council P.C. 1265, 19 July 1924. For commentary, see Titley, *A Narrow Vision*, at 145–61.

145 Indian Act, R.S.C. 1927, c. 98, s. 114. For commentary, see Titley, *A Narrow Vision*, at 59.

146 *Delgamuukw* at 1098 (S.C.C.).

147 Definition of 'crystallize' found in *Funk and Wagnalls Standard College Dictionary*, Can. ed. (Toronto: Fitzhenry and Whiteside, 1974), at 325.

148 *Delgamuukw* at 1116–17 (S.C.C.).

149 Ibid. at 1107–14.

150 Ibid. at 1088–91.

151 'Alchemy brings to its end that which has not come to an end ...' Peracelsus, a sixteenth-century German physician, cited in Marie Boas, *The Scientific Renaissance, 1494–1669* (London: Collins, 1962) at 177.

152 A brief intellectual background of the societies that developed this tradition is found in John Hale, *The Civilization of Europe in the Renaissance* (Toronto: Macmillan, 1994), at 355–72.

153 The Greek didactic poet Hesiod, who recorded the economic, political, and legal values of the archaic period of Greek history, commented on the arbitrary fables and fictions of princes and nobles who dispossessed other peoples. See David Tandy and Walter Neale, *Hesiod's Works and Days* (Berkeley: University of California Press, 1996), at lines 202–12.

   Ancient Rome also provides numerous examples of fictions used to deprive other nations of political and legal rights. The myth of Romulus and Remus endeavoured to absolve Romans from taking jurisdiction over Sabian and Etruscan peoples and lands. See Inez Scott Ryberg, trans., 'Selections from Livy's History of Rome,' in Paul MacKendrick and Herbert M. Howe, eds., *Classics in Translation*, vol. 2 (Madison: University of Wisconsin Press, 1980), at 284–7. This myth bred power, and Rome expanded at the expense of other nations. In AD 14, Augustus recorded the raw fact of his nation's power: 'I extended the frontiers of all those provinces of the Roman People which bordered nations not obedient to our command.' C.F. Edson and C. Schuler, trans. 'The Deeds of the Deified Augustus,' in ibid., 302 at 306. Eventually Rome's power was disseminated through law, and was effective in controlling the rights of others. For one example, see John Paul Heironimus, trans., 'Selected Letters of the Younger Pliny,' in ibid., 361 at 366–7 (Pliny to the Emperor Trajan).

154 For example, see Niccolo di Bernardo Machiavelli, *The Prince*, 77 at 82–4, 133–6 and *The Discourses* 167 at 193–6, 200–1, 208, 210, 216, 314–16, 412–13, in Peter Bondanella and Mark Musa, eds. and trans., *The Portable Machiavelli* (New York: Penguin Books, 1979). Machiavelli argued for the use of fictions in the affairs of state. In the seventeenth century, Thomas Hobbes also identified the importance of fictions and created the myth of the 'Leviathan' to support the extension of civil authority over people. See Thomas Hobbes, *Leviathan*, ed. R. Tuck (Cambridge: Cambridge University Press, 1991), at 120.

155 Plato wrote about the myth of the metals to explain why some people could claim rights and enforce laws over others in G.M.A. Grube, trans., *Plato's Republic* (Indianapolis: Hackett, 1974), at line 415a–e.:

... but the God who fashioned you mixed gold in the creation of those of you who are fit to rule, so that they are the most precious; and in the guardians, silver; and iron and bronze in the farmers and craftsmen ...

Can you suggest any device which will make our citizens believe this story?

I can not see any way, he said, to make them believe it themselves, but their sons and later generations might ...

But let us leave this matter to later tradition. Let us now arm our earthborn and lead them forth with rulers in charge. And as they march let them look for the best place in the city to have their camp, a site from which they could most easily control those within, if anyone is unwilling to obey the laws ...

156 Pope Innocent IV, 'Commentaria Doctissima in Quinque Libros Decreta-lium,' in James Muldoon, ed., *The Expansion of Europe: The First Phase* (Phila-delphia: University of Pennsylvania, 1977), 191 at 191–2, cited in David Getches, Charles Wilkinson and Robert A. Williams Jr, eds., *Federal Indian Law: Cases and Materials* (St Paul, MN: West Publishing, 1993), at 43–4.

157 See James Muldoon, *Popes, Lawyers, and Infidels* (Philadelphia: University of Pennsylvania, 1979). Similar assertions were also used by those who resisted the Christians. See Mohammed Pickthall, *The Meaning of the Glorious Koran* (New York: New American Library, 1953), at 64, 72, 86, 139–44. An Islamic perspective on law (the Shari'ah) and war can be found in Seyyed Hossein Nasr, *Ideals and Realities of Islam* (Boston: Beacon Press, 1966) at 31, 93–118.

158 See Sidney Z. Ehler and John B. Morral, eds. and trans., *Church and State through the Centuries* (London: Burns and Oates, 1967), at 142, 153–7, cited in Getches, Wilkinson, and Williams, *Federal Indian Law*, at 45–7. See also Felix S. Cohen, 'The Spanish Origins of Indian Rights in the Law of the United States' (1942) 31 *Georgetown Law Journal* 1.

159 Getches, Wilkinson, and Williams, *Federal Indian Law*, at 46.

160 See Lewis Hanke, *The Spanish Struggle for Justice in America* (Philadelphia: University of Pennsylvania Press, 1949), 34, cited in Getches, Wilkinson, and Williams, *Federal Indian Law*, at 50: 'A complete list of the events that occurred when the Requirements' formalities ordered by King Ferdinand were carried out in America, more or less according to law, might tax the reader's patience and credulity, for the Requirement was read to stress and empty huts when no Indians were to be found. Captains muttered its theo-logical phrases into their beards on the edge of sleeping Indian settle-ments, or even a league away before starting the formal attack, and at times some leather-lunged Spanish notary hurled its sonorous phrases after the Indians as they fled into the mountains.'

161 Charles Gibson, ed., *The Spanish Tradition in America* (Columbia: University of South Carolina Press, 1968), at 58–60.

162 For a detailed study of this phenomenon in North America see Francis Jennings, *The Invasion of America: Indians, Colonialism and the Cant of Conquest* (New York: W.W. Norton, 1976).

163 In *Calvin's Case* (1608), 77 Eng. Rep. 377 (K.B.), Lord Chief Justice Edward Coke observed: 'if a King come to a Christian kingdom ... he may at his pleasure alter and change the laws of that kingdom; but until he doth make an alteration of those laws the ancient laws of that kingdom remain. But if a Christian King should conquer a kingdom of an infidel, and bring them under his subjection, there *ipso facto* the laws of the infidel are abrogated, for that they be not only against Christianity, but against the law of God, and of nature ...'

164 The Royal Proclamation of 1763 (U.K.), repr. in R.S.C. 1985, App. II, No. 1, states: 'And whereas it is just and reasonable, and essential to our Interest, and the Security of our Colonies, that the several Nations or Tribes of Indians with whom we are connected, and who live under our protection, should not be molested or disturbed in the Possession of such Parts of *Our Dominions and Territories* as, *not having been ceded to or purchased by US*, are reserved to them ...'

165 Chief Justice Marshall in *McIntosh v. Johnson* at 573–4: 'Those relations which were to exist between the discoverer and the natives, were to be regulated by themselves ... In the establishment of these relations, the rights of the original inhabitants were, in no instance entirely disregarded; but were necessarily, to a considerable extent impaired ... their rights to complete sovereignty, as independent nations were necessarily diminished ...'

166 For an excellent discussion of this process see Robert Williams, Jr, *The American Indian in Western Legal Thought: The Discourses of Conquest* (New York: Oxford University Press, 1990).

167 *St. Catherines Milling and Lumber Co. v. The Queen* (1888), 14 App. Cas. 46 at 54.

168 *Delgamuukw* at 1098 (S.C.C.).

169 See *R. v. Guerin*, [1984] 2 S.C.R. 355 at 378: 'The principle of discovery ... gave ultimate title in the land in a particular area to the nation which had discovered and claimed it. In that respect at least the Indians' rights in the land were obviously diminished.'

170 See *R. v. Sparrow*, [1990] 1 S.C.R. 1075 at 1103: 'there was from the outset never any doubt that sovereignty and legislative power, and indeed the underlying title, to such lands vested in the Crown.'

171 *Delgamuukw* at 1098 (S.C.C.).

172 *Van der Peet* at 547.

173 The former Chief Justice of the United States Supreme Court noted: 'The extravagant and absurd idea that the feeble settlements made on the sea coast, or the companies under whom they were made, acquired legitimate power by them to govern the people, or occupy the lands from sea to sea, did not enter the mind of any man.' *Worcester v. Georgia*, 31 U.S. (6 Pet.) 515 *Georgia* at 544–5.

174 *Delgamuukw* at 1098 (S.C.C.), per Lamer C.J.C.

175 Ibid.

176 Ibid. at 1083.

177 Ibid. at 1081.

178 Ibid. at 1083.

179 In characterizing the Aboriginal right in question (in this case, title) as sui generis, the Court continued a trend made explicit in *R. v. Guerin*. For further discussion see Borrows and Rotman, 'The Sui Generis Nature of Aboriginal Rights.'

180 *Delgamuukw* at 1081 (S.C.C.).

181 Ibid. The reliance on the sui generis nature of Aboriginal title affirms the Supreme Court's earlier pronouncement in *St. Mary's Indian Band v. Cranbrook*, [1997] 2 S.C.R. 657 at 667, that 'native land rights are in a category of their own, and as such, traditional real property rules do not aid the Court in resolving' Aboriginal land rights cases.

182 *Delgamuukw* at 1081 (S.C.C.), per Lamer C.J.C.

183 Ibid. at 1081. Various dimensions of that title include its inalienability except to the Crown, its source, and the communal nature of its holding. Inalienability is referenced to assertions of sovereignty because 'lands held pursuant to aboriginal title cannot be transferred, sold or surrendered to anyone other that the Crown.' Ibid. Its source is referenced to assertions of sovereignty because it 'arises from possession *before* the assertion of British sovereignty.' Ibid. at 1082. Its communal nature is referenced to British sovereignty because 'aboriginal title cannot be held by individual aboriginal persons,' which is a common law legal fiction created to ensure that only the Crown receives title from an Aboriginal nation. Ibid.

184 See Darlene Johnston, *The Taking of Indian Lands: Consent or Coercion?* (Saskatoon: University of Saskatoon Native Law Centre, 1989).

185 *Delgamuukw* at 1107 (S.C.C.), citing Lamer C.J.C. in *R. v. Gladstone* at 774.

186 *Delgamuukw* at 1107–8 (S.C.C.), citing Lamer C.J.C. in *R. v. Gladstone* at 774–5 (emphasis omitted).

187 As Nisga'a people observed in 1887: 'The land was given to us by our forefathers by the great God above, who made both the white man and the

Indian, and our forefathers handed it down and we have not given it to anyone. It is still ours and will be ours until we sign a strong paper to give part of it to the Queen.' Tennant, *Aboriginal Peoples and Politics*, at 62. See Tennant generally, as his entire book deals with this issue.

188 See Robert Howse and Alissa Malkin, 'Canadians are a Sovereign People: How the Supreme Court Should Approach the Reference on Quebec Secession' (1997) 76 *Canadian Bar Review* 186 at 192, where they observe: 'If the constitution can only defend itself through self-assertion of its bindingness then this invites an opposite self-assertion of those who seek to reject the constitutional order as a whole, and the matter cannot but be resolved except through an implicitly violent struggle of wills. This is the dangerous and fateful implication of the positivistic approach [to constitutional interpretation].'

189 *St. Catherines Milling and Lumber Co. v. The Queen* at 55, 54.

190 *Delgamuukw* at 284 (B.C.S.C.).

191 Ibid. at 285.

192 Ibid.

193 Ibid. at 342. The United States Supreme Court expressed a similar sentiment when it wrote 'Every American schoolboy knows that the savage tribes of this continent were deprived of their ancestral ranges by force and that, even when the Indians ceded millions of acres by treaty in return for blankets, food and trinkets, it was not a sale but the conquerors' will that deprived them of their land.' *Tee-Hit-Ton Indians v. United States* at 289–90.

194 In Monet and Wilson, *Colonialism on Trial*, at 196, Skanu'u (Ardythe Wilson-Gitksan) responded to such notions with the following observation: 'the reality is that, historically and to the present, we have been active in our resistance to be silenced and made invisible. The reality is that we have never given up, never sold, nor lost in battle, our ownership and jurisdiction to our territories. Our right and title is inherited from our ancestors who lived and governed themselves for thousands of years before Columbus emerged from his mother's womb and drew his first breath. The reality is that *Delgamuukw v. The Queen* is only one of the many simultaneous activities undertaken by the Gitksan and Wet'suwet'en to protest the abuses of the Agents of the Crown since their first encroachment on to our territories. The reality is that our societies, our cultures and our systems are alive and well. They have sustained us through more than 150 years of the darkest, most destructive years that our people have ever known and will continue to sustain us ...'

195 See Lisa Disch, 'More Truth than Fact: Storytelling as Critical Understanding in the Writing of Hannah Arendt' (1993) 21 *Political Theory* 665 at 682:

'Political events are contingent and so cannot be named or known in terms of existing conceptual categories. In Third Critique, Kant introduces "crystallization" as a metaphor for contingency ... Crystallization describes the formation of objects that come into being not by a gradual, evolutionary process but suddenly and unpredictably "by a *shooting together*, i.e. by a sudden solidification." ... In calling totalitarianism "the final crystallizing catastrophe" that constitutes its various "elements" into a historical crisis, [Hannah] Arendt makes an analogy between contingent beauty and unprecedented evil' (emphasis in original). Could the Supreme Court's acceptance of the Crown's crystallization of title be analogized as an acceptance of an act of totalitarianism by the Crown, an evil which constitutes its various elements into a historical crisis? For further discussion of Arendt's work see Lisa Disch, *Hannah Arendt and the Limits of Philosophy* (Ithaca, N.Y.: Cornell University Press, 1994).

196 *Delgamuukw* at 1107 (S.C.C.), per Lamer C.J.C.

197 Ibid. at 1103.

198 Ibid. at 1111 (emphasis in original). For commentary see Catherine Bell, 'New Directions in the Law of Aboriginal Rights' (1998) 77 *Canadian Bar Review* 36 at 62. For a critique of the infringement of constitutional Aboriginal rights see Kent McNeil, 'How Can the Infringements of the Constitutional Rights of Aboriginal Peoples Be Justified?' (1997) 8 *Constitutional Forum* 33.

199 I am paraphrasing Joseph Conrad, who wrote 'The conquest of the earth, which mostly means the taking it away from those who have a different complexion or slightly flatter noses than ourselves, is not a pretty thing when you look into it.' *Heart of Darkness*, 2nd ed., ed. D.C.R.A. Goonetilleke (Peterborough, ON: Broadview Press, 1999). See also Machiavelli, *The Prince*, at 82–3.

200 *Delgamuukw* at 1108 (S.C.C.).

201 '[B]oth the federal and provincial governments' can exercise this power. Ibid. at 1107. For further critique of the court's test for infringement see Kent McNeil, *Defining Aboriginal Title in the 90's: Has the Supreme Court Finally Got It Right?* (North York, ON: Robarts Centre for Canadian Studies, York University, 1998).

202 The United States Supreme Court in *Cherokee Nation v. Georgia*, 30 U.S. (5 Pet.) 1 at 26–7 (1831) observed: 'They have in Europe sovereign and semi-sovereign states and states of doubtful sovereignty. But this state [Indian Nations], if it be a state, is still a grade below them all: for not to be able to alienate without permission of the remainder-man or lord, places them in a state of feudal dependence.'

203 *Delgamuukw* at 1096 (S.C.C.).

204 Ibid. at 1085–6.

205 Ibid. at 1083.

206 Feudal tenure gave important rights to the lord, vis-a-vis the tenant, which are analogous to the Crown/Aboriginal relationship. See Stroud Milsom, *Historical Foundations of the Common Law,* 2nd ed. (Toronto: Butterworths, 1981), at 100.

207 See Kent McNeil, *Common Law Aboriginal Title* (Oxford: Clarendon Press, 1989), at 107, where he refuted this assertion.

208 *Delgamuukw* at 1085 (S.C.C.), per Lamer C.J.C.

209 Ibid.

210 Ibid., citing s. 18(2) of the Indian Act.

211 Ibid.

212 Ibid. at 1085–6.

213 Ibid. at 1087–8. For a critique of the restriction on Aboriginal rights by reference to Aboriginal pre-contact practices see Russel Barsh and James Youngblood Henderson, 'The Supreme Court *Van der Peet* Trilogy: Native Imperialism and Ropes of Sand' (1997) 42 *McGill Law Journal* 993; Bradford Morse, 'Permafrost Rights: Aboriginal Self-Government and the Supreme Court in *R. v. Pamajewon*' (1997) 42 *McGill Law Journal* 1011.

214 *Delgamuukw* at 1088 (S.C.C.).

215 Ibid. at 1091. An example of the increased powers Aboriginal people might enjoy relative to participation and consultation in lands and resources is found in *Nunavut Tunngavik Inc. v. Canada* (1997), 149 D.L.R. (4th) 519 (F.C.T.D.), where the Minister of Fisheries and Oceans' allocation of fish was set aside because it did not conform to consultation requirements set out in the Nunavut Agreement. While this case may be distinguished from issues of title because consultation between the minister and the Aboriginal group was mandated by agreement, one might find courts taking a similar stance given *Delgamuukw*'s strong requirement for Aboriginal participation where title is found to exist. If British Columbia courts were to review ministerial decision making as the Federal Court did, then resource allocation and management in the province would eventually undergo substantial changes.

216 For discussion of this point, see the Honourable Mr Justice Douglas Lambert, '*Van der Peet* and *Delgamuukw*: Ten Unresolved Issues' (1998) 32 *University of British Columbia Law Review* 249 at 258–9.

217 *Delgamuukw* at 1089 (S.C.C.). The court went on to add that these 'elements of aboriginal title,' referring to the traditional activities and use of the land by Aboriginal peoples, 'create' the 'inherent limitation on the uses to which the land, over which such title exists, may be put.'

218 The court said: 'For example, if occupation is established with reference to the use of the lands as a hunting ground' it cannot strip mine it. 'Similarly, if a group claims a special bond with the land because of its ceremonial or cultural significance, it may not use the land in such a way as to destroy that relationship (e.g., by developing it in such a way that the bond is destroyed, perhaps by turning it into a parking lot).' Ibid.

219 Ibid. at 1091.

220 When did Aboriginal peoples in British Columbia ever agree to the Crown being able to receive and redesignate their lands if they were used for 'unauthorized' (as defined by non-Aboriginal courts) purposes?

221 The definition of Aboriginal rights according to traditional activities is criticized in Barsh and Henderson, 'The Supreme Court *Van der Peet* Trilogy'; Morse, 'Permafrost Rights.'

222 *Delgamuukw* at 1095 (S.C.C.).

223 Ibid.

224 One can anticipate numerous judicial contests concerning the elements of Aboriginal title that prohibit its use 'in a way that aboriginal title does not permit.' Ibid. at 1091.

225 Ibid. at 1097.

226 Ibid. (emphasis added).

227 Ibid. at 1100.

228 The court said, ibid. at 1101, citing McNeil, *Common Law Aboriginal Title*, at 201–2, that since at common law physical occupation is proof of possession, title 'may be established in a variety of ways, ranging from the construction of dwellings through cultivation and the enclosure of fields to regular use of definite tracts for hunting, fishing or otherwise exploiting its resources.' The court further noted, citing Slattery, 'Understanding Aboriginal Rights,' at 758, that 'In considering whether occupation sufficient to ground title is established, "one must take into account the group's size, manner of life, material resources, and technological abilities and the character of the lands claimed."'

229 In *Delgamuukw* at 1104 (S.C.C.), the court wrote: 'The requirement for exclusivity flows from the definition of aboriginal title itself, because I have defined aboriginal title in terms of the right to exclusive use and occupation of land. Exclusivity, as an aspect of aboriginal title, vests in the aboriginal community which holds the ability to exclude others from the lands held pursuant to that title. The proof of title must, in this respect, mirror the content of the right' (emphasis omitted).

230 I am paraphrasing the judgment of the Australian High Court in *Mabo v. Queensland* at 42: 'Whatever the justification advanced in earlier days for

refusing to recognize the rights and interests in land of the indigenous inhabitants of settled colonies, an unjust and discriminatory doctrine of that kind can no longer be accepted.'

231 David McKay, cited in *Calder v. A.G.B.C.* at 150.

232 Prime Minister Pierre Trudeau's speech, which is quoted throughout this paragraph, is found in Peter Cumming and Neil Mickenburg, *Native Rights in Canada*, 2nd ed. (Toronto: Indian-Eskimo Association, 1972), at appendix IV.

233 Cardinal, *The Unjust Society.*

234 Weaver, *Making Canadian Indian Policy.*

235 *Calder v. A.G.B.C.* (S.C.C.).

236 *Delgamuukw* at 1114 (S.C.C.).

237 Ibid.

238 Ibid.

239 The principle of equality before the law was explained in *Canada (A.G.) v. Lavell*, [1974] S.C.R. 1349 at 1366: ' "equality before the law" ... is frequently invoked to demonstrate that the same law applies to the highest official of government as to any other ordinary citizen, and in this regard Professor F.R. Scott, in delivering the Plaunt Memorial Lectures on Civil Liberties and Canadian Federalism in 1959, speaking of the case of *Roncarelli v. Duplessis* [(1959), 16 D.L.R. (2d) 689], had occasion to say: "It is always a triumph for the law to show that it is applied equally to all without fear or favour. That is what we mean when we say that all are equal before the law." '

240 *Delgamuukw* at 1115 (S.C.C.).

241 For an examination of the unequal treatment of Aboriginal and non-Aboriginal sovereignty in the United States see Joseph Singer, 'Sovereignty and Property' (1991) *Northwestern University Law Review* 1.

242 *Nisga'a Final Agreement*, initialed 4 August 1998 at 1; now Nisga'a Final Agreement Act, S.B.C. 1999, c. 2.

243 For differing opinions on the Nisga'a Agreement see the special issue of (1998/99) 120 *B.C. Studies.*

244 Nisga'a Final Agreement Act, Chapter 3, s. 4(a).

245 While it may seem unlikely that Nisga'a people will lose access to their land given the government power they will retain over alienated land, its potential future loss to them should not be entirely dismissed. The Alaska Land Claims Settlement provided that Indian lands would be held in fee simple, and while the provisions there were given in a different context, many groups lost their lands. See Thomas Berger, *Village Journey* (Vancouver: Douglas and McIntyre, 1988).

246 The Nisga'a have agreed to release any Aboriginal rights that are not dealt

with in the Agreement to Canada: 'If, despite this Agreement and the settlement legislation, the Nisga'a Nation has an Aboriginal right, including Aboriginal title, in Canada, that is different in attributes or geographical extent from, the Nisga'a section 35 rights as set out in this Agreement, the Nisga'a Nation releases that Aboriginal right to Canada ...' Nisga'a Final Agreement Act, General Provisions, s. 26.

247 Many of the responsibilities of wilps will be effectively replaced by the Nisga'a Lisims Government and Nisga'a Village Governments. While this is not expressly in the agreement a review of the powers of these governments makes this evident. Nisga'a Final Agreement Act, Chapter 11, Nisga'a Government, ss. 2–8.

248 See the Nisga'a Final Agreement Act, at 25 (incidental impact provisions), 66–8 (forestry equivalency provisions), 159 (federal/provincial paramountcy in environmental protection).

249 See the Nisga'a Final Agreement Act at 162–3 (judicial review of administrative decisions by Nisga'a Institutions), 193 (appeal from Nisga'a court to the B.C.S.C.).

250 See Nisga'a Final Agreement Act at page 217.

251 See ibid. at 239.

252 David Black, owner of Black Newspapers (which publishes forty-eight papers in British Columbia), expressed this view in an interview with Ben Meisner, CKPG Radio in Prince George on Friday, 23 October 1998. Dr Keith Martin, a Reform Party MP from the riding of Esquimalt-Jaun de Fuca, has expressed similar views: 'Apartheid or separate development failed in South Africa, and it will fail in B.C.' See Craig McInnes, *Globe and Mail*, 24 July 1998. Aboriginal people do not themselves want to be victims of racism and apartheid. Chief Louis Stevenson of the Peguis First Nation tried to bring this to the world's attention. See Mallea, *Aboriginal Law*, at 1–7; Richardson, *People of Terra Nullius*, at 126.

253 See Resolutions from the 12th Annual Convention of the Nisga'a Tribal Council in a letter from Frank Calder to Jean Chretien, 10 November 1969 (DIAND file 1/24–2–16, vol. 2). See also Gordon Campbell, *Policy Positions: One Law for All*, 5 October 1998, http://www.bcliberals.bc.ca/platform/policy/positions/treaty /html. Gordon Campbell is the leader of the provincial Liberal Party. In 2001 he was elected premier of British Columbia.

254 Chief Joe Mathias has lamented racist policies in Canada that deny Aboriginal people ownership of land. See Frank Cassidy, ed., *Reaching Just Settlements: Land Claims in British Columbia* (Lantzville, BC: Oolichan Books, 1991), at 14–17. Mel Smith has also deplored the use of race to separate people. See *Our Home or Native Land?* (Vancouver: Stoddart, 1995).

255 Preston Manning, then leader of the Official Opposition in the House of Commons, expressed a similar view in the *Globe and Mail*, Tuesday, 16 June 1998 at A23; editorialist Trevor Lautens said the Supreme Court's *Delgamuukw* decision 'drastically undermined the Crown ownership of 94 per cent of the land mass of BC,' *Vancouver Sun*, Saturday, 28 February 1998; Terry Morley labelled the decision 'imprudent,' *Vancouver Sun*, Saturday, 20 December 1998; writer Gordon Gibson called it a 'breathtaking mistake,' *Globe and Mail*, 16 December 1998.

256 The Reform Party of Canada made this point, and the ones that follow in the next few sentences, in a document entitled, 'What the Nisga'a Deal Means to You,' http://www.reform.ca/duncan/whatdeal.html. The Assembly of First Nations has made similar points about the government before and, in 1990, wrote: 'important policy frameworks should not be dictatorily or unilaterally imposed.' See Assembly of First Nations, 'A Critique of Federal Land Claims Policies,' in Cassidy, *Aboriginal Self-Determination*, 232 at 246.

257 Gordon Gibson has asked this question. *Globe and Mail*, 21 July 1998, at A15.

258 See Select Standing Committee on Aboriginal Affairs, *Towards Reconciliation: Nisga'a Agreement-in-Principle and British Columbia Treaty Process* (Thirty-sixth Parliament, Legislative Assembly of British Columbia, 3 July 1997).

259 Those in favour of a referendum are numerous. The Liberal Party of British Columbia initiated legal action to force a referendum on the treaty, while editorials in many newspapers, such as the *Financial Post*, 23 October 1998, and the *Globe and Mail*, Friday, 24 July 1998, have likewise called for a referendum. Mel Smith has said, 'In my view, the Nisga'a Agreement attempts to establish a third order of government without benefit of a formal constitutional amendment.' *Merritt Herald*, 21 October 1998 at 23. The Federal Reform Party and its successor, the Canadian Alliance Party, have also come out in support of a referendum on the treaty. See 'Federal Reform Joins Bid to Force Nisga'a Vote,' *Vancouver Sun*, Friday, 24 July 1998.

Aboriginal people in British Columbia similarly wonder about significant constitutional changes that effect the structure of their society by including them in the province without their consent. It would be interesting to see the question of their consent to inclusion in British Columbia put to a referendum. Allowing Aboriginal people to vote on this question separately, while the rest of the province votes on the Nisga'a treaty, should satisfy those who wish to see true representative participation in a referendum. The Cree in Quebec assert a similar point in Grand Council of the Cree, *Sovereign Injustice: Forcible Inclusion of the James Bay Crees and Cree Territory into a Sovereign Quebec* (Nemaska, James Bay, QC: Grand Council of the Cree [of Quebec], 1995), at 297–350.

260 Mel Smith, *Vernon Morning Star,* 12 October 1998, at 12. Harold Cardinal also wrote about the importance of not turning back the clock: 'Positive Indian identity does not ... mean a desire to return to the days of yesteryear.' *The Unjust Society,* at 24.

261 Ovide Mercredi, Former Chief of the Assembly of First Nations, expressed these views in Assembly of First Nations, *First Peoples and the Constitution: Conference Report of March 13–15, 1992* (Ottawa: Supply and Services, 1992), at 34 and in Mercredi and Turpel, *In the Rapids,* at 24, 245–8.

262 It was unilateral in the sense that Aboriginal peoples did not participate in its creation and their political will in the matter was actively suppressed. For a discussion of the implications of unilateral assertions of sovereignty see the *Reference Re Secession of Quebec* at 264–6.

263 The court noted in *Sparrow,* at 1099, that '[t]he consent to its extinguishment before the *Constitution Act 1982,* was not required ... The test of extinguishment to be adopted, in our opinion, is that the Sovereign's intention must be clear and plain if it is to extinguish an aboriginal right.' The court has also suggested that, prior to 1982, negotiated treaty rights can be unilaterally modified without the consent of the Aboriginal group which claims the protection of the treaty. See *R. v. Badger,* [1996] 1 S.C.R. 771 (S.C.C.).

264 In *Delgamuukw* at 1115 (S.C.C.) the court noted that '[r]ights which were extinguished by the sovereign before that time are not revived' by s. 35(1) of the Constitution Act, 1982.

265 *Delgamuukw* at 1116 (S.C.C.).

266 *Van der Peet* at 547.

267 *Delgamuukw* at 1115 (S.C.C.).

268 The submergence of Aboriginal jurisdiction within federal/provincial disputes is also found in other areas of Aboriginal rights jurisprudence. See Turpel 'Home/Land.'

269 The court expressed no opinion concerning extinguishment of Aboriginal title in British Columbia prior to 1871. Since there were numerous proclamations and ordinances prior to 1871 in this area (which some courts have interpreted as extinguishing Aboriginal title in British Columbia), the court's failure to address this question leaves a very wide door open for those who would claim that Aboriginal title in the province was extinguished before British Columbia entered Confederation.

270 The Supreme Court of Canada recently determined that band councils could grant long-term interests in reserve land without extinguishing their rights in the parcel. In *Opetchesaht Indian Band v. Canada* (1997), 147 D.L.R.

(4th) 1, the court found that under s. 28(2) of the Indian Act, R.S.C. 1952, c. 149, bands have the authority to 'grant limited indeterminate rights in reserve lands' without securing the consent of their membership.

271 For a case that demonstrates the role of Aboriginal consent in the alternation of their legal interests see *Semiahmoo Indian Band v. Canada* (1997), 148 D.L.R. (4th) 523 (F.C.A.). The court's attention was focused on the Crown's fiduciary obligations that attached to surrenders of lands under ss. 37 and 38 of the Indian Act, S.C. 1951, c. 29. In the *Semiahmoo* case, the court found the Crown had a 'post-surrender' fiduciary duty to act in the best interests of the band, and that it had violated this duty when it failed to return the land to the band as requested at a later date. The case is significant because it demonstrates some courts' concerns regarding the Crown's treatment of Indian consent. For commentary see Bob Freedman, '*Semiahmoo Indian Band v. Canada*' (1997) 36 *Alberta Law Review* 218. See also Eugene Meehan and Elizabeth Stewart, 'Developments in Aboriginal Law: The 1995–96 Term' (1997) 8 *Supreme Court Law Review* 1 at 7, commenting on *Blueberry River Indian Band v. Canada* (1995), 130 D.L.R. (4th) 193 (S.C.C.).

272 *Delgamuukw* at 1117 (S.C.C.).

273 Ibid.

274 Ibid. at 1119. The court continued, at 1120–1: 'As a result, a provincial law could never, proprio vigore, extinguish aboriginal rights, because the intention to do so would take the law outside of provincial jurisdiction.' For further commentary on the jurisdictional implications of *Delgamuukw* see Nigel Bankes, '*Delgamuukw*, Division of Powers and Provincial Land and Resource Laws: Some Implications for Provincial Resource Rights' (1998) 32 *University of British Columbia Law Review* 317.

275 *Delgamuukw* at 1122 (S.C.C.).

276 The cases of *Haida Nation v. British Columbia (Minister of Forests)* (1997), 153 D.L.R. (4th) 1 (B.C.C.A.); *Halfway River First Nation v. British Columbia (Minister of Forests)*, [1998] 1 C.N.L.R. 14 (B.C.S.C.); and *R. v. Paul (T.P.)* (1998), 196 N.B.R. (2d) 292 (C.A.) demonstrate that Aboriginal peoples' interest in their lands can affect the province's use and management of that resource. For instance, in *Haida*, the Haida claimed Aboriginal title to a large area subject to a tree farm licence. The issue was whether the Haida's claim was capable of constituting an encumbrance within the meaning of s. 28 of the Forest Act, R.S.B.C. 1996, c. 157. The British Columbia Court of Appeal held in *Haida* at 5, that there was 'no reason to doubt that, as a matter of plain or grammatical meaning, the aboriginal title claimed by the Haida Nation, if it exists, constitutes an encumbrance on the Crown's title to the

timber.' This case, coupled with *Delgamuukw*, demonstrates the significant impact that Aboriginal title could have on the use and management of provincial Crown lands.

277 *Sparrow* at 1112.

278 *Delgamuukw* at 519 (B.C.C.A.), citing the trial judgment of McEachern J. in *Delgamuukw* at 473 (B.C.S.C.)

279 *R. v. Cote* at 407.

280 To quote the words of Brennan J. in *Mabo v. Queensland* at 42: 'Whatever the justification advanced in earlier days for refusing to recognize the rights and interests in land of the indigenous inhabitants of settled colonies, an unjust and discriminatory doctrine of that kind can no longer be accepted.'

Chapter 5

1 John Borrows, 'A Genealogy of Law: Inherent Sovereignty and First Nations Self-Government' (1992) 30 *Osgoode Hall Law Journal* No. 2 at 291–354.

2 *R. v. Sparrow*, [1990] 1S.C.R. 1075 at 1103.

3 See the statement of David McKay, cited in *Calder v. A.G.B.C.* at 150. For other Aboriginal perspectives questioning Crown title, see Leroy Little Bear, Menno Boldt, and J. Anthony Long, *Pathways to Self-Determination: Canadian Indians and the Canadian State* (Toronto: University of Toronto Press, 1984), at 5–56; Menno Boldt, and J. Anthony Long, eds., *The Quest for Justice: Aboriginal Peoples and Aboriginal Rights* (Toronto: University of Toronto Press, 1986) at 17–70; Michael Asch, *Home and Native Land: Aboriginal Rights and the Canadian Constitution* (Toronto: Methuen, 1984), esp. at 26–40.

4 See *Reference Re Language Rights Under s. 23 of the Manitoba Act, 1870 and s. 133 of Constitution Act, 1867*, [1985] 1 S.C.R. 721 at 748–9.

5 The Royal Commission on Aboriginal Peoples was initiated in the months following the failure of constitutional reform in the Meech Lake Accord in 1987 and the armed confrontation between the Mohawks and the Canadian state at Oka, Quebec, in 1990. It was established on 26 August 1991 and issued its final report five years later, in November 1996. The mandate of the commission was to 'investigate the evolution of the relationship between aboriginal peoples ... the Canadian government, and Canadian society as a whole.' The commission was further asked to 'propose specific solutions rooted in domestic and international experience, to the problems that have plagued those relationships ...' *Report of the Royal Commission on Aboriginal People*, Volume 1, *Looking Forward, Looking Back* (Ottawa: Supply and Services, 1996), at 2. One of its foundational recommendations, which

it regarded as central to constructing a better relationship between Aboriginal peoples and the Crown, was for Canadian governments to acknowledge the lack of legal or moral justification for the dispossession of Aboriginal peoples in Canada. See recommendation 1.16.2 at page 696: 'Federal, provincial and territorial government further the process of renewal by: (a) acknowledging that concepts such as terra nullius and the doctrine of discovery are factually, legally and morally wrong.'

6 *Report of the Royal Commission on Aboriginal People*, volume 1, *Looking Forward, Looking Back*, at 245–544.

7 Differences between Aboriginal and Crown interpretations in this regard have been documented in each province and territory in Canada: in British Columbia, see Tennant, *Aboriginal Peoples and Politics*; in Alberta, see Richard Price, *The Spirit of Alberta Indian Treaties* (Edmonton: Pica Pica Press, 1987); in Saskatchewan, see Harold Cardinal, *My Dream: That We Will One Day Be Recognized as First Nations* (Saskatoon: Office of the Treaty Commissioner, 1998); in Manitoba, see Paul Chartrand, *Manitoba's Métis Settlement Scheme of 1870* (Saskatoon: Native Law Centre, 1991); in Ontario, see David McNab, *Circles of Time: Aboriginal Land Rights and Resistance in Ontario* (Waterloo: Wilfrid Laurier University Press, 1999); in Quebec, see Grand Council of the Crees (of Quebec), *Sovereign Injustice*; in New Brunswick, Nova Scotia, and Prince Edward Island, see L.F.S. Upton, *Micmacs and Colonists: Indian-White Relations in the Maritimes* (Vancouver: UBC Press, 1979); in Newfoundland, see Donald McCrae, *Report of the Complaints of the Innu of Labrador to the Canadian Human Rights Commission* (Ottawa: Supply and Services, 1993); in the North, see Royal Commission on Aboriginal Peoples, *The High Arctic Relocation*.

8 For these perspectives see generally Frank Cassidy, ed., *Aboriginal Self-Determination* (Lantzville, BC: Oolichan Books, 1991); Boyce Richardson, ed., *Drum-Beat: Anger and Renewal in Indian Country* (Toronto: Summerhill Press, 1989); Taiaiake Alfred, *Peace, Power, Righteousness: An Indigenous Manifesto* (Toronto: Oxford University Press, 1999); Patricia Monture-Angus, *Journeying Forward: Dreaming First Nations Independence* (Halifax: Fernwood, 1999).

9 A close examination of the numbered treaties covering Alberta, Saskatchewan, Manitoba, and northern and western Ontario shows many problems of deception and dishonesty; see Treaty 7 Elders and Tribal Council et al., 'Aboriginal and Government Objectives in the Treaty Era,' in *The True Spirit and Intent of Treaty 7* (Montreal: McGill-Queen's University Press, 1996), esp. at 210–12; Rene Fumoleau, *As Long as This Land Shall Last: A History of Treaty 8 and 11* (Toronto: McClelland and Stewart, 1976). For problems with treaties on Vancouver Island, see Chris Arnett, *The Terror of the*

Coast: Land Alienation and Colonial War on Vancouver Island and the Gulf Islands, 1849–1863 (Burnaby, BC: Talonbooks, 1999). For problems with treaties in Ontario see Janet Chute, *The Legacy of Shingwaukonse* (Toronto: University of Toronto Press, 1998), at 137–59, 195–221; for problems with the treaties in Atlantic Canada, see William Wicken, 'Re-examining Mi'kmaq-Acadian Relations 1635–1755,' in Sylvie Departie, et al., eds., *Vingt an après, Habitants et marchands: Lectures de l'histoire des XVIIe et XVIIIe siècles canadiens* (Montreal: McGill-Queen's University Press, 1998); William Wicken, 'Heard It from My Grandfather: Mi'kmaq Treaty Tradition and the Syliboy Case of 1928' (1995) 44 *University of New Brunswick Law Journal* 146; William Wicken, 'The Mi'kmaq and Wuastukwiuk Treaties' (1994) 43 *University of New Brunswick Law Journal* 43.

10 In fact, in one notable case concerning Treaty 11, *Paulette v. Register of Titles (No. 2)*, the court held: 'it was almost unbelievable that the Government party could have ever returned from their efforts [to sign a treaty] with any impression but that they had given an assurance in perpetuity to the Indians in their territories that their traditional use of land was not affected.' (1973), 42 D.L.R. (3d) 8 (N.W.T.S.C.); reversed on other grounds, 63 D.L.R. (3d) 1 (N.W.T.C.A.); affirmed on other grounds, 72 D.L.R. (3d) 161 (S.C.C.).

11 Large portions of British Columbia, Quebec, and the north fit into this category.

12 Canada is described as a free and democratic society in section 1 of the Charter.

13 Williams, *The American Indian in Western Legal Thought*; Peter Fitzpatrick, *The Mythology of Modern Law* (London: Routledge, 1992); Bruce Clark, *Native Liberty-Crown Sovereignty* (Montreal: McGill-Queen's University Press, 1990); A.C. Hamilton and C.M. Sinclair, *The Justice System and Aboriginal People: Report of the Aboriginal Justice Inquiry in Manitoba*, vol. 1 (Winnipeg: Queen's Printer, 1991), at 130–42; Dara Culhane, *The Pleasure of the Crown* (Vancouver: Talon Books, 1998).

14 From 1996 to 2000 Canada ranked as the number one country in the world on the United Nations Human Development Index. The index, compiled by the United Nations Development Program (UNDP), measures such areas as life expectancy, education, income. However, if Aboriginal peoples in Canada were included as a separate group they would rank sixty-third in the world. This gap is one indicator of the disparity between Aboriginal peoples and others in Canada. For a description of the socio-economic challenges Aboriginal peoples face in Canada see Royal Commission on Aboriginal Peoples, *Renewal: A Twenty Year Commitment*, vol. 5 (Ottawa: Supply and Services, 1996), at 23–54.

15 See Royal Commission on Aboriginal Peoples, *Bridging the Cultural Divide: A Report on Aboriginal Peoples and the Criminal Justice System* (Ottawa: Supply and Services, 1996). The Supreme Court of Canada in *R. v. Gladue*, [1999] 1 S.C.R. 688 noted that Canada is in 'crisis' with Aboriginal peoples and the justice system.

16 Kent McNeil, *Common Law Aboriginal Title* (Oxford: Clarendon Press, 1989).

17 Royal Commission on Aboriginal Peoples, *Treaty Making in the Spirit of Co-existence: An Alternative to Extinguishment* (Ottawa: Supply and Services, 1995).

18 For an affirmation of the importance of property and contractual rights in society see James W. Ely, *The Guardian of Every Other Right: A Constitutional History of Property Rights* (New York: Oxford University Press, 1998); Charles Fried, *Contract as Promise: A Theory of Contractual Obligation* (Cambridge: Harvard University Press, 1991).

19 Mel Smith, *Our Home or Native Land?* (Vancouver: Stoddart, 1995).

20 Matthew 7:24.

21 For critiques of the uses of the rule of law in this regard see articles in Alan Hutchinson and Patrick Monahan, eds., *The Rule of Law: Idea or Ideology* (Toronto: Carswell, 1987).

22 Ernest Barker, ed., *The Politics of Aristotle* (New York: Oxford University Press, 1958) at 126–7.

23 Ibid. Throughout *Delgamuukw*, the Supreme Court of Canada reveals an internal conflict as it vests final sovereignty in both the Crown and the rule of law. This conflict threatens the sovereignty of law in Canada. The vesting of final sovereignty in the Crown may produce a bias in the law in favour of Canada's non-Aboriginal population, which traces its rights to the Crown. Aboriginal people do not find their rights rooted in assertions of Crown sovereignty and thus could experience great difficulties in having their entitlements placed on an equal footing with those derived from the Crown. Furthermore, vesting final sovereignty in the Crown may pervert the constitution and its expression regarding the rule of law, in which final sovereignty is placed.

24 An interesting discussion about the appropriate distribution of legal entitlements between Aboriginal peoples and others in North America is found in Macklem, 'Distributing Sovereignty.'

25 See Preamble to the Charter.

26 *Reference Re Language Rights Under s. 23 of the Manitoba Act, 1870 and s. 133 of the Constitution Act, 1867*, [1985] 1 S.C.R. at 748–9.

27 The laws were of no force because they failed to comply with s. 23 of the Manitoba Act, 1870, U.K. 32 & 33 Vict. c. 3 (which is part of the Constitution of Canada, Constitution Act, 1871, U.K., c. 28). The laws of Alberta and

Saskatchewan suffered the same defect. See *R. v. Mercure*, [1988] 1 S.C.R. 234; *R. v. Paquette*, [1990] 2 S.C.R. 1103.

28 Patrick Monahan, *Essentials of Canadian Law: Constitutional Law* (Toronto: Irwin Law, 1997), at 128.

29 See Christopher Moore, *1867: How the Fathers Made a Deal* (Toronto: McClelland and Stewart, 1997).

30 The non-recognition of Aboriginal title, the creation of small inadequate reserves, the denial of the vote, the passage of anti-potlach laws, the denial of the right to pre-empt land, the replacement of systems of government through the Indian Act, the out-lawing of land claims support, the horror of residential schools, and numerous other actions taken as a result of this assertion.

31 Joe Rabin, 'Job Security and Due Process: Monitoring Administrative Discretion Through a Reasons Requirement' (1976) 44 *University of Chicago Law Review* 60 at 77–8.

32 *Island of Palmas Case* (1928), 2 R.I.A.A. 829, where the court held that a claim based on discovery is incomplete until accompanied by the effective occupation of the region claimed to be discovered; *Western Sahara Case*, (1975) ICJ Reports 12, in which the court precludes a region from being termed uninhabited if nomadic or resident tribes with a degree of social or political organization are present in the area.

33 See *Mabo v. Queensland* at 42, where Justice Brennan wrote, 'the common law of this country would perpetuate injustice if it were to continue to embrace the enlarged notion of terra nullius.'

34 *Status of Eastern Greenland Case* (1933), 3 W.C.R. 148 at 171: '[the doctrine of conquest] only operates as a cause of lack of sovereignty when there is a war between two states, and by reason of defeat of one of them sovereignty over territory passes from the loser to the victorious state.' Piecemeal encroachment on Aboriginal land in Canada does not fit this description.

35 Under the doctrine of adverse possession, one state can acquire title to part of another state's land by occupying it for an extended period of time with the acquiescence of the original owner. In order for the claim to be valid, there must be a de facto sovereignty that is peaceful and unchallenged. Canada did not acquire territory in this way as there has been continual Aboriginal resistance to Crown assertions of possession.

36 For further discussion see generally Sharon Venne, *Our Elders Understand Our Rights: Exploring International Law Regarding Indigenous Rights* (Penticton, BC: Theytus, 1998); James Anaya, *Indigenous Peoples in International Law* (New York: Oxford University Press, 1996).

37 For an insight into Aboriginal possession of land prior to British assertions of sovereignty in northern North America, see Cole Harris and Geoffrey

Matthews, eds., *Historical Atlas of Canada*, vol. 1, *From the Beginning to 1800* (Toronto: University of Toronto Press, 1987).

38 John Borrows, 'Wampum at Niagara: The Royal Proclamation, Canadian Legal History and Self-Government,' in Asch, *Aboriginal and Treaty Rights in Canada*, 155–72.

39 To understand how vagueness and unintelligibility relate to the rule of law see *R. v. Nova Scotia Pharmaceutical Society*, [1992] 2 S.C.R. 606 at 643: 'A law will be found unconstitutionally vague if it so lacks in precision as not to give sufficient guidance for legal debate.'

40 *Reference Re Language Rights* at 749.

41 A landmark report describing the encumbrances Aboriginal governments function within. See Keith Penner, *Indian Self-Government in Canada: Report of the Special Committee* (Ottawa: Queen's Printer, 1983). Other accessible descriptions include Howard Adams, *Prison of Grass: Canada from a Native Point of View* (Toronto: General, 1975); Cardinal, *The Unjust Society*; Miller, *Skyscrapers Hide the Heavens*; Richardson, *DrumBeat*; Richardson, *People of Terra Nullius*; Weaver, *Making Canadian Indian Policy*.

42 *Reference Re Language Rights* at 750–1. For examples of how the Canadian government acted contrary to the rule of law in displacing Aboriginal peoples' own purposive ordering of their own laws and social relations see *Report of the Royal Commission on Aboriginal People*, volume 1, *Looking Forward, Looking Back* at 137–200, 245–604.

43 *Reference Re Language Rights* at 753.

44 Ibid.

45 Ibid. at 757.

46 Ibid. at 768.

47 In order to enjoy the rule of law, both Aboriginal and non-Aboriginal peoples must live by legal frameworks that are extensions of themselves. A review of Canada's law and history reveals that Aboriginal peoples have not enjoyed this recognition. Is this a form of despotism? Aboriginal and non-Aboriginal people must be permitted to create structures that recognize the importance of both Aboriginal and Crown sovereignty in Canada. People will find greater dignity in laws that facilitate this objective. See Charles Taylor, *Philosophical Arguments* (Cambridge: Harvard University Press, 1995), at 187. See the Nisga'a treaty for one possible model in creating this proper legal framework.

48 *Calder* at 210.

49 Ibid.

50 Ibid. at 211.

51 Some might contend, however, that the Act of State doctrine should be

extended to prevent the court from reviewing the very assertion of Crown sovereignty. This may be called for on the ground that such review (despite not being an issue of treaty of conquest) would nevertheless be a challenge to an Act of State. In support, they may cite the rationale of the doctrine, which is a 'recognition of the Sovereign prerogative to acquire territory in a way that cannot be later challenged in municipal court.' *Calder* at 211. For those who make this argument, it should be remembered that the history of the development of parliamentary democracy involves a sustained attempt to restrict and constrain the Crown's prerogative powers. See Christopher Hill, *The Century of Revolution, 1603–1714* (New York: W.W. Norton, 1980) 34–74, 119–44, 222–41, 275–90. The extension of the Crown's prerogative to mere 'assertions' may be a dangerous precedent that undermines the hard fought struggles to bridle Crown power.

52 For commentary on the differences between institutional and individual independence of the judiciary see the observations of the Chief Justice of Manitoba, Richard J. Scott, 'Accountability and Independence' (1996) 45 *University of New Brunswick Law Journal* 27.

53 See *R. v. Lippe*, [1991] 2 S.C.R. 114 at 139: 'judicial independence is critical to the public's perception of impartiality. Independence is the cornerstone, a necessary prerequisite, for judicial impartiality.'

54 Luc Tremblay, *The Rule of Law, Justice and Interpretation* (Montreal: McGill-Queen's University Press, 1997) at 3.

55 (1985), 20 D.L.R. (4th) 399 at 401. Judicial independence also applies in Canada, as the court noted at 402: 'In inheriting a constitution similar to that of the United Kingdom we have also inherited the fundamental precept that the courts represent a separate and independent branch.'

56 See *Reference Re Secession of Quebec* at 258.

57 A leading constitutional scholar has observed: 'The independence of the judge from the other branches of government is especially significant, because it provides an assurance that the state will be subjected to the rule of law. If the state could count on the courts to ratify all legislative and executive actions, even if unauthorized by the state, the individual would have no protection against tyranny.' Peter Hogg, *Constitutional Law of Canada* (Scarborough, ON: Carswell, 1997), at 172. It may be asked why the court should even have this power as an alien political body on Aboriginal land. One answer to this question is that Canadian courts are courts of law (not politics), and as such should equally examine principles of law from Canadian and Aboriginal societies, to deliver a judgment based on these criteria. Their jurisdiction does not flow from legislatures, but rather flows from their grounding decisions on legal principles.

58 See *Reference Re Language Rights*. For an excellent article examining the distinctions between constitutional principles and provisions in the rule of law see Patrick Monahan, 'Is the Pearson Airport Legislation Unconstitutional? The Rule of Law as a Limit on Contract Repudiation by Government' (1995) 33 *Osgoode Hall Law Journal* 411. For an alternative argument regarding the importance of the distinction between constitutional principles and provisions see Joel Bakan and David Scheiderman, 'Submission to the Standing Senate Committee on Legal and Constitution Affairs Concerning Bill C-22' (unpublished, on file with author).

59 *Reference Re Language Rights* at 753.

60 John Locke, *The Second Treatise on Government* (New York: Macmillan, 1985), at 9–10.

61 As the Supreme Court said in *Reference Re Secession of Quebec* at 260: 'Canadians have never accepted that ours is a system of simple majority rule.'

62 'It is inherent in the concept of adjudication, at least as understood in the western world, that the judge must not be an ally or supporter of one of the contending parties.' Hogg, *Constitutional Law of Canada*, at 172.

63 See Locke, *The Second Treatise on Government*, at 9–10. However, for a discussion of how a judge may never be compelled to arrive at a certain result because of the interpretive nature of law and the value-laden character of the judicial role see Duncan Kennedy, 'Toward a Critical Phenomenology of Judging,' in Hutchinson and Monahan, *The Rule of Law*, at 141.

64 William R. Lederman, 'Judicial Independence and Court Reform in Canada for the 1990's' (1987) 12 Queen's Law Journal 385 at 397, n. 25.

65 Chief Justice Antonio Lamer observed: 'The rule of law, interpreted and applied by impartial judges is the guarantee of everyone's rights and freedoms ... Judicial independence is at its root, concerned with impartiality in appearance and fact. And these, of course, are elements essential to an effective judiciary. Independence is not a perk of judicial office. It is a guarantee of the institutional conditions of impartiality.' Martin Friedland, *A Place Apart: Judicial Independence and Accountability in Canada* (Ottawa: Canadian Judicial Council, 1995) at 1. For further discussions of impartiality and judicial independence see *Valente v. The Queen*, [1985] 2 S.C.R. 673 at 685; *R. v. Genereux*, [1992] 1 S.C.R. 259 at 283; *R. v. Beauregard*, [1986] 2 S.C.R. 56 at 69; *Liteky v. U.S.*, 510 U.S. 540 at 552 (1994), cited with approval in *R.D.S. v. The Queen* at para. 105; Richard Devlin, 'We Can't Go On Together With Suspicious Minds: Judicial Bias and Racialized Perspective in *R. v. R.D.S.*' (1995) 18 *Dalhousie Law Review* 408.

66 In *R.D.S.*, at para. 106, Justice Cory cited with approval *R. v. Bertram*, [1989] O.J. 2123 (H.C.J.), online: QL (OJ): 'In common usage bias describes a lean-

ing, inclination, bent or predisposition towards one side or another in a particular result. In its application to legal proceedings, it represents a predisposition to decide an issue or cause in a certain way that does not leave the judicial mind perfectly open to conviction. Bias is a condition or state of mind which sways judgment and renders a judicial officer unable to exercise his or her judicial functions impartially in a particular case.'

67 The fictive exchange between Thomas More and William Roper in the play 'A Man For All Seasons' illustrates this idea:

> MORE: ... What would you do? Cut a great road through the law to get after the Devil?
> ROPER: I'd cut down every law in England to do that!
> MORE: Oh? And when the last law was down, and the Devil turned round on you – where would you hide, Roper, the laws all being flat? This country's planted thick with laws from coast to coast – Man's laws, not God's – and if you cut them down – and you're the man to do it – d'you really think you could stand upright in the winds that would blow then? Yes, I'd give the Devil benefit of the law, for my own safety's sake.

Robert Bolt, *A Man For All Seasons: A Play of Sir Thomas More* (Toronto: Irwin, 1963), at 39.

68 Different perspectives on this case can be found in David Schneiderman, *The Quebec Decision: Perspectives on the Supreme Court Ruling on Secession* (Toronto: Lorimer, 1999).

69 *Reference Re Secession of Quebec* at 240.

70 *Sparrow* at 1106.

71 *Reference Re Secession of Quebec* at 247.

72 Ibid. at 240.

73 Ibid. at 247.

74 See John Borrows, 'Constitutional Law From a First Nations Perspective': Self-Government and The Royal Proclamation' (1994) 28 *University of British Columbia Law Review* 1.

75 See Brian Slattery, 'The Organic Constitution: Aboriginal Peoples and the Evolution of Canada' (1996) 34 *Osgoode Hall Law Journal* 101.

76 Though the court has written of the importance of Aboriginal oral traditions (*Delgamuukw* at 1064–79 (S.C.C.)), law (*Van der Peet* at 545), and perspectives (*Sparrow* at 1112). For academic commentary on the implications of Aboriginal normative values for constitutional law see John Borrows and Len Rotman, 'The Sui Generis Nature of Aboriginal Rights: Does it Make a Difference? (1977) 36 *Alberta Law Review* 9; Sakej Henderson, 'Empowering Treaty Federalism' (1995) 58 *Saskatchewan Law Review* 241; Brian Slattery,

'Understanding Aboriginal Rights' (1987) 66 *Canadian Bar Review* 727; James Tully, *Strange Multiplicity: Constitutionalism in an Age of Diversity* (Cambridge: Cambridge University Press, 1995); Jeremy Webber, 'Relations of Force and Relations of Justice: The Emergence of Normative Community Between Colonies and Aboriginal Peoples' (1995) 33 *Osgoode Hall Law Journal* 623; Mark Walters, 'The Golden Thread of Continuity: Aboriginal Customs at Common Law and Under the Constitution Act, 1982 (1999) 44 *McGill Law Journal* 711.

77 *Reference Re Secession of Quebec* at 240.

78 Ibid. at 249.

79 See ibid. at 248, where Lamer C.J.C. wrote: 'These defining principles function in symbiosis. No single principle can be defined in isolation from the others, nor does any one principle trump or exclude the operation of any other.'

80 Ibid. at 250.

81 Ibid.

82 For a discussion of the centralist orientation of the Constitution Act, 1867, see Donald Creighton, *Confederation: Essays* (Toronto: University of Toronto Press, 1967).

83 *Reference Re Secession of Quebec* at 250, citing *Northern Telecom Canada Ltd. v. Communication Workers of Canada*, [1983] 1 S.C.R. 733 at 741.

84 *Reference Re Secession of Quebec* at 251.

85 Alan Cairns, 'The Judicial Committee and its Critics' (1971) 4 *Canadian Journal of Political Science* 301; Murray Greenwood, 'Lord Watson, Institutional Self-Interest, and the Decentralization of Canadian Federalism in the 1890's' (1974) 9 *University of British Columbia Law Review* 244; Richard Risk, 'Constitutional Scholarship in the Late Nineteenth Century: Making Federalism Work' (1996) 46 *University of Toronto Law Journal* 427.

86 See *Citizens Insurance Company v. Parsons* (1881), 7 A.C. 96 (J.C.P.C.); *Hodge v. The Queen* (1883), 9 A.C. 117 (J.C.P.C.); *A.G. Ontario v. A.G. Canada* (The Local Prohibition Reference), [1896] A.C. 348 (J.C.P.C.); *Montreal v. Montreal Street Railway*, [1912] A.C. 333 (J.C.P.C.); *A.G. Canada v. A.G. Alberta* (The Insurance Reference), [1916] 1 A.C. 598 (J.C.P.C.); *Reference Re the Board of Commerce Act 1919 and the Combines and Fair Prices Act, 1919*, [1922] 1 A.C. 191 (J.C.P.C.); *King v. Eastern Terminal Elevator Co.*, [1925] S.C.R. 434; *A.G. Canada v. A.G. Ontario* (Labour Conventions), [1937] A.C. 326 (J.C.P.C.); *A.G. Canada v. A.G. Ontario* (the Employment and Social Insurance Act), [1937] A.C. 355 (J.C.P.C.); *A.G. British Columbia v. A.G. Canada* (the Natural Products Marketing Act), [1937] A.C. 377 (J.C.P.C.). For further discussion of the strengthening of provincial powers under the constitution through judicial interpretation see Gerald P. Browne, *The Judicial Committee and the British North American Act* (Toronto: University of Toronto Press, 1967).

87 See Ryder, 'The Demise and Rise of the Classical Paradigm in Canadian Federalism.'

88 Dominion jurisdiction in relation to Aboriginal peoples is found in s. 91(24) of the Constitution Act, 1867, which provides federal power in matters of 'Indians and Lands reserved for the Indians.' Problems of application of s. 91(24) which 'threaten to undermine the autonomy of Aboriginal Peoples' are discussed in Menno Boldt and J. Anthony Long, *Governments in Conflict* (Toronto: University of Toronto Press, 1985).

89 *Reference Re Secession of Quebec* at 249, citing *Reference Re Remuneration of Judges of the Provincial Court of Prince Edward Island,* [1997] 3 S.C.R. 3 at 75.

90 *Reference Re Secession of Quebec* at 252.

91 Ibid. at 247.

92 Johnson persuaded the Algonquin and Nippising Nations of the Ottawa and French River valleys to be messengers in inviting other Nations to attend a peace council at Niagara in the summer of 1764. Representatives of these two Nations travelled throughout the winter of 1763–4 with a printed copy of King George III's Royal Proclamation, and with various strings of wampum, in order to request the various First Nations to this council. Public Archives of Canada (PAC), Sulpician Documents, M. 1644, No. 70.

93 In the early 1760s Minavavana, an Ojibway Chief from west of Manitoulin at Michilimackinac, declared:

> Englishman, although you have conquered the French you have not yet conquered us! We are not your slaves. These lakes, these woods and mountains, were left to us by our ancestors. They are our inheritance; and we will part with them to none. Your nation supposes that we, like the white people, cannot live without bread, and pork and beef! But, you ought to know, that He, the Great Spirit and Master of Life, has provided food for us, in these spacious lakes, and on these woody mountains.
>
> Englishman, our Father, the king of France, employed our young men to make war upon your nation. In this warfare, many of them have been killed; and it is our custom to retaliate, until such time as the spirits of the slain are satisfied. But, the spirits of the slain are to be satisfied in either of two ways; the first is the spilling of the blood of the nation by which they fell; the other, by covering the bodies of the dead, and thus allaying the resentment of their relations. This is done by making presents.
>
> Englishman, your king has never sent us any presents, nor entered into any treaty with us, wherefore he and we are still at war; and, until he does these things, we must consider that we have no other father or friend among the white man, than the king of France ...

... you have ventured your life among us, in the expectation that we should not molest you. You do not come armed, with an intention to make war, you come in peace, to trade with us, to supply us with necessities, of which we are in much want. We shall regard you therefore as a brother; and you may sleep tranquilly, without fear of the Chipeways. As a token of our friendship we present you with this pipe, to smoke.

Quoted in Wilbur R. Jacobs, *Wilderness Politics and Indian Gifts: The Northern Colonial Frontier, 1748–1763* (Lincoln: University of Nebraska Press, 1966), at 75.

94 Sir William Johnson noted regarding Aboriginal governance '... I am well convinced, they never mean or intend anything like it, and that they can not be brought under our laws, for some Centuries, neither have they any word which can convey the most distant idea of subjection, and it should be fully explained to them, and the nature of subordination punishment ettc [sic], defined, it might produce infinite harm ... and I dread its consequences, as I recollect that some attempts towards Sovereignty not long ago, was one of the principal causes of all our troubles ...' See Paul Williams, 'The Chain' (LL.M. thesis, York University, 1982), at 83, quoting Sir William Johnson.

95 The purpose of the meeting was to create a political relationship that would, in Johnson's words, ensure a 'Treaty of Offensive and Defensive Alliance' that would include promises to 'assure them of a Free Fair & open trade, at the principal Posts, & a free intercourse & passage into our Country, That we will make no Settlements or Encroachments contrary to Treaty, or without their permission. That we will bring to justice any persons who commit Robberys or Murders on them & that we will protect and aid them against their and our Enemys & duly observe our engagements with them.' C. Flick, ed., *The Papers of Sir William Johnson*, vol. 4 (Albany: State University of New York Press, 1925), at 328.

96 Transcripts of a meeting at Drummond Island in Lake Huron to the west of Manitoulin on July 1818 between Anishnabe peoples and representatives of the British Crown contain articulate references to the Treaty of Niagara. An account of the meeting is as follows:

The Chiefs did de camp, laying down a broad Wampum Belt, made in 1764; one made in 1786; and one marked Lieutenant M'Dowal, Commanding Michilimackinac, with the pipe of peace marked on it.
Orcarta [Anishnabe] speaker:
Father, Your children now seated round you, salute you sincerely, they intend to talk to you a great deal, and beg you will listen to them with patience, for they intend to open their hearts to you ...

Holding the Belt of 1764 in his hand he said:

Father, This my ancestors received from our Father, Sir W. Johnson. You sent word to all your red children to assemble at the crooked place (Niagara). They heard your voice – obeyed the message – and the next summer met you at the place. You then laid this belt on a mat, and said – 'Children, you must all touch this Belt of Peace. I touch it myself, that we may all be brethren united, and hope our friendship will never cease. I will call you my children; will send warmth (presents) to your country; and your families shall never be in want. Look towards the rising sun. My Nation is as brilliant as it is, and its word cannot be violated.'

Father, Your words were true – all you promised came to pass. On giving us the Belt of Peace, you said – 'If you should ever require my assistance, send this Belt, and my hand will be immediately stretched forth to assist you.'

Here the speaker laid down the Belt.

Cptn. T.G. Anderson, 'Report on the Affairs of the Indians of Canada, Section III,' Appendix No. 95 in App. T of the *Journals of the Legislative Assembly of Canada*, vol. 6.

97 For example, see Arthur Ray, J.R. Miller, and Frank Tough, *Bounty and Benevolence: A History of Saskatechewan Treaties* (Montreal: McGill-Queen's University Press, 2000); Harold Cardinal and Walter Hildebrandt, *Treaty Elders of Saskatchewan: Our Dream is That Our People Will One Day be Clearly Recognized as Nations* (Calgary: University of Calgary Press, 2000).

98 For example, this is evidenced in a treaty on Manitoulin Island in 1836 where Sir Francis Bond Head, lieutenant governor of Upper Canada, started negotiations with the Anishinabek by noting 'Seventy snow seasons have now passed away since we met in council at the crooked place (Niagara) at which time your Great Father, the King and the Indians of North America tied their hands together by the wampum of friendship.' Canada, *Indian Treaties and Surrenders, from 1680–1890* (Ottawa: Printer to the Queen's Most Excellent Majesty, 1891–1912 [Toronto: Coles, 1971]), at 112.

99 Johnson proposed, on behalf of the British, that, 'at this treaty ... we should tie them down (in the Peace) according to their own forms of which they take the most notice, for example, by exchanging a very large belt with some remarkable & intelligible figures thereon. Expressive of the occasion which should always be shown to remind them of their promises.' Ibid. at 329.

100 Donald Braider, *The Niagara* (New York: Holt, Rinehart and Winston, 1972), at 137.

101 William G. Godfrey, *Pursuit of Profit and Preferment in Colonial North America: John Bradstreet's Quest* (Waterloo: Wilfrid Laurier University Press, 1982), at 197.

102 William Warren, an Ojibway writer, records that 'twenty-two different tribes were represented' at the council at Niagara. William Warren, *History of the Ojibway of Lake Superior* (St Paul: Minnesota Historical Society, 1885; repr. Minneapolis: Ross and Haines, 1970), at 219.

103 Williams, 'The Chain,' at 79.

104 Flick, ed., *The Papers of Sir William Johnson*, vol. 2, at 278–81, 481, 511–14.

105 Alexander Henry, *Travels and Adventures in Canada and the Indian Territories between the years 1760–1776* (Toronto: Morang, 1901), at 157–74.

106 Another author has recorded the attendance at the treaty: 'Deputys from almost every nation to the Westward viz Hurons, Ottawaes, Chippawaes, Meynomineys or Folles avoins, Foxes, Sakis, Puans, ettc. with some from the north side of Lake Superior and the neighbourhood of Hudson's Bay.' The Delawares and Shawnees were not in attendance at the treaty. William Johnson to the Lords of Trade, 8 October 1764, in E.B. O'Callaghan, ed., *Documents Relative to the Colonial History of the State of New York*, vol. 7 (Albany: Weed, Parsons, 1856), at 648.

107 G. Johnson to T. Faye, 16 March 1764, in Flick, ed., *The Papers of Sir William Johnson*, vol. 2, at 487.

108 Presents were exchanged to certify the binding nature of the promises being exchanged. The expenditure for the provisions and presents at Niagara were enormous for that day and age, and signify that the assembly was an unique and extraordinary meeting. Johnson's papers lists 'Expence [sic] of provisions for Indians only ... £25,000 New York Currency Besides the Presents ... £38,000 Sterling. Williams, 'The Chain,' at 82. Johnson's generous bestowal of presents demonstrates that he followed the principles of First Nations diplomacy in ratifying their agreement. Furthermore, the extravagance and value of these presents illustrates that he did not want the Indians to soon forget the treaty.

109 Braider, *The Niagara*, at 137.

110 Robert A. Williams, Jr, 'The Algebra of Federal Indian Law: The Hard Trail of Decolonizing and Americanizing the White Man's Indian Jurisprudence' (1986) *Wisconsin Law Review* 219 at 291.

111 F.W. Major, *Manitoulin: Isle of the Ottawas* (Gore Bay: Recorder Press, 1974), at 11–15 ('An Indian Council').

112 *Reference Re Secession of Quebec* at 251.

113 '... the two memoranda (wampum) which they hold; the one being a pledge of perpetual friendship between the N.A. Indians, and the British Nations,

and was delivered to the Tribe at a Council convened for that purpose, by Sir William Johnson, at Niagara in 1764.' Thomas G. Anderson, Superintendent of Indian Affairs at Manitoulin Island, Indian Department Report, *Report of Indian Affairs* (1845), at 269.

114 Ibid.

115 Flick, ed., *The Papers of Sir William Johnson*, vol. 2, at 309–10.

116 John Borrows, 'Wampum at Niagara: The Royal Proclamation, Canadian Legal History and Self-Government,' in Michael Asch, ed., *Aboriginal and Treaty Rights in Canada: Essays in Law, Equality and Respect for Difference* (Vancouver: UBC Press, 1997), at 155.

117 Ibid. at 253.

118 Ibid.

119 Ibid. at 253–6.

120 For example, see the discussion in Harris, *The Resettlement of British Columbia*, at 68–102; and Tennant, *Aboriginal Peoples and Politics*, at 39–52, 96–113.

121 Ian Getty and Antoine Lussier, *As Long as the Sun Shines and the Water Flows: A Reader in Canadian Native Studies* (Vancouver: UBC Press), at 29–190 (development of the Indian Act); James R. Miller, *Shingwauk's Visions: A History of Native Residential Schools* (Toronto: University of Toronto Press, 1996), at 151–216 (assimilation through residential school policy).

122 See the voluminous transcripts from the Royal Commission on Aboriginal Peoples, where these viewpoints were continuously expressed, recorded on CD-ROM, The Royal Commission on Aboriginal Peoples, *For Seven Generations: Report of the Royal Commission on Aboriginal Peoples* (Montreal: Libraxus, 1997).

123 Peter was the hereditary chief of the Nawash but had also to maintain his position through the consent of the people. While George Copway noted: 'The rulers of the Ojibway were inheritors of the power they held ...' at 140, this statement should be compared with the following quotation, which indicates that hereditary power was not always the means for a person to become a chief: 'leadership was not always offered to those who trained for it or to those who were born into the leadership totem. Merit was the criteria for assessing the quality of the candidate. Thus, if a person, born of another totemic group were deemed to possess a greater capacity for leadership than one so prepared, he would be preferred.' Basil Johnston, *Ojibway Heritage* (Toronto: McClelland and Stewart, 1976), at 63.

124 Lawrence A. Keeshig, 'Historical Sketches of the Cape Croker Indians' *Canadian Echo* [Newspaper, Wiarton, Ont.] (8 January, 1931).

125 Margret arrived at Nawash with her mother, brother, and sister.

126 A collection of recipes for traditional Native medicines compiled at the turn of the twentieth century preserves many of these remedies. It was written by a Christian missionary living among our people but taken from interviews with Native women and the ingredients are written in the Ojibway language. See Ontario Provincial Archives, OPA Box 103, Cape Croker Reserve Papers, MS 108.

127 Verna Patronella Johnston, *Tale of Nokomis* (Toronto: Musson Book Company, 1975); see Preface (Nokomis translated means 'grandmother'). The book consists of stories remembered by Verna and told to her by Margret McLeod, who heard them from her great-grandparents (36).

128 *Reference Re Secession of Quebec* at 256.

129 George Watts, Chairman of the Nuu-Chah-Nulth Nation on Vancouver Island said: 'There is this term being tossed around about aboriginal title. Well, I even disagree with this term ... What we have in our area is the Ha Houlthee, which is not aboriginal title. Ha Houlthee is very different from the legal term of aboriginal title. And you can't extinguish my title because it comes from my chief. You have to destroy us as a people if you want to extinguish our title. That is the only possible way to extinguish our title, to get rid of us as a people.' Frank Cassidy, ed., *Reaching Just Settlements: Land Claims in British Columbia* (Lantzville, BC: Oolichan Press, 1991), at 22.

130 *Reference Re Secession of Quebec* at 257.

131 A paradigmatic expression of Aboriginal resentment towards Canadian law and policy relative to Aboriginal peoples is Cardinal, *The Unjust Society*. This book continues to have great relevance, although it was written over thirty years ago, because many of the issues identified have not been resolved, but instead have grown worse.

132 Anne McGillivray and Brenda Comaskey, *Black Eyes All of the Time* (Toronto: University of Toronto Press, 1999), 22–52; Dara Culhane Speck, *An Error in Judgement* (Vancouver: Talonbooks, 1987).

133 For treatment of these issues see, generally, Cassidy, *Reaching Just Settlements*.

134 *Reference Re Secession of Quebec*

135 *Reference Re Quebec Secession*, [1998] 2 S.C.R at para. 74.

136 *Logan v. Styres* (1959), 20 D.L.R. (2d) 416 (Ont. H.C.) (upholding forceable eviction of traditional Haudenosaunee government).

137 For example, Joseph Trutch, in denying Aboriginal title in British Columbia observed: 'The title of the Indians in the fee of the public lands, or any portion thereof, has never been acknowledged by Government, but, on the contrary, is distinctly denied.' *British Columbia, Papers Connected with the Indian Land Question, 1850–1875* (Victoria: Government Printer, 1875), at appendix, 11.

138 John S. Milloy, *A National Crime: The Canadian Government and the Residential School System, 1879–1986* (Winnipeg: University of Manitoba Press, 1999).

139 Aborignal people are constantly charged with criminal offences for hunting and fishing in traditional economic pursuits. Some high-profile cases are *R. v. Syliboy*, [1929] 1 D.L.R. 307 (N.S. Co. Ct.); *R. v. Simon* (1985), 24 D.L.R. (4th) 390 (S.C.C.); *R. v. Horseman*, [1990] 1 S.C.R. 901; *R. v. Côté* (1996), 138 D.L.R. (4th) 185 (S.C.C.); *R. v. Badger* (1996), 133 D.L.R. (4th) 324 (S.C.C.); *R. v. Marshall*, [1999] 2 S.C.R. 456.

140 *Thomas v. Norris*, [1992] 2 C.N.L.R. 139 (B.C.S.C.) (Aboriginal spirit dancing not protected by Charter); *Jack and Charlie v. The Queen* (1986), 21 D.L.R. (4th) 641 (S.C.C.) (taking fresh deer meat for Aboriginal death ceremony not protected).

141 Many bands were kept apart or relocated to prevent their association because of a government fear they would organize to resist impingements of their rights.

142 A Crown fiduciary duty has recently been articulated in an attempt to cure violations of Aboriginal rights stemming from differences in the way Aboriginal people hold and access their rights. Significant cases in this regard are *Guerin v. The Queen* (1984), 13 D.L.R. (4th) 321 (S.C.C.); *Kruger v. The Queen* (1985), 17 D.L.R. (4th) 591 (F.C.A.); *Blueberry River Indian Band v. Canada* (1995), 130 D.L.R. (4th) 193 (S.C.C.). For a fuller discussion see Len Rotman, *Parallel Paths: Fiduciary Doctrine and the Crown-Native Relationship in Canada* (Toronto: University of Toronto Press, 1996).

143 *Canada (A.G.) v. Lavell*, [1974] S.C.R. 1349 (invidious distinctions in the Indian Act on the basis of sex upheld).

144 *Reference Re Secession of Quebec* at 259.

145 Ibid.

146 Ibid.

147 The Indian Act, S.C. 39 Vict., c. 18., now as amended, R.S.C. 1985, c. I-5.

148 'This band requests the Indian department to pay expenses incurred by Peter Nadjiwan and Chief Jones to Walkerton in regard to timber carried.' 20 July 1914, motion 7, Reserve Records.

149 'That hand bills be printed and circulated announcing the willingness of the band to open the pasture cattle in the vacant land of the reserve at the rate of fifty cents pr month pr head ... that any cattle trespassing on the reserve shall be put in the pound when it is ascertained that the fees required has not been paid.' 2 June 1902, 267. Reserve Records.

150 'That owing to some of our people being in want of seed and no means to obtain it the Department is asked if they would be willing to grant a sum of money out of our funds not to exceed one thousand dollars to be given to

those who would make good use of same and paying it back with interest out of their shares if interest money in two payments ...' 5 March 1900, Reserve Records.

151 'That with a view to encourage the pursuit of agriculture and make use of the vast area of pasture lands in the reserve & assisting in making the homes industrious Indians more comfortable and attractive We ask the department to allow our agent to obtain good stock, in cows, sheep & pigs or even horses etc. and have it so arranged that they cannot sell the same for a certain time, this privilege to be given to those deserving of help and to those who attain a proficiency in economy or may be helped to get lumber in the same way.' Dec. 1898, Reserve Records.

152 'That we appoint Ed Johnston to act as fishery overseer on the north westerly side of Cape Croker & on the Easterly side Paul Johnson to act & see that no white man nor a french man to fish on Indian fishing grounds. Carried.' 7 October 1907, Reserve Records.

153 For a detailed and extensive record of community decisions relative to our community maintenance and development one should refer to the Cape Croker Reserve Records, MS 108, microfilmed and preserved at the Ontario Archives.

154 For the text of Treaty 72 see Canada, *Canada: Indian Treaties and Surrenders* (Ottawa: Queen's Printer, 1891–1912), at 195–6.

155 For text see ibid. at 213.

156 Enemikeese (Conrad Van Dusen), *The Indian Chief: An Account of the Labours, Losses, Sufferings and Oppressions of Ke-zig-ko-e-ne-ne (David Sawyer), A Chief of the Indians of Canada West* (London: William Nichols Printer, 1867), at 51.

157 'When we surrendered our land, and made a treaty with Mr. Oliphant in October last, Mr. Oliphant, with ourselves, walked upon a road open from our village (Saugeeng) about one mile in a straight line to the shore of Lake Huron. This road, we supposed, ran northward; and was to be the boundary between the land we surrendered, and that which we reserved adjoining Saugeeng village. But when the surveyors commenced their work, it was found that a line running due north from the village, does not reach the shore of Lake Huron till it extends about five miles and a half from the boundary agreed on by Mr. Oliphant and ourselves. By this survey we are shut out from the water of the Lake, greatly to our inconvenience and damage.' Ibid. at 84–6.

158 'In a former Treaty made with Captain Anderson last summer, it was fully expressed and understood that when our land would be sold, actual settlement should be required; and we thought the same condition was implied in the Treaty made with Mr. Oliphant last October.' Ibid. Notice that the

Indians felt the negotiations with Anderson and Oliphant constituted the same treaty.

159 'Having no more hunting ground, from choice, as well as from necessity, we wish to turn our attention, more than ever before, to the cultivation of our land; and therefore hope our great father will encourage us in this, by giving to each in our tribe a title deed of one hundred acres of land, as prayed for in our memorial of last April.' Ibid.

160 'We also beg the privilege of speaking to our great father about the propriety of taking steps towards establishing at Saugeeng, and at Newash, "manual schools" for the benefit of our youth.' Ibid.

161 We also wish to present a 'requisition' for one hundred pounds, for the payment of our expenses and c., according to the decision of our General Council held at Saugeeng on the 5th inst., a copy of the proceedings which we have to present.' Ibid. Note the exercise of self-government in holding meetings to decide how to allocate funds from their interest.

162 'We also wish to make some statements to our great father, setting forth our wishes to secure his sanction to the acts of our General Councils from time to time, when considered by the Governor in Council, calculated to secure the harmony, and promote the interest, of our tribe.' Ibid.

163 Ibid. at 261–2.

164 Ibid. at 262.

165 Ibid.

166 *Van der Peet* at 547, citing Mark Walters, 'British Imperial Constitutional Law, and Aboriginal Rights: A Comment on *Delgamuukw v. B.C.*' (1992) 17 *Queen's Law Journal* 350 at 413.

167 *Côté* at 407.

168 For the Supreme Court's discussion of similar issues in Quebec's claim of the right to secede on the principles of self-determination see *Reference Re Secession of Quebec* at 284–6. The exploitation and colonization of Aboriginal peoples occurred through, inter alia: the imposition of band councils over hereditary governments; the criminalization of their social, economic, and spiritual relations through the enactment of the laws against potlach; the fragmentation of their territorial integrity through the denial and/or infringement of land rights and the creation of small inadequate reserves; the century-long denial of the right to vote in federal and provincial elections; the traumatic removal of whole generations of children through residential schools and insensitive child welfare laws; and the restricted access to their traditional food sources through the imposition of discriminatory fishing and hunting licences.

169 *Reference Re Secession of Quebec* at 287.

170 Ibid. at 284–5, citing Antonio Cassese, *Self-Determination of Peoples: A Legal Reappraisal* (Cambridge: Cambridge University Press, 1995), at 334.

171 *Reference Re Secession of Quebec* at 285, citing the *Declaration on Principles of International Law concerning Friendly Relations and Co-operation among States in accordance with the Charter of the United Nations*, GA Res. 2625 (XXV), UN GAOB, 25th Sess., Supp. No. 28, UN Doc. A/8082 (1970) 121 at 123–4.

172 *Reference Re Secession of Quebec* at 285, citing the *Vienna Declaration and Programme of Action*, adopted by the World Conference on Human Rights (14–25 June 1993), A/CONF.157/23 (12 July 1993), at 4 (I.2).

Chapter 6

1 For a description of these conditions see *A Survey of the Contemporary Indians of Canada: A Report on Economic, Political, Education Needs and Policies in Two Volumes*, ed. Harry B. Hawthorn (Ottawa: Indian Affairs Branch, 1966).

2 The government set out this plan in the 1969 White Paper. See Department of Indian Affairs and Northern Development, *Statement of the Government of Canada on Indian Policy, 1969* (Ottawa: Queen's Printer, 1969). The White Paper was designed to reduce and minimize political and 'lawful obligations' owed to Indian people. The leading work examining the White Paper is Sally Weaver, *Making Canadian Indian Policy: The Hidden Agenda 1968–1970* (Toronto: University of Toronto Press, 1981).

3 Harold Cardinal, *The Unjust Society: The Tragedy of Canada's Indians* (Edmonton: Hurtig, 1969), at 139.

4 Indian organizations were to 'restore and revitalize a sense of direction, purpose and being for Indians' and 'work to weld communities together into dynamic, growing forces that can participate in their twentieth century environment.' Ibid. at 162–5.

5 Ibid. at 163.

6 Cardinal observed: 'Since the introduction of formal white education to the Indians of Canada, their original educational processes have either been shunted completely aside or discouraged. The only purpose in educating the Indian has been to create little brown white men, not what it should have been, to help develop the human being or to equip him for life in a new environment.' Ibid. at 166.

7 On the restructuring of social institutions Cardinal wrote: 'there must be created, within these communities, structures that attack the problem at their source. Ideally, most of the services within a community should be provided by the community itself. Before this can happen, huge sums of money must be provided, aimed at community problems. No outside

bureaucracy, whether in Ottawa or in a provincial capital, is flexible
enough ...' Ibid. at 168.

8 Economic development was to require 'huge sums of money ... to enable
Indian groups to take advantage of ... opportunities on our own reserves.'
Ibid. at 169.

9 In securing Indian rights through existing and renewed treaties Cardinal
suggested: 'The negotiations for this must be undertaken in a new and different spirit by both sides. The treaties must be maintained. The treaties
must be interpreted in light of needs that exist today ... The Indian simply
cannot afford to allow the government to renege on its obligations because,
if he does, he commits cultural suicide.' Ibid. at 166.

10 Writing representative of this approach can be found in Leroy Little Bear,
Menno Boldt, and J. Anthony Long, *Pathways to Self-Determination: Canadian
Indians and the Canadian State* (Toronto: University of Toronto Press, 1984);
Menno Boldt and J. Anthony Long, *The Quest for Justice: Aboriginal Peoples and
Aboriginal Rights* (Toronto: University of Toronto Press, 1986); J. Anthony
Long and Menno Boldt, eds., *Governments in Conflict: Provinces and Indian
Nations and Canada* (Toronto: University of Toronto Press, 1988); Boyce
Richardson, ed., *DrumBeat: Anger and Renewal in Indian Country* (Toronto:
Summerhill Press, 1989); Cassidy, *Aboriginal Self-Determination.*

11 *Report of the Royal Commission on Aboriginal Peoples*, vols. 1–5 (Ottawa: Supply
and Services Canada, 1996).

12 Recommendation 2.3.27 of the Royal Commission states:

The Parliament of Canada enact an Aboriginal Nations Recognition
and Governance Act to

(a) establish the process whereby the government of Canada can recognize the accession of an Aboriginal group or groups to nation status
and its assumption of authority as an Aboriginal government to
exercise its inherent self-governing jurisdiction;

(b) establish criteria for the recognition of Aboriginal nations, including [there follows a list of six criteria]

(c) authorize the creation of recognition panels under the aegis of the
proposed Aboriginal and Lands Tribunal to advise the government
of Canada on whether a group meets recognition criteria;

(d) enable the federal government to vacate its legislative authority
under section 91(24) of the *Constitution Act, 1867* with respect to
core powers deemed needed by Aboriginal nations and to specify
which additional areas of federal jurisdiction the Parliament of
Canada is prepared to acknowledge as being core powers to be
exercised by Aboriginal governments; and

(e) provide enhanced financial resources to enable recognized Aboriginal nations to exercise expanded governing powers for an increased population base in the period between recognition and the conclusion or reaffirmation of comprehensive treaties.

13 Recommendation 2.3.45 of the Royal Commission states: 'The government of Canada present legislation to abolish the Department of Indian Affairs and Northern Development and replace it by two new departments: a Department of Aboriginal Relations and a Department of Indian and Inuit Services.'

14 See recommendations 3.5.1 to 3.5.44.

15 See recommendations 3.2.1 to 3.4.15.

16 See recommendations 2.5.1 to 2.5.52.

17 See recommendations 2.2.2 to 2.2.17.

18 For instance, in early January 1998 the Minister of Indian Affairs responded to some of the Royal Commission's recommendations regarding residential schools. She stated that the Government of Canada 'expresses profound regret' for past actions which have contributed to some of the difficulties Aboriginal people currently experience.

19 For example, see *R. v. Pamajewon*, [1996] 2 S.C.R. 821, where the Supreme Court of Canada refused to consider broad rights to self-government under s. 35(1) of the constitution.

20 While the message of greater participation within Canada did appear in Cardinal and the commission's proposals, this message did not receive the same emphasis and pursuit as 'Aboriginal control of Aboriginal affairs.'

21 See Bryan Schwartz, 'A Separate Aboriginal Justice System?' (1990) 28 *Manitoba Law Journal* 77 at 78–80, where he argued that 'separatism leads to indifference from the larger community instead of supportive interaction.'

22 A survey conducted by Southam News and Compas Poll asked: 'Do you feel the federal government should put more money in the following areas?' It then listed sixteen categories and elicited a response which accorded national defence and Aboriginals the lowest priority. See Giles Gherson, 'Defense, Native Programs Get Least Support,' *Vancouver Sun* (12 December 1997), A1.

23 *Report of the Royal Commission on Aboriginal People*, volume 1, *Looking Forward, Looking Back*, at 17–20.

24 Will Kymlicka and Wayne Norman, 'Return of the Citizen: A Survey of Recent Work on Citizenship Theory' (1994) 104 *Ethics* 352. Aristotle commented on the contested nature of citizenship when he observed: 'a state is a compound made up of citizens; and this compels us to consider who should properly be called a citizen and what a citizen really is. The nature of citizen-

ship, like that of the state, is a question which is often disputed: there is no general agreement on a single definition ...' Aristotle, *The Politics of Aristotle*, trans. Ernest Barker (Oxford: Oxford University Press, 1962), at 93.

25 Alan Cairns, 'The Fragmentation of Canadian Citizenship,' in William Kaplan, ed., *Belonging: The Meaning and Future of Canadian Citizenship* (Montreal: McGill-Queen's University Press, 1993), at 181.

26 Thomas H. Marshall, *Class, Citizenship and Social Development* (Chicago: University of Chicago Press, 1964). Marshall was influential in outlining this view of citizenship in the 1940s in his attempt to catalogue the benefits which flowed from the democratic developments in the eighteenth, nineteenth, and twentieth centuries. He stated that civil rights developed late in the eighteenth century with the rise of the centralized nation state and included entitlements to things like 'life, liberty and the pursuit of happiness.' He wrote that political rights developed in the nineteenth century and granted status to people to participate in the nation state through the franchise; freedom of speech, association, and the press; and the right to run for political office. Finally, he observed that social rights were a product of the late nineteenth and early twentieth centuries and include rights to public education, health care, unemployment insurance, old age pensions, and so forth.

27 Kymlicka and Norman, 'Return of the Citizen,' at 354. Of course, resort can always be had to the common law, which may protect people's participation in the community.

28 See Stephen Macedo, *Liberal Virtues: Citizenship, Virtue and Community* (Oxford: Oxford University Press, 1990), at 39, for praise of the strength with which rights-oriented notions of citizenship are held in Western societies.

29 My own view on this topic can be found in Borrows, 'Contemporary Traditional Equality: The Effect of the Charter on First Nations Politics' (1994) *University of New Brunswick Law Journal* 19.

30 Kylimcka and Norman, 'Return of the Citizen,' at 357.

31 Ibid., quoting Jürgen Habermas, 'Citizenship and National Identity: Some Reflections on the Future of Europe' (1992) 12 *Praxis International* at 10–11.

32 Alexis de Toqueville, *Democracy in America*, vol. 2 (New York: Arlington House, 1840) is a major work celebrating this conception; for a contemporary synthesis of citizenship theory in this tradition see Thomas Janoski, *Citizenship and Civil Society: A Framework of Rights and Obligations in Liberal, Traditional and Social Democratic Regimes* (Cambridge: Cambridge University Press, 1998).

33 Michael Ignatieff, *The Needs of Strangers* (Toronto: Viking, 1985); Michael Ignatieff, *The Warrior's Honor: Ethnic War and Modern Conscience* (Toronto: Viking, 1998), at 4–5.

34 Tocqueville, *Democracy in America*, at 123–8.
35 For an excellent discussion of the need to actively tolerate autonomous associations in democracy see Michael Walzer, *On Toleration* (New Haven, CT: Yale University Press, 1997).
36 Their existence also depends upon active encouragement in settings beyond and outside the courts.
37 James Tully, *Strange Multiplicity: Constitutionalism in an Age of Diversity* (Cambridge: Cambridge University Press, 1995).
38 Alan Cairns, *Citizens Plus: Aboriginal Peoples and the Canadian State* (Vancouver: UBC Press, 2000).
39 See Charles Taylor, 'The Politics of Recognition,' in Amy Gutman and Charles Taylor, eds., *Multiculturalism and the Politics of Recognition* (Princeton: Princeton University Press, 1952).
40 Kymlicka and Norman, 'Return of the Citizen,' at 370.
41 Paraphrasing Charles Taylor, *Philosophical Arguments* (Cambridge: Harvard University Press, 1985), at 225.
42 For example, the *Sparrow* court's observation that 'there was from the outset never any doubt that sovereignty and legislative power, and indeed underlying title, vested in the Crown' (1103) is fatal to establishing Aboriginal peoples as full citizens with their land and with others. One of the strongest manifestations of Aboriginal identity is 'doubt' about the particular effects of that assertion. See the various similar positions taken by Aboriginal peoples in Cassidy, ed., *Aboriginal Self-Determination*; Richardson, *DrumBeat*; Don Monet and Ardythe Wilson, eds., *Colonialism on Trial: Indigenous Land Rights and the Gitksan and Wet'suwet'en Sovereignty Case* (Philadephia: New Society, 1992); Grand Council of the Crees (of Quebec), *Sovereign Injustice: Forcible Inclusion of the James Bay Cree and Cree Territory into a Sovereign Quebec* (Newcastle, Que.: Grand Council of the Cree, 1995). The failure to effectively consider Aboriginal understandings from this perspective distances Aboriginal peoples from the Canadian state. This approach does not foster a sense of citizenship because it excludes important subjective elements of who Indians 'feel they are' in relationship to others in society. If courts and other Canadians do not engage Aboriginal people in a direct conversation on how Crown sovereignty displaced Aboriginal title, many Indigenous peoples will continue to feel excluded from national life. In fact, continued silence may cause some Aboriginal people to wonder if their exclusion as underlying owners and governors of land is necessary to national life, as considerations of an underlying Aboriginal title and Indigenous sovereignty in Canada are so conspicuously absent. The neglect in addressing Aboriginal issues at this level prevents Aboriginal peoples from opening up their iden-

tity to include notions of Canadian citizenship. In a democratic society, people must be mindful of the diverse constituencies they must persuade in promulgating their opinions. The bonds of belonging are diminished when people do not see their approach to any given issue reflected in the public resolution of disputes.

43 An excellent compilation of writers addressing issues in simultaneous cultural participation is found in Bill Ashcroft, Gareth Griffiths, and Helen Tiffin, eds., *The Post-Colonial Studies Reader* (New York: Routledge, 1996).

44 The intercultural nature of Canadian society has been examined in Tully, *Strange Multiplicity*.

45 *Report of the Royal Commission on Aboriginal People*, volume 1, *Looking Forward, Looking Back*, at 14. In 1961 the Aboriginal population was estimated to be 220,000.

46 Ibid. at 17–20.

47 Cairns, *Citizens Plus*.

48 'Although the life expectancy of Aboriginal people throughout North America as measured from birth is significantly lower than for non-Aboriginal people, it has improved since the second world war.' *Report of the Royal Commission on Aboriginal People*, volume 3, at 119.

49 However, this expansion in income did not keep pace with that experienced by non-Aboriginal people. See James Frideres, *Native Peoples in Canada: Contemporary Conflicts* (Scarborough, ON: Prentice-Hall, 1993), at 159–62. Also disturbing is the fact that Aboriginal unemployment increased in this period, *Report of the Royal Commission on Aboriginal People*, volume 2, at 804.

50 Department of Indian and Northern Affairs, *Aboriginal Education: The Path to Empowerment* (Ottawa: Supply and Services, 1994).

51 Ibid.

52 *Report of the Royal Commission on Aboriginal People*, vol. 2, at 817.

53 The potential for the narrative of Aboriginal control of Canadian affairs to effect these changes will be strengthened as the notion of Aboriginal control of Aboriginal affairs remains strong and vibrant. I am not advocating that Aboriginal control of Aboriginal affairs be neglected.

54 I recognize that considering land as a party to citizenship in its own right would initially seem strange to people who are not used to considering land as having an agency of its own. There would be questions and concerns about how to detect this agency and how to protect its functioning in the light of demanding, competing interests. After all, even if Aboriginal peoples were able to exercise sufficient influence to momentarily convince other Canadians that land should have a place of its own in decision making, it

may be fairly asked who would articulate the land's concerns. There is a substantial non-Native literature that concerns itself with these questions in the non-Aboriginal context; an influential, thoughtful, and representative piece is Christopher Stone, *Earth and Other Ethics: The Case for Moral Pluralism* (New York: Harper and Row, 1987).

55 For a general discussion of this issue see Jaroslav Pelikan, *The Vindication of Tradition* (New Haven, CT: Yale University Press, 1984).

56 See John Borrows, 'A Genealogy of Law: Inherent Sovereignty and First Nations Self-Government' (1992) 30 *Osgoode Hall Law Journal* 291.

57 It is first important to note that what is 'traditional' or constitutes a central cultural value will differ between First Nations. These differences make it difficult to anticipate which precise issues may be of concern in Aboriginal control of Canadian affairs.

58 See Eric Wolf, *Europe and the People without History* (Berkeley: University of California Press, 1982), at 387. While I have observed that identity is not fixed, I would not argue it is not infinitely fluid. Peoples' interpretations of their cultures' meaning is restrained by their sense of 'how we do things here.' Taylor, 'The Politics of Recognition.'

59 Edward Said, *Culture and Imperialism* (New York: Vintage Books, 1993), at 336. I would like to thank Natalie Oman for bringing this quotation to my attention in her dissertation, 'Sharing Horizons,' at 42.

60 For a discussion of how identity is formed through this interactive, dialogical process, see Mikhail M. Bakhtin, *Discourse in the Novel*, in *The Dialogical Imagination: Four Essays*, ed. Michael Holquist (Austin: University of Texas Press, 1981), at 354.

61 John Borrows, 'Wampum at Niagara: The Royal Proclamation, Canadian Legal History and Self-Government,' in Michael Asch, ed., *Aboriginal and Treaty Rights in Canada: Essays in Law, Equality, and Respect for Difference* (Vancouver, UBC Press, 1997). The principles found in the two-row wampum were over a hundred years old by the time they were received in this area. They were first established by the Haudenosaunee with the Dutch in 1664, and with the English not too many years later.

62 Haudenosaunee Confederacy, oral presentation, *Minutes and Proceedings and Evidence of the Special Committee on Indian Self-Government*, issue 31 (31 May–1 June, 1983), at 13.

63 Ibid.

64 Thomas G. Anderson, 'Report on the Affairs of the Indians of Canada, Section III' Appendix No. 95, in App. T. of the *Journal of the Legislative Assembly of Canada*, vol. 6.

65 For example, I know most of the Aboriginal judges in Canada. Almost every

one of them undertakes his or her role on the bench in a way which upholds and respects Canadian legal values while at the same time infusing the system with insight and understanding formed through personal educational and life experiences.

66 My identification of widespread agreement on certain precepts among Canadian Aboriginal peoples does not stem from some essentialized notion of the Aboriginal psyche. Rather, Aboriginal peoples have been positively socialized and negatively racialized to interpret the world differently from many non-Aboriginals. If exposed to different contexts, Aboriginal peoples can hold as many different views on life as other people nurtured and educated in such environments. However, the process of socialization and racialization currently operating structures the formation of ideas and identity for Aboriginal peoples in certain ways. While many Aboriginal peoples may be able to question or separate themselves from these influences, strong societal forces nevertheless exist both within and outside Aboriginal communities to structure their development. For readings on the social nature of racialization see Peter Li and Singh Bolaria, *Racial Oppression in Canada* (Toronto: Garamond Press, 1988), esp. chap. 1.

67 See *Delgamuukw* (S.C.C.).

68 *R. v. White and Bob*; *R. v. Taylor and Williams* (1981), 62 C.C.C. (2d) 228 (Ont. C.A.); *R. v. Simon* (1985), 24 D.L.R. (4th) 390; *R. v. Horseman*, [1990] 1 S.C.R. 901 (S.C.C.); *R. v. Badger*, [1996] 1 S.C.R. 771; *R. v. Sundown*, [1999] 1 S.C.R. 393; Sakej Henderson, 'Empowering Treaty Federalism' (1995) 58 *Saskatchewan Law Review* 241; Harold Cardinal, 'Livelihood Lands under Treaty Eight' (LL.M. thesis, Harvard Law School, 1997).

69 See the Supreme Court of Canada's comments in *Reference Re Secession of Quebec* at 250–2.

70 The fact that this discourse has developed in the face of the strong holistic perspectives that many Aboriginal peoples possess makes this exclusion even more striking.

71 *Black v. Law Society of Alberta*, [1989] 1 S.C.R. 591.

72 See the case *Jacobs v. Mohawk Council of Kahnawake*, [1998] 3 C.N.L.R. 68 (Can. H.R. Trib.).

73 General Conference of the United Nations Education, Scientific and Cultural Organization, 20th Session, *Declaration on Race and Racial Prejudice* E/CN.4/Sub.2/1982/Add.1, annex V (1982).

74 Aboriginal control through Canadian affairs also has the potential to check the abuse and disregard for women that can occur within communities. Enough of our people have now raised these concerns to allow a response. Of course, abuse and disregard of women's rights occur in the wider Cana-

dian society and Aboriginal people taking control in Canadian affairs will not end these problems. But their most poignant effects may be diffused if alternatives for shelter, participation, and criticism lie within both Aboriginal and wider Canadian circles. While the potential for criticism on these issues may trouble some Aboriginal leaders, these reproaches may themselves result in greater attention and accountability. For further discussion see Emma Laroque, 'Re-examining Culturally Appropriate Models in Criminal Justice Applications,' in Asch, *Aboriginal and Treaty Rights in Canada.*

75 Will Kymlicka and Wayne Norman, *Citizenship in Diverse Societies* (New York: Oxford University Press, 2000), 1.

76 Ibid. at 31. This notion has also become a theme in some of Michael Ignatieff's recent writings. See Michael Ignatieff, *Blood and Belonging: Journeys Into the New Nationalism* (New York: Farrar, Straus and Giroux, 1994); Ignatieff, *The Warrior's Honor.*

77 For a general comment in this regard see Mel Smith, *Our Home and Native Land* (Vancouver: Stoddart, 1995).

78 See David Frum, The Dissolution of Canadian Churches,' *National Post,* 19 August 2000.

79 Tom Flanagan, *First Nations? Second Thoughts* (Montreal: McGill-Queen's University Press, 2000), at 8–9.

80 Ibid. at 194–5.

81 See a short review by Taiaiake Alfred, *Windspeaker,* May 2000.

82 Cairns, *Citizens Plus,* at 200.

83 Ibid. at 212, quoting Adeno Addis, 'On Human Diversity and the Limits of Toleration' in I. Shapiro and W. Kymlicka, eds., *Ethnicity and Group Rights* (New York: New York University Press, 1997), at 126. For a similar thesis see Tully, *Strange Multiplicity.*

84 Cairns, *Citizens Plus,* at 213.

85 Kymlicka and Norman, *Diverse Societies,* at 39.

86 Sharon Venne, *Our Elders Understand Our Rights: Exploring International Law Regarding Indigenous Rights* (Vancouver: Theytus Books, 1998), at 68–96; Dale Turner, 'Liberalism's Last Stand: Aboriginal Sovereignty and Minority Rights,' in Curtis Cook and Juan Lindau, eds., *Aboriginal Rights and Self-Government* (Montreal: McGill-Queen's University Press, 2000), at 135–47.

87 Ibid. at 40.

88 *Delgamuukw* at 1089 (S.C.C.), per Lamer C.J.C.

Afterword

1 For a description of the Two-Row Wampum belt see chapters 5 and 6.

Bibliography

Books and Dissertations

Adams, Howard. *Prison of Grass: Canada from a Native Point of View.* Toronto: General, 1975.

Ainslie, George. *Picoeconomics: The Strategic Interaction of Successive Motivational States with the Person.* Cambridge: Cambridge University Press, 1993.

Alfred, Taiaiake. *Peace, Power, Righteousness: An Indigenous Manifesto.* Toronto: Oxford University Press, 1999.

Allen, Carleton Kemp. *Law in the Making.* 7th ed. Oxford: Clarendon Press, 1964.

Allen, Robert S. *His Majesty's Indian Allies: British Indian Policy in the Defence of Canada, 1774–1815.* Toronto: Dundurn Press, 1993.

Anaya, James. *Indigenous Peoples in International Law.* New York: Oxford University Press, 1996.

Anderson, Eugene N. *Ecologies of the Heart: Emotion, Belief and the Environment.* New York: Oxford University Press, 1996.

Aristotle. *The Politics of Aristotle.* Trans. Ernest Barker. Oxford: Oxford University Press, 1962.

Arnett, Chris. *The Terror of the Coast: Land Alienation and Colonial War on Vancouver Island and the Gulf Islands, 1849–1863.* Burnaby, BC: Talonbooks, 1999.

Arthurs, Harry W. *Without the Law.* Toronto: University of Toronto Press, 1985.

Asch, Michael. *Home and Native Land: Aboriginal Rights and the Canadian Constitution.* Toronto: Methuen, 1984.

Ashcroft, Bill, Gareth Griffiths, and Helen Tiffin, eds. *The Post-Colonial Studies Reader.* New York: Routledge, 1996.

Atkinson, Ronald F. *Knowledge and Explanation in History.* London: Macmillan Press, 1978.

Bakan, Joel. *Just Words: Constitutional Rights and Social Wrongs*. Toronto: University of Toronto Press, 1997.

Baker, John H. *An Introduction to English Legal History*, 3rd ed. London: Butterworths, 1990.

Barker, Ernest, ed. *The Politics of Aristotle*. New York: Oxford University Press, 1958.

Barlett, Richard H. *The Mabo Decision: Commentary and Text*. Toronto: Butterworths, 1993.

Barsh, Russel, and James Youngblood Henderson. *The Road: Indian Tribes and Political Liberty*. Berkeley: University of California Press, 1980.

Benton-Banai, Edward. *The Mishomis Book: The Voice of the Ojibway*. Hayward, WI: Indian Country Communications, 1988.

Berger, Thomas. *A Long and Terrible Shadow: White Values and Native Rights in the Americas, 1492–1992*. Toronto: Douglas and McIntyre, 1991.

– *Village Journey*. Vancouver: Douglas and McIntyre, 1988.

Berman, Harold J. *Law and Revolution: The Formation of the Western Legal Tradition: The Folklaw*. Cambridge: Harvard University Press, 1983.

Bishop, Charles. *The Northern Ojibwa and the Fur Trade: An Historical and Ecological Study*. Toronto: Holt Rinehart and Winston, 1974.

Black, Henry Campbell. *Black's Law Dictionary*, 5th ed. St Paul, MN: West Publishing, 1979.

Blackstone, William. *Commentaries on the Laws Of England*. Vol. 1. Ed. S.G. Tucker. New York: W.E. Dean, 1845.

Blais, André, and Elisabeth Gidengil. *Making Representative Democracy Work*. Toronto: Dundurn Press, 1991.

Blondin, George. *When the World was New: Stories of the Sahtu Dene*. Yellowknife: Outcrop, 1990.

Boas, Marie. *The Scientific Renaissance, 1454–1669*. London: Collins, 1962.

Boldt, Menno. *Surviving as Indians: The Challenge of Self-Government*. Toronto: University of Toronto Press, 1993.

Boldt, Menno, and J. Anthony Long. *Governments in Conflict*. Toronto: University of Toronto Press, 1985.

Boldt, Menno, and J. Anthony Long, eds. *The Quest for Justice: Aboriginal Peoples and Aboriginal Rights*. Toronto: University of Toronto Press, 1986.

Bolt, Robert. *A Man for All Seasons: A Play of Sir Thomas More*. Toronto: Irwin, 1963.

Bondanella, Peter, and Mark Musa, eds. and trans. *The Portable Machiavelli*. New York: Penguin Books, 1979.

Boyer, Patrick. *Lawmaking by the People: Referendums and Plebiscites in Canada*. Toronto: Butterworths, 1982.

Braider, Donald. *The Niagara*. New York: Holt, Rinehart and Winston, 1972.

Bright, William. *American Indian Linguistics and Literature*. New York: Mouton, 1984.

Brody, Hugh. *Maps and Dreams: Indians and the British Columbia Frontier*. Toronto: Douglas and McIntyre, 1988.

Brooks, Peter, and Paul Gonitz, *Law's Stories: Narrative and Rhetoric in the Law*. New Haven, CT: Yale University Press, 1996.

Brown, Dee. *Bury My Heart at Wounded Knee*. Toronto: Bantam Books, 1970.

Brown, Lester R., et al. and Worldwatch Institute, *Vital Signs: The Trends That are Shaping Our Future*. New York: W.W. Norton, 1995.

Browne, Gerald P. *The Judicial Committee and the British North America Act*. Toronto: University of Toronto Press, 1967.

Bullard, Robert. *Dumping in Dixie: Race, Class and Environmental Quality*. Boulder, CO: Westview Press, 1990.

Burnett, James A. et al., *On the Brink: Endangered Species in Canada*. Saskatoon: Western Producer Prairie Books, 1989.

Butler, David, and Austin Ranney, eds. *Referendums: A Comparative Study of Practice and Theory*. Washington: American Enterprise Institute for Public Policy Research, 1978.

Cairns, Alan. 'The Fragmentation of Canadian Citizenship.' In William Kaplan, ed. *Belonging: The Meaning and Future of Canadian Citizenship*. Montreal: McGill-Queen's University Press, 1993.

Cairns, Alan, John Courtney, Peter MacKinnon, Hans Michelmann, David Smith, eds. *Citizenship, Diversity and Pluralism*. Montreal: McGill-Queen's University Press, 1999.

Citizens Plus: Aboriginal Peoples and the Canadian State. Vancouver: UBC Press, 2000.

Cardinal, Harold. 'Livelihood Lands under Treaty Eight.' LL.M. thesis, Harvard Law School, 1997.

– *My Dream: That We Will One Day Be Recognized as First Nations*. Saskatoon: Office of the Treaty Commissioner, 1998.

– *The Unjust Society: The Tragedy of Canada's Indians*. Edmonton: Hurtig, 1969.

Cardinal, Harold, and Walter Hildebrandt. *Treaty Elders of Saskatchewan: Our Dream Is That Our People Will One Day Be Clearly Recognized as Nations*. Calgary: University of Calgary Press, 2000.

Carter, Sarah. *Lost Harvests: Prairie Indian Reserve Farmers and Government Policy*. Montreal: McGill-Queen's University Press, 1990.

Cassese, Antonio. *Self-Determination of Peoples: A Legal Reappraisal*. Cambridge: Cambridge University Press, 1995.

Cassidy, Frank, ed. *Aboriginal Self-Determination*. Lantzville, BC: Oolichan Books, 1991.

– *Reaching Just Settlements: Land Claims in British Columbia.* Lantzville, BC: Oolichan Books, 1991.

Cassidy, Frank, and Norman Dale. *After Native Claims: The Implications of Comprehensive Claims Settlements for Natural Resources in British Columbia.* Lantzville, BC: Oolichan Books and Institute for Research on Public Policy, 1988.

Chartrand, Paul. *Manitoba's Métis Settlement Scheme of 1870.* Saskatoon: Native Law Centre, 1991.

Chute, Janet. *The Legacy of Shingwaukonse.* Toronto: University of Toronto Press, 1998.

Clark, Bruce. *Native Liberty, Crown Sovereignty: The Existing Aboriginal Right of Self-Government in Canada.* Montreal: McGill-Queen's University Press, 1990.

Cleland, Charles. *The Prehistoric Animal Ecology and Ethnozoology of the Upper Great Lakes Region.* Ann Arbor: University of Michigan Press, 1966.

Cohen, Felix. *Handbook of Federal Indian Law.* Washington, DC: U.S. Government Printing Office, 1942.

Cole, Douglas, and Ira Chaikin. *An Iron Hand Upon the People: The Law Against the Potlatch on the Northwest Coast.* Vancouver: Douglas and McIntyre, 1990.

Conley, John, and William O'Barr. *Rules versus Relationships: The Ethnography of Legal Discourse.* Chicago: University of Chicago Press, 1990.

Conrad, Joseph. *Heart of Darkness.* 2nd ed. Ed. O.C.R.A. Goonetilleke. Peterborough, ON: Broadview Press, 1999.

Cook, Curtis, and Juan Lindau, eds. *Aboriginal Rights and Self-Government.* Montreal: McGill-Queen's University Press, 2000.

Copyway, G. or Kah-ge-ga-gah-bowh. *The Traditional History and Characteristic Sketches of the Ojibway Nation.* 1850; repr. Toronto: Coles, 1972.

Creighton, Donald. *Confederation: Essays.* Toronto: University of Toronto Press, 1967.

Cronin, Thomas. *Direct Democracy: The Politics of Initiative, Referendum and Recall.* Cambridge: Harvard University Press, 1989.

Cronon, William. *Changes in the Land: Indians, Colonists and the Ecology of New England.* New York: Hill and Wang, 1983.

– *Nature's Metropolis: Chicago and the Great West.* New York: W.W. Norton, 1991.

Culhane, Dara Speck. *An Error in Judgement.* Vancouver: Talon Books, 1987.

– *The Pleasure of the Crown.* Vancouver: Talon Books, 1998.

Cumming, Peter, and Neil Mickenburg. *Native Rights in Canada.* 2nd ed. Toronto: Indian-Eskimo Association, 1972.

Davies, Norman. *The Isles: A History.* New York: Oxford University Press, 1999.

De Lahontan, Baron. *New Voyages to North American.* Vol. 1. New York: Burt Franklin, 1905.

Delgado, Richard, and Jean Stephani. *Failed Revolutions: Social Reform and the Limits of Legal Imagination.* Boulder, CO: Westview Press, 1994.

Dicey, Albert Venn. *Law of the Constitution.* 10th ed. London: Macmillan, 1959.

Dickason, Olive P. *Canada's First Nations: A History of Founding Peoples from Earliest Times.* Toronto: McClelland and Stewart, 1992.

Disch, Lisa. *Hannah Arendt and the Limits of Philosophy.* Ithaca, NY: Cornell University Press, 1994.

Dockstator, Mark. 'Towards An Understanding of First Nations Self-Government.' D.Jur.Thesis, Osgoode Hall Law School, 1994.

Doern, G. Bruce, ed. *The Environmental Imperative: Market Approaches to the Greening of Canada.* Toronto: C.D. Howe Institute, 1990.

Doherty, R. *Disputed Waters: Native Americans and the Great Lakes Fishery.* Lexington: University of Kentucky Press, 1990.

Dorson, Richard. *Bloodstoppers and Bearwalkers.* Cambridge: Harvard University Press, 1952.

Duff, Wilson. *The Indian History of British Columbia.* Vol. 1. *The Impact of the White Man.* Victoria: Provincial Museum of British Columbia, 1964.

Dworkin, Ronald. *Law's Empire.* London: Fontana, 1986.

– *A Matter of Principle.* Cambridge: Harvard University Press, 1985.

– *Taking Rights Seriously.* Cambridge: Harvard University Press, 1977.

Edgerton, Robert. *Sick Societies: Challenging the Myth of Primitive Harmony.* Toronto: Maxwell Macmillan, 1992.

Ehler, Sidney Z., and John B. Morral, eds. and trans. *Church and State through the Centuries.* London: Burns and Oates, 1967.

Ellickson, Robert. *Order without Law: How Neighbors Settle Disputes.* Cambridge: Harvard University Press, 1991.

Elshtain, Jean Bethke. *Democracy on Trial.* Don Mills, ON: Anansi, 1995.

Ely, James W. *The Guardian of Every Other Right: A Constitutional History of Property Rights.* New York: Oxford University Press, 1998.

Enemikeese (Conrad Van Dusen). *The Indian Chief: An Account of the Labours, Losses, Sufferings, and Oppressions of Ke-zig-ko-e-ne-ne (Daniel Sawyer), A Chief of the Indians of Canada West.* London: William Nichols Printer, 1867.

Erdrich, Louise. *The Bingo Palace.* New York: Harper Collins, 1994.

Fairfield, R.P., ed. *The Federalist Papers* No. 10. Garden City, NJ: Anchor Books, Doubleday, 1966.

Firth, Raymond. *We, the Tikopia.* Boston: Beacon Press, 1936.

Fisher, Robin. *Contact and Conflict: Indian European Relations in British Columbia.* Vancouver: UBC Press, 1992.

Fitzpatrick, Peter. *The Mythology of Modern Law.* New York: Routledge, 1992.

Flanagan, Tom. *First Nations? Second Thoughts.* Montreal: McGill-Queen's University Press, 2000.

Flick, C., ed. *The Papers of Sir William Johnson.* Vols. 2, 4. Albany: State University of New York Press, 1925.

Francis, Daniel. *The Imaginary Indian: The Image of the Indian in Canadian Culture.* Vancouver: Arsenal Pulp Press, 1992.

French, Laurence A., ed. *The Winds of Injustice: American Indians and the U.S. Government.* New York: Garland Publishers, 1994.

Frideres, James. *Native Peoples in Canada: Contemporary Conflicts.* 4th ed. Scarborough, ON: Prentice-Hall, 1993.

Fried, Charles. *Contract as Promise: A Theory of Contractual Obligation.* Cambridge: Harvard University Press, 1991.

Friedland, Martin. *A Place Apart: Judicial Independence and Accountability in Canada.* Ottawa: Canadian Judicial Council, 1995.

Funk, Jack, and Gordon Lobe, eds., *... And They Told Us Their Stories: A Book of Indian Stories.* Saskatoon: Saskatoon District Tribal Council, 1991.

Fumoleau, René. *As Long as This Land Shall Last: A History of Treaty 8 and 11.* Toronto: McClelland and Stewart, 1976.

Furmston, M.P., ed. *Cheshire, Fifoot and Furmston's Law of Contract.* 11th ed. London: Butterworths, 1986.

Gaffen, Fred. *Forgotten Soldiers.* Penticton, BC: Theytus Books, 1985.

Getches, David, Charles Wilkinson, and Robert Williams Jr. *Federal Indian Law.* 4th ed. Minneapolis: West Publishing, 1998.

Getty, Ian, and Antoine Lussier, eds. *As Long as the Sun Shines and the Water Flows: A Reader in Canadian Native Studies.* Vancouver: UBC Press, 1990.

Gibson, Charles, ed. *The Spanish Tradition in America.* Columbia: University of South Carolina Press, 1968.

Gluckman, Max. *Politics, Law and Ritual in Primitive Society.* Chicago: Aldine Publishing, 1965.

Goddard, John. *Last Stand of the Lubicon Cree.* Vancouver: Douglas and McIntyre, 1991.

Godfrey, William G. *Pursuit of Profit and Preferment in Colonial North America: John Bradstreet's Quest.* Waterloo, ON: Wilfrid Laurier University Press, 1982.

Gosse, Richard, James Youngblood Henderson, and Roger Carter, eds. *Continuing Poundmaker and Riel's Quest: Presentations Made at a Conference on Aboriginal People and Justice.* Saskatoon: Purich Publishing, 1994.

Goudie, Andrew. *The Human Impact on the Natural Environment.* 4th ed. Cambridge, MA: MIT Press, 1994.

Grand Council of the Cree. *Sovereign Injustice: Forcible Inclusion of the James Bay*

Crees and Cree Territory into a Sovereign Quebec. Nemasta, James Bay, QC: Grand Council of the Cree [of Quebec], 1995.

Greenhouse, Carol, et al. *Law and Community in Three American Towns.* Ithaca, NY: Cornell University Press, 1994.

Grube, G.M.A., trans., *Plato's Republic.* Indianapolis: Hackett, 1974.

Habermas, Jürgen. *Justification and Application: Remarks on Discourse Ethics.* Cambridge, MA: MIT Press, 1993.

Haig-Brown, Celia. *Resistance and Renewal: Surviving the Indian Residential School.* Vancouver: Tillicum Library, 1988.

Hale, John. *The Civilization of Europe in the Renaissance.* Toronto: Macmillan, 1994.

Hale, Sir Matthew. *The History of the Common Law of England.* 5th ed. Chicago: University of Chicago Press, 1974.

Haltiner, Gerald. *Stories the Red People Told.* Aspena, MI: G. Haltiner, 1951.

Hamilton, A.C., and C.M. Sinclair. *The Justice System and Aboriginal People: Report of the Aboriginal Justice Inquiry in Manitoba.* Vol. 1. Winnipeg: Queen's Printer, 1991.

Hanke, Lewis. *The Spanish Struggle for Justice in America.* Philadelphia: University of Pennsylvania Press, 1949.

Hardoy, Jorge, and David Satterthwaite, eds. *Small and Intermediate Cities: Their Role in Regional and Natural Development in the Third World.* Boulder, CO.: Westview Press, 1995.

Harring, Sidney. *White Man's Law: Native People in Nineteenth-Century Jurisprudence.* Toronto: University of Toronto Press, 1998.

Harris, Cole. *The Resettlement of British Columbia: Essays on Colonialism and Geographical Change.* Vancouver: UBC Press, 1997.

Harris, Cole, and Matthews, Geoffrey, eds. *Historical Atlas of Canada.* Vol. 1. *From the Beginning to 1800.* Toronto: University of Toronto Press, 1987.

Harris, Chief Kenneth B. *Visitors Who Never Left: The Origin of the People of Damelhamid.* Vancouver: UBC Press, 1974.

Hasager, Ulla, et al. *Ka Ho'okololonui Kanaka Maoli: The People's International Tribunal Hawai'i MANA'O.* Honolulu: Honolulu Publishing, 1993.

Hawkes, David, ed. *Aboriginal Peoples and Government Responsibility: Exploring Federal and Provincial Roles.* Ottawa: Carleton University Press, 1989.

Hedican, Edward. *Applied Anthropology in Canada: Understanding Aboriginal Issues.* Toronto: University of Toronto Press, 1995.

Heidegger, Martin. *Being and Time.* Trans. John Macquarrie and Edward Robinson, New York: Harper and Row, 1962.

Henderson, James Youngblood, Marjorie Benson, and Isobel Findlay. *Aboriginal Tenure in the Constitution of Canada.* Scarborough, ON: Carswell, 2000.

Henry, Alexander. *Travels and Adventures in Canada and the Indian Territories between the Years 1760–1776*. Toronto: Morang, 1901.

Hickerson, Harold. *The Chippewa and Their Neighbours: A Study in Ethnohistory*. New York: Holt, Rinehart and Winston, 1970.

Hill, Christopher. *The Century of Revolution, 1603–1714*. New York: W.W. Norton, 1980.

Hiss, Tony. *The Experience of Place*. New York: Random House, 1990.

Hobbes, Thomas. *Leviathan*. Ed. R. Tuck. Cambridge: Cambridge University Press, 1991.

Hoebel, E. Adamson. *The Law of Primitive Man*. New York: Atheneum, 1974.

Hogg, Peter. *Constitutional Law of Canada*. Toronto: Carswell, 1997.

Hohfeld, Wesley N. *Fundamental Legal Conceptions, as Applied in Judicial Reasoning and Other Legal Essays*. Walter W. Cook. New Haven, CT: Yale University Press, 1964.

Hooker, M.B. *Legal Pluralism*. Oxford: Clarendon Press, 1975.

Hughes, J. Donald. *American Indian Ecology*. El Paso: Texas Western University Press, 1983.

Hutchinson, Alan. *Waiting for Coraf: A Critique of Law and Rights*. Toronto: University of Toronto Press, 1995.

Hutchinson, Alan, and Patrick Monahan, eds. *The Rule of Law: Idea or Ideology*. Toronto: Carswell, 1987.

Ignatieff, Michael. *Blood and Belonging: Journeys into the New Nationalism*. New York: Farrar, Straus and Giroux, 1994.

– *The Needs of Strangers*. Toronto: Viking, 1985.

– *The Warrior's Honor: Ethnic War and Modern Conscience*. Toronto: Viking, 1998.

Imai, Shin. *The 1997 Annotated Indian Act*. Toronto: Carswell, 1996.

Inglis, Julian T., ed. *Traditional Environmental Knowledge: Concepts and Cases*. Ottawa: Canadian Museum of Nature, 1993.

Innis, Harold Adams. *The Fur Trade in Canada: An Introduction to Canadian Economic History*. Toronto: University of Toronto Press, 1962.

Jacobs, Jane. *The Death and Life of Great American Cities*. New York: Modern Library, 1992.

– *The Economy of Cities*. New York: Random House, 1988.

Jacobs, M. *The Green Economy: Environment, Sustainable Development and the Politics of the Future*. Vancouver: UBC Press, 1991.

Jacobs, Wilbur R. *Wilderness Politics and Indian Gifts: The Northern Colonial Frontier, 1748–1763*. Lincoln: University of Nebraska Press, 1966.

Jaenen, Cornelius. *Friend and Foe: Aspects of French-Amerindian Cultural Contact in the Sixteenth and Seventeenth Centuries*. New York: Columbia University Press, 1976.

Janoski, Thomas. *Citizenship and Civil Society: A Framework of Rights and Obligations in Liberal, Traditional and Social Democratic Regimes.* Cambridge: Cambridge University Press, 1998.

Jennings, Francis. *The Ambiguous Iroquois Empire.* New York: W.W. Norton 1984.

– *The Invasion of America: Indians, Colonialism and the Cant of Conquest.* New York: W.W. Norton, 1976.

Jennings, Francis et al., eds. *The History and Culture of Iroquois Diplomacy.* Syracuse, NY: Syracuse University Press, 1985.

Johnson, Nevil. 'Types of Referendum.' In Austin Ranney, ed., *The Referendum Device: A Conference.* Washington: American Institute for Public Policy Research, 1981.

Johnson, Rebecca, John McEnroy, Thomas Kuttner, and Wade MacLauchlan, eds. *Gerard v. LaForest at the Supreme Court of Canada, 1985–1997.* Ottawa. Canadian Historical Association, 2000.

Johnston, Basil. *Ojibway Heritage.* Toronto: McClelland and Stewart, 1976.

Johnston, Darlene. *The Taking of Indian Lands: Consent or Coercion?* Saskatoon: University of Saskatoon Native Law Centre, 1989.

Johnston, Verna Patronella. *Tales of Nokomis.* Toronto: Stoddart, 1975.

Kairys, David, ed. *The Politics of Law: A Progressive Critique.* Rev. ed. New York: Pantheon Books, 1990.

Kiralfy, Albert K.R., ed. *Potter's Historical Introduction to English Law and its Institutions.* London: Sweet and Maxwell, 1962.

Knudston, Peter, and David Suzuki. *Wisdom of the Elders.* Toronto: Stoddart, 1993.

Kohn, K.A., ed. *Balancing on the Brink of Extinction: The Endangered Species Act and Lessons for the Future.* Washington, DC: Island Press, 1991.

Kresh III, Shepard. *The Ecological Indian: Myth and History.* New York: W.W. Norton, 1999.

Kulchyski, Peter. *Unjust Relations: Aboriginal Rights in Canadian Courts.* Toronto: Oxford University Press, 1994.

Kymlicka, Will, and Wayne Norman. *Citizenship in Diverse Societies.* New York: Oxford University Press, 2000.

Ladd, Everett D. *The American Polity: The People and Their Government.* New York: W.W. Norton, 1985.

Laidlaw, George E. 'Ojibway Myths and Tales.' *Twenty-Seventh Annual Archeological Report* 86. Ontario: Ministry of Education, 1915.

Landes, Ruth. *The Ojibway Woman.* New York: W.W. Norton, 1971.

Lasch, Christopher. *The Revolt of Elites and the Betrayal of Democracy.* New York: W.W. Norton, 1995.

Leopold, Aldo. *Sand County Almanac and Sketches Here and There.* New York: Oxford University Press, 1949.

Lewis, Martin. *Green Delusions: An Environmental Critique of Radical Environmentalism.* Durham, NC: Duke University Press, 1992.

Li, Peter, and Singh Bolaria. *Racial Oppression in Canada.* Toronto: Garamond Press, 1988.

Little Bear, Leroy, Menno Boldt, and J. Anthony Long, eds. *Pathways to Self-Determination: Canadian Indians and the Canadian State.* Toronto: University of Toronto Press, 1984.

Llewellyn, Karl N., and E. Adamson Hoebel. *The Cheyenne Way: Conflict and Case Law in Primitive Jurisprudence.* Norman: University of Oklahoma Press, 1941.

Locke, John. *The Second Treatise on Government.* New York: Macmillan, 1985.

Long, J. Anthony, and Menno Boldt, eds. *Governments in Conflict: Provinces and Indian Nations in Canada.* Toronto: University of Toronto Press, 1988.

Lopez, Barry. *Crow and Weasel.* San Fransico: North Point Press, 1990.

Lutz, Hartmut. *Contemporary Challenges: Conversations with Canadian Native Authors.* Saskatoon: Fifth House, 1991.

Macedo, Stephen. *Liberal Virtues: Citizenship, Virtue and Community.* Oxford: Oxford University Press, 1990.

MacKendrick, Paul, and Herbert M. Howe. *Classics in Translation.* Vol. 2. Madison: University of Wisconsin Press, 1980.

Macklem, Partrick. *Indigenous Difference and the Constitution of Canada.* Toronto: University of Toronto Press, 2001.

Maclaren, Virginia. *Sustainable Urban Development in Canada.* Vol. 1. *Summary Report.* Toronto: Incurr Press, 1992.

Maitland, Frederic W. *The Forms of Action at Common Law.* Cambridge: Cambridge University Press, 1948.

Maitland, Frederic W., and Francis C. Montague. *A Sketch of English Legal History.* London: G.P. Putnam and Sons, 1915.

Major, F.W. *Manitoulin: Isle of the Ottawas.* Gore Bay, ON: Recorder Press, 1974.

Mallea, Paula. *Aboriginal Law: Apartheid in Canada?* Brandon, MB: Bearpaw Publishing, 1994.

Manuel, George, and Michael Posluns. *The Fourth World.* Don Mills, ON: Collier-Macmillan, 1974.

Marchak, M. Patricia. *Logging the Globe.* Montreal: McGill-Queen's University Press, 1995.

Marshall, Thomas H. *Class, Citizenship and Social Development.* Chicago: University of Chicago Press, 1964.

Matsuda, Mari, Charles Lawrence, and Richard Delgado, eds., *Words That Wound: Critical Race Theory, Assaultive Speech, and the First Amendment.* Boulder, CO: Westview Press, 1993.

McCrae, Donald. *Report of the Complaints of the Innu of Labrador to the Canadian Human Rights Commission.* Ottawa: Supply and Services, 1993.

McGillivray, Anne, and Brenda Comaskey. *Black Eyes All of the Time.* Toronto: University of Toronto Press, 1999.

McMillan, Alan. *Native Peoples and Cultures of Canada.* Toronto: Douglas and McIntyre, 1988.

McNab, David. *Circles of Time: Aboriginal Land Rights and Resistance in Ontario.* Waterloo: Wilfrid Laurier University Press, 1999.

McNeil, Kent. *Common Law Aboriginal Title.* Oxford: Clarendon Press, 1989.

– *Defining Aboriginal Title in the 90's: Has the Supreme Court Finally Got it Right?* North York, ON: Robarts Centre for Canadian Studies, York University, 1998.

– *Emerging Justice: Essays on Indigenous Rights in Canada and Australia.* Saskatoon: Native Law Centre, 2001.

Mercredi, Ovide, and Mary Ellen Turpel. *In the Rapids: Navigating the Future of First Nations.* Toronto: Viking Books, 1993.

Milen, Robert A., ed. *Aboriginal Peoples and Electoral Reform in Canada.* Ottawa: Dundurn Press, 1991.

Miller, James R. *Shingwauk's Visions: A History of Native Residential Schools.* Toronto: University of Toronto Press, 1996.

– *Skyscrapers Hide the Heavens: A History of Indian White Relations in Canada.* Toronto: University of Toronto Press, 1989.

Milloy, John S. *A National Crime: The Canadian Government and the Residential School System, 1879–1986.* Winnipeg: University of Manitoba Press, 1999.

Mills, Antonio. *Eagle Down Is Our Law: Witsuwit'en Law, Feasts and Land Claims.* Vancouver: UBC Press, 1994.

Milsom, Stroud F.C. *Historical Foundations of the Common Law.* 2nd. ed. Toronto: Butterworths, 1981.

Monahan, Patrick. *Essentials of Canadian Law: Constitutional Law.* Toronto: Irwin Law, 1997.

Monet, Don, and Ardythe Wilson, eds. *Colonialism on Trial: Indigenous Land Rights and the Gitksan and Wet'suwet'en Sovereignty Case.* Philadelphia, New Society, 1992.

Monture-Angus, Patricia. *Journeying Forward: Dreaming First Nations Independence.* Halifax: Fernwood, 1999.

Moore, Christopher. *1867: How the Fathers Made a Deal.* Toronto: McClelland and Stewart, 1997.

Morrison, Bruce R., and C. Roderik Wilson, eds. *Native Peoples: The Canadian Experience.* 2nd ed. Toronto: McClelland and Stewart, 1992.

Morse, Bradford, and Gordon Woodman, eds. *Indigenous Law and the State.* Providence, RI: Foris, 1988.

Muldoon, James, ed. *The Expansion of Europe: The First Phase.* Philadelphia: University of Pennsylvania Press, 1977.

– *Popes, Lawyers, and Infidels.* Philadelphia: University of Pennsylvania Press, 1979.

Nasr, Seyyed Hossein. *Ideals and Realities of Islam.* Boston: Beacon Press, 1966.

Newell, Diane. *Tangled Webs of History: Indians and the Law in Canada's Pacific Coast Fisheries.* Toronto: University of Toronto Press, 1993.

Nock, David A. *A Victorian Missionary and Canadian Indian Policy: Cultural Synthesis vs. Cultural Replacement.* Waterloo: Wilfrid Laurier University Press, 1988.

Noss, Reed, and Allen Cooperrider. *Biodiversity.* Washington, DC: Island Press, 1994.

Notzke, Claudia. *Aboriginal People and Natural Resources in Canada.* North York, ON: Captus Press, 1993.

O'Callaghan, E.B., ed. *Documents Relative to the Colonial History of the State of New York.* Vol 7. Albany: Weed, Parsons, 1856.

Ogilvie, Margaret H. *Historical Introduction to Legal Studies.* Toronto: Carswell, 1982.

Olson, Mancur. *The Rise and Decline of Nations: Economic Growth, Stagflation and Social Rigidities.* New Haven, CT: Yale University Press, 1982.

Oman, Natalie. 'Sharing Horizons: A Paradigm for Political Accomodation in Intercultural Settings.' PhD thesis, McGill University, 1997.

Orkin, Andrew. *Sovereign Injustice: Forcible Inclusion of the James Bay Crees and Cree Territory into a Sovereign Quebec.* Fullicit, QC: Grand Council of Crees, 1996.

Pearce, David, and R. Kerry Turner. *Economics of Natural Resources and the Environment.* Brighton: Harvester Wheatsheaf, 1990.

Pelikan, Jaroslav. *The Vindication of Tradition.* New Haven, CT: Yale University Press, 1984.

Penner, Keith. *Indian Self-Government in Canada: Report of the Special Committee.* Ottawa: Queen's Printer, 1983.

Petrone, Penny. *Native Literature in Canada: From Oral Tradition to the Present.* Toronto: Oxford University Press, 1990.

Pettipas, Katherine. *Severing the Ties That Bind: Government Repression of Indigenous Religious Ceremonies on the Prairies.* Winnipeg: University of Manitoba Press, 1994.

Pickthall, Mohammed. *The Meaning of the Glorious Koran.* New York: New American Library, 1953.

Pinder, Leslie Hall. *The Carriers of No: After the Land Claims Trial.* Vancouver: Lazara Press, 1991.

Pinkerton, Evelyn, ed. *Cooperative Managament of Local Fisheries.* Vancouver: UBC Press, 1989.

Portelli, Alesssandro. *The Death of Luigi Trastulli: Form and Meaning in Oral History.* Albany: State University of New York Press, 1991.

Pospisil, Leopold. *Anthropology of Law.* New York: Harper and Rowe, 1971.

Post, Robert, ed. *Law and the Order of Culture.* Los Angeles: University of California Press, 1991.

Price, Richard. *The Spirit of Alberta Indian Treaties.* Edmonton: Pica Pica Press, 1987.

Rappaport, Roy. *Pigs For Ancestors: A Ritual Ecology of a New Guinea People.* 2nd ed. New Haven, CT: Yale University Press, 1984.

Raush, Jonathan. *Demosclerosis: The Silent Killer of American Government.* New York: Times Books, 1994.

Ray, Arthur J. *Indians in the Fur Trade: Their Role as Trappers, Hunters and Middlemen in the Lands Southwest of Hudson Bay, 1660–1870.* Toronto: University of Toronto Press, 1974.

Ray, Arthur, J.R. Miller, and Frank Tough. *Bounty and Benevolence: A History of Saskatchewan Treaties.* Montreal: McGill-Queen's University Press, 2000.

Reddy, Marlite A. *Statistical Record of Native North Americans.* Washington, DC: Gale Research, 1993.

Reid, Dorothy M., ed. *Tales of Nanabozho.* Toronto: Oxford University Press, 1963.

Richardson, Boyce, ed. *DrumBeat: Anger and Renewal in Indian Country.* Toronto: Summerhill Press, 1989.

– *People of Terra Nullius: Betrayal and Rebirth in Aboriginal Canada.* Vancouver: Douglas and McIntyre, 1993.

Riddington, Robin. *Little Bit Know Something.* Vancouver: Douglas and McIntyre, 1990.

Riker, William. *Liberalism against Populism: A Confrontation between the Theory of Democracy and the Theory of Social Change.* San Francisco: W.H. Freeman, 1982.

Roach, Kent. *Due Process and Victims' Rights: The New Law and Politics of Criminal Justice.* Toronto: University of Toronto Press, 1999.

Rose, Alex, ed. *Nisga'a: People of the Nass River.* Vancouver: Douglas and McIntyre, 1993.

Rotman, Leonard. *Parallel Paths: Fiduciary Doctrine and the Crown-Native Relationship in Canada.* Toronto: University of Toronto Press, 1996.

Sagoff, Mark. *The Economy of the Earth: Philosophy, Law and the Environment.* Cambridge: Cambridge University Press, 1988.

Said, Edward. *Culture and Imperialism.* New York: Vintage Books, 1993.

– *Orientalism.* New York: Vintage Books, 1978.

Sarat, Austin, and Thomas Kearns. *Law in Everyday Life.* Ann Arbor: University of Michigan Press, 1993.

Schmalz, Peter. *The History of the Ojibwa of Southern Ontario.* Toronto: University of Toronto Press, 1990.

– 'The Saugeen-Ojibway Fishery: Historic Use and Contemporary Practice.' Unpublished, 1990.

Schneiderman, David. *The Quebec Decision: Perspectives on the Supreme Court Ruling on Secession.* Toronto: Lorimer, 1999.

Seagle, William. *The Quest for Law.* New York: Knopf, 1941.

Seneca, Joseph, and Michael Taussig, *Environmental Economics.* 3rd ed. Englewood Cliffs, NJ: Prentice-Hall, 1984.

Smith, Donald B. *Sacred Feathers.* Toronto: University of Toronto Press, 1987.

Smith, Mel. *Our Home or Native Land?* Vancouver: Stoddart, 1995.

Stephenson, M.A., and Suri Ratnapala, eds. *Mabo: A Judicial Revolution.* St Lucia, Queensland: University of Queensland Press, 1993.

Stewart, A. *The Initiative, Referendum and Recall: Theory and Applications.* Monticello, IL: Vance Bibliographies, 1983.

Stewart, George. *Canada Administration of the Earl of Dufferin.* Toronto: Rose-Belford, 1878.

Stone, Christopher. *Earth and Other Ethics: The Case for Moral Pluralism.* New York: Harper and Row, 1987.

Stren, Richard, et al., eds. *Sustainable Cities: Urbanization and the Environment in International Perspective.* London: J. Kingsley Publishers, 1992.

Tallian, Laura. *Direct Democracy: An Historical Analysis of the Initiative, Referendum and Recall Process.* Los Angeles: Los Angeles Peoples Lobby, 1977.

Tandy, David, and Walter Neale. *Hesiod's Works and Days.* Berkeley: University of California Press, 1996.

Taylor, Charles. *Philosophical Arguments.* Cambridge: Harvard University Press.

– *Philosophy and the Human Sciences.* Cambridge: Cambridge University Press, 1985.

Tennant, Paul. *Aboriginal Peoples and Politics: Indian Land Question in British Columbia, 1849–1989.* Vancouver: UBC Press, 1990.

Thompson, E.P. *Customs in Common.* London: Merlin Press, 1991.

– *Whigs and Hunters.* London: Allen Press, 1975.

Thornton, Russell. *American Indian Holocaust and Survival: A Population History Since 1942.* Norman: University of Oklahoma Press, 1987.

Titley, Brian. *A Narrow Vision: Duncan Campbell Scott and the Administration of Indian Affairs in Canada.* Vancouver: UBC Press, 1986.

Toqueville, Alexis de. *Democracy in America.* Vol. 2. New York: Arlington House, 1840.

Tremblay, Luc. *The Rule of Law, Justice and Interpretation.* Montreal: McGill-Queen's University Press, 1997.

Trevor-Roper, Hugh. *The Rise of Christian Europe*. London: Thames and Hudson, 1965.

Trigger, Bruce. *Natives and Newcomers: Canada's Heroic Age Reconsidered*. Montreal: McGill-Queen's University Press, 1985.

Tully, James. *Strange Multiplicity: Constitutionalism in an Age of Diversity*. Cambridge: Cambridge University Press, 1995.

Upton, Leslie F.S. *Micmacs and Colonists: Indian-White Relations in the Maritimes*. Vancouver: UBC Press, 1979.

Vansina, Jan. *Oral Tradition as History*. Madison: University of Wisconsin Press, 1985.

Venne, Sharon. *Our Elders Understand Our Rights: Exploring International Law Regarding Indigenous Rights*. Penticton, BC: Theytus, 1998.

Vescey, Chris, and Robert Venables, eds. *American Indian Environments: Ecological Issues in Native American History*. Syracuse, NY: Syracuse University Press, 1980.

Vescey, Christopher. *Traditional Ojibway Religion and Its Historical Changes*. Philadelphia: American Philosophical Society, 1983.

Vizenor, Gerald. *The People Named the Chippewa: Narrative Histories*. Minneapolis: University of Minnesota Press, 1984.

– *The Trickster of Liberty: Tribal Heirs to a Wild Baronage*. Minneapolis: University of Minnesota Press, 1988.

Wa, Gisday, and Delgam Uukw. *The Spirit in the Land*. Gabriola Island, BC: Reflections Press, 1992.

Wackernagel, Mathis, and William Rees, *Our Ecological Footprint: Reducing Human Impact on the Earth*. Gabriola Island, BC: New Society Publishers, 1996.

Walker, Louise J. *Legends of Green Sky Hill*. Grand Rapids, MI: Eerdmans, 1959.

Wall, Steve, and Harvey Arden, *Wisdom Keepers: Meetings with Native American Spiritual Elders*. Hillsboro, OR: Beyond Words, 1990.

Walzer, Michael. *On Toleration*. New Haven, CT: Yale University Press, 1997.

Warren, William. *History of the Ojibway of Lake Superior*. St Paul: Minnesota Historical Society, 1885; repr. Minneapolis: Ross & Haines, 1970.

Weaver, Sally. *Making Canadian Indian Policy: The Hidden Agenda, 1968–1970*. Toronto: University of Toronto Press, 1981.

Whaley, Rick, and Walter Bresette. *Walleye Warriors: An Effective Alliance against Racism and for the Earth*. Philadelphia: New Society Publishers, 1994.

White, James Boyd. *Justice as Translation*. Chicago: University of Chicago Press, 1990.

White, Richard. *The Middle Ground: Indians, Empires and Republics in the Great Lakes Region, 1650–1815*. Cambridge: Cambridge University Press, 1991.

Wiget, Andrew. *Critical Essays on Native American Literature.* Boston: G.K. Hall, 1985.

Wilkinson, Charles. *American Indians, Time and the Law: Native Societies in a Modern Constitutional Democracy.* New Haven, CT: Yale University Press, 1987.

Williams, Paul. 'The Chain.' LL.M. thesis. York University, 1982.

Williams, Robert A. Jr. *The American Indian in Western Legal Thought: The Discourses of Conquest.* New York: Oxford University Press, 1990.

Wittgenstein, Ludwig. *Philosophical Investigations.* 2nd ed. Trans. G.E.M. Anscombe. Oxford: Basil Blackwell, 1967.

Wolf, Eric. *Europe and the People without History.* Berkeley: University of California Press, 1982.

Woodward, Jack. *Native Law.* Scarborough, ON: Carswell, 1990.

Wright, Ronald. *Stolen Continents: The New World through Indian Eyes.* Toronto: Penguin Books, 1992.

Wunder, John R. *Retained by the People: The History of American Indians and the Bill of Rights.* New York: Oxford University Press, 1994.

Yarnell, Richard. *Aboriginal Relationships between Culture and Plant Life in the Upper Great Lakes Region.* Ann Arbor: University of Michigan Press, 1964.

Zimmerman, Joseph P. *Participatory Democracy: Populism Revived.* New York: Praeger, 1986.

Zukin, Sharon. *Landscapes of Power: From Detroit to Disney World.* Berkeley: University of California Press, 1991.

Articles

Adams, Barbara Babcock. 'A Tolerated Margin of Mess: The Trickster and His Tales Reconsidered' (1975) 11 *Journal of Folklore Institute* 147.

Allen, Douglas W. 'Homesteading and Property Rights: or How the West Was Really Won' (1991) 34 *Journal of Law and Economics* 1.

Anaya, James. 'Native Land Claims in the United States: The Un-Atoned-for Spirit of Place' (1994) 18 *Cultural Survival Quarterly* 52.

Anderson, Terry, and Peter Hill, 'The Race for Property Rights' (1990) 33 *Journal of Law and Economics* 177.

Asch, Michael, and Catherine Bell. 'Definition and Interpretation of Fact in Canadian Aboriginal Title Litigation: An Analysis of *Delgamuukw*' (1993–4) 19 *Queen's Law Journal* 503.

Asch, Michael, and Patrick Macklem. 'Aboriginal Rights and Canadian Sovereignty: An Essay on *R. v. Sparrow*' (1991) 29 *Alberta Law Review* 498.

Assier-Andrieu, Louis. 'Anthropology as the Eye of the Law' (1993) 33 *Journal of Legal Pluralism* 179.

Auger, Donald. 'Crime and Control in Three Nish-nawbe-Aski Nation Communities' (1992) 34 *Canadian Journal of Criminology* 317.

Bakan, Joel, Bruce Ryder, David Schneiderman, and Margot Young. 'Developments in Constitutional Law: The 1993–1994 Term' (1995) 6 *Supreme Court Law Review* 67.

Bankes, Nigel. '*Delgamuukw*, Division of Powers and Provincial Land and Resource Laws: Some Implications for Provincial Resource Rights' (1998) 32 *University of British Columbia Law Review* 317.

Barnes, Robin D. 'Race Consciousness: The Thematic Content of Racial Distinctiveness in Critical Race Scholarship' (1990) 103 *Harvard Law Review* 1864.

Barsh, Russel, and James Youngblood Henderson. 'The Supreme Court *Van der Peet* Trilogy: Native Imperialism and Ropes of Sand' (1997) 42 *McGill Law Journal* 993.

Bartlett, Katherine T. 'Tradition, Change and the Idea of Progress in Feminist Legal Thought' [1995] *Wisconsin Law Review* 303.

Bartlett, Richard. 'The Fiduciary Obligation of the Crown to the Indians' (1989) 53 *Saskatchewan Law Review* 301.

Bell, Catherine. 'New Directions in the Law of Aboriginal Rights' (1998) 77 *Canadian Bar Review* 36.

Bell, Derrick. 'Racial Reflections: Dialogues in the Direction of Liberation' (1990) 37 *UCLA Law Review* 1037.

– 'The Referendum: Democracy's Barrier to Racial Equality' (1978) 54 *Washington Law Review* 1.

Bishop, Alan J. 'Western Mathematics: The Secret of Cultural Imperialism' (1990) 32 *Race and Class* 51.

Bluehouse, Philmer, and James Zion. 'Hozhooji Naat'aanii: The Navajo Justice and Harmony Ceremony' (1993) 10 *Mediation Quarterly* 329.

Booth, A.L., and H.M. Jacobs. 'Ties That Bind: Native American Beliefs as a Foundation for Environmental Consciousness' (1990) 12 *Environmental Ethics* 27.

Borrows, John. 'Constitutional Law From a First Nations Perspective: Self-Government and the Royal Proclamation' (1997) 28 *University of British Columbia Law Review* 1.

– 'Contemporary Traditional Equality: The Effect of the Charter on First Nations Politics' (1994) 43 *University of New Brunswick Law Journal* 19.

– 'Domesticating Doctrines: Aboriginal Peoples after the Royal Commission' (2000) 46 *McGill Law Journal* 571.

– 'Frozen Rights in Canada: Constitutional Interpretation and the Trickster' (1997) 22 *American Indian Law Review* 37.

– 'A Genealogy of Law: Inherent Sovereignty and First Nations Self-Government' (1992) 30 *Osgoode Hall Law Journal* 291.

- 'Listening for a Change: The Courts and Oral Tradition' (2001) 39 *Osgoode Hall Law Journal* 1.
- 'Living between Water and Rocks: First Nations, the Environment and Democracy' (1997) 47 *University of Toronto Law Journal* 417.
- 'Negotiating Treaties and Land Claims: The Impact of Diversity within First Nations Property Interests' (1992) 12 *Windsor Yearbook of Access to Justice* 179.
- 'Reliving the Present: Title, Treaties and the Trickster in British Columbia' (1999) 120 *BC Studies* 99.
- 'Sovereignty's Alchemy: An Analysis of *Delgamuukw v. The Queen*' (1999) 37 *Osgoode Hall Law Journal* 537.
- 'The Trickster: Integral to a Distinctive Culture' (1997) *Constitutional Forum* 29.
- 'Uncertain Citizens: The Supreme Court and Aboriginal Peoples' (2001) 80 *Canadian Bar Review* 15
- 'With or Without You: First Nations' Law (in Canada)' (1996) 41 *McGill Law Journal* 629.

Borrows, John, and Len Rotman. 'The Sui Generis Nature of Aboriginal Rights: Does it Make a Difference?' (1997) 36 *Alberta Law Review* 9.

Bourgeois, Donald J. 'The Role of the Historian in the Litigation Process' (1986) 67 *Canadian Historical Review* 2.

Bowman, Margaret. 'The Reburial of Native American Skeletal Remains: Approaches to the Resolution of a Conflict' (1989) 13 *Harvard Environmental Law Journal* 147.

Brant, Clare. 'Native Ethics and Rules of Behaviour' (1990) 35 *Canadian Journal of Psychiatry* 534.

Brock, Kathy. 'The Politics of Aboriginal Self-Government: A Canadian Paradox' (1991) 34 *Canadian Public Administration* 272.

Bullard, Robert. 'The Threat of Environmental Racism' (1993) 7 *Natural Resources and the Environment* 23.

Cairns, Alan. 'The Judicial Committee and Its Critics' (1971) 4 *Canadian Journal of Political Science* 301.

Carillo, Jo. 'Identity as Idiom: Mashpee Reconsidered' (1995) 28 *Indiana Law Review* 517.

- 'Surface and Depth: Some Methodological Problems with Bringing Native American-centred Histories to Light' (1993) 20 *New York University Review of Law and Social Change* 405.

Chang, Williamson. 'The Wasteland in the Western Exploitation of Race and the Environment' (1992) 63 *University of Colorado Law Review* 849.

Chartrand, Paul. 'Aboriginal Rights: The Dispossession of the Métis' (1991) 29 *Osgoode Hall Law Journal* 457.

Christie, Gordon. 'Aboriginal Rights, Aboriginal Culture and Protection' (1998) 36 *Osgoode Hall Law Journal* 447.

Cleland, Charles. 'The Inland Shore Fishery of the North Great Lakes: Its Development and Importance in Pre-History' (1982) 47 *American Antiquity* 761.

Cohen, Felix. 'The Spanish Origins of Indian Rights in the Law of the United States' (1942) 31 *Georgetown Law Journal* 1.

– 'Transcendental Knowledge and the Functional Approach' (1935) 35 *Columbia Law Review* 809.

Coleman, J., and John Freejohn. 'Democracy and Social Choice' (1986) 97 *Ethics* 11.

Collins, Nancy B., and Andrea Hall. 'Nuclear Waste in Indian Country: A Paradoxical Trade' (1994) 12 *Law and Inequality Journal* 267.

Cook, Nancy L. 'Outside the Tradition: Literature as Legal Scholarship' (1994) 63 *University of Cincinnati Law Review* 95.

Cover, Robert M. 'The Folktales of Justice: Tales of Jurisdiction' (1985) 14 *Capital University Law Review* 179.

– 'Foreword: Nomos and Narrative' (1983) 97 *Harvard Law Review* 11.

Cowlishaw, Gillian. 'Did the Earth Move for You? The Anti-Mabo Debate' (1995) 6 *Australian Journal of Anthropology* 32.

Coyle, Michael. 'Traditional Indian Justice in Ontario: A Role for the Present?' (1986) 24 *Osgoode Hall Law Journal* 605.

Cruickshank, Julie. 'Invention of Anthropology in British Columbia's Supreme Court: Oral Tradition as Evidence in *Delgamuukw v. BC*' (1992) 95 *BC Studies* 25.

Delgado, Richard. 'Rodrigo's Final Chronicle: Cultural Power, the Law Reviews, and the Attack on Narrative Jurisprudence' (1995) 68 *Southern California Law Review* 545.

Deloria, Sam, and Robert Laurence, 'What's an Indian? A Conversation about Law School Admissions, Indian Tribal Sovereignty and Affirmative Action' (1991) 44 *Arkansas Law Review* 1107.

Devlin, Richard. 'Judging and Diversity: Justice or Just Us?' (1996) 20 *Provincial Court Judges Journal* 4.

– 'We Can't Go on Together with Suspicious Minds: Judicial Bias and Racialized Perspective in *R. v. R.D.S.*' (1995) 18 *Dalhousie Law Review* 408.

DeWalt, Billie. 'Using Indigenous Knowledge to Improve Agricultural and Natural Resource Management' (1994) 53 *Human Organization* 123.

Dickinson, G.M., and R.D. Gidney, 'History and Advocacy: Some Reflections on the Historian's Role in Litigation' (1987) 68 *Canadian Historical Review* 576.

Dickson-Gilmore, Jane. 'Finding the Ways of the Ancestors: Customary Change and Invention of Tradition in the Development of Separate Legal Systems' (1992) 34 *Canadian Journal of Criminology* 479.

Disch, Lisa. 'More Truth than Fact: Storytelling as Critical Understanding in the Writing of Hannah Arendt' (1993) 21 *Political Theory* 665.

Elder, P.S. 'Legal Rights for Nature: The Wrong Answer to the Right(s) Question' (1984) 22 *Osgoode Hall Law Journal* 309.

Elgie, Stewart. 'Injunctions, Ancient Forests and Irreparable Harm: A Comment on *Western Canada Wilderness Committee v. A.G. British Columbia*' (1991) 25 *University of British Columbia Law Review* 387.

Elliot, David. 'Aboriginal Peoples in Canada and the United States and the Scope of the Fiduciary Relationship' (1996) 24 *Manitoba Law Journal* 137.

Ellwanger, Kimberly T. 'Money Damages for the Breach of the Federal-Indian Trust Relationship after Mitchell II' (1983–4) 59 *Washington Law Review* 675.

Espeland, Wendy. 'Legally Mediated Identity: *The National Environmental Policy Act* and the Bureaucratic Construction of Interests' (1994) 28 *Law and Society Review* 1149.

Eule, Julian. 'Judicial Review of Direct Democracy' (1990) 99 *Yale Law Journal* 1503.

Fisher, Robin. 'Joseph Trutch and Indian Land Policy' 12 (1971–2) *BC Studies*.

– 'Judging History: Reflections on the Reasons for Judgment in *Delgamuukw v. B.C.*' (1992) 95 *BC Studies* 43.

Fitzpatrick, Peter. 'Law and Societies' (1984) 22 *Osgoode Hall Law Journal* 115.

Ford, Richard Thompson. 'The Boundaries of Race: Political Geography in Legal Analysis' (1994) 107 *Harvard Law Review* 1843.

Fortune, Joel. 'Construing *Delgamuukw*: Legal Arguments, Historical Argumentation and the Philosophy of History' (1992) 51 *University of Toronto Faculty of Law Review* 80.

Freedman, Bob. 'Semiahmoo Indian Band v. Canada' (1997) 36 *Alberta Law Review* 218.

– 'The Space for Aboriginal Self-Government in British Columbia: The Effect of the Decision of the British Columbia Court of Appeal in *Delgamuukw v. British Columbia*' (1994) 28 *University of British Columbia Law Review* 49.

Freudenburg, William. 'Addictive Economies: Extractive Industries and Vulnerable Localities in a Changing World Economy' (1992) 57 *Rural Sociology* 305.

Frickey, Philip. 'Marshalling the Past and Present: Colonialism, Constitutionalism and Interpretation in Federal Indian Law' (1993) 107 *Harvard Law Review* 381.

Frug, Gerald. 'The City as a Legal Concept' (1980) 93 *Harvard Law Review* 1059.

Glenn, Patrick. 'The Common Law in Canada' (1995) 74 *Canadian Bar Review* 261.

Gover, Kevin, and Jana Walker. 'Escaping Environmental Paternalism: One Tribe's Approach to Developing a Commercial Waste Project in Indian Country' (1992) 63 *University of Colorado Law Review* 933.

Grammond, Sabastien. 'Aboriginal Treaties and Canadian Law' (1994) 20 *Queen's Law Journal* 57.

Greenwood, Murray. 'Lord Watson, Institutional Self-Interest, and the Decentralization of Canadian Federalism in the 1890's' (1974) 9 *University of British Columbia Law Review* 244.

Griffiths, J. 'What is Legal Pluralism?' (1986) 24 *Journal of Legal Pluralism and Unofficial Law* 1.

Gunn, Angus, and Ira Nishisato. 'Holwood and Wymilwood' (1993–4) *Nexus* 20.

Habermas, Jürgen. 'Address: Multiculturalism and the Liberal State' (1995) 47 *Stanford Law Review* 849.

– 'Citizenship and National Identity: Some Reflections on the Future of Europe' (1992) 12 *Praxis International* 1.

Hahn, Robert, and Gordon Hester. 'Marketable Permits: Lessons for Theory and Practice' (1989) 16 *Ecology Law Quarterly* 361.

Harring, Sid. 'The Liberal Treatment of Indians: Native People in Nineteenth Century Ontario Law' (1992) 56 *Saskatchewan Law Review* 297.

Harris, Angela. 'Race and Essentialism in Feminist Legal Theory' (1990) 42 *Stanford Law Review* 581.

Hasio, Douglas. 'Invisible Cities: The Constitutional Status of Direct Democracy in a Democratic Republic' (1992) 41 *Duke Law Journal* 1267.

Henderson, Sakej. 'Empowering Treaty Federalism' (1995) 58 *Saskatchewan Law Review* 241.

– 'First Nations Legal Inheritances: The Mikmaq Model' (1996) 23 *Manitoba Law Journal* 1.

– 'Mikmaw Tenure in Atlantic Canada' (1995) 18 *Dalhousie Law Journal* 196.

Hogg, Peter, and Mary Ellen Turpel. 'Implementing Aboriginal Self-Government: Constitutional and Jurisdictional Issues' (1995) 74 *Canadian Bar Review* 187.

Hoskins, David. 'Acid Rain, Emissions Trading and the Clean Air Act Amendments of 1989' (1990) 15 *Columbia Journal of Environmental Law* 329.

Howse, Robert, and Alissa Malkin. 'Canadians Are a Sovereign People: How the Supreme Court Should Approach the Reference on Quebec Secession' (1997) 76 *Canadian Bar Review* 186.

Hunt, Alan. 'Law, Community, and Everyday Life: Yngvesson's Virtuous Citizens and Disruptive Subjects' (1996) 21 *Law and Social Inquiry* 179.

Hutchins, Peter W., David Schulze, and Carol Hilling. 'When Do Fiduciary Obligations to Aboriginal Peoples Arise?' (1995) 59 *Saskatchewan Law Review* 97.

Jackson, Michael. 'In Search of the Pathways to Justice: Alternative Dispute Resolution in Aboriginal Communities' (1992) (Special issue) *University of British Columbia Law Review* 41.

– 'Locking Up Natives in Canada' (1989) 23 *University of British Columbia Law Review* 205.

Kapashesit, Randy, and Murray Klippenstein. 'Aboriginal Group Rights and Environmental Protection' (1991) 36 *McGill Law Journal* 925.

Karno, Valerie. 'Bringing Fiction to Justice: Including Individual Narrative in Judicial Opinions' (1990) 2 *Hastings Women's Law Journal* 77.

Kline, Marlee. 'The Colour of Law: Ideological Representations of First Nations in Legal Discourse' (1994) 3 *Social and Legal Studies* 451.

Kymlicka, Will, and Wayne Norman. 'Return of the Citizen: A Survey of Recent Work on Citizenship Theory' (1994) 104 *Ethics* 352.

Lambert, Honourable Mister Justice Douglas. '*Van der Peet* and *Delgamuukw*: Ten Unresolved Issues' (1998) 32 *University of British Columbia Law Review* 249.

Lederman, William R. 'Judicial Independence and Court Reform in Canada for the 1990's' (1987) 12 *Queen's Law Journal* 385.

Lester, Geoffrey S. 'Aboriginal Land Rights: Some Remarks upon the Ontario Lands Case (1885–1888)' (1988) 13 *Queen's Law Journal* 132.

Lilles, Heino. 'A Plea for More Human Values in Our Justice System' (1992) 17 *Queen's Law Journal* 328.

Llewellyn, Karl. 'Some Realism about Legal Realism: Responding to Dean Pound' (1931) 44 *Harvard Law Review* 1222.

Lowery, Daniel. 'Developing a Tribal Common Law Jurisprudence: The Navajo Experience' (1993) 18 *American Indian Law Review* 379.

Lowie, Robert. 'Oral Tradition and History' (1915) 17 *American Anthropologist* 597.

– 'Oral Tradition and History' (1917) 30 *Journal of American Folklore* 161.

Macklem, Patrick. 'Distributing Sovereignty: Indian Nations and Equality of Peoples' (1993) 45 *Stanford Law Review* 1311.

– 'First Nations Self-Government and the Borders of the Canadian Legal Imagination' (1991) 36 *McGill Law Journal* 382.

– 'Normative Dimensions of an Aboriginal Right to Self-Government' (1995) *Queen's Law Journal* 173.

Mandamin, Leonard, et al. 'The Criminal Code and Aboriginal People' (1992) (Special issue) *University of British Columbia Law Review* 5.

Matsuda, Mari. 'Affirmative Action and Legal Knowledge: Planting Seeds in Plowed Up Ground' (1988) 11 *Harvard Women's Law Journal* 1.

- 'Looking to the Bottom: Critical Legal Studies and Reparations' (1987) 22 *Harvard Civil Rights–Civil Liberties Law Review* 323.
McChesney, Fred S. 'Government as Definer of Property Rights: Indian Lands, Ethnic Externalities and Bureaucratic Budgets' (1990) 19 *Journal of Legal Studies* 297.
McDonnell, Roger F. 'Contextualizing the Investigation of Customary Law in Contemporary Native Communities' (1992) 34 *Canadian Journal of Criminology* 299.
McLeod, Clay. 'The Oral Histories of Canada's Northern Peoples, Anglo-Canadian Evidence Law, and Canada's Fiduciary Duty to First Nations: Breaking Down the Barriers of the Past' (1992) 30 *Alberta Law Review* 1276.
McNeil, Kent. 'How Can Infringements of the Constitutional Rights of the Aboriginal Peoples Be Justified?' (1997) 8 *Constitutional Forum* 33.
- 'A Question of Title: Has the Common Law Been Misapplied to Dispossess the Aboriginal?' (1990) 16 *Monash University Law Review* 91.
Meehan, Eugene, and Elizabeth Stewart. 'Developments in Aboriginal Law: The 1995–96 Term' (1997) 8 *Supreme Court Law Review* 1 at 7.
Merry, Sally Engle. 'Law and Colonialism' (1991) 25 *Law and Society Review* 889.
- 'Resistance and the Cultural Power of Law' (1995) 29 *Law and Society Review* 11.
Mezey, Naomi. 'The Distribution of Wealth, Sovereignty and Culture through Indian Gaming' (1996) 48 *Stanford Law Review* 711.
Monahan, Patrick. 'Is the Pearson Airport Legislation Unconstitutional? The Rule of Law as a Limit on Contract Repudiation by Government' (1995) 33 *Osgoode Hall Law Journal* 411.
Monture, Patricia. '*Ka-Nin-Geh-A-Sa-Nonh-Ya-Gah*' (1986) 2 *Canadian Journal of Women and the Law* 159.
Morse, Bradford. 'Permafrost Rights: Aboriginal Self-Government and the Supreme Court in *R. v. Pamajewon*' (1997) 42 *McGill Law Journal* 1011.
Moses, Daniel David. 'The Trickster Theatre of Tomson Highway' (1987) 60 *Canadian Fiction Magazine* 88.
Otis, Ghislain. 'Opposing Aboriginality to Modernity: The Doctrine of Aboriginal Rights in Canada' (1997) 12 *British Journal of Canadian Studies* 1.
Pentney, William. 'The Rights of the Aboriginal Peoples of Canada and the Constitution Act 1982, Part I: The Interpretive Prism of s. 25' (1988) 22 *University of British Columbia Law Review* 21.
Pommersheim, Frank. 'The Contextual Legitimacy of Adjudication in Tribal Courts and the Role of the Bar as an Interpretive Community' (1988) 18 *New Mexico Law Review* 49.
- 'Liberation, Dreams and Hard Work: An Essay on Tribal Court Jurisprudence' [1992] *Wisconsin Law Review* 411.

Pue, W. 'Wrestling with Law: (Geographical) Specificity v. (Legal) Abstraction' (1990) 11 *Urban Geography* 566.

Puri, Kamal. 'Cultural Ownership and Intellectual Property Rights Post-*Mabo*: Putting Ideas into Action' (1995) 9 *Intellectual Property Journal* 293.

Rabin, Joe. 'Job Security and Due Process: Monitoring Administrative Discretion through a Reasons Requirement' (1976) 44 *University of Chicago Law Review* 60 at 77–8.

Radin, Max. 'A Restatement of Hohfeld' (1938) 51 *Harvard Law Review* 1145.

Ragsdale, John. 'Law and Environment in Modern America and among the Hopi Indians: A Comparison of Values' (1986) 10 *Harvard Environmental Law Review* 417.

Ray, Arthur J. 'Creating the Image of the Savage in Defence of the Crown' (1990) 6 *Native Studies Review* 13.

Rees, William. 'Economics, Ecology, and the Limits of Conventional Analysis' (1991) 40–1 *Journal of the Air and Waste Management Association* 1.

Reynolds, Glenn H. 'Is Democracy Like Sex?' (1995) 48 *Vanderbilt Law Review* 1635.

– 'Prenumbral Reasoning on the Right' (1992) 140 *University of Pennsylvania Law Review* 1333.

Risk, Richard. 'Constitutional Scholarship in the Late Nineteenth Century: Making Federalism Work' (1996) 46 *University of Toronto Law Journal* 427.

Rorty, Richard. 'On Ethnocentrism: A Reply to Clifford Geertz' (1986) 25 *Michigan Quarterly Review* 525.

Ross, Rupert. 'Leaving Our White Eyes Behind: The Sentencing of Native Accused' [1989] 3 Canadian Native Law Reporter 1.

Ross, Thomas. 'The Richmond Narratives' (1989) 68 *Texas Law Review* 381.

Rotman, Leonard. 'Provincial Fiduciary Obligations to First Nations: The Nexus between Governmental Power and Responsibility' (1994) 32 *Osgoode Hall Law Journal* 736.

Royster, Judith V., and Rory Snow Arrow Fausett. 'Control of the Reservation Environment: Tribal Primacy, Federal Delegation, and the Limits of State Intrusion' (1989) 64 *Washington Law Review* 581.

Rychlak, Ronald J. 'People as Part of Nature: Reviewing the Law of the Mother' (1994) 13 *Stanford Environmental Law Journal* 451.

Ryder, Bruce. 'The Demise and Rise of the Classical Paradigm in Canadian Federalism: Promoting Autonomy for the Provinces and First Nations' (1991) 36 *McGill Law Journal* 308.

Sarat, Austin, and Roger Berkowitz. 'Disorderly Differences: Recognition, Accommodation, and American Law' (1994) 6 *Yale Journal of Law and the Humanities* 285.

Saxe, Diane. 'Reflections on Environmental Restoration' (1992) 2 *Journal of Environmental Law and Policy* 77.

Schwartz, Bryan. 'A Separate Aboriginal Justice System?' (1990) 28 *Manitoba Law Journal* 77.

Scott, Richard J. 'Accountability and Independence' (1996) 45 *University of New Brunswick Law Journal* 27.

Shamir, Ronen. 'Suspended in Space: Bedouins under the Law of Israel' (1996) *Journal of Law and Society* 231.

Sherrott, Geoff. 'The Court's Treatment of the Evidence in *Delgamuukw v. B.C.*' (1992) 56 *Saskatchewan Law Review* 441.

Sierra, Maria Teresa. 'Indian Rights and Customary Law in Mexico: A Study of the Nahuas in the Siera de Puebla' (1995) 29 *Law and Society Review* 227.

Singer, Joseph. 'Sovereignty and Property' (1991) *Northwestern University Law Review* 1.

Slattery, Brian. 'The Independence of Canada' (1983) 5 *Supreme Court Law Review* 369.

– 'Making Sense of Aboriginal Rights' (2000) 79 *Canadian Bar Review* 196.

– 'The Organic Constitution: Aboriginal Peoples and the Evolution of Canada' (1996) 34 *Osgoode Hall Law Journal* 101.

– 'Rights, Communities and Tradition' (1991) 41 *University of Toronto Law Journal* 447.

– 'Understanding Aboriginal Rights' (1987) 66 *Canadian Bar Review* 727.

Soifer, Aviam. 'Objects in the Mirror are Closer Than They Appear' (1994) 28 *Georgia Law Review*.

Stone, Christopher. 'Should Trees Have Standing?' (1972) 45 *Southern California Law Review* 450.

Strickland, Rennard. 'A Tale of Two Marshalls: The Cherokee Cases and the Cruel Irony of Supreme Court Victories' (1994) 47 *Oklahoma Law Review* 111.

Suchman, Mark. 'Invention and Ritual: Notes on the Interrelation of Magic and Intellectual Property in Preliterate Societies' (1989) 89 *Columbia Law Review* 1264.

Teubner, G. 'Rethinking Legal Pluralism (1992) 13 *Cardozo Law Review* 1443.

Trackman, Leon. 'Native Cultures in a Rights Empire: Ending the Dominion' (1997) 45 *Buffalo Law Review* 189 at 196–212.

Tribe, Lawrence. 'Ways Not to Think about Plastic Tress: New Foundations for Environmental Law' (1974) 83 *Yale Law Journal* 1315.

Trope, Jack, and Walter Echo Hawk. '*Native American Graves Protection and Repatriation Act*: Background and Legal History' (1992) 24 *Arizona State Law Journal* 35.

Tso, Chief Justice Tom. 'The Process of Decision Making in Tribal Courts' (1989) 31 *Arizona Law Review* 225.

Turpel, Mary Ellen. 'Aboriginal Peoples and the Canadian Charter: Interpretive Monopolies, Cultural Differences' (1989–90) 6 *Canadian Human Rights Yearbook* 3.

– 'Home/Land' (1991) 10 *Canadian Journal of Family Law* 17.

Valencia-Weber, Gloria. 'Tribal Courts: Custom and Innovative Law' (1994) 24 *New Mexico Law Review* 227.

Van Dyke, Brennan. 'Emissions Trading to Reduce Acid Deposition' (1991) 100 *Yale Law Journal* 2707.

Vitousek, Peter, et al. 'Human Appropriation of the Products of Photosynthesis' (1986) 34 *Bioscience* 368.

Wallingford, James. 'The Role of Tradition in the Navajo Judiciary: Re-emergence and Revival' (1994) 19 *Oklahoma City University Law Review* 141.

Walters, Mark. 'The Golden Thread of Continuity: Aboriginal Customs at Common Law and Under the Constitution Act, 1982' (1999) 44 *McGill Law Journal* 711.

– 'British Imperial Constitutional Law and Aboriginal Rights: A Comment on *Delgamuukw v. B.C.*' (1992) 17 *Queen's Law Journal* 350.

Watson, Alan. 'An Approach to Customary Law' [1984] *University of Illinois Law Review* 561.

Weaver, Russell. 'Langdell's Legacy: Living with the Case Method' (1991) 36 *Villanova Law Review* 517.

Webber, Jeremy. 'The Jurisprudence of Regret: The Search for Standards of Justice in Mabo' (1995) 17 *Sydney Law Review* 5.

– 'Relations of Force and Relations of Justice: The Emergence of Normative Community between Colonists and Aboriginal Peoples' (1995) 33 *Osgoode Hall Law Journal* 623.

Wells, Matthew D. 'Sparrow and Lone Wolf: Honoring Tribal Rights in Canada and the United States' (1991) 66 *Washington Law Review* 1119.

Wicken, William. 'Heard It from My Grandfather: Mi'kmaq Treaty Tradition and the Syliboy Case of 1928' (1995) 44 *University of New Brunswick Law Journal* 146.

– 'The Mi'kmaq and Wuastukwiuk Treaties' (1994) 43 *University of New Brunswick Law Journal* 43.

Wilkinson, Charles. 'Cross-Jurisdictional Conflicts: Analysis of Legitimate State Interests on Federal and Indian Lands' (1982) 2 *UCLA Journal of Environmental Law and Policy* 145.

– 'Home Dance, the Hopi, and the Black Mesa: Conquest and Endurance in the American Southwest' (1996) *Brigham Young University Law Review* 449–82.

Williams Jr, Robert A. 'The Algebra of Federal Indian Law: The Hard Trail of Decolonizing and Americanizing the White Man's Indian Jurisprudence' (1986) *Wisconsin Law Review* 219.

- 'Large Binocular Telescopes, Red Squirrel Pinatas, and Apache Sacred Mountains: Decolonizing Environmental Law in a Multicultural World' (1994) 95 *West Virginia Law Review* 1133.
- 'Sovereignty, Racism, Human Rights: Indian Self-Determination and the Postmodern World Legal System' (1995) 2 *Review of Constitutional Studies* 146.
- 'Taking Rights Aggressively: The Perils and Promise of Critical Legal Theory for People of Color' (1987) 5 *Law and Inequality Journal* 103.

Worthen, Kevin. 'Two Sides of the Same Coin: The Potential Normative Power of American Cities and Indian Tribes' (1991) 44 *Vanderbilt Law Review* 1273.

Worthen, Kevin, and Wayne Farnsworth. 'Who Will Control the Future of Indian Gaming? "A Few Pages of History Are Worth a Volume of Logic"' (1996) *Brigham Young University Law Review* 407.

Yazzie, Robert. Chief Justice of the Navajo Supreme Court. 'Life Comes From It: Navajo Justice Concepts' (1994) 24 *New Mexico Law Review* 175.

Zuni, Christine. 'The Southwest Intertribal Court of Appeals' (1994) 24 *New Mexico Law Review* 304.

Essays

Alverson, William, et al. 'Zoning for Diversity.' In *Wild Forests: Conservation Biology and Public Policy*. Washington, DC: Island Press, 1990.

An-Na'im, Abdullahi Ahmed. 'Problems of Universal Cultural Legitimacy for Human Rights.' In Abdullahi Ahmed An-Na'im and Francis Deng, eds., *Human Rights in Africa: Cross-Cultural Perspectives*. Washington: Brookings Institute, 1990.

Asch, Michael. 'Errors in Delgamuukw: An Anthropological Perspective.' In Frank Cassidy, ed., *Aboriginal Title in British Columbia: Delgamuukw v. The Queen*. Lantzville, BC: Oolichan Press, 199.

Asch, Michael, and Cathy Bell. 'Challenging Assumptions: The Impact of Precedent in Aboriginal Rights Litigation.' In Michael Asch, ed., *Aboriginal and Treaty Rights in Canada: Essays in Law, Equality, and Respect for Difference*. Vancouver: UBC Press, 1997.

Bakhtin, Mikhail M. 'Discourse in the Novel.' In *The Dialogical Imagination: Four Essays*, ed. Michael Holquist. Austin: University of Texas Press, 1981.

Black, Jerome H. 'Reforming the Context of the Voting Process in Canada: Lessons from Other Democracies.' In Herman Bakvis, ed., *Voter Turnout in Canada*. Toronto: Dundurn Press, 1991.

Borrows, John. 'Because It Does Not Make Sense: Sovereignty's Power in R. v.

Delgamuukw.' In Diane Kirby and Catherine Coleborne, eds., *Law, History and Colonialism: The Reach of Empire*. Manchester: University of Manchester Press, 2001.

– 'Landed Citizenship: Narratives of Aboriginal Political Participation.' In Will Kymlicka et al., eds., *Citizenship in Diverse Societies*. Oxford: Oxford University Press, 2000.

– 'Wampum at Niagara: The Royal Proclamation, Canadian Legal History and Self-Government.' In Michael Asch, ed., *Aboriginal and Treaty Rights in Canada: Essays in Law, Equality and Respect for Difference*. Vancouver: UBC Press, 1997.

– 'Colonialism, Canadian Legal History and *Delgamuukw v. The Queen*.' In Diane Kirby, ed., *Law, History and Colonialism: Empire's Reach*. Manchester: Manchester University Press, 2001.

Cairns, Alan. 'The Fragmentation of Canadian Citizenship.' In William Kaplan, ed. *Belonging: The Meaning and Future of Canadian Citizenship*. Montreal: McGill-Queen's University Press, 1993.

Christenson, P. 'Increasing Returns and Ecological Sustainability.' In Robert Costanza, ed., *Ecological Economics: The Science and Management of Sustainability*. New York: Columbia University Press, 1991.

Cloud, Peter Blue. 'Resistance at Oka.' In Peter Nabov, ed., *Native American Testimony: A Chronicle of Indian-White Relations from Prophecy to the Present, 1492–1992*. New York: Viking Press, 1992.

Dahl, Gudrun. 'Environmentalism, Nature, and Otherness: Some Perspectives on Our Relations with Small Scale Producers in the Third World.' In Gudrun Dahl, ed., *Green Arguments and Local Subsistence*. Stockholm: Stockholm Studies in Anthropology, 1993.

Daly, Herman. 'Sustainable Development: From Concept and Theory towards Operational Principles.' In *Steady State Economics*. 2nd ed. Washington: Island Press, 1991.

Dumont, James. 'Justice and Aboriginal People.' In *Aboriginal Peoples and the Justice System: Report of the National Roundtable on Aboriginal Issues*. Ottawa: Supply and Services, 1993.

Eliot, T.S. 'Tradition and the Individual Talent.' In *Selected Essays*. London: Faber, 1953.

Erasmus, Georges, and Joe Sanders. 'Canadian History: An Aboriginal Perspective.' In Diane Engelstad and John Bird, eds., *Nation to Nation: Aboriginal Sovereignty and the Future of Canada*. Concord, ON: Anansi Press, 1992.

Favel, Chief Blaine. 'First Nations Perspectives on the Split in Jurisdiction.' In Richard Gosse, James Youngblood Henderson, and Roger Carter, eds., *Continuing Poundmaker and Riel's Quest: Presentation Made at a Conference on Aboriginal People and Justice*. Saskatoon: Purich Publishing, 1994.

Gower, Barry S. 'What Do We Owe Future Generations?' In David Cooper and Joy Palmer, eds., *The Environment in Question: Ethics and Global Issues.* New York: Routledge, 1992.

Holtzkamm, Tim E., et al. 'Rainy River Sturgeon: An Ojibway Resource in the Fur Trade Economy.' In Kerry Abel and Jean Friesen, eds., *Aboriginal Resource Use in Canada: Historical and Legal Aspects.* Winnipeg: University of Manitoba Press, 1991.

Jackson, Michael. 'The Case in Context.' In Don Monet and Ardythe Wilson, eds., *Colonialism on Trial: Indigenous Land Rights and the Gitksan and Wet'suwet'en Sovereignty Case.* Philadelphia: New Society, 1992.

Jeffery, Chief Alice. 'Remove Not the Landmark.' In Frank Cassidy, ed., *Aboriginal Title in British Columbia.* Lantzville, BC: Oolichan Books, 1991.

Johnson, Nevil. 'Types of Referndum.' In Austin Ranney, ed., *The Referendum Device: A Conference.* Washington, DC: American Institute for Public Policy Research, 1981.

Johnston, Basil. 'One Generation from Extinction.' In Daniel David Moses and Terry Goldie, eds., *An Anthology of Canadian Literature in English.* Toronto: Oxford University Press, 1992.

King, Thomas. 'The One about Coyote Going West.' In Thomas King, ed., *All My Relations: An Anthology of Canadian Native Fiction.* Toronto: McClelland and Stewart, 1990.

LaDuke, Winona. 'A Society Based on Conquest Cannot Be Sustained: Native Peoples and the Environmental Crisis.' In Richard Hofrichter, ed., *Toxic Struggles: The Theory and Practice of Environmental Justice.* Philadelphia: New Society Publishers, 1993.

Little Bear, Leroy. 'What's Einsten Got to do With It?' In Richard Gosse, James Youngblood Henderson, and Roger Carter, eds., *Continuing Poundmaker and Riel's Quest: Presentations Made at a Conference in Aboriginal People and Justice.* Saskatoon: Purich Publishing, 1994.

MacDonald, David. 'Referendums and Federal General Elections in Canada.' In Michael Cassidy, ed., *Democratic Rights and Electoral Reform in Canada.* Ottawa: Dundurn Press, 1991.

MacDonald, Roderick A. 'Recognizing and Legitimating Aboriginal Justice: Implications for a Reconstruction of Non-Aboriginal Legal Systems in Canada.' In Royal Commission on Aboriginal Peoples, *Aboriginal Peoples and the Justice System.* Ottawa: Supply and Services, 1993.

Mandell, Louise. 'Native Culture on Trial.' In Kathleen Mahoney and Sheila Martins, eds., *Equality and Judicial Neutrality.* Toronto: Carswell, 1989.

McNeil, Kent. 'The Meaning of Aboriginal Title.' In Michael Asch, ed., *Aboriginal and Treaty Rights in Canada: Essays on Law, Equality and Respect for Difference.* Vancouver: UBC Press, 1997.

Minow, Martha. 'Stories in Law.' In Peter Brooks and Paul Gewirtz, eds., *Law's Stories*. New Haven, CT: Yale University Press, 1996.

Mitchell, Grand Chief Michael. 'An Unbroken Assertion of Sovereignty.' In Boyce Richardson, ed., *DrumBeat: Anger and Renewal in Indian Country*. Toronto: Summerhill Press, 1985.

Monture-Okanee, Patricia. 'Alternative Dispute Resolution: A Bridge to Aboriginal Experience?' In C. Morris and Andrew Perie, eds., *Qualifications for Dispute Resolution: Perspectives on the Debate*. Victoria: University of Victoria Dispute Resolution Centre. 1994.

Nissenbaum, Paul, and Paul Shardle. 'Building a System for Land-Use Planning: A Case Study for the Puyallup Tribe.' In Stephen Cornell and Joseph Kalt, eds., *What Can Tribes Do? Strategies and Institutions in American Indian Economic Development*. Los Angeles: American Indian Studies Center, 1992.

Perrot, Nicolas. 'Memoir on the Manners, Customs, and Religion of the Savages of North America.' In Emma Blair, ed., *The Indian Tribes of the Upper Mississippi Valley and Region of the Great Lakes*. Vol. 1. Cleveland: Arthur H. Clark, 1911.

Pope Innocent IV. 'Commentaria Doctissima in Quinque Libros Decretalium.' In James Muldoon, ed., *The Expansion of Europe: The First Phase*. Philadelphia: University of Pennsylvania Press, 1997.

Porter, Tom. 'Traditions of the Constitution of the Six Nations.' In Leroy Little Bear, Menno Boldt and J. Anthony Long, eds., *Pathways to Self-Determination: Canadian Indians and the Canadian State*. Toronto: University of Toronto Press, 1984.

Power, Thomas Michael. 'Thinking about Natural Resource Dependent Economies: Moving beyond the Folk Economics of the Rear View Mirror.' In Richard Knight and Sarah Bates, eds., *A New Century for Natural Resources Management*. Washington, DC: Island Press, 1995.

Rapport, D. 'The Interface of Economics and Ecology.' In Ann-Mari Jansson, ed., *Integration of Economy and Ecology: An Outlook for the Eighties*. Stockholm: Asko Laboratory, University of Stockholm, 1984.

Ray, Arthur. 'Fur Trade History and the Gitksan and Wet'suwet'en Comprehensive Claim: Men of Property and the Exercise of Title.' In Kerry Abel and Friesen, eds., *Aboriginal Resource Use in Canada*. Winnipeg: University of Manitoba Press, 1991.

Ridington, Robin. 'Cultures in Conflict: The Problem of Discourse.' In W.H. New, ed., *Native Writers and Canadian Writing*. Vancouver: UBC Press, 1990.

– 'Fieldmark in Courtroom 53.' In Frank Cassidy, ed., *Aboriginal Title in British Columbia. Delgamuukw v. The Queen*. Lantzville, BC: Oolichan Press, 1992.

Roman, Andrew. 'From Judicial Economy to Access to Justice: Standing and

Class Actions.' In Canadian Bar Association, *Environmental Law: An Environmental Primer.* Toronto: Canadian Bar Association, 1991.

Ryan, Joan, and Bernard Ominayak. 'The Cultural Effects of Judicial Bias.' In Kathleen Mahoney and Sheilah Martin, eds., *Equality and Judicial Neutrality.* Toronto: Carswell, 1989.

Ryberg, Inez Scott. 'Selections from Livy's History of Rome.' In Paul McKendrick and Herbert M. Howe, eds., *Classics in Translation.* Vol. 2. Madison: University of Wisconsin Press, 1980.

Sanders, Douglas. 'The Indian Lobby.' In Keith Banting and Richard Simeon, eds., *And No One Cheered: Federalism, Democracy and the Constitution Act.* Toronto: Methuen, 1983.

Schoolcraft, Henry Rowe. 'Historical and Methodological Perspective.' In Andrew Wiget, ed., *Critical Essays on Native American Literature.* Boston: G.K. Hall, 1985.

Schwartz, Bryan. 'Unstarted Business: Two Approaches to Defining s. 35 – What's in the Box, and What Kind of Box?' In *First Principles, Second Thoughts.* Montreal: Institute for Research on Public Policy, 1986.

Schwartz, O.D. 'Plains Indian Influence on the American Environmental Movement: Ernest Thompson and Ohiyesa.' In Paul A. Olsen, ed., *The Struggle for the Land: Indigenous Insight and Industrial Empires in the Semi-Arid World.* Lincoln: University of Nebraska Press, 1990.

Simpson, Brian. 'The Common Law and Legal Theory.' In William Twining, ed., *Legal Theory and Common Law.* Oxford: Basil Blackwell, 1986.

Smith, Joseph H., ed. 'The Mohegan Indians v. Connecticut.' In *Appeals to the Privy Council from the American Plantations.* New York: Octagon Books, 1965.

Spry, Irene. 'The Tragedy of the Loss of the Commons in Western Canada.' In Ian Getty and Antoine Lussier, eds., *As Long as the Sun Shines and the Water Flows: A Reader in Canadian Native Studies.* Vancouver: UBC Press, 1990.

Taylor, Charles. 'The Politics of Recognition.' In Amy Gutman and Charles Taylor, eds., *Multiculturalism and the Politics of Recognition.* Princeton, NJ: Princeton University Press, 1992.

Tennant, Paul. 'The Place of Delgamuukw in British Columbia History and Politics – And Vice Versa.' In Frank Cassidy, ed., *Aboriginal Title in British Columbia: Delgamuukw v. The Queen.* Lantzville, BC: Oolichan Books, 1992.

Tobias, John. 'Protection, Civilization and Assimilation: An Outline History of Canada's Indian Policy.' In James Miller, ed., *Sweet Promises: A Reader on Indian-White Relations in Canada.* Toronto: University of Toronto Press, 1991.

Treaty 7 Elders and Tribal Council et al. 'Aboriginal and Government Objectives in the Treaty Era.' In *The True Spirit and Intent of Treaty 7*. Montreal: McGill-Queen's University Press, 1996.

Wicken, William. 'Re-examining Mi'kmaq–Acadian Relations 1635–1755.' In Sylvie Departie, et al., *Vingt an après, Habitants et marchands: Lectures de l'histoire des XVIIe et XVIIIe siècles canadiens*. Montreal: McGill-Queen's University Press.

Documents

Assembly of First Nations. *First Peoples and the Constitution: Conference Report of March 13–15, 1992*. Ottawa: Supply and Services, 1992.

British Columbia. *List of Proclamations for 1858 ... 1864*. New Westminster: Government Printing Office, n.d.

– *Papers Connected with the Indian Land Question, 1850–1875*. Victoria: Government Printer, 1875.

Brundtland, G.H., and World Commission on Environment and Development. *Our Common Future*. Oxford: World Commission on Environment and Development, 1987.

Canada. *Canada: Indian Treaties and Surrenders*. Ottawa: Queen's Printer, 1891–1912.

Department of Indian Affairs and Northern Development. *Statement of the Government of Canada on Indian Policy, 1969*. Ottawa: Queen's Printer, 1969.

Department of Indian and Northern Affairs. *Aboriginal Education: The Path to Empowerment*. Ottawa: Supply and Services, 1994.

Hawthorn, Harry B., ed. *A Survey of the Contemporary Indians of Canada: A Report on Economic, Political, Education Needs and Policies in Two Volumes*. Ottawa: Indians Affairs Branch, 1966.

Moyer, Sharon, and Lee Axon. *An Implimentation Evaluation of the Native Community Council Project of the Aboriginal Legal Services of Toronto*. Toronto: Ministry of the Attorney General, 1993.

Royal Commission on Aboriginal Peoples. *Aboriginal Peoples and the Justice System: A Report of the National Roundtable on Aboriginal Justice Issues*. Ottawa: Supply and Services, 1993.

– *Bridging the Cultural Divide: A Report on Aboriginal People and Criminal Justice in Canada*. Ottawa: Supply and Services, 1996.

– *For Seven Generations: Report of the Royal Commission on Aboriginal Peoples*. Montreal: Libraxus, 1997.

– *The High Arctic Relocation: A Report on the 1953–1955 Relocation*. Ottawa: Supply and Services, 1994.

– *Partners in Confederation: Aboriginal Peoples, Self-Government, and the Constitution*. Ottawa: Supply and Services, 1993.

- *Report of the Royal Commission on Aboriginal People.* Vols. 1–6. Ottawa: Supply and Services Canada, 1996.
- *Report of the Royal Commission on Aboriginal People.* Volume 1. *Looking Forward, Looking Back.* Ottawa: Supply and Services, 1996.
- *Report of the Royal Commission on Aboriginal People.* Volume 2. *Restructuring the Relationship.* Ottawa: Supply and Services, 1996.
- *Treaty Making in the Spirit of Co-existence: An Alternative to Extinguishment.* Ottawa: Supply and Services, 1995.
Select Standing Committee on Aboriginal Affairs. *Towards Reconciliation: Nisga'a Agreement-in-Principle and British Columbia Treaty Process.* Thirty-sixth Parliament, Legislative Assembly of British Columbia, 3 July 1997.
Solicitor General Canada, Corrections Branch. *Community Holistic Healing: Hollow Water First Nation.* Ottawa: Solicitor General, 1993.
World Resources Institute. *UNEP and UNDP's Biannual World Resources Report.* New York: Oxford University Press, 1996.

Cases

A.G. British Columbia v. A.G. Canada. The Natural Products Marketing Act), [1937] A.C. 377 (J.C.P.C.).
A.G. Canada v. A.G. Alberta. (The Insurance Reference), [1916] 1 A.C. 598 (J.C.P.C.).
A.G. Canada v. A.G. Ontario (Labour Conventions), [1937] A.C. 326 (J.C.P.C.).
A.G. Canada v. A.G. Ontario (The Employment and Social Insurance Act), [1937] A.C. 355 (J.C.P.C.).
A.G. Canada v. Giroux (1916), 30 D.L.R. 123 (S.C.C.).
A.G. Ontario v. A.G. Canada (The Local Prohibition Reference), [1896] A.C. 348 (J.C.P.C.).
A.G. Quebec v. A.G. Canada (1920), 56 D.L.R. 373 (J.C.P.C.) (Star Chrome case).
Attorney General of Ontario v. Attorney General of Canada: Re Indian Claims, [1897] A.C. 199.
Augustine and Augustine v. R.; Barlow v. R., [1987] 1 C.N.L.R. 20 (N.B.C.A.).
Bank of Montreal v. Hall, [1990] 1 S.C.R. 121.
Beecher v. Wetherby, 95 U.S. 517 (U.S.S.C.).
Black v. Law Society of Alberta, [1989] 1 S.C.R. 591.
Blueberry River Indian Band v. Canada (1995), 130 D.L.R. (4th) 193 (S.C.C.).
Boyer v. Canada (1986), 26 D.L.R. (4th) 284, leave to appeal to S.C.C. refused (1986), 72 N.R. 365.
Brendale v. Confederated Tribes and Bands of the Yakima Nation, 492 U.S. 408 (1989).
British Columbia (A.G.) v. Canada (A.G.), [1906] A.C. 552.

B.C. Birth Registration No. 1994–09–040399, [1998] 4 C.N.L.R. 7 (B.C.S.C.).

Calder v. A.G.B.C. (1971), 13 D.L.R. (3d) 64 (B.C.C.A.).

Calder v. A.G.B.C. (1973), 34 D.L.R. (3d) 145 (S.C.C.).

Campbell v. Hall (1774), 1 Cowp. 204.

Canada (A.G.) v. Lavell, [1974] S.C.R. 1349.

Casimel v. I.C.B.C., [1992] 1 C.N.L.R. 84 (B.C.S.C.).

Champneys v. Buchan (1857), 4 Drew. 104.

Cherokee Nation v. Georgia, 30 U.S. (5 Pet.) 1 (1831).

Citizens Insurance Company v. Parsons (1881), 7 A.C. 96 (J.C.P.C.).

Connolly v. Woolrich (1867), 17 R.J.R.Q. 75 (Quebec Superior Court), affirmed as
    Johnstone v. Connelly (1869), 17 R.J.R.Q. 266 (Que. Q.B.).

Delaware Tribal Business Committee v. Weeks, 430 U.S. 73 (1977).

Delgamuukw v. British Columbia (1991), 79 D.L.R. (4th) 185 (B.C.S.C.).

Delgamuukw v. British Columbia (1993), 104 D.L.R. (4th) 470.

Delgamuukw v. British Columbia, [1997] 3 S.C.R. 1010.

Ex Parte Crow Dog, 109 U.S. 556 (U.S.S.C. 1888).

Guerin v. The Queen (1984), 13 D.L.R. (4th) 321 (S.C.C.).

Haida Nation v. British Columbia (Minister of Forests) (1997), 153 D.L.R. (4th) 1
    (B.C.C.A.).

Halfway River First Nation v. British Columbia (Minister of Forests), [1998] 1 C.N.L.R.
    14 (B.C.S.C.).

Hammerton v. Honey (1876), 24 W.R. 603.

Hodge v. The Queen (1883), 9 A.C. 117 (J.C.P.C.).

Husky Oil v. M.N.R., [1995] 3 S.C.R. 453.

In Re Calvin's Case (1608), 77 Eng.Rep. 377 (K.B.).

In Re Certified Question II: Navajo Nation v. MacDonald (1989), 16 Indian Law
    Reporter 6086 (Navajo Supreme Court).

In Re Estate of Belone v. Yazzie (1987), 5 Navajo Reporter 161.

Isaac et al. v. Davey (1974), 51 D.L.R. (3d) 170 (C.A.), affirmed 77 D.L.R. (3d)
    481 (S.C.C.).

Island of Palmas Case (1928), 2 R.I.A.A. 829.

Jack and Charlie v. The Queen (1986), 21 D.L.R. (4th) 641 (S.C.C.).

Jacobs v. Mohawk Council of Kahnawake, [1998] 3 C.N.L.R. 68 (Can. H.R. Trib.).

Johnson v. McIntosh, 21 U.S. (8 Wheat) 542 (U.S.S.C. 1823).

Jones v. Fraser (1886), 2 C.N.L.C. 203 (S.C.C.).

Jones v. Meehan, 175 U.S. 1 (1899).

King v. Eastern Terminal Elevator Co., [1925] S.C.R. 434.

Kruger v. The Queen (1985), 17 D.L.R. (4th) 591 (F.C.A.).

Liteky v. U.S., 510 U.S. 540 (1994).

Lockwood v. Wood, [1844] 6 Q.B. 50 (Ex.Ch.).

Logan v. Styres (1959), 20 D.L.R. (2d) 416 (Ont. H.C.).

Mabo v. Queensland (No. 2) (1992), 107 A.L.R. 1.

Milirrpum v. Nabalco Pty. Ltd. (1971), [1972–1973] A.L.R. 65 (N.T.Sp.Ct.)

Milpurrurru v. Indofurn Pty. Ltd. (1994), 130 A.L.R. 659 (Aust. F.C.).

Miller v. The King, [1950] 1 D.L.R. 513 (S.C.C.).

Mitchell v. Canada (M.N.R.), [1999] 1 C.N.L.R. 112 (F.C.A.)

Mitchell v. Dennis, [1984] 2 C.N.L.R. 91 (B.C.S.C.).

Mitchell v. M.N.R., [2001] 3 C.N.L.R. 122.

Monarch Steamship Co. Ltd. v. Karlshamns Oljefabriker (A/B), [1949] A.C. 196.

Montreal v. Montreal Street Railway, [1912] A.C. 333 (J.C.P.C.).

Morton v. Mancari, 417 U.S. 535 (1974).

Multiple Access Ltd. v. McCutcheon, [1982] 2 S.C.R. 161.

Native Communications Society of B.C. v. M.N.R., [1986] 3 F.C. 471 (C.A.).

Newman v. State of Florida, 174 So. 2d 479, 483 (Fla. Dist. Ct.). App., 1965).

New Windsor Corp. v. Mellor, [1975] 1 Ch. 380 (C.A.).

Northern Telecom Canada Ltd. v. Communication Workers of Canada, [1983] 1 S.C.R. 733.

Nowegijick v. The Queen (1983), 144 D.L.R. (3d) 193.

Nunavut Tunngavik Inc. v. Canada (1997), 149 D.L.R. (4th) 519 (F.C.T.D.).

Oklahoma State Tax Comm'r v. Citizens Band of Potawatomi Indian Tribe of Oklahoma, 498 U.S. 505 (1991).

Opetchesaht Indian Band v. Canada (1997), 147 D.L.R. (4th) 1.

Otineka Development Corp. v. The Queen, [1994] 2 C.N.L.R. 83 (T.C.C.).

Paul v. Canadian Pacific Ltd., [1988] 2 S.C.R. 654.

Paulette v. Register of Titles (No. 2) (1973), 42 D.L.R. (3d) 8 (N.W.T.S.C.); reversed on other grounds 63 D.L.R. (3d) 1 (N.W.T.C.A.); affirmed on other grounds 72 D.L.R. (3d) 161 (S.C.C.).

Pawis v. The Queen (1979), 102 D.L.R. (3d) 602 (F.C.T.D.)

R. v. Adams (1996), 138 D.L.R. (4th) 657.

R. v. Badger, [1996] 1 S.C.R. 771.

R. v. Bear's Shin Bone (1899), 3 C.C.C. 329 (N.W.T.S.C.).

R. v. Beauregard, [1986] 2 S.C.R. 56.

R. v. Bertram, [1989] O.J. 2123.

R. v. Cheekinew (1993), 80 C.C.C. (3d) 143 (Sask. Q.B.)

R. v. Côté (1996), 138 D.L.R. (4th) 385.

R. v. Genereux, [1992] 1 S.C.R. 259.

R. v. Gladstone, [1996] 2 S.C.R. 723.

R. v. Gladue, [1999] 1 S.C.R. 688.

R. v. Guerin, [1984] 2 S.C.R. 335 (S.C.C.).

R. v. Horseman, [1990] 1 S.C.R. 901.

R. v. Howard, [1994] 2 S.C.R. 299.

R. v. Jones and Nadjiwon, [1993] 3 Canadian Native Law Reporter 182 (Ont. Prov. Div.).

R. v. Khan, [1990] 2 S.C.R. 531.

R. v. Lewis (1996), 133 D.L.R. (4th) 700.

R. v. Lippe, [1991] 2 S.C.R. 114.

R. v. Marshall, [1999] 2 S.C.R. 456.

R. v. Mercure, [1988] 1 S.C.R. 234.

R. v. Morin (1993), 114 Sask. R. 2 (Sask. Q.B.), reversed (1995) 101 C.C.C. (3d) 124 (Sask. C.A.).

R. v. Moses (1992), 71 C.C.C. (3d) 347 (Y.Terr.Ct.).

R. v. Nan-e-quis-a Ka (1899), 1 Territories Law Reports 211 (N.W.T.S.C.).

R. v. Nikal (1996), 133 D.L.R. (4th) 658.

R. v. Nova Scotia Pharmaceutical Society, [1992] 2 S.C.R. 606.

R. v. Pamajewon, [1996] 2 S.C.R. 821.

R. v. Paquette, [1990] 2 S.C.R. 1103.

R. v. Paul (T.P.) (1998), 196 N.B.R. (2d) 292 (C.A.).

R. v. Roberts, [1989] 2 C.N.L.R. 146 (S.C.C.).

R. v. Sikyea (1964), 43 D.L.R. (2d) 150.

R. v. Simon (1985), 24 D.L.R. (4th) 390 (S.C.C.).

R. v. Sioui, [1990] 1 S.C.R. 1025.

R. v. Smith, [1992] 2 S.C.R. 915.

R. v. Smokehouse, [1996] 2 S.C.R. 672.

R. v. Sparrow, [1990] 1 S.C.R. 1075.

R. v. Stienhuaer, [1985] 3 C.N.L.R. 187 (Alta. Q.B.).

R. v. Sundown, [1999] 1 S.C.R. 393.

R. v. Syliboy, [1929] 1 D.L.R. 307 (N.S.Co.Ct.).

R. v. Taylor and Williams (1981), 62 C.C.C. (2d) 228 (Ont. C.A.).

R. v. Van der Peet, [1996] 2 S.C.R. 507.

R. v. Webb, [1993] 1 C.N.L.R. 148 (Y.Terr.Ct.).

R. v. Wells, [2000] 1 S.C.R. 207.

R. v. White and Bob (1964), 50 D.L.R. (2d) 613 (B.C.C.A.), affirmed (1965) 52 D.L.R. (2d) 481n (S.C.C.).

R. v. Willcocks (1995), 22 O.R. (3d) 552 (Gen. Div.)

R. v. Williams (1921), 4 C.N.L.C. 421.

R. v. Williams, [1995] 2 C.N.L.R. 299 (B.C.C.A.).

R.D.S. v. The Queen (1997), 10 C.R. (5th) 1 (S.C.C.).

Read v. Bishops of Lincoln, [1892] A.C. 644 (P.C.).

Re Beaulieu's Petition (1969), 67 W.W.R. 669 (N.W.T.Terr.Ct.).

Re Deborah (1972), 28 D.L.R. (3rd) 483 (N.W.T.C.A.).

Reference Re the Board of Commerce Act 1919 and the Combines and Fair Prices Act, 1919, [1922] 1 A.C. 191 (J.C.P.C.).

Reference Re Language Rights Under s. 23 of the Manitoba Act, 1870 and s. 133 of Constitution Act, 1867, [1985] 1 S.C.R. 721.

Reference Re Remuneration of Judges of the Provincial Court of Prince Edward Island, [1997] 3 S.C.R. 3.

Reference Re Secession of Quebec, [1998] 2 S.C.R. 217.

Re Noah Estate (1961), 32 D.L.R. (2d) 686 (N.W.T.T.C.).

Re Tagornak Adoption Petition, [1984] 1 C.N.L.R. 185 (N.W.T.S.C.).

Re Wah-Shee (1975), 21 R.F.L. 156 (N.W.T.S.C.).

Robb v. Robb (1891), 3 C.N.L.C. 613.

Roncarelli v. Duplessis (1959), 16 D.L.R. (2d) 689.

Ross v. Registrar of Motor Vehicles, [1975] 1 S.C.R. 5.

St. Catherines Milling and Lumber Co. v. The Queen (1888), 14 App. Cas. 46.

St. Mary's Indian Band v. Cranbrook, [1997] 2 S.C.R. 657.

Semiahmoo Indian Band v. Canada (1997), 148 D.L.R. (4th) 523 (F.C.A.).

Sero v. Gault (1921), 50 O.L.R. 27.

Sheldon v. Ramsay (1852), 9 U.C.R. 105.

Smith et al. v. The Queen (1983), 147 D.L.R. (3d) 237 (S.C.C.).

Smith v. Young (1898), 3 C.N.L.C. 656.

Status of Eastern Greenland Case (1933), 3 W.C.R. 148.

Tee-Hit-Ton Indians v. United States, 348 U.S. 272 (U.S.S.C., 1955).

Thomas v. Norris, [1992] 2 C.N.L.R. 139 (B.C.S.C.).

Tucktoo v. Kitchooalik, [1972] 5 W.W.R. 203 (N.W.T.C.A.), affirming [1972] 3 W.W.R. 194.

United States v. Sandoval, 231 U.S. 28 (U.S.S.C., 1913).

United States v. Santa Fe Pacific Ry. Co., 314 U.S. 339 (U.S.S.C., 1941).

U.S. v. Sandoval, 231 U.S. 28 (U.S.S.C., 1913).

U.S. v. Wheeler, 435 U.S. 313, 319 (1978).

Valente v. The Queen, [1985] 2 S.C.R. 673.

Vielle v. Vielle, [1993] 1 C.N.L.R. 165 (Alta. Q.B.).

Washington v. Davis, 426 U.S. 229 (1976).

Western Australia v. Commonwealth of Australia (1995), 128 A.L.R. 1 (H.C.).

Western Industrial Contractors Ltd. v. Sarcee Developments Ltd. (1979), 98 D.L.R. (3d) 424 (S.C.C.).

Western Sahara Case, [1975] ICJ Reports 12.

Worcester v. Georgia, 31 U.S. (6 Pet.) 515 (1832).

Index